More Building
Classic Small Craft

More Building
Classic Small Craft

John Gardner

International Marine Publishing Company
Camden, Maine

Printed in hardbound 1984
First paperback printing 1990

Published by International Marine Publishing Company

10 9 8 7 6 5 4 3 2

Library of Congress Cataloging-in-Publication Data

Gardner, John, 1905–
    More building classic small craft : how to build 23 traditional
boats / John Gardner.
        p.   cm.
    Rev. ed. of: Building classic small craft. c1977-c1984.
    Includes bibliographical references.
    ISBN 0-87742-274-5
    1. Boatbuilding.   I. Gardner, John, 1905–   Building classic
small craft.   II. Title.
    VM351.G35   1990
    623.8'202—dc20   89-24691
                                                              CIP

International Marine Publishing Company offers software for sale. For
information and a catalog, please contact TAB Software Department, Blue
Ridge Summit, PA 17294-0850.

Questions regarding the content of this book should be addressed to:

International Marine Publishing Company
Division of TAB Books
P.O. Box 220
Camden, ME 04843

To Fred Dion, a good boss who knew boats; Kenneth Durant, a historian who wanted the facts; Dave Getchell, editor, who always has given me scope; and Mystic Seaport Museum, a haven for classic small craft and conservator of the skills that built them.

CONTENTS

PREFACE

The selection of small boats in this book includes a diversity of types for markedly different needs and uses. They are good boats and will be appreciated, I hope, even by those who have no immediate plans to build. But it is primarily for the prospective builder—itching to get to work on a boat in his garage, shed, cellar, or backyard—that this book is intended.

The dories, tenders, skiffs, peapod, duckboat, pilot gig, modified Herreshoff 17-foot rowboat, and other boats in these pages are all tried and proven models that have passed the test of use and are not forbiddingly difficult for nonprofessionals to tackle. Indeed, the directions for building and the explanations of boatbuilding procedures given here have been worked out first and foremost for inexperienced nonprofessionals. Through writing how-to-build articles for amateur boatbuilders for the past 33 years and instructing upwards of a thousand of them in my

classes in recreational boatbuilding at Mystic Seaport Museum over the past 14 years, I have come to understand and respect their needs.

With one exception, all of the boats were subjects of articles written by me for the *National Fisherman* within the past 10 years. The exception is the article on the McInnis "bateau," which appeared originally in *WoodenBoat* magazine. Those articles have been revised, expanded, and in a couple of cases completely rewritten for inclusion here.

The most notable feature of this book is its large number of detailed construction drawings, 125 such drawings in all, representing on the order of a thousand hours or more of exacting work bent over the drawing board. How many weekends were spent in this way I hesitate to say and am reluctant to recall, sometimes working into the wee hours of Monday morning when there were deadlines to meet for the *National*

Fisherman. Had it not been that the bulk of this work had already been done, this book would probably never have been written. To have produced this bulk of drawings from scratch and all of a piece would have been impossible.

In addition to their specific application to the boats in this book, these drawings taken together also constitute something of a reference manual of wooden boatbuilding practices and procedures, a manual of wide general application. Considerable is to be learned from it even though none of the boats included are built.

Finally, it should be understood that this book, unlike so many books offering boats to build, contains *all the information* needed for the building procedures. There are no additional plans to buy. There are no blueprints. None are needed. Everything required in the way of directions and information is between these covers, although sometimes some careful study may be necessary to dig it out. It is the same with blueprints. As long as drawings are legible, it is a waste of time and paper to blow them up to blueprint size. A tip to builders: Xerox the pages that you will be referring to frequently, and use them in place of the book. It will save wear and tear on your book and keep it clean.

"Classic small craft," "vintage boats," "heritage boats," "traditional small craft"—these expressions are not-entirely-satisfactory attempts to name and characterize a special kind of small boat that has made a spectacular comeback in the last 25 or 30 years and is now enjoying well-deserved popularity and acclaim.

The 19th century in America was an era of rapid material progress and unprecedented technical innovation. When the century drew to a close, our native small craft had attained a diversity of form and an elegance of design combined with functional utility that was previously unknown and is unexcelled to this day. These developments carried over into the early decades of the present century, but by 1940, for reasons too involved to go into here, the tide had turned sharply and had ebbed far out. The old boats had slipped out of use and out of sight, and were almost forgotten. Few if any Whitehalls, Swampscott dories, wherries, peapods, Adirondack guide-boats, St. Lawrence River skiffs, Rangeley boats, or others like them continued to be built and used. Rowing had become a thing of the past. Wood as a boatbuilding material seemed well on the way out.

That is how it appeared on the surface. Underneath a ferment was working. Following the lead of Howard Chapelle and Francis Herreshoff, more and more small craft enthusiasts, from 1950 on, turned their efforts to the revival of our small craft heritage. This revival built up steam during the 1960s and swept the country in the 1970s. Classic small craft have now come into their own again and are here to stay.

It is always possible to go to extremes. There are some who make a fetish out of wood, and others make a fetish out of what is old, simply because it is old. Some antique boats were better left undisturbed on the rubbish heap of the past. And while I cherish and value wood as much as anyone and prefer it above all other boatbuilding materials, I cannot deny that thermoplastics are worthy materials for some boatbuilding applications when properly used. Epoxy glue and similar thermoplastic adhesives are a boon to boatbuilders, and had they come along earlier they would most certainly have been adopted by 19th century boatbuilders, who were realists and not blind to a good thing. But good things can be abused, and I have to take a dim view of the current fad for slobbering messy, expensive, ineffectual plastic all over wooden construction that would be perfectly adequate without it. Very much on the plus side, however, are the better grades of marine plywood, which has proved itself a superior material for lapstrake planking even though some purists still tend to look down their noses at it.

Nothing is more central to the American boatbuilding tradition than a readiness to try new things and to accept worthy innovations when they appear. From time immemorial boatbuilders have been looking for shortcuts and improvements. The best way and the easiest way. It is the sailors who are more apt to be the conservatives, being understandably reluctant to go to sea in untried experiments that could drown them. Boatbuilders who are true to their trade are conservatives in the best sense of that word, holding steadfastly to the ways of the past when they are good ways, and prefering the old ways, perhaps, but displaying realism enough to adopt the new when it proves better. *The best of the old with the best of the new.* That is the motto and the spirit of this book.

Occasionally I am asked why anyone would go to all the bother of building a boat—especially a classic boat using wood and hand tools—when there are any number of boats you can buy. Why, indeed! To ask the question is to miss the point, and all the fun.

People build all sorts of boats for all sorts of reasons.

I doubt if they always could tell you why. Maybe in part it is because they like the feel of sharp tools cutting into wood. Wasn't it Francis Herreshoff who said there was nothing nicer than the tangy smell of cedar shavings fresh from the plane, and their springy feel underfoot? Building a boat is a grand way to relax, let down, and get away from it all, as in the case of one overworked physician in a mid-American city who revealed that in off hours he would escape to the attic of his house, where he had a trimaran under construction. Building a boat is a challenge for some, an opportunity to prove themselves; others find a way to realize their individuality, and still others find a temporary retreat to earlier, simpler ways from a time when machines seem to be closing in on us. And there is the end product, the completed boat itself, unique and resplendent, the apple of the builder's eye.

John Gardner
Mystic, Connecticut

More Building
Classic Small Craft

1

HERRESHOFF ROWBOAT
AND
MODIFIED McINNIS BATEAU

HERRESHOFF ROWBOAT

In October 1947, the lines of a rowboat were offered to the readers of *Rudder* magazine by its most illustrious contributor, L. Francis Herreshoff. In those days *The Rudder* was riding the crest of a wave of unprecedented popularity and interest on the part of the boating public, the like of which has not been seen since.

Every month brought new articles by Herreshoff. Some issues contained as many as three separate contributions, which a widening circle of readers awaited with the keenest anticipation and received as inspired doctrine.

The wave set in motion then was the wave of the future, and its force is still felt. Much that has taken place on the boating scene since, and is taken for granted today, dates back to Herreshoff's writing of a

generation ago and to the views and ideas he expressed then. The immense and instant response of his readers leaves no doubt that many people had only been waiting for someone to express publicly with force, logic, and authority the substance of their own inner feelings and convictions, yearnings and intuitions.

In that time, rowing for recreation was almost unknown in this country. With the exception of a highly specialized form engaged in as a competitive sport by an elite of college athletes, rowing in the United States had all but disappeared. Why should anyone row when motors were so cheap and so readily available?

Herreshoff thought otherwise, and when he announced that what America needed, among other things, was a good rowboat, he spoke a radical doctrine. Today it is not necessary to make a case for recreational rowing, or to recapitulate the arguments

1

A modified Herreshoff rowboat built by Myron Young, of Laurel, New York, from plans and construction details in this chapter. "There have been no problems with the construction," Young reported. "Herreshoff's lines and your changes and construction methods worked very well."

put forth in Herreshoff's classic book *The Common Sense of Yacht Design*. But the rowboat he advocated is worth some consideration, falling as it does, somewhere between the fragile racing scull and what Herreshoff characterized as the "heavy, ill-shaped rowboat of several hundred pounds."

What Herreshoff had in mind was "a good seaboat," very easy to row and not difficult to plank. The lines of such a boat he presented to us in Figure 357 of *Common Sense*. Like so many others back in the 1940s, I subscribed to *The Rudder* to make sure I saw Herreshoff's latest contribution as soon as it appeared in print and to have all his articles on file for frequent rereading. Entranced by the rowboat lines in the October 1947 issue, I immediately scaled off an enlargement as best I could, from which I made a scale half-model, the one now tacked over the entrance to the small-boat shop at Mystic Seaport. Ever since I first saw its lines, it has been high on my list of boats to build some day. In the summer of 1979 I received a request for offsets, and soon after I received a second request. I finally had the incentive to work out the details for building this boat, or at least one very much like it.

The First Model Worked Up from Herreshoff's Lines

Although Herreshoff did not provide offsets, construction details, or anything in the way of scantling dimensions or other specifications, he certainly intended that the lines should be built from, or at least that they should provide basic proportions and design characteristics for boats subsequently to be built. The only hint given for construction is that the 17-foot boat with its 42-inch beam should be light—under 100 pounds. The boat I worked up in 1979 and presented in the February 1980 issue of *National Fisherman* would be a bit heavier, but still it would not weigh much more than 100 pounds.

The alterations I made in the lines were minor and would not affect the performance perceptibly. I made them solely to simplify the building of the round hull shape by an inexperienced amateur.

First, I made my version of this boat a true double-ender. Her stems are exactly the same, so that duplicate molds can be used at corresponding stations forward and aft of the midsection. The differences between the bow and stern ends of a boat built exactly

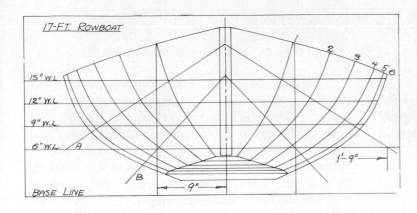

17-FT. ROWBOAT

15" W.L.
12" W.L.
9" W.L.
6" W.L. A

BASE LINE

9"

1'-9"

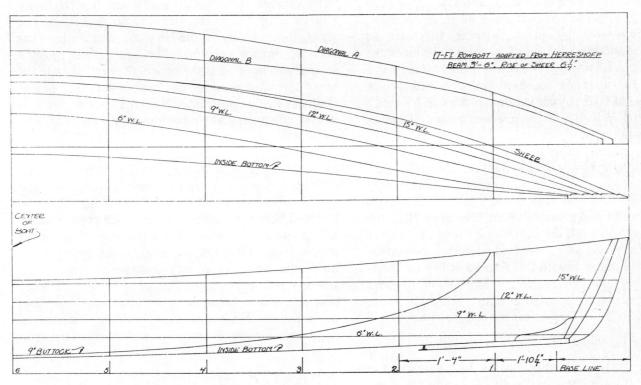

DIAGONAL B

DIAGONAL A

17-FT. ROWBOAT ADAPTED FROM HERRESHOFF
BEAM 3'-6". RISE OF SHEER 6½"

6" W.L.

9" W.L.

12" W.L.

15" W.L.

SHEER

INSIDE BOTTOM ?

CENTER
OF
BOAT

15" W.L.

12" W.L.

9" W.L.

6" W.L.

9" BUTTOCK ?

INSIDE BOTTOM ?

1'-4"

1'-10¼"

BASE LINE

17-FT. DOUBLE-ENDED ROWBOAT ADAPTED FROM HERRESHOFF
OFFSETS TO INSIDE OF PLANKING AND BOTTOM. FEET, INCHES, EIGHTHS.

		STEM	1	2	3	4	5	6
HEIGHTS	SHEER	1-9-7	1-7-7	1-6-4	1-5-3	1-4-4	1-3-7	1-3-5
	INSIDE BOTTOM	0-5-3	0-4-7	0-4-2	0-3-6	0-3-2	0-2-7	0-2-5
	9" BUTTOCK	SHEER 1-7-7	—	0-9-6	0-6-3	0-4-6	0-3-6	0-3-1
HALF-BREADTHS	BOTTOM	0-0-3	0-1-3	0-3-1	0-5-0	0-6-3	0-7-4	0-8-0
	6" W.L.	0-0-3	0-2-0	0-5-0	0-8-4	0-11-2	1-1-5	1-2-6
	9" W.L.	0-0-3	0-4-3	0-8-3	0-11-7	1-3-0	1-5-1	1-6-1
	12" W.L.	0-0-3	0-6-1	0-10-6	1-2-3	1-5-3	1-7-2	1-7-7
	15" W.L.	0-0-3	0-7-5	1-0-3	1-4-1	1-6-7	1-8-4	1-9-0
	SHEER	0-0-3	0-8-7	1-1-6	1-5-0	1-7-2	1-8-5	1-9-1
	DIAGONAL A	0-0-7	0-8-7	1-1-2	1-4-1	1-6-5	1-8-2	1-8-7
	DIAGONAL B	0-1-1	0-7-4	0-10-5	1-0-7	1-2-3	1-3-4	1-4-1

DIAGONAL A UP 1-7-6 ABOVE B.L. AND OUT 1-9-0 ON 6" W.L.
DIAGONAL B UP 1-3-4 ABOVE B.L. AND OUT 9" ON 6" W.L.

to the lines Herreshoff drew would be so slight as to have no discernible effect on performance, but those differences would add work in building.

The evolution of the Adirondack guideboat took the same course. The first double-enders were slightly asymmetrical fore and aft, but when the guideboat attained the peak of its development, bow and stern were built exactly alike. Performance was not altered, but a substantial saving in building labor was gained.

The basic hull shapes of the Adirondack guideboat and the Herreshoff rowboat have much in common. Both boats have flat, plank bottoms. In short, the guideboat and the Herreshoff rowboat have much the same sectional shapes. The boat Herreshoff drew is a foot longer than the standard full-size Adirondack guideboat of 16 feet. In maximum beam the difference is greater—42 inches for the rowboat against 38 inches for the guideboat.

Bottom widths differ even more. For the rowboat, inside width amidships of the flat bottom is 16 inches; for most 16-foot guideboats the corresponding bottom width is normally between 8 and 9 inches. This extra width should make the rowboat less tippy than the guideboat, although the latter was adequately stable and entirely safe when handled correctly. Nevertheless, in comparison with flat-floored utility rowboats and wide, outboard craft, the Herreshoff rowboat might appear to be somewhat tiddly. After all, it was intended to be an easy, fast-moving rowboat, not a working skiff the side of which one can sit on with impunity.

Inside depth amidships scales 12 inches in the Herreshoff lines compared with 11½ inches in a 16-foot Grant guideboat. In my initial model (as well as in my second and final model) I increased the sheer height uniformly throughout by 1 inch, making the inside depth amidships 13 inches. I counted on this increase to improve seakeeping qualities without increasing windage significantly.

One major difference between the Herreshoff rowboat and the Adirondack guideboat is the amount of bottom rocker, or fore-and-aft camber. In the former it is 2¾ inches, as I drew it, while in the latter it is barely more than 1 inch for a 16-foot boat.

As mentioned above, my biggest departure from the original Herreshoff lines was in the shape and construction of the stems. I drew the same shape and dimensions at either end, although I suggested that builders could lower the height at the stern by an inch

or so if they thought this would improve the appearance.

Herreshoff did not indicate a stem construction, but the curved shape he drew suggests a conventionally rabbeted stem and a rabbeted sternpost. Further, the amount of stem curve might require curved timber or a steam-bent stempiece.

Instead, I chose a stem very similar to that found in the Rangeley Lakes boat, although the one I used is even simpler (see the drawing on page 10). Consisting of two pieces, it can be sawn to shape from ordinary straight-grain plank and requires no rabbeting. The inner piece is easily beveled in place after the boat has been set up for planking. The outer piece may be shaped and beveled at the bench, then attached to the inner part after planking has been completed. This is the most easily constructed stem that I know, yet it is wholly adequate and pleasing in appearance, at least to my eye.

I worked up the boat to be clinker-planked with eight strakes got out of standard 4-by-8-foot panels of ¼-inch marine plywood, spliced as required. Laps and splices would be glued with a flexible adhesive and fastened between frames with clinched copper tacks. Strakes would be fastened to the frames with screws or copper rivets. Glued laps can add much strength and make the boat completely and permanently tight whether left in or taken out of the water, a most desirable feature in any boat that is to be hauled about on a trailer. More complete building instructions applicable to both this and my second model begin on page 9.

The Second Model

My first article about the Herreshoff rowboat, in *National Fisherman*, February 1980, brought a highly encouraging response. Buzz Nichols of Beach Haven Gardens, New Jersey, was one of those dropping a favorable word:

I enjoyed reading your article about the Herreshoff boat. . . .In May of 1978 I was living in Long Beach, California, and had the impulsive desire to buy a rowing dory for recreation. By a stroke of good fortune I came across a fellow named Ellis E. St. Rose, in Venice, California. He built such a boat as you describe in your article. It was after that design by Herreshoff, and the only difference from what you describe that I can detect is that the laps of the clinker planking were fastened with brass screws, not copper rivets.

While in California, I made a number of cross-channel trips from Catalina Island to Long Beach, a distance of 28 miles. In one crossing, August 1978, I made the trip rowing single in 5 hours 47 minutes. The boat is excellent in the open ocean, and does very well trolling while running offshore.

Certainly this was a highly favorable report. One that was just as favorable but much more detailed can be found in an article by Allan H. Vaitses in *Rudder*, January 1955. Somehow I overlooked this article until Bill Davis of Virginia Beach, Virginia, kindly sent me a copy. Davis, who works for the Farrell Steamship Lines in Norfolk, was one of those who initially suggested a how-to series for the construction of this boat. Anyone interested in the Herreshoff rowboat would be well rewarded to find Vaitses's very interesting account. Some of the salient points follow.

On "every decent work day" of a 32-month span — to avoid a lengthy roundabout trip around the harbor — Vaitses rowed one of the Herreshoff boats back and forth across the mile-wide harbor between his home on Mattapoisett Neck and the Burr Brothers' Boat Yard on Neds Point. Vaitses figures this amounted to 1,200 miles under oars, and at the end the boat was in good shape and none the worse for nearly three years of continual use. Before settling on the Herreshoff rowboat, Vaitses tried or considered various craft, but for one reason or another none proved suitable. Round-bottomed yacht tenders drew too much water. Semidories weighed too much. A flat-bottomed skiff was too slow, very wet, and "a bear in a crosswind."

The boat had to be light because the beach at Mattapoisett was rocky and shoal, not over 3 inches deep for a distance of 200 feet offshore. Planked semidory fashion with ⅜-inch cedar, this 17-foot boat weighed no more than 125 pounds soaking wet.

According to Vaitses, this boat was at least twice as fast as an ordinary rowboat and would outdistance anything under oars except racing shells. In a moderate breeze most ordinary small sailboats were no faster. Frequent timing of trips across the harbor indicated a top average speed of 6 m.p.h. with ordinary 7½-foot oars and a stationary thwart. A speed of 4 to 5 m.p.h. could be kept up indefinitely, and short bursts of 7 m.p.h. were possible. With spoon oars and a sliding seat she would undoubtedly do better.

Vaitses pointed out certain limitations in the type. When the boat is pulled straight on into a steep chop, her sharp bow tends to knife into solid water, and without decking at her ends she will fill unless slowed down. Second, she lacks initial stability to some extent, though not as dramatically as an Adirondack guideboat or a canoe. Her apparent tenderness may bother some not used to such boats, but it is no problem if one keeps in the middle. Certainly it would be possible to tip her over through carelessness on the part of the occupants, but blame should not be attached to the boat.

Vaitses thought that because of her low sides, 500 pounds was about the limit of his boat's load capacity, but he feared that making her more high sided would increase her windage unduly. I considered this also, but I decided the boat would benefit from the inch of freeboard I had added, while the increase in windage would be too small to matter.

After reading Vaitses's article, I made a second and final revision of the lines drawn by Herreshoff. The new section lines and the accompanying table of offsets that appear herewith represent quite a lot of work and thoughtful study. These 12 sectional outlines, numbered .5 to 6, represent all of the required frame shapes. This body plan of sectional shapes and their measurements recorded in the table of offsets was taken from a full-size laydown of lines that was thoroughly worked over and faired. This work hardly needs to be done again. Laying out the sectional shapes full size from the offsets as given should suffice, and the shapes should be accurate enough to build from.

Note that the offsets are measured in sixteenths rather than the usual eighths of inches, and that in some cases pluses are used when a measurement runs a bit over. When the sections are laid out, the diagonals rather than the waterline measurements should govern if significant discrepancies between the two arise. I don't anticipate any such discrepancies.

The principal difference between the first lines that I drew up for this boat and the revised lines presented herewith is a considerable increase in the sheer beam, particularly forward. This has meant filling out the topsides significantly. This has been accomplished, however, without the slightest alteration in the underbody shape. Thus, below the load waterline the

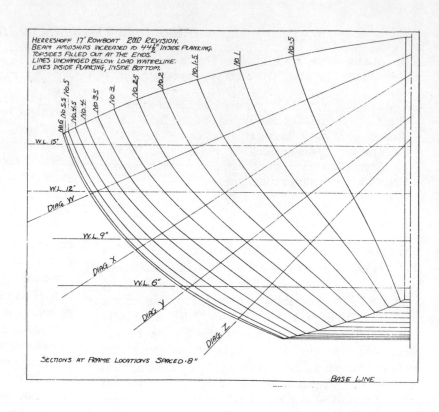

HERRESHOFF 17' ROWBOAT. 2ND REVISION.
BEAM AMIDSHIPS INCREASED TO 44½" INSIDE PLANKING.
TOPSIDES FILLED OUT AT THE ENDS.
LINES UNCHANGED BELOW LOAD WATERLINE.
LINES INSIDE PLANKING, INSIDE BOTTOM.

SECTIONS AT FRAME LOCATIONS SPACED 8"

	STATIONS	STEM	No.5	No.1	No.1.5	No.2	No.2.5	No.3	No.3.5	No.4	No.4.5	No.5	No.5.5	No.6
HEIGHTS	SHEER	1-10-2	1-8-13	1-8-0	1-7-4+	1-6-8+	1-5-15	1-5-5	1-4-13	1-4-7	1-4-2	1-3-14	1-3-11+	1-3-10
	INSIDE BOTTOM	0-5-5	0-5-2	0-4-12	0-4-7	0-4-2	0-3-13	0-3-8	0-3-4+	0-3-0+	0-2-14+	0-2-12+	0-2-11+	0-2-11+
HALF-BREADTHS	INSIDE BOTTOM	0-0-6	0-0-10	0-1-6	0-2-4	0-3-2	0-4-0+	0-5-0	0-5-14	0-6-10	0-7-2	0-7-10	0-7-15	0-8-1
	6" W.L.	0-0-6	0-0-15+	0-2-3+	0-3-11	0-5-2+	0-6-13	0-8-8	0-10-0	0-11-7	1-0-10	1-1-12	1-2-7	1-2-11+
	9" W.L.	0-0-6	0-2-4	0-4-6	0-6-9	0-8-9+	0-10-10	1-0-6	1-2-0	1-3-6	1-4-8	1-5-6+	1-6-0	1-6-2
	12" W.L.	0-0-6	0-3-12	0-6-12+	0-9-6	0-11-13+	1-1-15	1-3-10	1-5-2+	1-6-5	1-7-3	1-7-14	1-8-5	1-8-7+
	15" W.L.	0-0-6	0-5-4+	0-8-12+	0-11-9	1-2-1	1-4-0	1-5-12	1-7-0+	1-8-1	1-8-14+	1-9-7+	1-9-12	1-9-14
	SHEER	0-0-6	0-7-8	0-10-15	1-1-10+	1-3-13+	1-5-7	1-6-14	1-7-15	1-8-12	1-9-6	1-9-13	1-10-0	1-10-2
DIAGONALS	DIAG. W	0-0-8	0-7-4+	0-10-9+	1-1-2	1-3-4+	1-5-0	1-6-7+	1-7-10	1-8-9	1-9-5+	1-9-14	1-10-3+	1-10-5+
	DIAG. X	0-0-8	0-6-14	0-9-14+	1-0-3+	1-2-3	1-3-11	1-4-15	1-6-0+	1-6-15	1-7-11	1-8-5+	1-8-13	1-8-15
	DIAG. Y	0-0-8	0-5-12	0-8-6	0-10-6	0-11-14+	1-1-4	1-2-6	1-3-6	1-4-4+	1-5-0+	1-5-11	1-6-1+	1-6-3+
	DIAG. Z	0-0-9	0-5-4	0-7-9	0-9-4+	0-10-9	0-11-12	1-0-13	1-1-10+	1-2-7	1-3-1	1-3-9	1-3-13	1-3-15

HERRESHOFF 17' ROWBOAT. 2ND REVISION. FRAME STATIONS SPACED 8" APART. BOTH ENDS OF BOAT ALIKE.

DIAGONAL W UP 21", OUT 20" ON 12" W.L. DIAGONAL X UP 19¾", OUT 21" ON 6" W.L. DIAGONAL Y UP 17" OUT 14" ON 6" W.L. DIAGONAL Z UP 15½", OUT 9" ON 6" W.L. MEASUREMENTS IN FEET, INCHES, AND SIXTEENTHS.

boat remains exactly the same as before, whereas above the load waterline the topsides are substantially fuller. The profile is unchanged.

In my first set of lines, when I raised the sheer by one inch, I nevertheless maintained Herreshoff's original beam, which pulled in the side flare. In the revision, I have let the side flare out, and as it runs forward from amidships I have progressively increased it, so that at station 1, which is only 22¼ inches aft of the forward edge of the stem, the sheer beam has been increased from 17¾ inches to 21⅛ inches, a net increase of 4⅛

inches. This is a lot! And the reason for it is to give more buoyancy and lift to the ends.

Allan Vaitses stressed the tendency of his boat with its sharp bow to knife into waves and take water when running into a head sea. He cautioned that in such circumstances it was necessary to hold back on the oars and slow down; otherwise the boat would fill.

This boat, as originally designed, did not have much buoyancy in its ends. What I have attempted to do here is to add buoyancy and lift but without slowing down the boat by spoiling Herreshoff's fine entrance at the

D.S. CONNELLY'S WIDENED VERSION HERRESHOFF/GARDNER ROWBOAT							
HALF-BREADTHS	STEM	1	2	3	4	5	6
INSIDE BOTTOM	0-0-6	0-1-5	0-4-0	0-6-7	0-8-6	0-10-2	0-11-0
+6" W.L.	0-0-6	0-2-2	0-5-7	0-10-3	1-1-5	1-4-3	1-5-6
+9" W.L.	0-0-6	0-4-5	0-9-2	1-1-6	1-5-3	1-7-7	1-9-1
+12" W.L.	0-0-6	0-6-3	0-11-5	1-4-2	1-7-6	1-9-0	1-10-7
+15" W.L.	0-0-6	0-7-7	1-1-2	1-6-0	1-9-2	1-11-2	2-0-0
SHEER	0-0-6	0-9-1	1-2-5	1-6-7	1-9-5	1-11-3	2-0-1
4-FOOT BEAM. HEIGHTS AS ORIGINALLY SHOWN. DIAGONALS TO BE DEVELOPED.							

load line. I do not say that the boat as now revised will not take water in a head sea, but I believe it will take considerably less, and with the addition of light end decks, or even temporary canvas coverings of some sort, this should be a much drier and safer boat. In my own boat, now in the planning stage, I am seriously considering installing very light end decks of ⅛-inch plywood with a small but adequate amount of foam flotation tucked away underneath.

Another reason for increasing the sheer beam was to give more purchase for the oars. The beam amidships to the inside of the planking is now 44½ inches. Add the thickness of the planking and that of outside gunwales, and you have between 46 and 47 inches. If the oarlock sockets are installed on the outside of the gunwales, as is the standard practice in the Adirondack guideboat, the rowing beam amidships will be not less than 46 inches, which in my estimation is ample for 8-foot sculls; for rough-water work I believe I would go with 7½-footers. For those who might want greater rowing span, folding outrigger oarlocks are now available. These would increase the effective rowing beam by several inches.

Of course, the rowing thwarts must be properly located, and this will be treated in detail below. Let me say now, however, that there should not be more than two rowing thwarts for this boat, and that they should be positioned in the center of the boat with only good arm reach between them—enough so that the oarsman on the forward thwart will have ample reach when two are rowing. If the two thwarts are properly located, the rowing span need not be less than 45 inches for either.

I consider this to be adequate, although Daniel S. Connelly of Cleveland Heights, Ohio, a knowledgeable connoisseur of small craft whose opinions I value and respect, feels that a 48-inch rowing span is better. Accordingly, he offers a widened version of this design, which opens up to 48 inches. I have copied his proposed table of half-breadths and submit it here for consideration.

It should be noted that Connelly's overall increase in beam derives basically from his increase of bottom width amidships from 16 to 22 inches. This will produce a somewhat slower boat, in my opinion, but one with increased initial stability. For those who desire a somewhat steadier boat and would not mind a slight loss of rowing speed, the Connelly boat might prove more satisfactory. Connelly's letter explaining his reasons and commenting on the design follows:

I am sure the Gardner/Herreshoff design is a winner, partly in view of your determination to keep weight on the low side.

I remembered Vaitses' article on commuting under oars, but had forgotten details including the boat used. I immediately reread it. His mild criticism of the boat regarding load-carrying capacity and initial stability emboldened me to forward a little experiment of my own.

Based on my feeling that a gunwale beam of 4 feet is about the minimum for a rowing boat, I simply expanded your design to reach this goal. As the method of achieving this with the least violence to your nice lines I simply expanded half-breadths of the flat bottom to increase maximum width of flat from 16 inches to 22 inches, and used your topsides as drawn for Stations 2 through 6. Stem siding was increased, and the added width at Station 1 was cut to one-half the geometric increase. I believe this would give fair lines within ⅛ inch when laid down full size on the scrieve board, depending on the quality of the batten used. For your file I attach the resulting half-breadths.

I have not had time to try these on the drafting board.

Regarding Vaitses' comment about the problem of water coming aboard in head seas—it ought to be possible to make a very lightweight, quickly detachable bow deck which would keep out 90 percent of the water without impeding maintenance.

Connelly had previously written to call my attention to the Reelfoot boat, which was developed on Reelfoot Lake in northwestern Tennessee and described in detail by George Laycock in the 1957 edition of *Sports Afield Boatbuilding Annual.* Laycock's article included a drawing by Edson I. Schock detailing lines and construction. Laycock claimed that the Reelfoot boats, which were built for many years by the Calhoun family of Tiptonville, Tennessee, numbered nearly 3,000 on Reelfoot Lake at the time he wrote the article, and had been exported all over the United States. This seems an awful lot of boats on a single lake, but I am not questioning that figure since I know nothing of that lake or the boats in question, except from the *Sports Afield* account.

Connelly forwarded a copy of the article to me, along with the following comments:

The striking similarity between your design and the Reelfoot Lake boat fascinates me. I am sure that the Reelfoot boat antedates October 1947 (date of the original Herreshoff article) by an appreciable interval, and the text of the enclosure tends to support this. It therefore appears to me that these are two designs of completely independent origin.

	Reelfoot	*Gardner*
LOA	15'10"	17'1"
Beam, inside	42¾"	42¼"
Depth, inside	12½"	13"
Max. width flat bottom	24"	16"
Bottom rocker	2⅞"	2¾"
Rise of sheer	5⅞"	6¼"

You will note that the Reelfoot drawings were prepared by Edson I. Schock—and thus, I presume, are properly faired. They are based on measurements by George Laycock in 1956. The photograph of one of these boats under bow-facing oars shows a rough job, but this may be a much abused livery boat. The photo of the completed boat shows what seems to be very acceptable workmanship. Apparently construction is carried out with hammer, saw and drawknife. Note the construction time quoted!

The article claimed that "two Reelfoot boatbuilders could build the entire boat in one day." I assume this meant they could assemble a boat in one day from pieces precut from patterns. Even then it would have been a long day, with a lot of hustle and not many smoke breaks.

The construction shown in the photos looked heavy—too heavy to produce a total weight for the boat of only 150 pounds, as claimed. And when the cypress with which many of them were planked soaked up, the weight was certainly more than 150 pounds. Apparently Reelfoot Lake is shallow, and so the bottoms of these boats were originally sheathed with a sheet of "tin"—presumably thin galvanized iron. Later, fiberglass was used. Because of the many stumps rising above the surface of the lake, hinged oars were used, permitting the oarsman to row facing forward.

Connelly's letter concluded with the following comments:

I am particularly pleased to see this latest of your designs. I feel that some of the builders of traditional rowing craft are not making realistic choices if rowing for recreation is their aim. Some of the boats are strictly working craft, intended to provide a working platform with load carrying capacity in fairly adverse weather conditions, with ease of propulsion important, but of secondary consideration.

I am also pleased to see you recommend plywood for planking. I have a 15-foot Lyman outboard, built in 1953, lapstrake-ply planked, and apparently as sound as the day it was completed, in spite of having been used by previous owners with a 40 h.p. engine.

This last comment, confirming my choice of marine plywood for planking, was most welcome inasmuch as there is still considerable unfounded prejudice against its use.

Before I go on to construction details, I'll excerpt one other letter that was sent soon after the appearance of the first of my articles on the Herreshoff rowboat. Bill Cannell, a boatbuilder in Camden, Maine, liked the Herreshoff rowboat so much he built one for his own use. How this came about and what came of it is related in Cannell's letter:

After you have looked at the accompanying...photograph you will understand that it was with no little interest that I read your article in the February *National Fisherman.*

Another close relative of the Herreshoff rowboat, this one built by Bill Cannell of Camden, Maine. The oarlock sockets for the after rowing position are very far aft. (Courtesy Bill Cannell)

The boat in Figure 357 of Mr. Herreshoff's *Common Sense of Yacht Design* has intrigued me for a long time, and two summers ago, having a slack period in building, I decided to do something about it. I called Muriel Vaughn and asked her to send up what she had on the boat, which was only that one drawing. She also mentioned that Allan Vaitses had built a boat to these lines and promised to send an article he had written on the boat for *Rudder*.

After waiting for the lines to arrive in the mail a couple of days, my enthusiasm gained such momentum that I said the hell with it and went ahead and began my own drawing of a very similar boat. I wanted to preserve the same basic proportions, but if possible further simplify her.

First of all, like you, I opted for waterlines symmetrical fore and aft to cut down the time of lofting and pattern making for the sawn frames. The sheer, however, is not symmetrical.

I made my design slightly wider on both the bottom and the sheer and gave the sections a bit more curve in the topsides. I also decided to eliminate the vertical keel that appears in Mr. Herreshoff's drawing for the sake of simplicity. For the same reason I ran the stem and bottomboards together in a sharp forefoot.

One design change I would make now is the arrangement of the rowing stations. Hoping to preserve perfect trim with either one or two oarsmen, I drew and built her with three rowing stations. When I went out for a spin with Maynard Bray to try her out for the first time for any distance with two rowing, it

became apparent that the oarlocks at the after rowing station lacked sufficient spread, and made rowing there very tiring. Two thwarts would have been better.

Mr. Herreshoff's description of Figure 357, "a good sea boat, very easy to row, and not difficult to plank up," is a good goal in the recreational rowing boat of today, and fortunately this boat seems to fulfill these requirements. There should be more boats of this type because they are so easy to row and are fast, and they are relatively simple to build, an advantage to the amateur builder and professional alike in terms of time and cost. As for seaworthiness, a boat of this type can handle any conditions which would be either fun or rational for the recreational oarsman to go out in.

Construction Details

As I stated earlier in the chapter, one of my primary considerations was to simplify construction as much as possible in the interest of the nonprofessional backyard builder while preserving the essential integrity of Herreshoff's design. Since Herreshoff provided no construction details, I felt justified in incorporating features from the Adirondack guideboat and the Rangeley Lakes boat. Both are craft of outstanding merit and ability proved through generations of use. Hundreds of each have been built and have given good service.

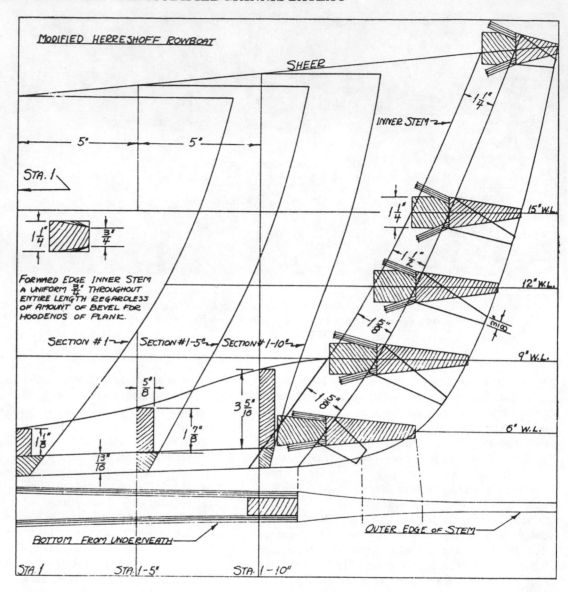

Note: *The stem bevels and related measurements in this drawing apply with precision only to the author's first revision of the Herreshoff boat. The author's second model, with flared topsides, requires somewhat greater stem bevels. In its general detail the drawing applies to either model. To get exact stem bevels for the second model, finish the bevels during the planking process.*

The stem construction adapted from the Rangeley boat could hardly be simpler or easier to make. There is no rabbet to lay out and cut, and no curved timber—either natural crook knees or steam-bent pieces—is required. Instead, the stem assembly is made up of three pieces cut out of ordinary straight-grain plank 1¼ inches thick. These are the forefoot, the inner stem, and the outer stem. Although the accompanying drawings show the stem construction in complete detail, it may be helpful to mention the order of construction and call attention to several details.

The forefoot and inner stempiece are fastened together, and this assembly is then fastened to the bottom board prior to making the setup for planking. In planking, no special care need be taken that the hood ends of the planks conform exactly to the shape of the

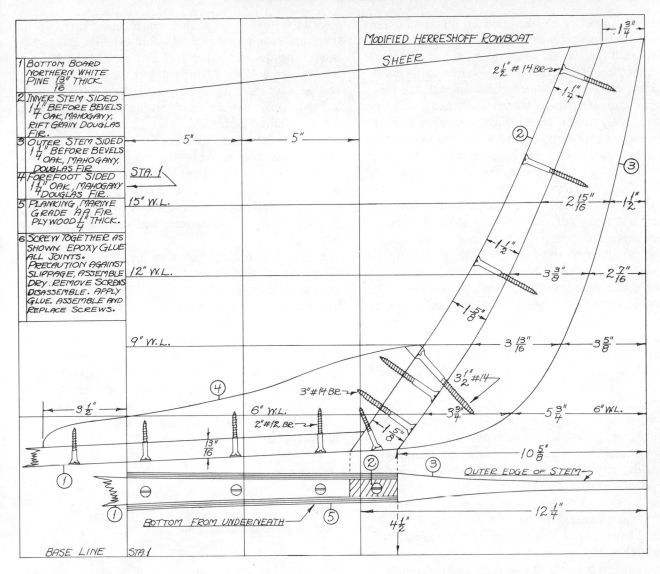

1	BOTTOM BOARD NORTHERN WHITE PINE 13/16" THICK
2	INNER STEM SIDED 1 1/4" BEFORE BEVELS OAK, MAHOGANY, RIFT GRAIN DOUGLAS FIR.
3	OUTER STEM SIDED 1 1/4" BEFORE BEVELS OAK, MAHOGANY, DOUGLAS FIR.
4	FOREFOOT SIDED 1 1/4" OAK, MAHOGANY, DOUGLAS FIR.
5	PLANKING, MARINE GRADE AA FIR PLYWOOD 1/4" THICK.
6	SCREW TOGETHER AS SHOWN. EPOXY GLUE ALL JOINTS. PRECAUTION AGAINST SLIPPAGE, ASSEMBLE DRY. REMOVE SCREWS. DISASSEMBLE. APPLY GLUE. ASSEMBLE AND REPLACE SCREWS.

outer edge of the inner stempiece. Provided the planks are not too short, this fit can be achieved after planking is completed by trimming the ends with a sharp block plane. The outer stempiece is then fastened on with screws from inside, as the drawing shows. It should be noted that in beveling the inner stempiece to receive the ends of the planking, its outer edge is held to a uniform width of ¾ inch throughout.

Although it is possible to determine the precise amount of bevel required for the ends of the planking from the laydown of lines, I suggest that inexperienced builders wait until after the setup for planking has been made before completing this bevel. By laying a batten across the frames to simulate planking, one can easily determine the exact amount of stem bevel, obviating any danger of cutting off too much.

It will add greatly to hull strength if the three members of the stem assembly are glued as well as screwed together. To prevent slippage, fasten the members together dry at first, then remove the screws, apply the glue, and finally, reseat the screws. Glue is slippery, and it is extremely difficult to keep joints properly aligned if glue is applied before fastening holes are bored.

This boat could be set up with the use of molds and planked in the ordinary way. It could be set up either right side up or upside down. Each of these two methods has advantages and disadvantages. With the boat right side up, it is easier for one person working alone to rivet the laps as planking proceeds. Most builders find it easier to fit the garboard and the laps with the boat upside down.

The boat might be planked bottom up on a ladder-frame setup with molds on 16-inch centers to correspond to an 8-inch frame spacing. As the planks were put on, they could be temporarily secured to the molds with long, slim, resin-coated nails through the laps. The nail heads are padded with round washers of thick leather slightly smaller than a dime. These press firmly on the lap without marring the wood, permitting the nails to be easily pulled with nippers when planking is completed and the molds are removed for timbering. This method, developed for the construction of the four-oared gig *General Lafayette* at Mystic Seaport, worked out very well for that boat. Frames could consist of steamed white oak bent in and riveted after the boat had been planked and turned right side up. In locations where suitable oak bending stock is not available, laminated ribs would be another way to go, and could be easier, lighter, and just as strong as steam-bent oak. Glued laminations of thin strips of spruce would be suitable.

Here, however, we shall consider quite a different approach to setting up and planking the Herreshoff rowboat. The method I have in mind was developed for building the Adirondack guideboat. With this method, no molds are required. The timbers or ribs, got out to shape ahead of time and fastened to the bottom board, serve as molds, and the planking is applied directly to them and permanently fastened in place as planking proceeds.

The 66 ribs or frames that are required for the standard guideboat are cut out of natural crooks obtained from large spruce stumps. They are so stiff and hold their shape so well that when they are set up and fastened to the bottom board all that is required is a spacer batten sprung around the sheer to equalize their fore and aft spacing at their upper ends. No internal cross bracing is needed.

The Herreshoff rowboat can be built in exactly the same way. Its foundation is a bottom board, like the guideboat's but wider. Although I am not suggesting that the frames for this boat be got out of large spruce stumps, I have found that stiff, preshaped frames or ribs can be laminated from thin spruce strips. At first, I assumed that it would be necessary to steam-bend these strips, which would have complicated the process. But I then found that strips ⅛ inch thick or slightly less and 1½ inches wide could be bent dry and glued on forms, and that once the glue had set they were completely rigid and stiff, with no springback whatever. The frames must be clamped to the forms until the glue has set.

With frames set 8 inches apart on centers, 48 of them are required for this 17-foot boat. Because the boat is the same at either end, and because both sides are the same, only 12 different shapes are required, and because the shape changes so slightly from frame to frame, only two or three short pieces of heavy plank will be required for the gluing forms, sawn to shape and altered as the shape changes. If 1½-inch strips are used, a matching pair of ⅝-inch by ⅝-inch frames is produced with each gluing. Making the frames for this boat turns out to be a relatively simple job. The material required can be rough spruce staging planks, obtainable almost anywhere, whereas good bending oak is not.

Bevels for the frames can be taken from the diagonals relative to the frame spacing of 8 inches. Only toward the ends of the boat will the frame bevels be great enough to matter. One way to make accurate plank forms on which to glue up the laminated frames is to lay out the sectional shapes, which is to say the body plan, on heavy paper (a good grade of detail paper would do nicely) and then with carbon paper trace the frame shapes on thin wood in order to make molds for each frame section. From these, the plank forms for gluing the laminated frames can be marked and cut to shape.

The method for gluing up laminated frames. In the foreground is a frame in the gluing form. In the background are three frames nearing completion. This method is also used for the modified McInnis bateau described later in this chapter. (Mary Anne Stets photo, Mystic Seaport)

All the frames for this boat can be made up piecemeal ahead of time and put aside until it is convenient to set up for planking. This is a schedule that lends itself to the home workshop, where circumstances often force the construction of a boat to be an intermittent and drawn-out process. Being able to build this boat without molds will cut not only the time required but the expense as well.

Although some may want to stick with the time-tested method of construction with molds, I intend to build this boat with preformed, laminated frames, and am already gluing them a few at a time when I can find the time to do so.

The boat should not be difficult to build, although it will not plank quite as easily as the original Herreshoff design. Its greater fullness in the topsides at the ends results in more bend and sny in the plank ends. In its construction, this boat resembles both the dory and the Adirondack guideboat, which, despite differences in shape, are closely related types. Both are planked on preshaped frames attached to flat bottom boards.

Before setting out to build this boat, the prospective builder would be well advised to review dory construction and, if possible, to read Kenneth and Helen Durant's *Adirondack Guide-Boat* (Camden, Maine: International Marine Publishing Co., 1980).

Dories are built both right side up and upside down, just as this boat can be. Advantages and disadvantages of the two methods have already been touched on. When the bottom-up method is followed, it is easier to fit the garboard to the bottom—and a good joint is essential if the boat is to be tight. Yet if rivets are used through the frames when the boat is bottom up, riveting becomes more difficult, generally requiring a helper to hold on. When the boat is built right side up, one person can do the riveting quite nicely.

If you should decide to build bottom up, the laps could be fastened to the frames with ¾-inch number 6 bronze flathead wood screws. This would be easier and faster than rivets, but considerably more expensive. On the other hand, if the holes through the frames for the rivets were bored snug, the nails might hold sufficiently well without burrs and peening until planking was completed and the boat turned over. Then one person could conceivably handle the heading over of the rivets. Even so, the services of a helper to hold on would be eminently desirable.

As I stated above, I am planning to build my boat with lapstrake planking of ¼-inch fir marine plywood. The plank laps will be glued with epoxy and pulled tight between the frames with copper tacks just long enough to clinch over about ⅛ inch on the inside and spaced 1¼ to 2 inches. Holes for the tacks will be made with an awl so that the soft copper will drive through the plywood without crippling. This is similar to the method used for fastening guideboat laps, except that the latter require two rows of tacks, one driven from either side.

It is easy to clinch over the ends against a smooth iron hold-on of some sort by reaching under and behind, even when the boat is being built bottom up. A boat constructed in this way, with plywood planking and glued laps, will remain perfectly tight both in the water and out. For keeping water absorption to a minimum, I cannot recommend too strongly that you saturate the planking inside and out with repeated applications of linseed oil, thinned about 20 percent with mineral spirits and applied boiling hot. The mixture should be heated in a double boiler in order to keep it below its flash point, and every sensible precaution should be employed. This ought not to be done until the glue has thoroughly cured, and the oil in such a saturation job will require several weeks to solidify and cure before the boat can be painted.

The accompanying construction drawings should be carefully studied. Most of the important points are indicated by the 24 numbered references, each of which is addressed in turn:

1, 19. The bottom, like those of the dory and the Adirondack guideboat, should be northern white pine, if possible, finished ¾ inch thick. Douglas fir, juniper, Port Orford cedar, or cypress could be substituted. The required width amidships is 16 inches, and since boards this wide are not easily obtained, two 3-inch strips may be glued with epoxy to the edges of a 10-inch board. There should be no difficulty in bending the planks to the very moderate rocker in the bottom.

2 – 4. The stem assembly, consisting of the inner and outer stems and the stem knee, is fully diagramed on pages 10 and 11. These pieces could be made of oak, but a lighter wood would save some weight. Good-quality rift or quarter-sawn Douglas fir would be excellent. Guideboat stems were spruce, and mahogany is another possibility.

This three-piece assembly should be made up and fastened together before it is incorporated in the boat. The inner stempiece and the stem knee are permanently glued and screwed together, but the outer stempiece is merely screwed on so that it can be taken

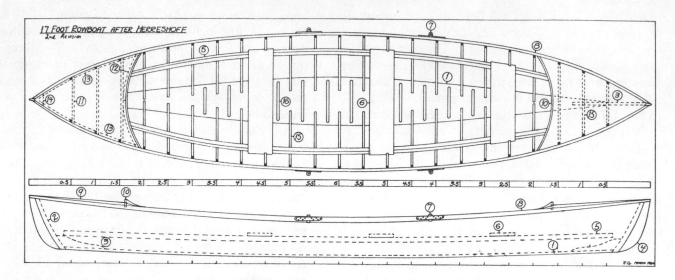

off when the boat is set up for planking. After the boat is planked, the outer stempiece is refastened.

Because the screw holes have already been bored, it will go back exactly where it is supposed to go and line up perfectly. One caution: Inexperienced builders had best not attempt to bevel the inner stem completely before planking, and should leave a little wood for a final fairing as planking proceeds.

5, 18. The seat risers and seat-riser doublers may be of pine, fir, or Port Orford cedar, sized ½ by 2½ inches. Besides supporting the thwarts, these are important structural members that greatly stiffen the hull. Risers are fastened to the frames with 1-inch number 8 bronze screws. Doublers span three frames and are glued and screwed to the risers. They support the ends of the thwarts and provide ample wood to receive three 2-inch number 12 screws put in through the ends of the thwarts.

6. Thwarts or seats are spruce, for stiffness with lightness. They are 8 inches wide and ⅞ inch thick. The under edges should be beveled for appearance.

7. Type and placement of the oarlock sockets are similar to those in the Adirondack guideboat. By locating the oarlock sockets on the outside of the outwale, a 4-foot spread is obtained for the forward rowlocks and a 45½-inch spread for the after rowing position.

8. The outwale is fir, spruce, or mahogany, 1¾ inches deep by 1¼ inches amidships. It is beveled to meet the flare of the sides, so that when fastened in place, the outer side stands plumb. The outwale tapers from 1¾ inches amidships to about 1 inch at the ends. It can be riveted through the timberheads or screw-fastened from the inside. It should be glued to the top strake of the planking as well as screwed or nailed with small anchor-fast annular nails driven through the planking from the inside.

9. End decks are plywood, ⅛ inch thick for lightness, although ¼-inch stock like the planking can be used without much of an increase in weight.

10. The coaming or *deck circles* (guideboat terminology) can be strips of oak ⅜ inch thick and 3 inches wide, steam-bent, and cut to shape to conform to the crown of the deck. Alternatively the coaming can be glue-laminated over a form with the use of thin strips of mahogany, ash, or other wood in the manner in which the frames are laminated. The coaming stands 1 inch above the deck. The radius for the deck circle is 28 inches from a center located 6 inches aft of station 3.

11. Deck beams are spruce, molded 1½ inches and sided ½ inch. There is 1 inch of crown in approximately 3 feet of length.

12. Backing for the coaming or deck circles is in two halves—sawn, bent, or laminated to shape. These two halves butt on the afterdeck beam to which they fasten and extend to the sides of the boat. They are curved both to correspond to the curvature of the deck and to fit the round of the deck circles, which are screwed to them.

13. Filler pieces are fitted between the frames and glued to the inner side of the top strake. These are pine,

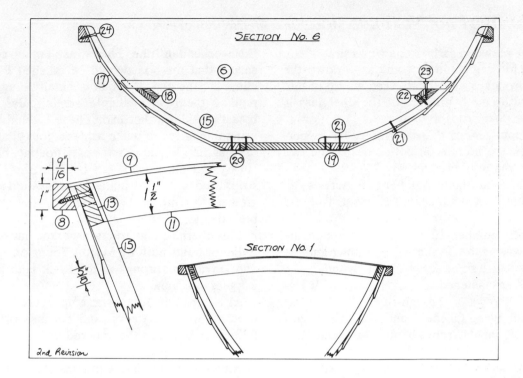

SECTION No. 6

SECTION No. 1

2nd Revision

1½ inches wide and ½ inch thick. Together with the ends of the frames, these filler pieces form a continuous shelf that is set below the sheerline by the thickness of the deck. The shelf supports the sides of the deck and is the structural member to which the edges of the deck are fastened. The filler pieces are also notched to receive the ends of the deck beams. The sheer plank is cut down by the thickness of the deck, which permits the outer edge of the deck to come flush with the outside of the planking. This edge is then covered and hidden by the outwale.

14. A breast cleat, hardly large enough to be dignified with the term breasthook, supports the outboard end of the deck and is fastened to the inner stem.

15. The method of laminating the frames in this boat has been explained above. The frames in the ends of the boat require considerable beveling and should be glued up ¾ inch thick to allow for this.

In gluing my frames I use 1½-inch-wide strips of seasoned, quarter-sawn Douglas fir, from which I can get out a matching pair of half-frames for either side of the boat. Since the boat is double-ended and there are 12 frame stations (or rather 11 on either side of the middle frame station), a total of 46 half-frames of 12 different shapes will be required. This will necessitate 12 differently shaped gluing forms.

Because the shapes change so gradually, however, slight alterations in the forms from station to station can be made, so that actually only about three separate pieces of 2-inch plank will be required for the gluing forms. Although I am using Douglar fir for my frames, spruce, which was used for the guideboat frames, would be excellent.

Some mahogany might do for gluing up frames. Oak does not glue very well as a rule, and it is heavy. Pine is too weak, as are cedar and juniper.

16. Bottom cleats are located as shown. They are of oak, laid on the flat, ⅝ inch by ⅞ inch, and screwed or riveted in place, the latter being stronger. Note the way the frames and bottom cleats are located: No limbers are required to drain the bottom, for water runs around the ends.

17. As stated above, planks are ¼-inch marine plywood, either fir or mahogany. One 10-foot sheet and one 8-foot sheet will be ample. Planks are put on in two and three pieces, glue-scarfed together. Splices should be located so as to break joints as much as possible. The 8-foot and 10-foot sheets are convenient for this.

18. The seat-riser doubler has been treated under 5.

19. The glued bottom joint has been dealt with in 1.

20. The edge of the garboard plank and the joint it makes with the bottom may be covered with a strip of fiberglass or Vectra tape put on with the same epoxy used for gluing the laps. This is needed to protect the

raw edge of the plywood garboard; a wood strip of any thickness would drag somewhat and slow down the boat. The Adirondack guideboats used a strip of thin iron put on with small screws, but the fiberglass is simpler, easier, and probably better.

21. It is recommended that the frames be copper-riveted through the bottom on both sides of the two glued joints in the bottom plank.

22. One-and-a-half-inch number 10 screws go through the seat-riser doubler into the seat riser and the frames.

23. Two-inch number 12 screws go through the ends of the thwarts into the seat-riser doubler and the seat riser. There are three screws in each end.

24. Frames are fastened to the outwales with 1¼-inch number 8 screws or through-rivets.

For glue I am using Chem-Tech T-88. Although I can no more guarantee it from a health standpoint than I can any epoxy glue, I have had no bad reports from those using it, and I find it the least caustic and irritating of any of the epoxies that I have tried.

Sequel

After concluding the series on the modified Herreshoff rowboat that I wrote for the *National Fisherman* in the spring of 1980, I started building one of the boats, intending to complete it for the Mystic Seaport Museum's Annual Small Craft Workshop, held the

first weekend in June. There wasn't much time, and to ensure that the boat would be finished I decided to eliminate the end decks as originally diagramed and replace them with simple semicircular laminated breasthooks at either end. These I glued on a form, using thin strips of white ash and epoxy, as shown in the diagram. White ash was used not only because it is strong and glues well, but because the Douglas fir strips used for the laminated frames would not take the greater amount of bend required for the circular breasthook.

This alternate construction worked out very well, as it did for boats built by Myron Young on Long Island and David Scarbrough at the Rock Hall Boat Shop, Burgess, Virginia.

As it turned out, there was ample bracing at the ends even without the decks, and because of the added fullness of the ends they proved to be sufficiently dry under reasonable conditions of use. Further, the elimination of the end decks resulted in appreciable savings in materials, labor, and weight.

To make a more versatile seating arrangement, the thwarts were relocated, and the two parts hinged as diagramed, so that they could accommodate long-legged rowers. The boat can now be correctly trimmed and rowed in either direction with one, two, or three occupants and with one or two oarsmen.

A recent builder, Allan Esenlohr of Newton, New Jersey, and Fishers Island, New York, has rigged his modified Herreshoff boat to sail. "Sailing is a good and pleasant change when one is tired of rowing," he

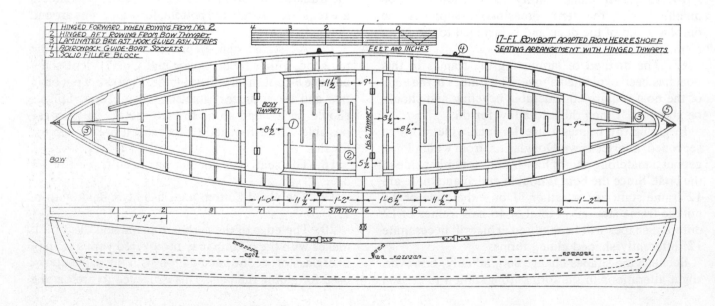

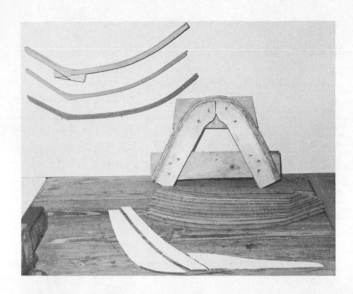

Components of the modified
Herreshoff rowboat. In the background is a breasthook being laminated over a form, and above it are
three frames taking shape. The stem
molds are also shown. (Mary Anne
Stets photo, Mystic Seaport)

Views of Myron Young's modified
Herreshoff rowboat. (Courtesy Myron
Young)

MODIFIED HERRESHOFF-PLANK WIDTHS-INCHES and EIGHTHS						
STATIONS	1	2	3	4	5	6
GARBOARD	5-4	5-4	5-3	4-7	4-4	4-2
NO. 2	3-4	4-1	4-3	4-4	4-6	4-6
NO. 3	2-6	3-1	3-3	3-5	3-4	3-5
NO. 4	2-7	3-1	3-3	3-4	3-4	3-5
SHEER	2-6	3-2	3-3	3-4	3-5	3-5
ADD BOTTOM THICKNESS TO GARBOARD WIDTHS.						
ADD LAP WIDTH TO NOS. 2, 3, 4 AND SHEER.						
WIDTHS TO BE ADJUSTED FAIR TO SUIT EACH						
INDIVIDUAL BOAT WITH FAIR LINING BATTEN.						

reports, "but this boat is a 'rower's' boat." And so it is. Sailing this boat is not particularly recommended.

Planking widths taken off my boat are given in the accompanying table. Such widths must be adjusted in the fairing process to suit each individual boat. Nevertheless, this table can save the builder a good deal of trouble. In building lapstrake, it is always desirable to have proven planking lines to work from, either taken from a good example of the boat already built or worked out on a scale half-model. The omission of planking lines from working plans for clinker-built boats is a grave defect. Even so, most plans now available for lapstrake boats fail to include them.

MODIFIED McINNIS BATEAU

This 12-foot 8-inch cartop boat, building directions for which follow, is intended to meet the needs of a broad segment of the boating public. Well adapted for hunting and fishing, it is equally well suited to a wide range of recreational uses. It is not a particularly difficult boat to build, nor will the materials required be hard to obtain or excessively expensive.

Both the hull design and the method of construction recommended here have been tried, tested, and found superior. The two are compatible, and their combination gives every indication of producing a craft of merit.

The hull shape has been adapted with only slight modifications from a multichine plywood design that Walter J. McInnis worked out in 1940 for Mumford Brothers, commercial builders in Amesbury, Massa-chusetts. McInnis called the boat a "voyageur's bateau," and clearly intended it primarily for hunting and fishing, and as a replacement for the ordinary canvas canoe. Construction was ultralight—especially for 1940, before the advent of thermoplastic adhesives. The three wide planks of the multichine sides were backed by ash seam battens, and ¼-inch Weldwood was used for its slightly rockered flat bottom. Weight of the completed boat is said to have been on the order of 63 pounds. After the company that was building them got into financial difficulties and shut down production, their stock of unsold boats was picked up by the Vermont fish and game wardens, which says something for the quality and character-istics of the boat!

Best known as one of this country's leading designers of large power craft, Walter McInnis is equally adept as a designer of small craft for the sportsman. An avid fly fisherman, McInnis is a longtime member of a famous Megantic sporting club in the Rangeley Lakes region. In the winter of 1949–50 Earle R. Rumery, then manager of the Marblehead Boat Yard Company in Biddeford, Maine, built one of these boats. He retained the shape but modified the construction considerably. Rounding the slightly knuckled shape of the sides, he framed them with flat ribs, covering the outside with canvas, canoe fashion. Weight was increased to about 75 pounds, but displacement, righting arm, stability, and other hull characteristics remained essentially unchanged.

McInnis commented on Rumery's boat in a letter published in *Outdoor Maine* in April 1960. He had this to say about its capacity and stability: "Three of us totaling in weight close to 600 pounds have fished from it, been able to stand up in it, fly cast or spin, all at the same time, using the alternate firing method, *without* danger of capsizing. She is a remarkable little boat." Responding to editorial comment on this letter, Rumery forwarded two photos of his boat, which were printed in *Outdoor Maine*'s June issue. "The first picture with the stern of the boat in the water," Rumery wrote, "was snapped on a trip taken by my son and me when we were carrying about 300 pounds of duffle across the lake. In the other picture we were just returning from a hunting trip, on which we had gotten a black bear and a large buck and doe, which we had carried across the lake in the boat." Perhaps in two trips, as all of this seems rather a lot for a single trip. In any case, an impressive performance for the little boat.

More than two decades later, Rumery wrote in response to my inquiry:

> I am glad to report that the boat is still in service at my wilderness camp in northern Maine. My son recanvased it this past year. . . .It has proved to be an ideal boat for fishing and hunting. Its stability is excellent, and—not that I recommend this for the general public—I have stood up in it a great many times, casting and fly fishing, while another person was rowing. The location of our camp makes it necessary for us to portage across the lake, since there are no roads to it. We have crossed the lake when it has been blowing hard, when in fact a larger boat, but of poor design, would have capsized. Our boat rows very easy and paddles very well.

So much for the boat's capacity, and for its handling and seakeeping characteristics.

The method of construction offered here, selected as the easiest and most suitable, is an adaptation of the building method developed over many years for the Adirondack guideboat. This adaptation of standard guideboat construction was first applied by me when I built the modified Herreshoff rowboat discussed earlier in this chapter. Apart from requiring some care and precision, this construction method is not difficult; it is well within reach of amateurs having basic woodworking experience and a minimum knowledge of lofting, spiling, and lapstrake planking. Though in no sense a boat to be stitched together in an afternoon or a weekend, it would go together more easily and quickly, I am convinced, than a Lawley yacht tender, a Delaware ducker, or a Rushton Wee Lassie, to cite several well-known classics that have been built successfully by amateurs.

No steam bending is required, no rabbeted keel or stems, no beveled chine strips, and no setup using molds, since planking is applied directly to the preshaped laminated frames. For this reason, the frames must be accurately shaped, and this requires an accurate full-size laydown of the frame sections, from which thin plywood patterns of the individual frame shapes are taken.

The materials required are readily obtainable almost anywhere. They consist of $\frac{3}{16}$-inch marine plywood for the planking and $\frac{3}{8}$-inch plywood for the bottom; spruce for the laminated frames, stems, and breasthooks and for the internal across-bottom intermediates, the outside fore-and-aft bottom runners, the thwarts, and the risers; mahogany, cherry, or other hardwood for the gunwales; small bronze screws, ring nails, rivets, and copper tacks for fastenings; epoxy adhesive; and a few yards of narrow fiberglass tape.

Spruce, the standard timber for framing Adirondack guideboats, is recommended for laminated frames and stems because it is stiff and strong yet light in weight, and because it glues well. Since it will be used in short pieces and thin strips, these can be cut to advantage, if one avoids knots, from rough eastern red spruce lumber, the kind widely sold for staging planks and ledger boards. Neither white pine nor white cedar is strong enough for this use. Clear, rift-sawn, old-growth Douglas fir makes a good substitute, but not the unseasoned, sappy, slash-sawn fir commonly supplied as construction lumber. The best marine-grade plywood that can be bought is none too good. Sapele ply is recommended as being strong and hard and having good abrasion resistance. Okoume plywood is lighter but softer, and has less impact strength. A good grade of marine fir would be quite adequate.

For the best results, one should observe the following order of construction. First comes the laydown of lines. An accurate full-size laydown is absolutely essential for obtaining the shapes of the bottom, the two stems, and the frames. Because the two ends of the boat are exactly alike, only one stem pattern is required, and only 10 different frame patterns, one for each station. From each of these 10 patterns four identical laminated frames will be made, one for each of the four identical quarters of the hull.

The gluing form and the procedure for laminating the stems are fully diagramed. Spruce strips $\frac{1}{8}$ inch thick, previously stripped on the circular saw, are coated with epoxy glue and clamped tightly into the curve of the gluing form, which will have been well

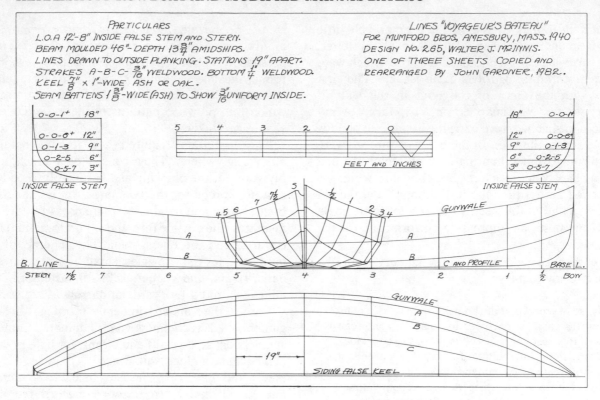

PARTICULARS
L.O.A 12'-8" INSIDE FALSE STEM AND STERN.
BEAM MOULDED 46"- DEPTH 13⅜" AMIDSHIPS.
LINES DRAWN TO OUTSIDE PLANKING. STATIONS 19" APART.
STRAKES A–B–C– ³⁄₁₆" WELDWOOD. BOTTOM ¼" WELDWOOD.
KEEL ⅞" x 1"-WIDE ASH OR OAK.
SEAM BATTENS 1⅜"-WIDE (ASH) TO SHOW ³⁄₁₆" UNIFORM INSIDE.

LINES "VOYAGEUR'S BATEAU"
FOR MUMFORD BROS, AMESBURY, MASS. 1940
DESIGN NO. 265, WALTER J. McINNIS.
ONE OF THREE SHEETS COPIED AND
REARRANGED BY JOHN GARDNER, 1982.

	STEM	½	1	2	3	4	5	6	7	7½	STERN
OFFSETS McINNIS BATEAU											
GUNWALE	1-11-2	1-7-6	1-5-5⁺	1-3-3	1-2-1⁺	1-1-6	1-2-0	1-2-7	1-4-7	1-6-6	1-9-5
A	1-5-0⁺	1-1-5⁺	0-11-2	0-8-4⁺	0-7-3	0-7-0	0-7-2⁺	0-8-3-0	0-10-6⁺	1-0-6⁺	1-4-1
B	0-11-1	0-7-7	0-5-3⁺	0-2-6	0-1-6-0	0-1-3	0-1-6	0-2-6-0	0-5-2⁺	0-7-3	0-10-2⁺
C			0-0-6⁺	0-0-3	0-0-1	0-0-0	0-0-1	0-0-3	0-0-6		
PROFILE		0-1-6	0-0-6⁺	0-0-3	0-0-1	0-0-0	0-0-1	0-0-3	0-0-6⁺	0-1-5	
GUNWALE	0-0-4	0-7-4	1-0-5⁺	1-7-0⁺	1-10-0⁺	1-11-0	1-10-2	1-7-1	1-0-7	0-8-2	0-2-4⁺
A	0-0-4	0-6-2	0-10-7	1-5-3	1-8-5	1-9-6	1-8-7	1-5-5⁺	0-11-4	0-6-7⁺	0-1-6
B	0-0-4	0-4-1	0-7-6⁺	1-1-4	1-4-6	1-5-7	1-4-7	1-1-6	0-8-2⁺	0-4-5	0-0-7⁺
C	0-0-4		0-2-6	0-7-1⁺	0-10-0	0-11-0	0-10-2	0-7-4	0-2-7		
½ FALSE KEEL	0-0-4	0-0-4		←		STRAIGHT		→		0-0-4	

waxed beforehand to prevent sticking. Later, a small block is glued to the stem blank and then trimmed so that it fills out the necessary sharp angle at the bottom of the stem. Dimensions are given for obtaining the bearding line, which governs the beveling of the stem. Prudence suggests not cutting back this bevel fully, but rather leaving a little wood to be trimmed later when the planking is fitted. This is glued and nailed in place. All that is needed to cover the ends of the ³⁄₁₆-inch planking is a strip of ⅝-inch bronze half oval.

The frames, which will finish ⁹⁄₁₆ inch sided and 1¹⁄₁₆ inch molded, are laminated in the same way. Gluing forms need not be as heavy as the one required for the stems, and if the frame laminations are made up in order, the form will need only slight recutting in changing from one frame to the next. If the strips are sawn from 1½-inch-thick stock, there will be plenty of wood for the glued-up frame blanks to be split on the saw and dressed to make two frames to go opposite each other in the boat. To fill out the sharp angle at the

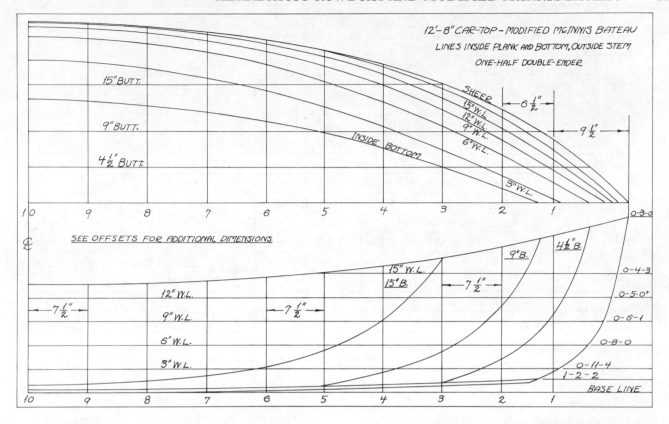

12'-8" CAR-TOP - MODIFIED McINNIS BATEAU
LINES INSIDE PLANK AND BOTTOM, OUTSIDE STEM
ONE-HALF DOUBLE-ENDER

15" BUTT.

9" BUTT.

4½" BUTT.

INSIDE BOTTOM

SHEER
15" W.L.
12" W.L.
9" W.L.
6" W.L.

3" W.L.

6½"

9½"

SEE OFFSETS FOR ADDITIONAL DIMENSIONS

15" W.L.

12" W.L.

9" W.L.

6" W.L.

3" W.L.

9" B.

15" B.

4½ B.

7½"

7½"

7½"

0-3-0

0-4-3

0-5-0⁺

0-6-1

0-8-0

0-11-4

1-2-2

BASE LINE

chine, small blocks are glued on and then trimmed to fill out the curve, as was done with the stems. This is done, of course, before the glued-up frame blank is split in two lengthwise. Bevels for the frames are obtained in the usual way from the laydown of section lines. Because of the considerable angle of bevel on the frames at stations 1, 2, 3, 4, and 5, the molded width of the blanks for these frames might well be increased by an additional ⅛-inch strip to allow for the wood that will be planed away in beveling.

Assuming the bottom is to be made up from standard 4-by-8 panels of ⅜-inch plywood, it will have to be spliced at one end. Scarf widths should be 12 times the thickness of the material, or 4½ inches here. Scarf surfaces should be accurately planed *almost* to a feather edge; a scant ¹⁄₃₂ inch of edge thickness should be left. Epoxy glue is applied to the two surfaces, and these are brought precisely together, tacked to prevent slippage, placed between two well-waxed boards wider than the scarf, and nailed through the scarf from one side to the other with enough large nails to bring everything tightly together. When the glue has fully cured, the nails are pulled, the boards removed, the nail holes through the scarf joint plugged, and the edges of the scarf sanded smooth.

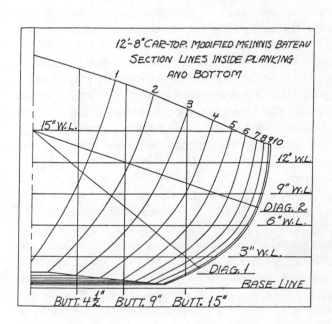

12'-8" CAR-TOP. MODIFIED McINNIS BATEAU
SECTION LINES INSIDE PLANKING
AND BOTTOM

1
2
3
4 5 6 7 8 9 10

15" W.L.

12" W.L.

9" W.L.

DIAG. 2

6" W.L.

3" W.L.

DIAG. 1

BASE LINE

BUTT. 4½"   BUTT. 9"   BUTT. 15"

STATIONS		STEM	1	2	3	4	5	6	7	8	9	10
HEIGHTS	SHEER	1-10-1	1-7-6	1-6-3	1-5-0+	1-4-0	1-3-1+	1-2-5	1-2-1+	1-1-7	1-1-6	1-1-6
	BOTTOM	0-1-5	0-2-4	0-1-4	0-1-1	0-0-7+	0-0-6	0-0-5	0-0-4	0-0-3+	0-0-3	0-0-3
	BUTT. 4½"	—	0-9-7	0-4-2	0-1-1	—	—	—	—	—	—	—
	BUTT. 9"	—	—	0-11-0	0-5-1	0-2-4	0-0-6+	—	—	—	—	—
	BUTT. 15	—	—	—	1-4-7	0-9-2	0-5-2+	0-3-2	0-2-1	0-1-4	0-1-1	0-0-7
HALF-BREADTHS	SHEER	0-0-0+	0-7-7+	0-11-5+	1-3-0	1-5-4+	1-7-3	1-8-5+	1-9-5+	1-10-3	1-10-7	1-11-0
	W.L. 15"	0-0-0+	0-6-4+	0-10-6	1-2-3	1-5-2	—	—	—	—	—	—
	W.L. 12"	0-0-0+	0-5-2+	0-9-3	1-1-1+	1-4-2	1-6-4	1-8-1+	1-9-3	1-10-2	1-10-6	1-10-7
	W.L. 9"	0-0-0+	0-4-0	0-7-7	0-11-5+	1-2-7	1-5-2+	1-7-1+	1-8-4+	1-9-5	1-10-1+	1-10-3
	W.L. 6"	0-0-0+	0-2-3+	0-6-0	0-9-5+	1-0-6	1-3-2+	1-5-4	1-7-1	1-8-1+	1-8-7	1-9-1
	W.L. 3"	0-0-0+	0-0-3	0-3-2+	0-6-5	0-9-5	1-0-1	1-2-1+	1-3-6	1-5-0	1-5-6+	1-6-1
	BOTTOM	—	0-0-0+	0-1-6	0-4-3+	0-6-7	0-8-6+	0-10-2	0-11-3	1-0-2	1-0-7	1-1-1
DIAGONAL 1		0-0-0+	0-6-3	0-10-0	1-1-1+	1-3-5	1-5-3+	1-6-6+	1-7-6	1-8-3	1-8-7	1-9-0
DIAGONAL 2		0-0-0+	0-6-1	0-9-7	1-1-2+	1-4-1	1-6-2	1-8-0+	1-9-3+	1-10-3	1-11-0	1-11-1

12'-8" CAR-TOP — MODIFIED McINNIS BATEAU

DIAGONAL 1 15" UP, OUT 15" ON 3" W.L. DIAG. 2 15" UP, OUT 18" ON 9" W.L.

OFFSET MEASUREMENTS, FEET, INCHES, EIGHTHS. INSIDE PLANK AND BOTTOM, O.S. STEM

Finally, in preparation for assembly, the bottom is cut out exactly to its faired *inside* shape. The locations of the frames and the across-bottom intermediates are lined across the inside surface of the bottom, and the stems are fastened on at the ends with glue and screws from the outside. Special care should be taken so that the two stems line up exactly with the centerline of the bottom. The bottom is not beveled until the setup on the ladder frame for planking has been made and the frames have been fastened in place. Beveling the bottom is part of the final fairing operation before planking.

The ladder frame and horses for the setup are made as diagramed. Required are several lengths of standard 2-by-6 floor joists and 1-inch spruce ledger board or the equivalent, to be nailed together. It is essential to pick out joists that are straight, and they should be seasoned and dry; otherwise they are likely to twist out of true. The uprights that support the bottom of the boat must vary in height, of course, so that they will conform to the designed fore-and-aft rocker of the bottom. The bottom is easily sprung down to rest on them and is secured with screws, which are fastened through the bottom with large washers under their heads. After the planked-up hull is removed from the form, the screw holes through the bottom are easily plugged.

When the bottom has been leveled athwartships, the stems are accurately plumbed and aligned before being secured in place. After this has been done, the frames and the cross-bottom intermediates are fastened in place at their respective locations, as previously marked on the inside of the bottom, with screws through the bottom. The frames are beveled before they are fastened to the bottom, and are placed so their heel bevels coincide with the curve of the bottom. This is also the time to fasten the bottom runners with screws (1½-inch number 8 wood screws) into the frames and intermediates inside. Not until all of this has been done is the bottom beveled to conform to the rake of the side frames—the object being a garboard that fits tightly when it is sprung in place along the chine knuckle and fastened.

The recommended approximate shape for the garboard, taken from a scale half-model of the hull, is shown. The dimensions given here will be close, but they should be relined on the boat with a fair batten just the same. If the bottom and ends of the plank stand a little proud when the plank is on, they are easily trimmed flush with a sharp block plane—the proper tool for trimming plywood.

Before planking starts, a fairly stiff batten is bent around the timberheads at the sheerline and attached at its ends to the stems. The frames are then correctly

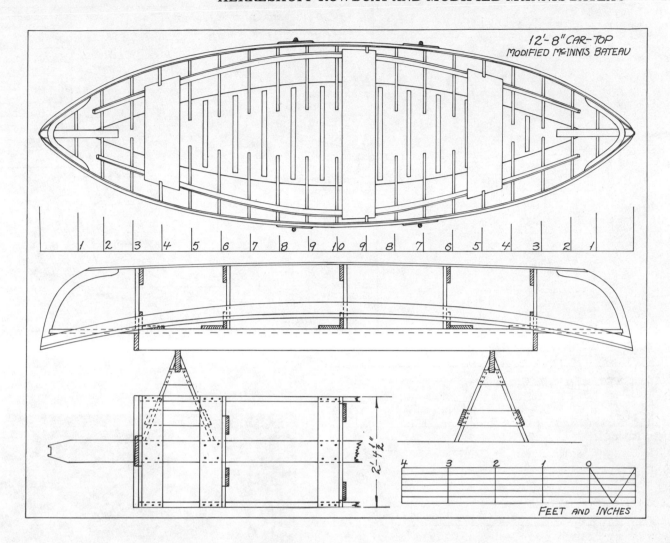

12'-8" CAR-TOP
MODIFIED McINNIS BATEAU

2'-4½"

FEET AND INCHES

spaced along this batten and temporarily attached to it. Twists of soft wire serve well for this. This is essentially the same procedure that is followed in planking an Adirondack guideboat. The laminated frames are stiff enough so that cross spalls or spreaders will probably not be necessary.

After the garboard is fastened in place, a stiff batten or ribband should be bent around the frames just above the turn of the bilge on either side and temporarily fastened to the stems at both ends. By this means the frames can be equalized. Any that bulge however slightly will be pushed back. Any that are slack can be pulled flush and wired. After the second and third plank from the bottom are on and fastened, this ribband will no longer be needed and can be removed. The reason that such a ribband may be needed is that ³⁄₁₆-inch plywood planking is not stiff enough by itself to pull the frames into line.

All of the planks, if gotten out of standard 4-by-8 panels, will have one splice. This can be done as the planking is put on the boat. Splices should be staggered as much as possible, starting with the garboard, which can be spliced amidships. All splices should be planned so that they land on frames, to which they should be fastened. Scarf length for ³⁄₁₆-inch plank is 2¼ inches. Splices are glued with epoxy. They will need to be clamped together until the glue sets, and this can be done with two small waxed blocks, one inside and one out, through-bolted with a small machine bolt. After the blocks and the bolt are removed, the hole through the splice is easily plugged.

The garboard shape with its wide ends is indicated by the shape of this particular hull with its ample sheer and the considerable width of its flat bottom. The wide end uses up space, tending to straighten out the run of the planks above and allowing them to diminish

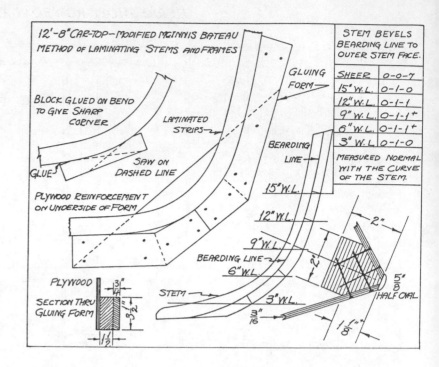

12'-8" CAR-TOP-MODIFIED McINNIS BATEAU
METHOD OF LAMINATING STEMS AND FRAMES

GLUING FORM

BLOCK GLUED ON BEND
TO GIVE SHARP
CORNER

LAMINATED
STRIPS

GLUE

SAW ON
DASHED LINE

BEARDING
LINE

PLYWOOD REINFORCEMENT
ON UNDERSIDE OF FORM

15" W.L.

12" W.L.

9" W.L.

BEARDING LINE

6" W.L.

PLYWOOD

SECTION THRU
GLUING FORM

3/4"

3 1/2"

1 1/2"

STEM

3" W.L.

3/16"

2"

2"

5/8"
HALF OVAL

1 1/8"

STEM BEVELS BEARDING LINE TO OUTER STEM FACE.	
SHEER	0-0-7
15" W.L.	0-1-0
12" W.L.	0-1-1
9" W.L.	0-1-1⁺
6" W.L.	0-1-1⁺
3" W.L.	0-1-0

MEASURED NORMAL WITH THE CURVE OF THE STEM.

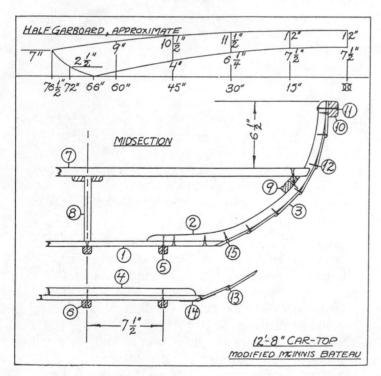

HALF GARBOARD, APPROXIMATE

7"   2 1/2"   9"   10 1/2"   11 1/2"   12"   12"
      4"   6 1/4"   7 1/2"   7 1/2"

76 1/2" 72" 66" 60"   45"   30"   15"   IX

MIDSECTION

6 1/2"

7 1/2"

12'-8" CAR-TOP
MODIFIED McINNIS BATEAU

A modified McInnis bateau built in Kansas by Robert McElroy, M.D., and his nephew, from the instructions presented in this chapter. "The boat required about three months of part-time work to construct," McElroy wrote. "It was a very good experience for both of us who had never built something of lapstrake construction."

slightly in width from amidships to the ends, which contributes to a pleasing appearance. The average width of the five planks above the garboard will be about 2⅞ inches amidships, diminishing to about 2½ inches at the ends, plus a ½-inch lap. A ½-inch lap is ample for a plank thickness of ³⁄₁₆ inch.

Laps are glued with an epoxy adhesive, thickened with Cab-O-Sil or something similar that will prevent running. Planks are nailed through the laps into the frames with ¾-inch bronze or stainless ring nails, except for the bottom edge of the garboard, where the molded width of the frame at the chine knuckle swells enough to take a 1-inch number 6 or number 7 screw. Between the frames the laps are pulled together, so the glue will have a chance to set, with ⅜-inch copper tacks spaced about 2 inches and clinched on the inside. A very fine, sharp awl, such as those used for guideboat tacks, would be just the thing to pierce the hard plywood and prevent the soft copper tacks from crippling. The ends of the planks are both glued and well nailed to the stems.

Where the bottom bevel is sufficiently wide to take tacks, they are put in the lower edge of the garboard between frames, just as they are in the laps. Otherwise, the screws into the bottoms of the frames should pull tight enough to ensure a tight glued joint along the chine edge between the frames. In any case, this joint is finally made permanently tight by being covered with a narrow strip of fiberglass tape set in epoxy.

The outside of the hull, even to a priming coat of paint, can be completed before it is removed from the form and set right side up. Some, however, might want to put the gunwale on after the hull is turned over, in order better to resight the sheerline and possibly to give it a final fairing.

There is nothing special about installing the risers and the thwarts. Information for locating them is given in the diagram. The thwarts have been located to accommodate either one or two occupants and to permit rowing or paddling. Oarlocks are the type standard for guideboats.

Laminated breasthooks are shown at the two ends. They are glued up on a form, which—to secure a good fit—should not be made until the gunwales are on. Because of the tight bend, the strips for laminating will have to be thinner than those for the frames. If white ash is available it can be used here, since it bends more easily than spruce and is stronger and heavier. These laminated breasthooks should be fastened with copper rivets through the gunwales.

No floorboards are required, and the bottom will drain easily around the ends of the intermediate cross cleats. Although the flat bottom is quite wide, it is more than adequately stiffened and reinforced by the outside bottom runners fastened through into the frame feet and the intermediates. Frames, intermediates, and runners are glued as well as screwed in place.

Weight should fall somewhere between 85 and 90 pounds. It could be made lighter if scantlings were shaved, but I like some safety factor.

Key to the numbered diagram:

1. *Plywood bottom:* ⅜ inch thick.
2. *Laminated spruce frames:* Sided ⁹⁄₁₆ inch, molded 1¹⁄₁₆ inch.
3. *Six plywood planks:* ³⁄₁₆ inch thick.
4. *Across-bottom intermediates:* Spruce, 1⅛ inches wide, 1¹⁄₁₆ inch thick.
5. *Bronze wood screws:* 1½-inch number 8.
6. *Bottom runners:* Spruce, 1⅛ inches wide, ¾ inch deep.
7. *Thwarts:* Spruce, 9 inches by ¾ inch.
8. *Post:* 1½ inches by ¾ inch.
9. *Riser:* Spruce, 1¾ inches by ¾ inch, tapering to 1 inch by ¾ inch at the ends.
10. *Gunwales:* Mahogany, cherry, or other hardwood, 1½ inches by ⅞ inch amidships, tapering to 1 inch by ¾ inch at the ends.
11. *Copper rivets:* Gunwale through frame heads, also gunwale through breasthooks.
12. *Lap fastenings into frames:* ¾-inch bronze or stainless ring nails.
13. *Copper tacks:* ⅜ inch, through laps between frames. Spaced about 2 inches.
14. *Fiberglass tape:* Two inches wide, set in epoxy.
15. *Bronze screws:* One-inch, number 6 or number 7, through bottom edge of garboard into frames.

Recommended epoxy glue: Chem-Tech T-88 thickened with Cab-O-Sil when necessary.

Suggested references: For a detailed explanation of guideboat construction, see *The Adirondack Guide-Boat* by Kenneth and Helen Durant. My book *Building Classic Small Craft* (this book's predecessor) offers guidance for lapstrake planking and spiling. The complete references are given in the Bibliography.

2

PILOT GIG

Late on Friday the 13th of December 1907, the seven-masted steel schooner *Thomas W. Lawson*, having lost her bearings in the fog, found herself in Broad Sound within the Western Rocks at the Isles of Scilly off England's Cornish coast.

The largest schooner ever built—over 400 feet long with her topmast head 155 feet above the deck—the *Lawson* had encountered two severe gales while crossing the Atlantic, which had blown out all but six of her sails and carried away all her lifeboats. And now on that fateful night she found herself in a perilous position close to a lee shore and in the direct sweep of a rising gale.

Pilot boats put out from Saint Marys and Saint Agnes islands, and the Saint Agnes boat got close enough to set William Cook Hicks, a Trinity House pilot, on board, but they could do nothing more in the

raging storm as darkness closed down. At about 1:15 in the morning of the 14th the 150-ton port anchor chain parted, and directly the starboard anchor gave way as well. As the helpless vessel was blown toward Annet the crew took to the rigging, and in less than 15 minutes she struck Shag Rock, rolling over and breaking in two between the number 4 and 5 holds. All hands were thrown into the sea except the pilot Hicks, who had lashed himself to the rigging and was carried down with the ship.

When day broke no sign of the *Lawson* was to be seen except a welter of wreckage floating off Saint Agnes and Annet. Although the gale still raged and seas were running mountain-high, the six-oared pilot gig *Slippen* put out with double-banked oars and a crew of 12. Of these, five were named Hicks. All morning they searched, finding only corpses, and

The pilot gig Treffry, *built in 1843, has survived generations of hard use despite her light build. (F.E. Gibson photo, Scilly Isles)*

finally one seriously injured crewman with his side badly mangled.

In the afternoon the search was continued. This time the *Slippen* apparently held a crew of six, and pulling as far as the Hellweather Ledges they spotted two survivors clinging to some rocks. Frederick Cook Hicks, eldest son of the drowned pilot, undaunted by the surf, swam a line to the exhausted men and brought both away safely. One was the captain, George W. Dow of Hancock, Maine, whose wrist was broken, and the other, Edward Rowe of Boston, the engineer. In recognition of his heroism that day, Fred Hicks was presented with gold watches by the U.S. government and the owners of the *Lawson*, and the members of the *Slippen*'s crew received gold medals.

This rescue is remembered because of the *Lawson* as well as the tragic involvement of the Hicks family. Yet it was but one of many gallant rescues carried out in Cornish pilot gigs. These superb seaboats, developed on the coast of Cornwall nearly 200 years ago, best demonstrated their unique qualities in the treacherous waters surrounding the Isles of Scilly.

In the bygone days of sail they competed as pilot boats, provided local transportation between the islands and the mainland, participated in rescue and salvage work, and were favored by smugglers when smuggling was rife along this stretch of coast. It has been said that at one time more rum and brandy were smuggled into Cornwall and Devon than lawfully entered the Port of London.

Situated 28 miles off Land's End at the convergence of two major sea-lanes—the English Channel and the Bristol Channel—the Scillies consist of some 145 low-lying islands and rocks. Many of the outer reefs and ledges are submerged at high tide, and the water around them is commonly 20 fathoms or more. Thus, vessels that strike them are likely to sink without leaving a trace.

The Western Rocks beyond Saint Agnes comprise 10 square miles of hidden perils. In fog, mist, and darkness this extended barrier of lethal rocks often went unperceived, because of its low silhouette, until the vessel struck. From the time of the Romans the Scillies were dreaded by mariners, yet because of their location merchantmen were forced near them.

In bygone centuries the Scillies were a favored haunt of pirates, buccaneers, and wreckers. It is said that at one time wrecking was a chief means of livelihood for the inhabitants. It is hard to realize that these islands, so peaceful today and bright with flowers grown for British florists, were once overrun with freebooters and cutthroats of many nationalities.

Smuggling lasted longer, well into the 19th century,

in fact. With the Channel Islands only 170 miles away and the coast of Brittany even closer, smuggling expeditions bringing back French lace, silks, brandy, and other contraband were well within the capability of these slim but seakindly six-oared gigs.

Richard Gillis of the Newquay Rowing Club, who has done so much to rescue and perpetuate these extraordinary boats, wrote in the journal *Country Life* that John Nance, a famous Scilly pilot born around 1800, made in his lifetime 25 smuggling trips to Roscoff on the French coast. The round trip aggregated about 250 miles of open sea, something of a feat for open boats averaging not more than 30 feet in length and about 5 feet in beam.

Some of these trips by Nance could have been made in *Bonnet*, built before 1833 and still sound and racing today after being restored in the 1950s. *Bonnet* was the boat used by John Nance's son, James, also a well-known Scilly pilot, born in 1831.

According to Gillis, on one of their smuggling trips John Nance and his crew kept at the oars for 30 hours straight, holding their gig head-on in seas when caught in an unexpected blow. These gigs were very fast and in a chase could usually outdistance Customs sail by hauling directly to windward. To discourage smuggling, England at one time prohibited the construction of eight-oared gigs.

Gillis believes that *Bonnet* was built by the Peters family who originated these pilot gigs. John Peters is credited with building the first one in 1790 or 1791 in the village of Saint Mawes, close by Falmouth on the Cornish coast. Three generations of Peters were responsible for the lion's share of boats built in the pilot gig's heyday, and the Polvarth yard whence they came belongs today to Frank Peters, a direct descendant, who is still building boats.

Gillis relates a tale about *Bonnet* that is too good to pass by. As the story goes, this gig took its name from an old lady who had a reputation for witchcraft. When the gigs pulled away for a job of pilotage, the old lady would run to the top of the hill and wave her bonnet to send the gig so named out ahead of the rest. After her death her son would carry the Old Lady's bonnet to the hilltop, place it on a bush, and say, "Now, Mother, do your best."

And for years after, apparently for reasons of superstition, the name *Bonnet* was never mentioned by the crew, who instead took care to refer to their boat as "the old hat."

In the days of sail these slim, sinewy, ultrafast gigs were active in pilotage and salvage along much of the Cornish coast, from Falmouth to Newquay and Padstow. At Newquay, Edgar March tells us, it was not unusual for competing gigs to race offshore as far as Lundy Island, some 50 miles and more, with expectation of picking up an inbound vessel.

But it is on their exploits in Scilly waters that their chief fame rests. At this dangerous crossroads of the sea-lanes the need in former times for pilots was continual and urgent. During prolonged spells of easterly weather, for instance, upward of 100 sail frequently would be found lying at anchor off the Roads, waiting to proceed.

For their skill and daring the local pilots were renowned among mariners everywhere. Their knowledge of the surrounding waters and the adjoining coast was minute. No risk daunted them, no weather was too bad to hold them ashore when their services were required.

The Bryher gig *Golden Eagle*, faster then either *Albion* or *March*, which she was built to supersede, carried out some notable rescue and salvage work. When the steamship *Sussex* was wrecked in December 1885, *Golden Eagle* rescued part of the crew and shared in the salvage of 200 bullocks and other cargo, including flour, lard, tinned beef, frozen geese, and turkeys.

A list of her exploits given by March includes saving the crew of the steamship *Brinkburn,* bound for Le Havre with cotton, in 1898; coming to the assistance of the French barque *Paranee,* stranded with a cargo of coconuts, a year later; and on the same night standing by the ship *Eric Rickmers* from Bangkok, loaded with rice.

When in April 1910 the Atlantic transport liner *Minnehaha* stranded on a hidden ledge in thick fog, *Golden Eagle* was on hand to assist in the rescue of passengers and crew. *Czar,* another Bryher gig, built to beat *Golden Eagle,* also participated in the salvage work on *Minnehaha,* which went on for three weeks and included the swimming ashore of 234 head of cattle.

Cattle were roped by the horns so their heads would be held above water, and towed to shore. When the Liverpool steamer *Castleford* was lost in June 1887, two pounds a head were paid for each steer landed on Annet. At that time *Gipsy,* a Scilly-built gig, was holed in the port side by the horn of a fractious bullock. The hole was still there, covered by a patch, when the Padstow Rowing Club refitted *Gipsy* in 1955.

O&M (after Obadiah and Mary, the names of her owners), another Scilly gig participating in that

The pilot gigs were sometimes rigged for sailing. The Nornour, *one of the surviving gigs, is shown with her lug rig off the Cornish coast. (F.E. Gibson photo, Scilly Isles)*

salvage operation, was not so lucky. Her whole bow was stove when a bullock fell on her from the deck. Mishaps of this sort were not uncommon. On one occasion, a bale of cotton being rolled into a gig slipped and crashed through the bilges of ¼-inch-thick elm plank.

In the estimation of March, who should know, no finer rescue effort is to be found in the annals of Scilly gigs than the one that saved two lives when the steamship *Delaware* went down off Fearing Ledge in December 1871. With engines stopped and sails blown out in the violent northwest gale, *Delaware* swung broadside on a mighty sea, then another close behind swept over her and she was gone. Sometime after, watchers from South Hill on Bryher spotted two men on half a boat, two on a spar, and one on some wreckage.

The gig *Albion,* 30 feet long with 5½ feet of beam and weighing close to half a ton, was picked as the best boat to go. Six oars were lashed crosswise to the thwarts, and this enabled 12 men to lift her up and carry her half a mile overland to Rushy Bay, where they launched her stern first into a following sea and wind. Running before the towering combers and gaining a little between each sea, they finally made the

lee of the North Hill on Samson, whence they could see that the two men previously seen on the half boat had managed to land. To reach them it was necessary for the nearly spent crew to carry the gig overland once again, some 200 yards across an isthmus of scrub and slippery rocks. Up a steep bank and down the other side they went, opposed by the full force of the December gale and in constant danger of dropping the boat and smashing her frail plank on the rocks.

But they managed to make it safely, and this time the launch went straight into the screaming blast, the huge waves standing the trembling gig nearly on end. Finally they reached White Island, picked up the two half-naked survivors, and returned to Samson. This time the exhausted crew did not attempt to carry their gig back over the high ground. With the two survivors they made their way to the East Par, where they huddled together for warmth and rest in the shelter of a rock to await the gig *March,* whose assistance had been signaled from the top of North Hill. Upon the arrival of *March,* the crew of *Albion* transferred to that boat and fought their way back to Bryher with the two survivors, who received hot drinks and were put to bed.

The crew that remained on Samson spent a cold

December night in the open, and in the morning had the task of manhandling *Albion* back across the isthmus. Regretfully we must add that those who carried out this heroic exploit received neither acknowledgment nor reward beyond the gratitude of the rescued men.

No account of these gigs should fail to mention that they were sometimes sailed, and that they were both fast and handy under canvas. March describes an urgent trip under sail from Bryher to Saint Marys and back to fetch a doctor on a wild night in rain and a hard sou'wester. The crew hugged the bottom of the boat— its mizzen set, its fore lug double-reefed, and several hundredweight of stone ballast aboard—bailing as the waves slopped over the rail. On one occasion, he relates, a mighty wave picked up the gig so that her rudder hung completely free, the boat spinning around with the lee gunwale buried and the crew bailing for their lives. The *Sussex* made the three-mile run in 15 minutes.

With the passing of merchant sail and ensuing changes in shipping and the development of improved aids for navigation, the heroic age of the pilot gig was brought to an end. Many came ashore for keeps and perished through neglect. The ignoble fate of one, it is said, was to become the roof of a chicken run. Others continued to find limited employment at the islands, such as transporting wedding parties—the last in 1929—and carrying loads of cut flowers and potatoes to the mainland.

In more recent years, going back to the 1950s, rowing clubs both on the Cornish mainland and on the Scillies have brought about a flourishing revival of gig racing. Not a few of the famous old gigs have been restored and are now racing. Prominent on this list are such names as *Bonnet, Shah, Dolly Varden, Nornour, Slippen, Czar, Golden Eagle, Dove, Newquay,* and *Treffry.* The Scilly gigs race regularly during the summer, with interisland and ladies' races once each week.

At Saint Marys, Tom Chudleigh has built several new gigs, including two completed in 1974, *Active* and *Good Intent. Active* is on the lines of *Treffry,* built by Peters in 1843. This was the longest pilot gig built until *Active,* and is generally considered the finest.

From Harold Kimber, who assisted Chudleigh in the construction of *Active*, I received the lines of *Treffry* and some of the construction details for *Active.* The process that led to this was set in motion when I read Edgar March's *Inshore Craft of Britain in the Days of Sail and Oar.*

Although I had been vaguely aware for a long time of the gigs variously employed for piloting, salvage, smuggling, and lifesaving along the English coast, it was not until I read the chapter on pilot gigs in March's book that I got a close-up look at these boats as they had been developed and used in Cornwall and particularly at the Isles of Scilly. These Cornish pilot gigs are all but incredible. If their capabilities and performance had not been fully and incontrovertibly attested, one would be obliged to reject as fanciful some of the feats attributed to them.

How well and how long they lasted in spite of the rough usage to which they were subjected is not the least remarkable thing about these remarkable boats. *Newquay,* built in 1812, is still afloat and racing albeit having undergone extensive repairs. And *Treffry,* also still alive, the gig whose lines are given here, was built in 1832.

Nor are these alone. At least 10 still in commission have lasted well over a century. As far as I know, no other class of boats anywhere can boast such a record of sheer endurance.

March's detailed account of these Cornish gigs was something of a revelation, yet my interest was further whetted by the realization that these gigs showed a number of similarities to early American Whitehall boats. *American Star,* the famous race boat given by the Whitehall boatmen of New York to General Lafayette on his last visit to the United States in 1826 and still preserved on the Lafayette estate in France, is a four-oared gig of 27 feet whose lines are surprisingly like those of the Cornish pilot gigs. Although she was built in Brooklyn, her builders were two brothers who had learned their trade in England.

To follow up this lead and see whether a closer and more definite connection could be made between American Whitehalls and British pilot gigs, I wrote to Harold Kimber in England, one who could likely provide additional information about these boats and perhaps even a set of lines. It was a shot in the dark, but as things turned out, it went straight to the mark.

Kimber, a master boatbuilder with over 50 years of the trade under his belt, had come out of retirement temporarily in 1972 when he was commissioned by the British National Maritime Museum to build a replica of a 26-foot 9th-century Viking *faeringen* (four-oared boat), one of the three king's boats found inside the Gokstad burial ship dug up near Oslo, Norway.

I visited Harold when he was engaged in this project at Cory's Bargeworks in Charlton, a London suburb,

The four-oared gig General Lafayette *skims over the Mystic River. Built by the author in the winter of 1974-75, she is a replica of the early American Whitehall boat* American Star, *which was presented to General Lafayette in 1826. The similarity to the Cornish gigs is remarkable. (Kenneth E. Mahler photo, Mystic Seaport)*

and was greatly impressed both by the difficulties of his undertaking and by the quality of his workmanship. Upon completing the faeringen, Harold went back to his home afloat, *Brue Gull,* a Griffiths-designed 28-foot centerboard cutter, which he had built in 1966 for his retirement.

His cruises up and down the English coast occasionally took him to the Isles of Scilly. Here, it seemed, was the place to go for lines, and Harold wrote, "I will try to get lines of the Scilly gigs, but am not at all sure that any exist. The Peters family who built most of them seem to have used one set of molds which were spaced a little differently, or padded out a bit or vice versa, in order to alter lines, as it appeared to be required. I know that this is what Tom Chudleigh does."

Imagine my surprise, not to mention elation, when in December 1973, after a long hiatus, word came from Harold that he had engaged to help his friend Tom Chudleigh and had sailed to Scilly, laid up *Brue Gull,* and was presently building a 32-foot gig—a reproduction of one built at Saint Mawes on the Cornish mainland in 1842.

His letter continued:

This brings me to the reason for writing so promptly [?]. I am enclosing herewith a very incomplete and crude lines plan and offset table of this boat. Both time and facilities to do better were just not available. In fact I made up molds in the actual boat, and the new one is now about one-third planked (clinker 5/16-inch elm), lovely, long, easy lines, but a bit of a headache using unstable wet wood. Can you possibly get the enclosed knocked into shape properly, and produce two sets of lines for me?

I laid out a preliminary draft of the boat and sent it to Harold with queries about a number of things that I questioned or did not understand. These he answered, besides making notes and additions on the drawing he returned. In particular I had suggested that section 1 seemed a bit too full, likewise section 8, and I had indicated with dotted lines the amount of easement I judged to be indicated.

Harold agreed: "This boat [*Treffry*] has been repaired and obviously forced outwards near Station 1. After setting up our molds we had to ease quite a bit off number 1 to fair it in. Numbers 1 and 8 as you show them dotted are probably correct." Further, he went on to say that "the deadrise [of the sections] is curved as shown—your sections are okay. Most of the gigs have camber on the keel. *Treffry* has more than others." As the drawing shows, the keel line is not

OFFSETS: FEET, INCHES, EIGHTHS TO INSIDE OF PLANK											
	STATIONS	1	2	3	4	5	6	7	8	9	TRAN.
HEIGHTS ABOVE BASE LINE	SHEER	3-9-0	3-5-1	3-2-2	3-1-2	3-1-0	3-1-6	3-4-0	3-8-0	3-9-7	4-0-0
	RABBET	1-1-2	1-0-7	1-0-7	1-1-0	1-1-4	1-2-1	1-3-1	1-3-7	1-4-4	1-4-6
	BOTTOM KEEL	0-10-0	0-9-5	0-9-5	0-9-6	0-10-2	0-10-7	0-11-5	1-0-5	1-1-1	1-1-4
	9" BUTTOCK	3-0-4	1-6-7	1-3-2	1-2-7	1-2-7	1-0-4	1-7-0	2-3-4	3-2-1	—
	18" BUTTOCK	—	2-6-5	1-7-7	1-5-5	1-4-7	1-7-0	2-2-0	—	—	—
HALF-BREADTHS	SHEER	0-9-6	1-7-7	2-1-5	2-4-0	2-4-1	2-3-0	1-11-0	1-3-2	0-11-4	0-7-4
	32" W.L.	0-8-1	1-6-3	2-0-7	2-3-2	2-3-5	2-2-0	1-9-2	0-11-5	0-6-1	0-0-5
	LOAD W.L.	0-5-1	1-2-2	1-9-4	2-1-0	2-1-3	1-10-5	1-4-3	0-6-2	0-2-7	0-0-5
	KEEL	0-0-7	0-0-7	0-0-7	0-0-7	0-0-7	0-0-7	0-0-7	0-0-7	0-0-7	0-0-5
DIAGONALS	DIAGONAL A	1-0-3	2-0-4	2-7-5	2-10-5	2-10-7	2-8-5	2-3-5	1-5-7	1-0-4	0-7-0
	DIAGONAL B	0-10-0	1-6-6	2-0-3	2-2-4	2-2-6	2-0-5	1-7-7	0-11-7	0-6-7	0-0-5
DIAG. A 4' ABOVE BASE LINE, OUT 2'-3" ON L.W.L. DIAG B 3' ABOVE B.L. OUT 1'-2" ON L.W.L.											

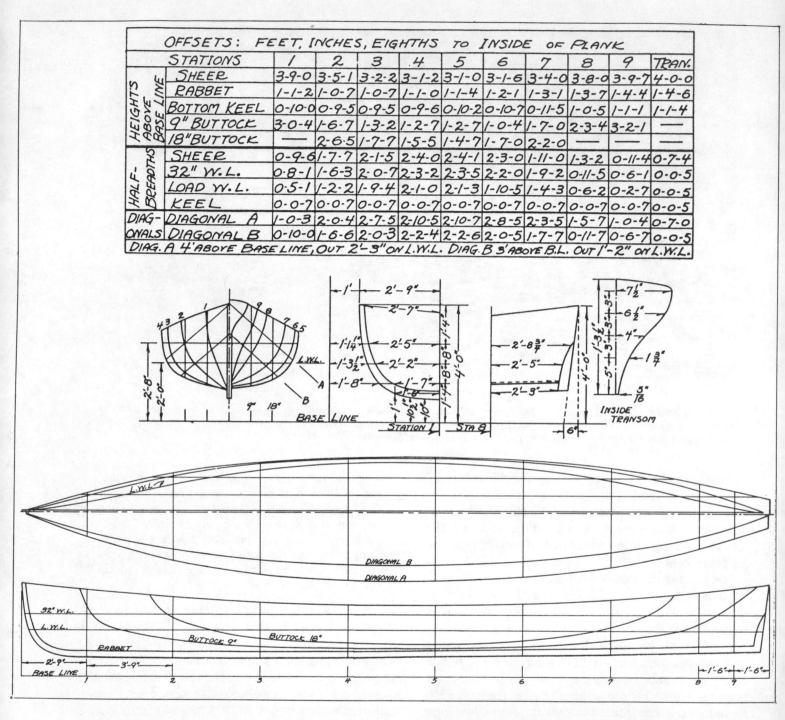

straight, as is usual in most other types, but rises considerably in a gradual curve as it moves aft.

Additional correspondence followed. In February 1974 Harold had the following comments:

With regard to your queries on *Treffry*, the ends of the thwarts fit the skin snugly, as do the hanging and the lodging knees. The undersides of the lodging knees are not notched to seat on the risings. At each end of each thwart there are two hanging knees which we call "thwart" knees. The planks lap three-quarters of an inch, and only the top edges are beveled. There are no solid floors, only bent frames and half frames. Stretchers ship into notches attached to margin planks screwed to the timbers. These also support the movable ceiling or bottom boards. *Treffry* has been retimbered at some time, and the replacements are not "joggled" over the plank lands as originally done, and as we are doing in the reproduction. Frank Gibson produced the enclosed photos yesterday. Will get some of the new boat on completion.

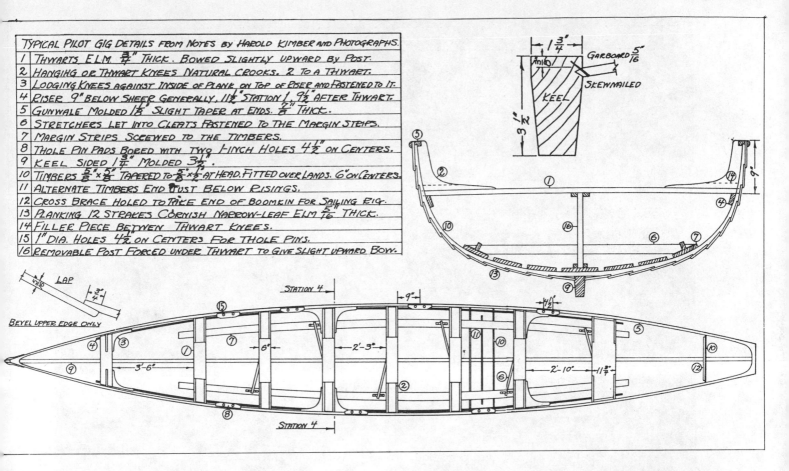

Typical Pilot Gig Details From Notes by Harold Kimber and Photographs.

1. Thwarts Elm ¾" Thick. Bowed Slightly Upward by Post.
2. Hanging or Thwart Knees Natural Crooks. 2 to a Thwart.
3. Lodging Knees against Inside of Plank on Top of Riser and Fastened to It.
4. Riser 9" Below Sheer Generally. 11½" Station 1. 9½" After Thwart.
5. Gunwale Molded 1⅝" Slight Taper at Ends. ⅞" Thick.
6. Stretchers Let Into Cleats Fastened to the Margin Strips.
7. Margin Strips Screwed to the Timbers.
8. Thole Pin Pads Bored with Two 1-Inch Holes 4½" on Centers.
9. Keel Sided 1¾" Molded 3½".
10. Timbers ⅝" × ⅝" Tapered to ⅝" × ½" at Head. Fitted over Lands. 6" on Centers.
11. Alternate Timbers End Just Below Risings.
12. Cross Brace Holed to Take End of Boomkin for Sailing Rig.
13. Planking 12 Strakes Cornish Narrow-Leaf Elm ⁵⁄₁₆" Thick.
14. Fillet Piece Between Thwart Knees.
15. 1" Dia. Holes 4½" on Centers for Thole Pins.
16. Removable Post Forced Under Thwart to Give Slight Upward Bow.

Tom Chudleigh had engaged to build not one but two gigs. Harold, however, was unable to remain in Scilly to see their completion. After he left there was difficulty in obtaining suitable materials, and so *Good Intent* was not finished until late in 1974. *Active,* however, did remarkably well in the interisland racing in the summer of 1974. "Nothing could come near her most of last season," Harold wrote at the time, "as her light weight and extra length stood her in good stead against the old shorter and heavier boats."

The lines given here are quite reliable, I believe. Of course, as mentioned, *Treffry* has changed shape somewhat, though only slightly, over the past 140 years. Besides, the boatbuilder's "eye" has the final say, and no two boats are ever built exacty alike, even on the same molds.

The drawing of the construction details that accompanies the lines attempts to be accurate as far as it goes, which, it must be said, is not very far. Note the heading "Typical Pilot Gig Details From Notes by Harold Kimber and Photographs." Only dimensions given by Harold are specified. This drawing is not intended to be scaled, and no scale is provided.

For instance, as to the laying out of plank, their number and thickness were given, as were the specifications that they were beveled on the top edge only and that the width of the lands or laps was ¾ inch. In addition, the length of the side to be covered was obtained from the lines. In the laying out of the plank widths, these were varied according to the amount of curvature.

Since the garboard and the sheer planks lie nearly flat, they were made 4½ inches, including the laps, whereas on the turn of the bilge, where there is maximum curvature, plank widths were reduced to 3½ inches. Whether the actual planking was lined in this manner I had no way of knowing, but this seemed logical and right. Generally the spacing and proportions of the planking are left to the boatbuilders and almost never appear in an architect's plans.

In March's book, plans but no offsets are given for the Newquay gig of the same name, but these are so small and badly reproduced as to be partly illegible and largely useless from a builder's standpoint. Furthermore, the source is not given, and we are not told whether full-size prints of the original drawings are available.

There appears to be a need to measure and record the details of these extraordinary boats much more accurately and fully than has so far been done. It is

Above: *Tom Chudleigh's shop in the Scilly Isles. On the right is the pilot gig* Treffry. *On the left is her replica,* Active, *under construction.* **Right:** *One of the two gigs built by Tom Chudleigh in 1974. (F.E. Gibson photos, Scilly Isles)*

hoped that this will not be put off until it is too late.

Although all of these gigs were built on the general model originated by the Peters family, there had to have been considerable minor variation from boat to boat. *Newquay*'s keel in the plan reproduced by March is shown to be quite straight, yet the keel for *Treffry,* as measured by Harold Kimber, has 4 inches of fore-and-aft camber or rocker.

As March explains, gigs from different islands or locations on the mainland raced for jobs, and when a gig was frequently beaten, the company that owned it would have another built in hopes of getting a faster boat. Thus *March* was built to beat *Albion, Golden Eagle* to beat *March,* and *Czar* to beat *Golden Eagle.*

March gives a list of scantlings, but does not say from what gig or gigs these measurements were taken.

This list is by no means complete, and varies somewhat from the dimensions provided by Kimber.

The keel, according to March, is molded 3½ inches and sided 2 inches; Kimber has it molded 3½ inches and sided 1¾ inches. March makes the planking ¼ inch thick, Kimber, ⁵⁄₁₆ inch.

Timbers, according to March, are ½ inch wide, ½ inch at their thickest, and ¼ inch at their thinnest section. In the two reproductions of *Treffry—Active* and *Good Intent*—timbers are ⅝ inch by ⅝ inch tapered to ½ inch molded at the head. It is not clear if the ⅝-inch-molded dimension applies before or after the timbers are notched or joggled to fit the lands.

March states that "notched timbers only were used. The men knew just where to cut each before steaming and when placed in position it exactly fitted every overlap." I must say this runs counter to my best judgment. My experience is that timbers so cut before steaming would almost certainly break at the notches when bent, no matter how well they were steamed and how superior the bending stock. The only feasible way, it seems to me, is first to bend the timbers to shape and then to notch them after they have cooled and dried to some extent.

How much the exceptional qualities of these gigs depended on the superiority of the planking material remains to be determined. The Peters clan who built most of the famous old gigs got their own lumber, selecting choice logs from young trees of narrow-leaf Cornish elm. These were buried in creek mud and left to season slowly for five years, after which they were removed, sawn, and stacked under cover for another year before they were used. As for the exceptional strength and flexibility of this elm planking, when *Slippen*, built about 1830, was repaired in 1953, a 4-foot strip of bilge planking had to be removed. Bent into a complete circle, this 120-year-old strip would spring back into shape when released, without the slightest distortion or damage. I doubt if any other planking material could meet this test. I have never seen any that could. Can it be that the signal superiority of these gigs derives ultimately from their unique planking timber?

This discussion of pilot gig construction could go on and on in spite of the relative paucity of exact data available to us at present. Much of March's lengthy chapter is given over to this subject, but without answering a fraction of the questions it raises. What is known for certain and recorded about these boats is only a small part of what remains to be determined.

A 1977 reproduction of the Treffry *on her sea trials. She was built from the plans in this chapter by Paul Schweiss (standing, with the tiller lines) of the Clinker Boat Works, Tacoma, Washington, for the Eureka Rowing Club, Eureka, California. There is growing interest in these gigs among amateur and professional boatbuilders. (Keith Bauer photo)*

3

MERRYMEETING BAY DUCKBOAT

If any class of traditional American small boats can lay claim to a native origin, certainly it is our duckboats, of which there is such a diversity. Duck hunting, first for market and subsistence and later for sport, has utilized over the years a variety of specialized craft. The earliest of record are the dugout log canoes obtained from the Indians and employed by the first settlers at Salem, Massachusetts, more than three and a half centuries ago. According to William Wood's *New England Prospect,* published in London in 1634, these were "made of whole pine trees, being about two foot & a half over and 20 foote long; in these likewise they go a fowling, sometimes two leagues to sea."

Three hundred years later the descendants of the settlers were still hunting ducks at sea—that is to say, from the islands in outer Marblehead Harbor—but they had given up log dugouts for light, double-ended gunning dories.

One of the more highly specialized gunning boats, one that has not been taken over for any use other than duck hunting, is the Merrymeeting Bay sneak float. The name comes from the large body of water formed by the confluence in a common estuary of Maine's Androscoggin and Kennebec rivers. This wide expanse of open water, long esteemed by duck hunters, requires a safe and seakindly craft that is also capable of stealthy approach to swimming ducks. The superior qualities of the Merrymeeting Bay sneak float as a gunning boat are widely known among duck hunters, yet as far as I can determine, its lines and construction details have never before been published.

The boat from which I have taken the lines and details presented here is probably as genuine a specimen of the type as has survived. It belongs to George Stadel, the Stamford, Connecticut, naval architect who had it built some 20 years ago. Stadel and his two sons have hunted extensively with this float in the area of Long Island Sound adjacent to Stamford, and attest to its superior qualities.

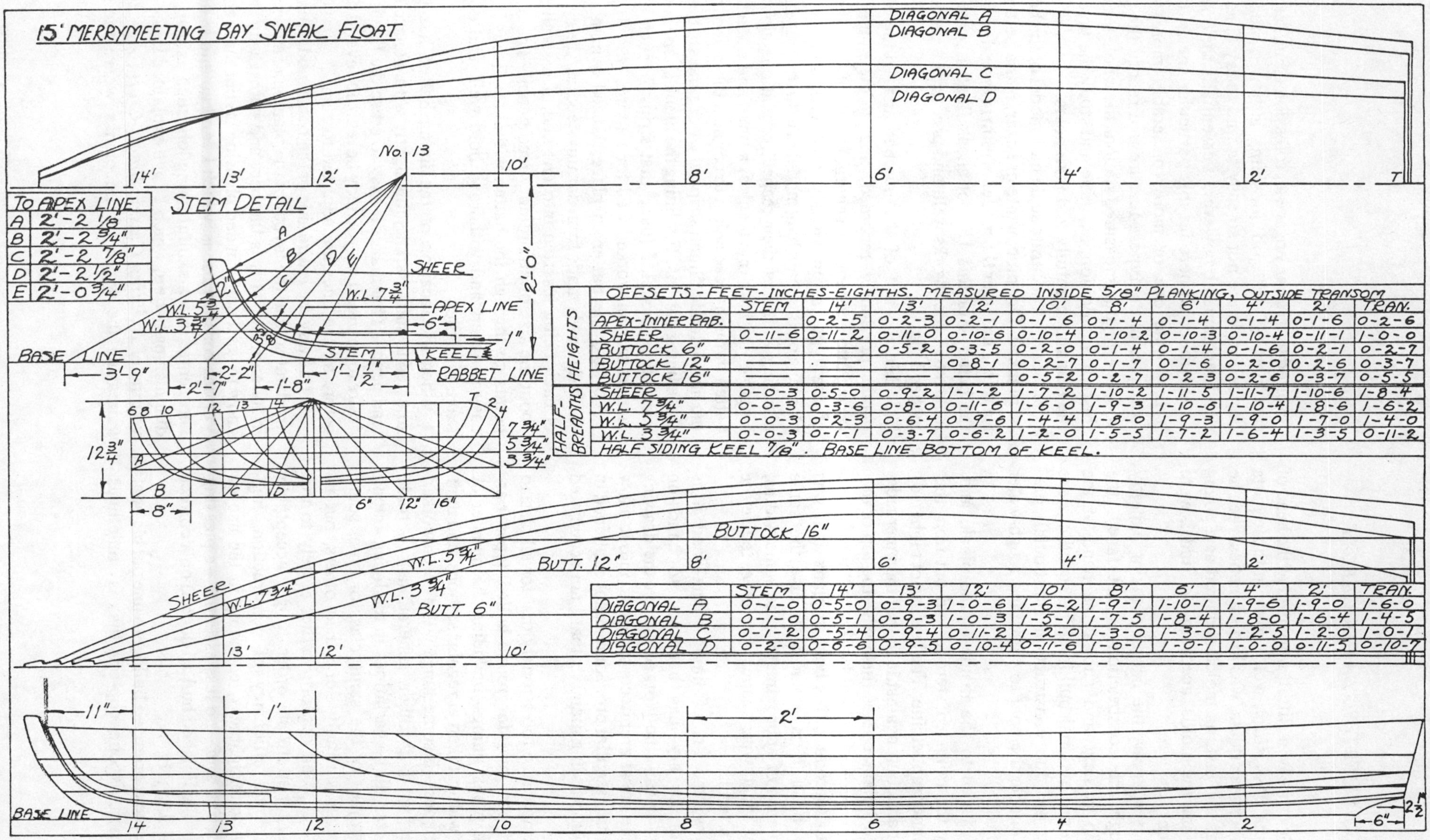

TO APEX LINE	
A	2'-2 1/8"
B	2'-2 3/4"
C	2'-2 7/8"
D	2'-2 1/2"
E	2'-0 3/4"

OFFSETS - FEET - INCHES - EIGHTHS. MEASURED INSIDE 5/8" PLANKING, OUTSIDE TRANSOM

		STEM	14'	13'	12'	10'	8'	6'	4'	2'	TRAN.
HEIGHTS	APEX-INNER RAB.	—	0-2-5	0-2-3	0-2-1	0-1-6	0-1-4	0-1-4	0-1-4	0-1-6	0-2-6
	SHEER	0-11-6	0-11-2	0-11-0	0-10-6	0-10-4	0-10-2	0-10-3	0-10-4	0-11-1	1-0-0
	BUTTOCK 6"	—	—	0-5-2	0-3-5	0-2-0	0-1-4	0-1-4	0-1-6	0-2-1	0-2-7
	BUTTOCK 12"	—	—	—	0-8-1	0-2-7	0-1-7	0-1-6	0-2-0	0-2-6	0-3-7
	BUTTOCK 16"	—	—	—	—	0-5-2	0-2-7	0-2-3	0-2-6	0-3-7	0-5-5
HALF-BREADTHS	SHEER	0-0-3	0-5-0	0-9-2	1-1-2	1-7-2	1-10-2	1-11-5	1-11-7	1-10-6	1-8-4
	W.L. 7 3/4"	0-0-3	0-3-6	0-8-0	0-11-6	1-6-0	1-9-3	1-10-6	1-10-4	1-8-6	1-6-2
	W.L. 5 3/4"	0-0-3	0-2-3	0-6-4	0-9-6	1-4-4	1-8-0	1-9-3	1-9-0	1-7-0	1-4-0
	W.L. 3 3/4"	0-0-3	0-1-1	0-3-7	0-6-2	1-2-0	1-5-5	1-7-2	1-6-4	1-3-5	0-11-2

HALF SIDING KEEL 7/8". BASE LINE BOTTOM OF KEEL.

	STEM	14'	13'	12'	10'	8'	6'	4'	2'	TRAN.
DIAGONAL A	0-1-0	0-5-0	0-9-3	1-0-6	1-6-2	1-9-1	1-10-1	1-9-6	1-9-0	1-6-0
DIAGONAL B	0-1-0	0-5-1	0-9-3	1-0-3	1-5-1	1-7-5	1-8-4	1-8-0	1-6-4	1-4-5
DIAGONAL C	0-1-2	0-5-4	0-9-4	0-11-2	1-2-0	1-3-0	1-3-0	1-2-5	1-2-0	1-0-1
DIAGONAL D	0-2-0	0-6-6	0-9-5	0-10-4	0-11-6	1-0-1	1-0-1	1-0-0	0-11-5	0-10-7

The builder was Will Rittal, who lived at the head of Merrymeeting Bay. Rittal, well known in those parts as a builder of sneak floats, was in his nineties when he built this one, his last, on molds acquired as a young apprentice, and the molds, according to Stadel, were old even then.

The hull is shapely, the carvel planking expertly lined. Though the construction is not fancy, the workmanship is neat and shows the hand of the experienced professional builder. The scantlings are quite heavy and the construction substantial, presumably to enable the boat to withstand rough-water use and to last.

Lines are drawn to the inside of the plank, and consequently the rabbeted stem is laid out from the apex line or inner rabbet line. The keel is not rabbeted, and the garboards butt against it so that the inner side of the garboard plank comes flush with the top of the keel; there is no covering keel batten or "hog."

In order to reproduce this boat in plank as it was traditionally built, it is essential to use the same number of planks of approximately the same widths, and the same lengthwise shapes, or *lining,* to use the boatbuilder's term.

Up to now, the art of lining plank—and it is something of an art—has been left to hands-on boatbuilders. It can't be worked out on the drawing board, and the naval architects do not go into it. How to go about this essential procedure is not explained in any of the boatbuilding manuals that I am acquainted with.

I cannot emphasize too strongly that for all classic small-craft types, and for round-hulled types particularly, the plank lining—including the number of planks, their widths taken at regular stations, and their lengthwise shapes—is something that has been worked out and perfected through generations of trade practice. There will be variations in the lining among different examples of the same class or type, some better and more skillfully done than others, but in general they must all conform rather closely to the same standard pattern in order to get acceptable results. Ease and efficiency of construction, hull strength and watertightness, economy in the use of planking material, and—no less essential—a pleasing appearance of the finished hull all depend on a correct and skillful lining job.

How is the inexperienced builder to line out his boat properly? There is one cop-out that is sometimes resorted to: He can engage a professional builder to do this part of the job for him, although qualified professionals are not so easy to find today. The way that I recommend, however, is essentially the one that I have followed here for this particular sneak float.

1. Locate one or more (preferably more) good examples of the type. Measure and record the plank widths at regular measured stations the whole length of the hull. In addition, examine and study the layout of the planking carefully and take notes.

2. Make an accurate scale half-model of the boat to be planked. Dry pine, white or sugar, is the best wood for this. The larger the model, within reasonable limits, the better. For this 15-foot sneak float a scale of 2 inches to 1 foot works well, and produces a model 30 inches long.

3. Making use of the number and width of the planks previously recorded, and at the same time taking into account the general layout of the planking of the type, as previously observed, line out the planking on the scale half-model. To do this, lay off the planking widths at their respective stations along the length of the hull, one plank at a time, and run a lining batten through these points to connect them and to fair the line so made. Small strips of white pine are best for these lining battens. For lining the plank shapes on the sneak-float model, I found that strips $\frac{7}{32}$ inch by $\frac{3}{32}$ inch in section worked well for battens.

To hold the batten in place, I used a number of miniature awls made from darning needles, the eye end of each being inserted into one end of a small stick about the size of an ordinary lead pencil. The needle points go through the batten without splitting it, are easy to insert and withdraw, hold well, and do not leave big holes.

When the location of the lining batten has been adjusted to suit, mark its line lightly with a sharp soft-lead pencil. This makes it easy to erase the line if you desire to change it, as you may have to do several times before all the lines are adjusted to suit.

In this way the entire side of the boat (model) can be lined out so that the layout of the planking can be seen in its entirety. This is the best and surest way that I know to get a uniform and pleasing layout throughout. Various considerations, which I can't go into in detail here, enter into a skillful lining job, such as using the diminishing batten, which I have explained in the first volume of *Building Classic Small Craft* (page 264), increasing the width of the planks where the hull

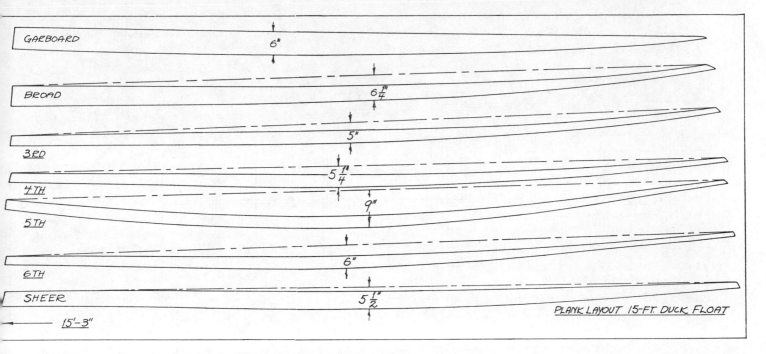

GARBOARD   6"

BROAD   6 1/4"

3RD   5"

4TH   5 1/4"

5TH   9"

6TH   6"

SHEER   5 1/2"

15'-3"

PLANK LAYOUT 15-FT. DUCK FLOAT

APPROXIMATE PLANK WIDTHS									
	TRANSOM	2'	4'	6'	8'	10'	12'	13'	14'
GARBOARD	5-7	5-12	5-12	5-10	5-3	4-10	3-14	2-6	1-4
2ND		5-3	4-14	4-10	4-3	3-11	2-15	2-4	1-14	1-9
3RD		2-9	2-14	3-0	3-6	3-1	2-9	2-1	1-10	1-7
4TH		2-4	2-10	3-0	3-4	3-0	2-9	2-1	1-11	1-6
5TH		2-4	2-10	2-15	3-0	2-14	2-10	1-14	1-9	1-2
6TH		2-4	2-8	2-14	3-2	2-14	2-8	1-12	1-7	1-5
SHEER		3-12	4-1	4-6	4-6	4-5	4-0	3-4	2-10	2-2

15' MERRYMEETING BAY DUCK FLOAT. WIDTHS IN INCHES & SIXTEENTHS. STATIONS MEASURED FROM AFTER PERP.

surface flattens out next to the keel, and decreasing the width where there is an increase in curvature, as at the turn of the bilge. Experience, experimentation, or both will help to avoid planking shapes that produce excessive sny (edgewise curvature) when laid out flat on the planking stock.

4. Once the scale half-model has been lined to suit, the planking shapes can be spiled from it and laid out flat, in miniature, on the drawing board, exactly as they would be laid out full size in planking the boat. Not only is it possible to tell in this way if adjustment in lining would be desirable, but you can also determine quite closely the widths of the boards required—no small consideration these days with the price of planking material as high as it is.

This is the procedure I have followed for the sneak float. Reproduced here is a layout of the planking showing the width of the boards required. As can be seen, all the planks are quite straight and call for boards not wider than 6 inches, except for number 5, which also could be got out of narrow boards if it were glue-spliced from two pieces.

In addition, a table of planking widths has been made up, from which the planking shapes can easily be lined out full size on the boat. A fair lining batten will be required for this, preferably one of white pine, say 1¼ or 1⅜ inches by ⅜ inch in section, tacked in place with small (number 2 common) nails.

Note that the planking widths given are specified *approximate*. This is because in lining out, some slight

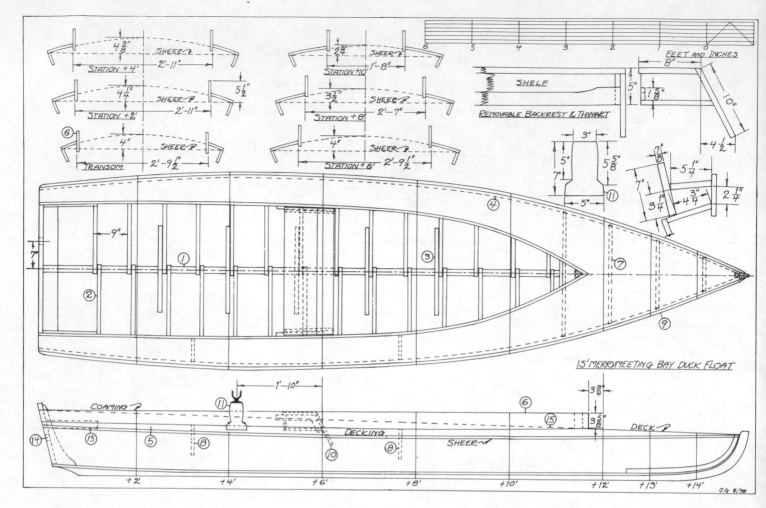

15' MERRYMEETING BAY DUCK FLOAT

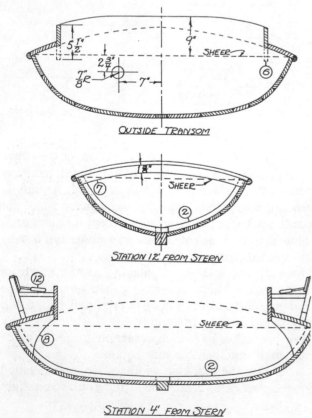

OUTSIDE TRANSOM

STATION 12' FROM STERN

STATION 4' FROM STERN

adjustments are always required in order to satisfy the discerning eye. The builder's eye is the final arbiter for fairness.

This layout of plank shapes with its accompanying table of plank widths is a new departure for how-to boat plans. Given the approximate width, shape, and lining of the strakes, the inexperienced builder need not hesitate to undertake carvel planking even for such a hull shape as this. It is my contention that building plans for planked boats cannot be considered complete unless they include plank widths and planking layout. A general study of planking widths and layout for traditional wooden small craft remains to be done and is much needed.

Because the boat is wide, flat, and low-sided, I would use a ladder-frame setup and plank the hull upside down. Resting the ladder frame on a couple of ordinary sawhorses would bring it to a convenient height for working. Conventional planking procedure is recommended. Molds from which the combined thickness of ribbands, steam-bent frames, and planking has been deducted are set up on two-foot stations, as laid off on the lines plan. The ribbands are fastened in place fore and aft, and close enough to keep the steam-bent frames from kinking. Next, the frames are

Left: *An interior view of George Stadel's sneak float shows the high position of the rowing thwart with storage box beneath, the flat run of the coaming, and the arrangement for the oarlocks. Less clearly visible are the lapping frames and the short floors.* **Below:** *Will Rittal was in his nineties when he built Stadel's float at the head of Merrymeeting Bay, Maine. The carvel planking is expertly lined. (John Gardner photos)*

bent in on 9-inch centers. Frames may be either continuous from one side to the other, or in two sections lapped across the keel, as shown. This done, the keel with the stem and the stern transom attached is laid in place and secured, and planking may proceed.

It appears that some of the later floats were strip-planked, perhaps by builders who lacked the confidence or skill for carvel planking. Because of the shape of the hull, which tapers toward the bow, strip planking would present some problems as well. I should want to reserve judgment on strip-built floats until I had a chance to inspect them. Nevertheless, to me strip planking suggests decadence.

The hull lines are well adapted to composite construction, such as the Gougeon Brothers' WEST System, which would result in a much lighter boat, and one that would remain tight when taken from the water for a considerable length of time. This might be worth

considering by someone intending to haul the boat from place to place on a trailer.

The construction drawings reproduced herewith, while not showing everything, contain sufficient information, I am sure, to build from authentically. Careful study of the drawings is recommended.

The following are numbered in the drawings for easy reference:

1. *Keel, stem, and sternpost or stern knee:* Oak, sided 1¾ inches and molded as shown in the lines plan. Stem can be got out of a width of oak plank, with some curved grain if possible. Lay out so that the cross grain comes at the stemhead end.

2. *Timbers:* Oak, steam-bent ¾ inch by ⅞ inch, laid on the flat. Spacing, approximately 9-inch centers. Ends lap over the keel and are nailed.

3. *Timbers:* Oak, steam-bent ¾ inch by ⅞ inch, laid on the flat. Five in all. Spaced as shown.

4. *Planking:* White pine finished ⅝ inch thick.

5. *Decking:* White pine ⅝ inch thick and canvas-covered.

6. *Coamings:* White pine ⁹⁄₁₆ inch by 5½ inches. Top lines straight when installed in boat. Coamings sit plumb.

7. *Deck beams:* Oak, sided ¾ inch, molded 1⅜ inches. Ends let into sheer plank ⅛ inch.

8. *Two deck supports:* ¾-inch pine, shaped as shown and fastened through the hull.

9. *Half-round trim:* Covers edges of deck canvas. One inch by ¾ inch, tapered slightly at bow end for appearance.

10. *Removable backrest and thwart:* Fits tightly against the inside of the coaming, resting on cleats fastened to the coaming. The forward side slopes at a convenient angle to serve as a backrest for a bow occupant seated in the bottom of the boat. Under the top, which forms a rowing thwart, there is a shelf and a shallow compartment that opens aft. Is lifted out easily.

11. *Supports for rowlocks:* Braced as shown and bolted on either side with ⁵⁄₁₆-inch carriage bolts through the deck.

12. Davis rowlocks number 3.

13. Cleats either side at the stern for removable seat or thwart.

14. *Hole for sculling oar:* Located as shown. Lined with leather. Diameter after lining, 1¾ inches.

15. Dotted line indicates deck camber. One beam mold will suffice for side decks.

Not shown are the gratings or platform in the bottom for occupants to sit on. They are located well above any seepage in the bottom.

4

15-FOOT FLATTIE SKIFF

At the late-winter small-craft gathering at Mystic Seaport in 1980, a teenager asked me to recommend a boat for quahogging. What he had in mind apparently was something simple and sturdy that would be easy and inexpensive to build, a utility workboat that he could knock around the shore in or take across the bay when the weather permitted.

He mentioned a length of 16 feet, but since then I have concluded that a foot or two less would probably be adequate, easier to handle, and somewhat cheaper to build. The boat that I am offering here will be only an inch or two under 15 feet overall, although it could easily be stretched out a foot longer—no longer, if it is to be planked with 16-foot boards. Also, it could be made a foot or so shorter without any difficulty.

What we have here is a variation on one of the most common and widespread small utility boats ever built, one that is found the entire length of the New England coast. Such flats belong to a very ancient type used widely in Europe centuries before fishermen brought them to the New World. In Maine it would be a large flatiron skiff; on the south shore of Connecticut, a small sharpie rowboat. Its wide, cross-planked bottom makes a steady working platform having great initial stability.

Admittedly, the flat bottoms of these boats do pound when driven into a chop, but this characteristic will be minimized in the design shown here, which has been made quite narrow and sharp forward for this reason. Some length is essential in order to achieve this narrow entrance. This is why such skiffs built as short as 12 feet or less almost invariably turn out to be overfull and stubby forward, tending to bang unmercifully when it gets the least mite lumpy.

Although these flats have great initial stability, they lack the seakindly characteristics of round-hull craft, and are not suited to go outside where the big ones roll. Under such conditions they could roll, or be thrown, completely over. Although the round hull might roll down, it would hang on and then roll back. As long as this limitation is recognized and respected, and as long as these flats stay in sheltered or semisheltered waters and are used with ordinary common sense, they are perfectly safe, as their continued use by the thousands over the years makes clear.

Because of its wood construction and large scantlings, the flat detailed here would float upright and quite high in the water should it ever fill. You could climb aboard over either the side or the stern if you ever fell overboard. Although I do not advise walking around inside a small boat, you could walk around inside this one without danger of tipping over. I am confident that this boat will pass Coast Guard level-flotation and stability requirements with flying colors.

The skiff detailed here is strictly for rowing, but it could easily be converted for sailing and would sail handily. To install a centerboard trunk and centerboard would be no great job, and this hull, rigged as a small sharpie, is capable of some speed.

I have gone to special pains to make this skiff as simple and inexpensive to build as possible in this time of inflated costs, and still have it hold together and last for a reasonable length of service. And how long is that? This is definitely not a Herreshoff yacht built to last a century, but I am certain that it will give good service for 10 years and even longer. And in 10 years of knocking around, this simple skiff will pay back its initial cost several times over. In this day of early obsolescence for nearly everything we use, 10 years is longer than the life of most cars and household appliances, and in 10 years the original owner will probably have graduated from quahogging and gone on to larger and more expensive vessels.

In any case, it is partly because of such considerations that I have specified fastening this skiff not with bronze screws that cost a king's ransom, or with old-type boat nails now almost impossible to find, but with ordinary hot-dipped galvanized common nails, available at almost any good lumberyard or hardware store. However, they must be hot-dipped galvanized nails, not the electroplated kind, which are worthless. Hot-dipped galvanized common nails in a wooden rowboat that is kept puttied and painted are certainly good for at least 10 years.

Because of the difficulty of finding sources of supply for special boat lumber, as well as its high cost, I call

for this skiff to be constructed almost entirely from number 2 common 1-inch white-pine boards. These are distributed throughout the country and available at most retail lumberyards. The only other lumber required is a 12-foot length of 2-inch-by-6-inch Douglas fir. So-called 1-inch boards of number 2 common white pine come planed and smooth on both sides and ¾ inch thick. They are used principally for interior finish, shelving, and simple furniture. They will have some knots. If these are sound and solid, not too large or too numerous, a board will be just as strong or even stronger for having them. In the cross-planked bottom, boards will be tougher with sound knots and will wear better.

Such boards require no surface planing. Sides, bottom, transom, keelson, thwarts, and various smaller members are all ¾ inch thick, and have only to be cut out to their molded shapes. In some places, for greater strength and more secure nailing, two ¾-inch thicknesses are doubled up to make 1½ inches. For joining these mating pieces solidly, epoxy glue is specified; I have also specified 1¾-inch copper clinch nails for pulling the two thicknesses together and reinforcing the glue joint. Only a relatively small quantity of these clinch nails is needed, and probably not more than a pint of epoxy glue. If care is taken to minimize skin contact, the short-term use of this small amount of glue will present no health hazard of any consequence.

The high cost of tools and the present scarcity of good ones are factors to be reckoned with. Unless you have machinery and a well-filled tool chest, some of the small-craft designs offered to inexperienced amateurs are simply out of the question. For this boat, no power tools whatsoever are necessary.

As for hand tools, the following minimum list will suffice: plane (smoothing or jack), handsaw, hammer, 1-inch chisel, rule, square, cheap plastic protractor, one or two 4-inch or 6-inch C-clamps, caulking iron of some sort (can be improvised), putty knife, and paintbrush. If you have a ripsaw in addition to a crosscut, this will make the job quite a bit easier. Of course the saws, plane, and chisel should be sharp and kept sharp, if at all possible. It hardly needs to be said that sharp tools make a tremendous difference.

Building should be started upside down on a flat floor or even the ground, which will give level support athwartships for the legs of the two molds. The surface need not be level fore and aft, although this would be desirable. In preparation for setting up, the stem is cut out and the stem cheeks glued and nailed on either

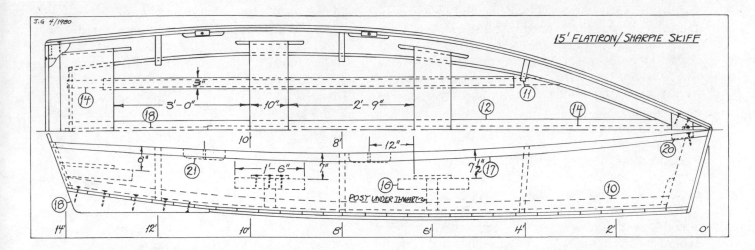

15' FLATIRON/SHARPIE SKIFF

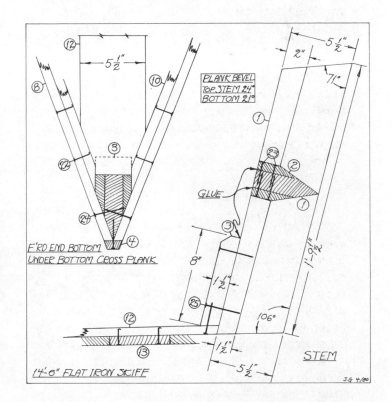

F'RD END BOTTOM
UNDER BOTTOM CROSS PLANK

PLANK BEVEL
TOP STEM 24°
BOTTOM 21°

GLUE

STEM

14'-6" FLAT IRON SKIFF

side. This assembly is beveled to receive the plank ends, and the keelson-to-stem block is nailed on as shown.

The bottom edges of the two garboards are marked out and cut to the line. Their forward ends are cut to match the rake of the stem, and the lap gains are cut at bow and stern. The transom is cut to shape and the bottom and side cleats are glued and nailed on the inside. The sides and bottom of the transom are beveled, and the recess that receives the after end of the keelson is cut in the bottom cleat.

Initially, in setting up, the forward ends of the garboards are nailed to the stem assembly with 2½-inch staging nails. These are double-headed nails whose inside heads hold while the outer heads stand out far enough from the board for easy pulling. Later, after the preliminary setup is completed, necessary adjustments for fairness have been made, and everything is correct, the temporary staging nails are pulled and replaced with the permanent fastenings. If you lack staging nails, ordinary common nails with thick leather washers under the heads make good substitutes.

Once the garboards are nailed to the stem, they are bent in place around the two molds and secured to them with staging nails. This done, the after ends of the two planks are pulled in and nailed to the transom assembly, which has been set at its proper rake and braced to the floor or the ground with temporary legs nailed with staging nails. At this stage in the construction the shape is established. The stem must be carefully plumbed and the molds leveled from side to side. Any appearance of twist or sag, any difference in

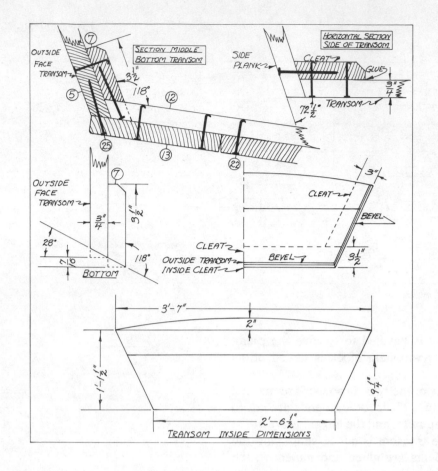

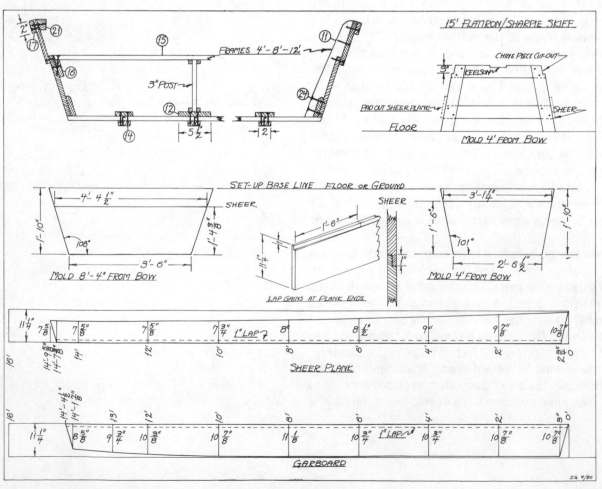

the sides, or any other unfairness must be corrected now.

When this has been done, the keelson is fitted at the bow and nailed to its block on the stem. Staging nails secure it for the time being in the notches cut for it in the two molds, and its after end is cut off so that it fits in the recess previously cut in the bottom cleat of the transom, where it is securely nailed.

The setup will now be solid and secure, and the chine pieces may be fitted against the inside bottom edges of the garboard planks. These chine pieces may be in two or even three lengths, which will make them easier to install. Their function is not to add longitudinal reinforcement, but to provide sufficient thickness for securely nailing the cross-planked bottom. Because of this, they must be glued to the inside of the garboards and have the additional reinforcement of copper clinch nails. A C-clamp or two will be useful here for pulling the chine pieces tight against the garboard as nailing proceeds. The nails hold the chine pieces in position until the glue sets.

Time—a day or more—should be allowed for the glue to set before the cross-planked bottom is fitted and nailed. Before this is done the meeting edges of the garboards and the chine pieces must be planed fair to receive the ends of the bottom cross planks, which, in order to be tight, must lie perfectly flat and touching throughout. Cross planks should be no less than 4 inches wide and no more than 6 inches. Planks wider than this will cup, and their seams tend to open too wide when the boat dries out.

For nailing the ends of the cross planking, 3-inch nails are used, with 1¾-inch copper clinch nails through the keelson at the center. Nails are driven through the plank ends into the chine pieces exactly as shown in the drawing. This keeps them a good distance away from the ends and minimizes the chance of splitting the chine pieces.

In some working skiffs of this type, there are no chine pieces and the garboard is made a full 1 inch thick on the bottom edge to receive the bottom nailing and is planed so that it tapers to a thickness of ¾ inch at the top edge. This is done most easily with a power surface planer, and requires stock a full inch or more thick, neither of which can be counted on here. Because the chine pieces must be depended upon to hold the bottom nailing, I can hardly overstress the importance of bonding them securely to the garboards with epoxy glue liberally reinforced with copper clinch nails.

Bottom cross planks should fit tightly together on the inside, and are beveled as diagramed to give ⅛ inch of open caulking seam on the outside. After several cross planks have been nailed on, a space the width of one plank and slightly narrower at one end than the other is skipped and several more planks are nailed on, and so on until the bottom is covered. After this is done, planks tapered to fit but longer than necessary are driven into the vacant spaces lengthwise, in the manner of long wedges. These planks produce an extra tight fit and wedge the planks tight on either side.

Further, to ensure tightness under the cross-plank ends, one may set them in a flexible bedding compound. Some, including the late Pete Culler, have used asphalt roofing and flashing cement for this. Because the first bottom plank at the bow narrows almost to a point, it would be advisable (in order to prevent splitting) to put it on with the grain running fore and aft and set it in epoxy glue in addition to nailing it. Before the bottom is put on, a caulking seam should be planed on the outside bottom edges of the garboards.

After the bottom is nailed, the heads of the nails should be set slightly below the surface for puttying and the ends of the cross planks planed flush with the rake of the sides. The bottom seams and the seam along the edge of the garboards are caulked with cotton set in tight with iron and mallet (or hammer), but not so hard as to break through into the inside. Seams should be filled with cotton to about 3⁄16 inch from the top. Seams so caulked are thoroughly soaked with thin oil paint, not latex. Red lead is best for this. When the seams have dried, they are filled to the surface with flexible bottom-seam compound.

The skeg and bottom rub strips can now be put on as diagramed. To minimize drag, bottom strips must be put on to run fore and aft and parallel with the centerline. Rub strips that are bent around the outside of the bottom drag water behind their curve and are unacceptable. The skeg, cut out of 2-inch-by-6-inch fir, is taper-planed from a thickness of 1½ inches where it fits against the bottom to ⅝ inch at the lower outside. This is to minimize drag.

The bottom can be finished even to final painting before the boat is turned right side up and the sheer planks bent on. To ensure a tight boat, the builder cannot be too painstaking in planking, caulking, and finishing the bottom.

The top edge of the garboard is perfectly straight, and the lower edge of the sheer plank will also be

A flattie under construction at Mystic Seaport as a maritime-skills project supplemental to a marine-educational program for college undergraduates. After several cross planks have been nailed on, a slightly wedge-shaped gap the width of one plank is incorporated. Then several more planks are nailed on, followed by another gap, and so on. Tapered planks are later driven lengthwise into the gaps to tighten the edge-to-edge fit of the planks. (Mary Anne Stets photos, Mystic Seaport)

straight if the molds under it are padded out with ¾-inch-thick strips as diagramed. There are no lap bevels, only the lap gains cut in at the ends so that the ends of the two planks will lie flush on the stem and transom. The 1-inch-wide laps are fastened with copper clinch nails spaced 2 inches to 2½ inches apart. After the sheer planks are on, their top edges, previously rough-cut to the diagramed widths, are carefully sighted and planed so that they give a fair sheerline throughout.

In the keyed references that follow, *pine* signifies number 2 common 1-inch white-pine boards, ¾-inch exact thickness. *Fir* is 2-inch-by-6-inch Douglas fir, select quality, rift-grain fir if possible, no sap. One 12-foot length of fir should be sufficient for the job.

1. *Stem:* Fir.
2. *Stem cheeks:* Pine.
3. *Keelson-to-stem block:* Fir.
4. *False stem:* Pine.
5. *Transom:* Pine.
6. *Transom side cleats:* Pine.
7. *Transom bottom cleat:* Pine.
8. *Garboard planks:* Two 16-foot, 12-inch-wide pine boards; exact dimensions: 11¼ inches wide and ¾ inch thick.
9. *Sheer planks:* Same as garboards.
10. *Chine pieces:* Pine.
11. *Side frames:* Fir.
12. *Keelson:* Pine.
13. *Bottom cross planks:* Pine.
14. *Bottom rub strips:* Pine.
15. *Thwarts:* Pine.
16. *Thwart cleats:* Pine.
17. *Outwales:* Pine.
18. *Skeg:* Fir.
19. *Quarter knees:* Fir.
20. *Breasthook:* Fir.
21. *Oarlock pads:* Fir.
22. *Copper clinch nails:* 9-penny, 1¾ inch.
23. 2-inch hot-dipped galvanized common nails.
24. 2½-inch galvanized nails.
25. 3-inch galvanized nails.

Sequel

A flattie skiff shortened to 14 feet was selected in 1981 for construction as a supplementary learning project in a special undergraduate program for college students. The choice proved to be a good one. The two skiffs built each semester are sold to cover the cost of materials, and there is a waiting list of would-be purchasers. From all reports received so far, the owners are well satisfied with them.

This solidly built skiff makes an excellent utility workboat, is unusually stiff and stable under conditions of ordinary use, and has unusual loading capacity. But it is too heavy to be easily handled and transported out of the water, and hence is unsuited for trailering. On the other hand, under a press of sail the boat would stand up well and would not prove to be a laggard.

Scaling the boat down from 15 to 14 feet was done simply by taking a foot out of the midsection while leaving the ends completely alone. That meant changing the location of the two thwarts in order to maintain sufficient rowing room between them, and making sure that the oarsman on the forward thwart would not be cramped for stretch, especially if he should have long arms.

If the skiff is built in a shop with a wood floor that can be nailed into, the setup for building will be easy. If there is a cement floor or no floor at all, it is recommended that the setup be made on two long planks—the heavier the better—laid parallel and flat, and far enough apart for the mold extensions, or "legs," to stand on them. The two planks are cleated together solidly with several lengths of board as cross members, the boards at the ends being positioned so as to support extensions from the stemhead and the transom stern. Such a building platform is easily leveled, provides secure nailing for the setup, and is easily taken apart and the lumber salvaged when the building job is completed.

It was previously suggested that because the first piece of bottom planking at the bow is narrow and triangular, it should be put on with its grain running fore and aft to reduce the danger of splitting when it is nailed. A good way to do this is to make up the piece from two identical triangular lengthwise pieces, with the grain in each running parallel to the hypotenuse (that is, the outer edge). The pieces are glued together so that the glue line follows the centerline of the boat. In this way the short grain in the two pieces will come on the inside, on the glue line, and the grain on the outside will run parallel with the chine of the boat.

The inner chine strips must be well bonded to the inside of the garboards so that the thickness at the bottom edge will be doubled and secure nailing for the bottom cross planking will be ensured. The importance of securing a perfectly solid bonding here cannot

College students provide the ash breeze for a 14-foot version of the 15-foot flattie described in this chapter. Power could also come from a dory sailing rig or a small outboard. For the latter, 10 h.p. would be plenty; much more than that would tend to make the stern squat and the boat pound in any sort of chop. (Mary Anne Stets photo, Mystic Seaport)

be overstated. Epoxy glue thick enough not to leak out of the joint is applied to the meeting surfaces of the chine strips and the garboards, which are pulled tightly together with C-clamps for fastening either with clinch nails or screws put in from the outside. If the latter are used, number 12 1¼-inch screws are recommended, with the heads set slightly below the surface for puttying. The garboard is bored for them, but not the inside pine chine strip, so that they will draw well.

When the bottom cross planking is nailed in place, holes slightly smaller than the nails should be bored through the ends of the cross planks, but not into the chine strips below, for maximum holding power. A slight bevel should be planed off the outside of the bottom edge of the garboard to provide a caulking seam not greater than ⅟₁₆ inch, in order that a strand of cotton may be driven between the lower edge of the garboard and the cross-planked bottom.

The directions given above for building this 14- or 15-foot flattie skiff are generally applicable to most cross-planked, flat-bottom skiffs, of which there are many variations.

If the builder finds he wants to adapt the flattie for sailing, the sailing rig with centerboard detailed for the 16-foot Swampscott dory (see Chapter 14) will do nicely. He will probably want to change the shape of the rudder, however, making it shorter and wider, the better to conform to the dimensions of the flattie's stern, while moderately increasing the area of its wetted surface. He need not be restricted to a spritsail, and could just as well employ a leg-o'-mutton or a sliding gunter. Also, the sail area could stand a modest increase, for this rather heavily built boat with its wide, flat bottom will stand up well and needs a fair amount of canvas to get her moving. But there must definitely be provision for reefing down, and anyone intending to sail this boat should not be averse to hiking out when conditions require it.

5

TWO 8-FOOT PRAMS

Ultrashort boats are not my cup of tea, and I should never think of designing a boat as short as 8 feet unless there was a demand for it. But over the years I have received a number of inquiries about building plans for dinghies, tenders, prams, and similar tabloid rowing craft of 8 feet and even less in length.

There is no substitute for length. Longer boats row and handle more easily, carry farther, and are better seaboats. They tend to be heavier, however, and they take up more room. For the owner of a small yacht these can be deciding factors in choosing a tender.

I do not recommend scaling down a 10-foot dory skiff to 8 feet because I think it would still be too heavy to cartop, but also because it is a sharp-ended model. In reducing the length of a sharp-ended boat to this extent, it would be unwise to decrease the beam in the same ratio, since to do so would likely result in too great a reduction both in stability and in carrying capacity. In order to ensure acceptable performance, it is generally necessary to leave the beam more or less alone or to reduce it only slightly. A relatively broader hull shape results, one that requires considerably more bend in the side planks to get them to land on the stem. This can greatly increase the difficulty of construction.

For a tender or dinghy as short as 8 feet the pram shape will produce a better boat with respect to capacity, stability, and seakindliness, and the properly designed pram will be easier to build than sharp-ended models. Whether such a pram will be pleasing to the eye is another matter, and depends to a large exent on whose eye is looking.

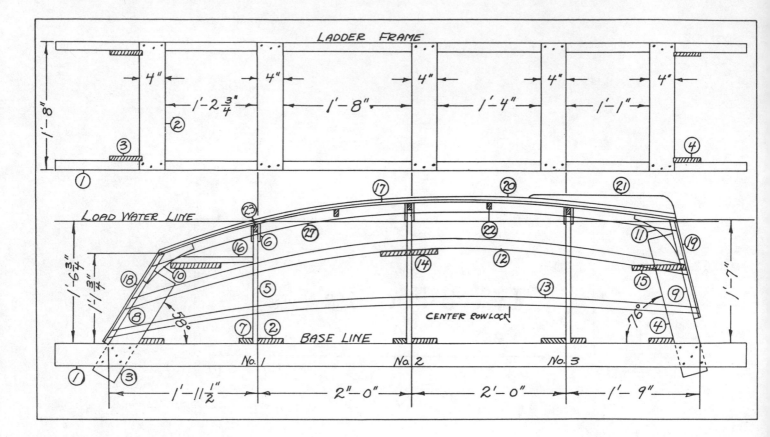

Yet the pram, even in short lengths, is far from being a box. Its heavily rockered bottom and slanting bow transom enable it to make headway with surprising ease, and for this reason prams generally tow well, a prime consideration, of course, if the boat is to be used as a yacht tender.

AN L. FRANCIS HERRESHOFF–INSPIRED PRAM

The little boat offered here is very close in shape to the pram that L. Francis Herreshoff designed as a tender for the *Nereia,* lines and construction details for which are to be found on pages 170–72 of his *Sensible Cruising Designs.* My attention was called to this design recently by a person who approached me with questions about building it.

Herreshoff recommended a type of dory construction that would have produced a nice solid boat, but a heavy one. His larger pram of similar construction, designed for *Marco Polo,* is extremely heavy. Further-more, I don't believe it would be possible to plank the bottom of the *Nereia* pram with ¾-inch pine boards without steaming them, because of the amount of rocker, and my guess is that even with steam you might have a tussle with that bottom curve.

Herreshoff said the *Nereia* pram would be heavy, and suggested that it could be built lighter with "laminated wood." Herreshoff had a thing against plywood, and seems not to have been able to bring himself to use the despised term.

Nevertheless, thousands of excellent small craft have been built out of plywood, and if it is used properly and is of good quality to start with, there is nothing the matter with using plywood for small boats. I have laid out the boat shown here to be built with plywood, which should produce a yacht tender light enough to be taken on deck without excessive straining.

Note that two standard 4-by-8-foot panels are ample for the sides, bottom, and ends. The thickness is ¼ inch. Marine grade is recommended because good-quality exterior fir is increasingly difficult to find.

The boat shown here is a couple of inches shorter

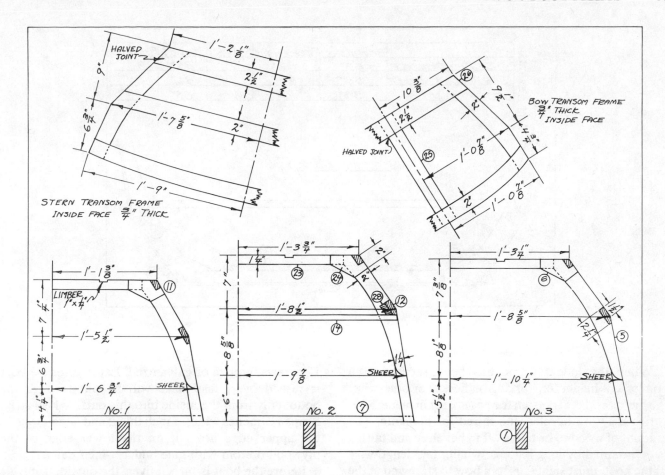

than the *Nereia* pram so that the sides can be gotten out of standard 8-foot panels. It is also slightly wider and slightly deeper, and the curve of the bottom toward the bow has been eased just a bit to give an easier bend, but not enough to hurt performance appreciably.

I have not given lines and offsets, but instead have provided actual dimensions for the bow and stern transoms and the three molds that remain in the boat as frames. This simplifies and shortens the building process a lot. The boat is set up for building on a ladder frame dimensioned to give the precise locations of the mold-frame assemblies, which are centered, plumbed, stayed in place, and then beveled for planking.

Materials in addition to the plywood include boards of ¾-inch finished thickness, epoxy glue, nails 1 inch, 1¼ inches, and 1½ inches long, and a few screws of assorted lengths. Small screws—say ¾-inch number 6 bronze wood screws for fastening the plywood to the chine strips and the seam battens—are optional.

The main dependence is upon glue, however, and small nails should be quite sufficient to hold the plywood in position until the glue has set. Annular

nails—also known as ring nails—are recommended. Where there is danger of going through, as with 1-inch nails through ¼-inch ply into the seam batten, these nails should be driven on somewhat of a slant, which also makes them hold better.

Epoxy glue is the only kind recommended. Those unacquainted with this adhesive would be well advised to familiarize themselves with its use before starting to build.

The frames, chines, seam battens, seats, skeg, bottom strip, and so forth are all dimensioned to be gotten out of ¾-inch thick lumber. Northern white pine, spruce, Douglas fir, mahogany, or Alaskan cedar may be used. White cedar and redwood are too soft. Ponderosa pine and sugar pine rot too easily. Oak might be used, although it is heavy.

For those who are not experienced boatbuilders, it will be helpful to outline an order of work. To start, the ladder frame, the frames for the bow and stern transoms, and the three molds that become frames and remain in the boat are made up in advance, as dimensioned.

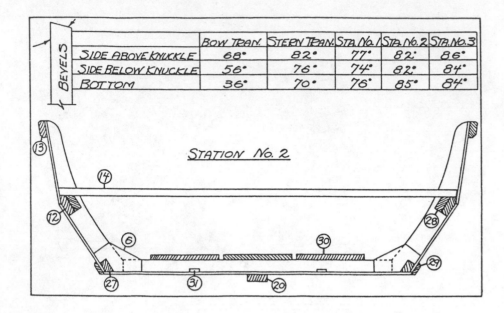

BEVELS		BOW TRAN.	STERN TRAN.	STA. NO.1	STA. NO.2	STA. NO.3
	SIDE ABOVE KNUCKLE	68°	82°	77°	82°	86°
	SIDE BELOW KNUCKLE	56°	76°	74°	82°	84°
	BOTTOM	36°	70°	76°	85°	84°

STATION No. 2

When the ladder frame has been secured at a convenient height for working on horses or otherwise, the molds and the transom frames are set in place, after which they are beveled and faired for planking. The amount of wood to be taken off in beveling and fairing is determined by long battens, which, laid lengthwise of the boat, must sight fair from bow to stern and at the same time touch the edges of the frame molds throughout.

This done, the chine strips and seam battens are cut in, fastened with screws and glue, and faired and beveled as necessary to conform to the rest of the framing. The chine strips and seam battens will bend in more easily if they are a few feet longer than the boat. The resulting overhang at either end need not be cut off until after the side planking is on and it is time to cover the bow and stern with plywood.

The side planks require spiling and are put on first. Next comes the bottom, but before this is put on it will be necessary to plane the chine strips fair, so that the bottom ply will lie with a fair and touching fit throughout. The bottom ply is glued on and nailed with 1½-inch nails into the chine strips and the bottom crosspieces throughout. The ends receive their plywood covering last.

Before the boat is turned right side up, a reinforcing strip is run down the center of the bottom the length of the boat and a small skeg is fastened to it at the stern end. This strip is bedded with glue and fastened into the inside bottom cross members with 2-inch number 12 screws, bronze or galvanized. Later, after the boat is turned over, fastenings will be put through the bottom ply from the inside into this outside keel strip. Strips 1½ inches wide, ⅜ inch thick, and chamfered on the upper edge are put on the lower edge of the plywood bottom with glue and 1¼-inch nails.

Before the boat is turned over, the outside gunwale strips are glued on and screwed into the frames. If this is done just before the boat is turned over, then as soon as the boat is right side up it will be easy to nail through the plywood from the inside before the glue sets. In any case, the glue should be tight throughout.

About all the woodwork that remains on the inside is the installation of the seats. These are important bracing members. The after thwart is supported by, and well fastened into, the center framing strip of the stern transom. On the inside of the bottom, several thin strips, ⅜ inch or ½ inch thick, may be extended fore and aft on top of the bottom crosspieces and fastened into them to serve as a walkway.

Although the final beveling and fairing of the frames, including the inside framing of the bow and stern transoms, will need to be tested and very likely adjusted after the frames have been set up (in order to fair them for planking), preliminary beveling of frames and transom framing should be done at the bench when the frames are assembled. The bevels provided for this were taken from a scale half-model, and will be found to be fairly accurate, if not exact.

When rowlocks are located, the center of the

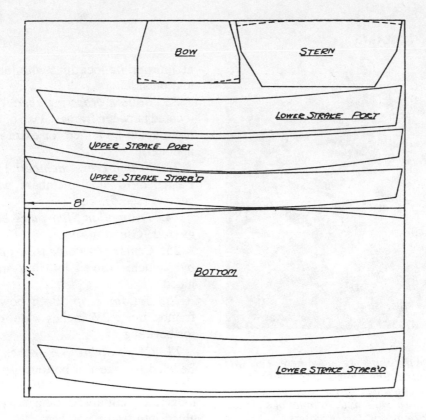

oarlock-pin socket should measure 10½ inches aft of the after edge of the center thwart.

For extra strength it might be well to make the frames, transom framing, chine strips, and seam battens of oak, although it is heavier than the other woods listed. The additional weight would probably not amount to more than 3 or 4 pounds in any case.

It is recommended that the boat be well saturated inside and out with hot linseed oil thinned with about 30-percent paint thinner or turps before painting. Heat the oil in a double boiler to keep it below the flash point. Several applications should be made, until the wood will not absorb any more. Allow the wood to dry thoroughly before painting it. Such treatment prevents rot and minimizes water absorption.

The comments that follow are keyed to numbers in the accompanying diagrams.

1. *Two 2 x 4s:* These should be dry and *must be straight.*

2. *Cross cleats:* One-inch pine or spruce. These are located so as to place the frame molds in the right location for beveling. Their locations must not be changed.

3. These two uprights, inclined at an angle of 58 degrees, support the bow transom frame in the correct position. If necessary, they should have additional bracing so that they hold firm.

4. Uprights for supporting the stern transom frame.

5. *The forward frame mold of three frame molds:* These are made from ¾-inch thick lumber. They are made long enough to reach the baseline occupied by the ladder frame. After the boat is planked and turned over they are cut off at the sheer and rounded.

6. *Plywood gussets either side of the frames for connecting the sides of the frames with the bottom cross members:* Glued and nailed; ¼-inch plywood scrap.

7. *Cross spall of 1-inch (¾ inch net) lumber for securing the ends of the frame molds:* Notch the ends for the frames to fit into them and nail, allowing the frame to come up flush against the cross cleat (2).

8. *Bow transom frame:* Made from ¾-inch lumber as diagramed. The pieces that make up the frame are halved together and glued. The outline in the diagram is made to the inside face of the frame, so that beveling will not change the shape. The frame pieces should be positioned as dimensioned on the diagram and temporarily fastened into the uprights (3) with screws until ready to be covered with plywood.

9. *Stern transom frame:* Same as *8.*

10. *Bow knee:* Put in before the bottom is put on in order to afford fastening for the outside keel strip (20).

11. *Stern knee:* Same as *10.*

12. *Seam battens:* 2¼ inches by ¾ inch.

A pram built in 1976 from the plans presented here. This was Ralph Carlsen's first boatbuilding project, and the boat has received much favorable comment over the years. The photograph was taken in the pram's sixth summer of hard use as a tender in New York and New Jersey waters.

13. *Outside gunwale strip:* 1¾ inches by ¾ inch, tapered slightly toward the ends. Glued to plywood topsides and screwed into frames.

14. *Center thwart:* Nine inches by ¾ inch. Notched around middle frame and glued and screwed to seam batten. Sufficient Styrofoam for flotation can be located under this thwart.

15. *Stern thwart:* Eight inches by ¾ inch. Important bracing member. Ends fastened to sides of the boat, after edge to the middle cleat and the inner face of the transom.

16. Short riser glued to sides of boat for supporting low bow seat.

17. *Quarter-inch-thick plywood bottom:* Fastened with glue and 1½-inch nails to chine strips and bottom cross members after the plywood sides are on.

18. *Quarter-inch plywood covering bow transom:* Glued and nailed to transom frame. Put on after sides and bottom.

19. *Plywood covering stern transom:* Same as *18.*

20. *Outside keel strip:* Two inches by ¾ inch. Glued to bottom. Nailed or screwed to inside bottom cross members and bow and stern knees.

21. *Skeg:* ¾-inch thick lumber. Securely fastened at appropriate locations with long screws from inside and outside.

22. *Bottom cross member:* 1⅛ inches by ¾ inch, located between frames: Two of these are shown. Two more could be added for extra reinforcement at bow and stern.

23. *Frame cross member:* 1⅛ inches by ¾ inch. Fastened to side members with ¼-inch plywood gussets (see *6).*

24. *Triangular filler piece between plywood side gussets:* Glued in place.

25. *Center strip bow transom frame:* Two inches by ¾ inch. Halved into top and bottom strips and glued.

26. *Bottom strip:* Both bow and stern transom frames; made 2½ inches wide to provide extra wood for beveling.

27. *Chine strips:* 1½ inches wide, ¾ inch thick. Beveled to take the bottom plywood sheet after the sides are on. Made 2 feet longer than the boat, or even longer, to facilitate bending into position. Screwed and glued into frame notches.

28. Short cleats of the same material as the seam battens *(12)* are glued and screwed or nailed to them to give extra support to the ends of the center thwart.

29. *Outside chine strips:* 1½ inches by ⅜ inch. Cover the exposed edges of the plywood bottom and are put on with glue and 1¼-inch nails.

30. *Sole flooring or walkway strips:* ½ inch thick and 6 to 7 inches wide amidships, tapering fore and aft to correspond to the shape of the boat.

31. *Limbers:* ½ inch by 1 inch, cut through all the frames and bottom cross members.

A PRAM OF SURPRISING ABILITY

This pram is functional and plain, perhaps, but not ugly. It is not intended to vie in looks with classic varnished yacht tenders by Lawley, Herreshoff, or Nevins, but I do believe it will hold its own in performance with any 8-foot version of such 10-foot and 12-foot round-hulled classics, and at the same time will be much easier and less expensive to build.

In the early 1960s I designed and built a pram for my own use. The family auto was a Falcon, which at that time was a small car, and I wanted a boat that could be loaded on top of it without a struggle, yet one

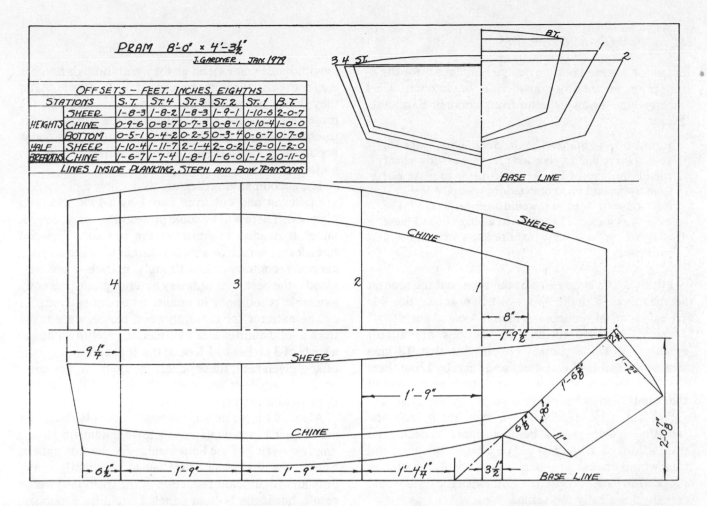

PRAM 8'-0" x 4'-3½"

J.GARDNER. JAN.1979

OFFSETS — FEET, INCHES, EIGHTHS						
STATIONS	S.T.	ST.4	ST.3	ST.2	ST.1	B.T.
HEIGHTS SHEER	1-8-3	1-8-2	1-8-3	1-9-1	1-10-6	2-0-7
HEIGHTS CHINE	0-9-6	0-8-7	0-7-3	0-8-1	0-10-4	1-0-0
HEIGHTS BOTTOM	0-5-1	0-4-2	0-2-5	0-3-4	0-6-7	0-7-0
HALF BREADTHS SHEER	1-10-4	1-11-7	2-1-4	2-0-2	1-8-0	1-2-0
HALF BREADTHS CHINE	1-6-7	1-7-4	1-8-1	1-6-0	1-1-2	0-11-0

LINES INSIDE PLANKING. STERN AND BOW TRANSOMS

that would take three persons in safety under reasonable conditions and without crowding.

The performance of this pram far surpassed my expectations. It rowed more easily, carried more, and proved a better seaboat than I had hoped for, yet it was light enough for me to load and off-load without assistance—that is, after I had worked out a procedure for doing it.

What is the explanation for this pram's exceptional carrying capacity, its stability, its restrained motion in a seaway, and the ease with which the boat rowed in spite of its abbreviated length of 9 feet 5 inches overall? After some consideration, I concluded that the pram's superior performance was due principally to two main characteristics of the hull shape: first, its deeply Veed bottom combined with extra wide beam, and second, the pronounced longitudinal curve of its bottom rocker. The deep V made for deep displacement, which steadied the boat, giving it a firm "hold" on the water that shallow, flat-bottomed craft sliding and bouncing around on the surface do not have. The exceptional amount of fore-and-aft bottom curve, continued in the upward slant of the raking bow transom, resulted in easy, unimpeded slippage through

the water, the boat tending to slip up and over rather than dig in and drag.

Because I was pleased with the pram's performance and found it relatively inexpensive and simple to build—lacking difficult planking bends due to its pram shape—I thought it an ideal craft for the amateur builder. The upshot was that I published lines, offsets, and building directions in the *National Fisherman* in 1963.

Since then many of the prams have been built, all with satisfactory results as far as I know. One reader who has an island in a large lake in Maine built two to transport supplies in. An upstate New York doctor who had never constructed a boat before was immensely pleased with one he built for his grandchildren. Several have been rigged to sail and apparently sail quite well, although the pram was designed for rowing.

More recently, those articles from the *National Fisherman* were reprinted as Chapter 3 in the first volume of *Building Classic Small Craft*. Although the materials from which this pram is built can hardly be called classic, the pram shape definitely is.

It was precisely from this book that the impetus

came for working out the design and details for the 8-foot pram we are now considering. In October 1978 I received the following letter from a man in Yarmouth, Maine:

> In your book, *Building Classic Small Craft,* page 36, your plans to build a plywood pram are exactly what I would like, except I'd like to get plans to make one from a standard piece of exterior plywood 4 feet by 8 feet, so the finished boat would be under 8 feet. I'd be using it as a means to get out to a larger boat. Please advise if you have these plans or know where I could get them.

I didn't have such plans at the time, but the request set me thinking. In the 9-foot-5-inch pram, section 4 is 18 inches aft of section 3, which is located slightly aft of amidships, and these two sections are almost exactly the same shape. To cut out that 18-inch section of hull between them and thereby bring them together could be done without disturbing the rest of the boat, and without changing the lines in any significant way except to shorten them, and the resulting length would be just under 8 feet. The proportions of the hull would be altered, it is true, and this would make the beam considerably greater in proportion to the length, but otherwise the lines would remain practically the same.

This is more or less what I have done. In addition to reducing the overall length to just under 8 feet, however, I have reduced the maximum beam from 55 inches to 51 inches, which would still seem ample for an 8-foot boat.

In general, the construction will be much the same as that described for the longer boat in *Building Classic Small Craft,* except that I have worked out a number of minor alterations that should make the boat easier to build, and lighter, but without any loss of strength or durability. These will be fully explained below. The ladder-frame setup is retained, and the building molds, or what serve as building molds, at stations 1, 2, 3, and 4 become part of the permanent hull structure and remain in the boat as frames.

The bow and stern transoms consist of internal framework covered with plywood, which is not put on until the boat is set up and ready for planking with keelson, chine, and full-length longitudinal risers fastened in place. This procedure makes for easy installation of these longitudinals, which previously were tricky to fit, cut, and bend in place after the finished transoms were on. Now the ends of these longitudinals can extend as they will through notches cut for them in the inner framing of the transoms. After they have been bent in place and fastened, the projecting ends are cut off flush with the surface of the transom framing, and the outer covering of plywood is applied. The side panels go on next, and finally the two bottom panels.

The accompanying diagram shows how these panels are laid out and cut from two 4-by-8-foot sheets of plywood. There will be some plywood to spare, almost all of it needed in finishing the interior. Plywood thickness is ¼ inch or a slightly thinner 5 millimeters. I cannot recommend too strongly marine-grade plywood—the best. The ordinary exterior grade presently available is too poor in quality to be considered.

The patterns for these plywood panels were taken from a solid quarter-size half-model, carefully made to a scale of 3 inches to 1 foot. If the boat conforms to the offsets given here, these panels should fit. In any case, prudence suggests that some checking of the boat be done before the plywood is cut.

Also, as I have noted, the bottom panels should be cut at least 1 inch oversize to allow for adjustment and ample covering of the bottom edges of the side panels. Should the side panels turn out to be slightly scant, only an insignificant reduction of the freeboard would result, but if the bottom panels should be undersize, that would be real trouble.

Spruce is recommended for longitudinals, frames and framing, thwarts, floors, and so forth. Spruce is strong and light, and it holds fastenings quite well. It also glues well, and glue is specified for use throughout, wherever wood meets wood. This is the strongest kind of construction, requiring a minimum of metal fastenings, particularly bronze wood screws, which are now priced all out of reason.

The keelson and the chines can be laminated from two or three thinner strips. Gluing is done when they are installed. They will be easier to bend that way, but stiffer and stronger when the glue sets than if put in solid.

The stern thwart will attach to the stern transom, serving to brace it and the whole stern. Likewise, a low seat will brace the bow.

These are some of the principal details and changes. Full details follow.

The pram is set up for building on a ladder frame, for which two 9-foot lengths of 2-inch-by-6-inch construction lumber will do nicely. Make sure they are

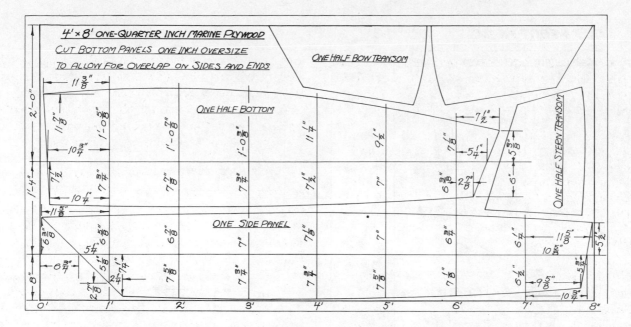

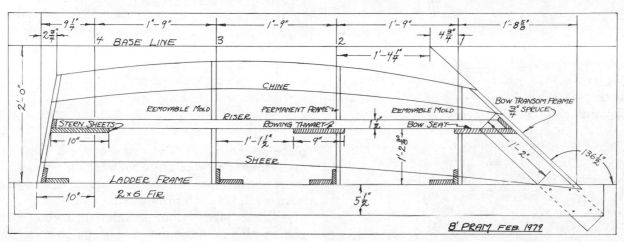

true, straight, and relatively dry. The ladder-frame setup is supported on horses at a convenient height for working, and is far and away the simplest and easiest method for building a boat of this size. Pay particular attention to the location of the cross cleats when locating the building molds (as dimensioned on the accompanying drawing), since the correct positioning of the molds depends on this.

The only kinds of lumber needed are ¼-inch marine plywood, either fir or mahogany, and spruce boards planed ¾ inch thick. One inexpensive source of spruce is the rough 1-inch spruce lumber now widely distributed and sold as spruce ledger boards. Frequently they are available relatively free of knots, so that in stripping them up on the saw to obtain the narrow widths required, it will be possible to obtain relatively clear stock.

For metal fastenings, screws, which would ordinar-

ily be used, can be largely replaced by bronze ring nails, sizes 12 and 14, which are much less expensive and entirely adequate in combination with glue. One advantage of spruce is that it takes and holds nails quite well for a softwood.

Although metal fastenings will play a part in holding this boat together, the main reliance will be on glue, and for that I especially recommend either of two formulations of epoxy: Chem-Tech T-88 or Cold-Cure. Cold-Cure will set at temperatures as low as 35° F. and will adhere to wet wood. Chem-Tech T-88 also cures at low temperatures and bonds damp wood. This property is important if lumber is not as dry as it should be, as sometimes happens. Both Chem-Tech T-88 and Cold-Cure are gap-filling to a reasonable extent, giving some tolerance in fitting joints.

If epoxy cannot be used, an adequate nonsensitizing substitute is Aerolite 306, which may be obtained

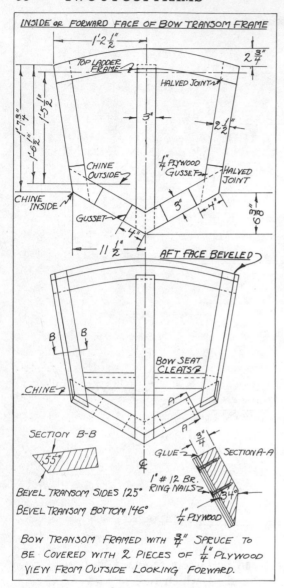

INSIDE or FORWARD FACE OF BOW TRANSOM FRAME

SECTION B-B

BEVEL TRANSOM SIDES 125°
BEVEL TRANSOM BOTTOM 146°

SECTION A-A
GLUE
1" # 12 BR. RING NAILS
1/4" PLYWOOD

BOW TRANSOM FRAMED WITH 3/4" SPRUCE TO BE COVERED WITH 2 PIECES OF 1/4" PLYWOOD VIEW FROM OUTSIDE LOOKING FORWARD.

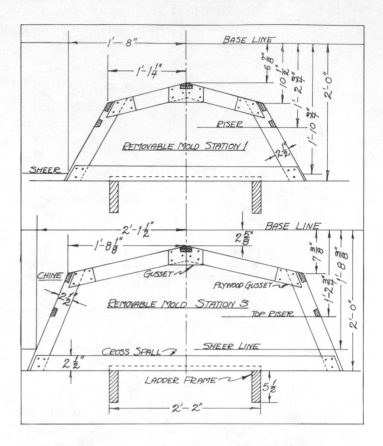

from Woodcraft Supply Corp., 313 Montvale Ave., Woburn, MA 01801. Cold-Cure epoxy is made by Industrial Formulators of Canada, 3824 William St., Burnaby, B.C. V5C 3H9, Canada. Chem-Tech T-88 is distributed by Chem-Tech, 4669 Lander Rd., Chagrin Falls, Ohio 44022. Also on the market are a number of other epoxy glues that would do quite adequately, but the builder is advised to do some testing before choosing one for the boat.

Every place where wood comes together in this boat should be glued as a way of compensating for the scaled-down dimensions of the scantlings. The keelson is a laminated member formed of two ½-inch thick strips of spruce glued together when they are bent into

place on the molds. The two strips will bend more easily than one 1-inch strip, but when the glue sets, the laminated member will be stiffer and stronger than if it were a solid, 1-inch thick piece.

Another place glue provides light but strong construction is in the covering of the bow and stern transom framing with ¼-inch plywood. Glue is used where the pieces constituting the transom frames are halved together and where these halved joints are reinforced on the inside with plywood gussets.

Before the boat can be set up on the ladder frame for planking, the internal framing for the bow and stern transoms must be assembled and glued and section molds made for stations 1, 2, and 3. Molds for stations 1 and 3 are temporary and are removed when the planked hull is lifted off the planking form.

The mold at station 2 remains in the boat and is the location of the rowing thwart. The thwart itself is removable, as is a dory thwart. The space beneath it is covered with plywood, which glues to the side frames to form a bulkhead that completely fills the area, supporting the thwart and bracing the sides and the bottom of the boat at this point.

The internal fore-and-aft stringers—namely the keelson, the two chine strips, and the two risers—are

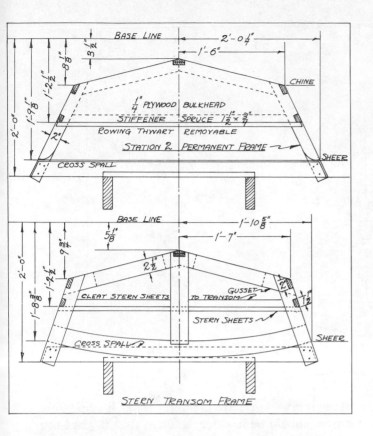

well after the stern transom is set up in place, it is not shown in the drawing. Also, it rakes so little that there is no need to go to the trouble of developing it.

Both the stern sheets and the seat in the bow are important structural members, bracing their respective ends of the boat and tying the sides to the end in one rigid unit. They are glued (1) to the risers that are glued to the sides of the boat and (2) to the cleats, which are in turn glued to the plywood covering of the transoms. The importance of these reinforcing assemblies and their careful installation cannot be overemphasized.

I suggest to prospective builders, especially if this happens to be their first venture at boatbuilding, that they spend some time studying the drawings. Time so spent will not be wasted. It is not possible to take in everything at a glance, and all too easy to miss important details the first time around.

The drawings have been numbered for easy reference. Every item should be considered in turn and located on the drawings. There should be an effort to visualize how each member is made, how it will fit into the finished structure of the boat, and how it will relate to adjoining members when it enters the building sequence. In a word, an effort should be made to build the boat in one's head as fully and completely as possible before picking up the tools.

As previously mentioned, this 8-foot pram is closely similar both in design and construction to my 9½-foot pram featured in the early 1960s in *National Fisherman* and since then widely and successfully built. It would help, I am sure, to review the *National Fisherman* articles for the plans, the building directions, and especially the photographs of the 9½-foot pram. These have since been reprinted in my *Building Small Boats for Oar and Sail* (now out of print) and in the first volume of *Building Classic Small Craft*.

1. *Side planking:* Quarter-inch or 5-mm first-quality marine plywood, fir or mahogany. After the ladder-frame setup has been made and the molds have been faired, and the risers, the chines, the inner keel or keelson, and the transom framing are in place, the side panels go on.

They go on first—that is, before the bottom panels—and are glued and nailed to the risers, chines, and transom framing. When applied, the side panels should be slightly larger, by ⅛ inch or so, than their finished size, so they can be planed to conform to the chines and the ends of the transoms after they are in place and fastened to the boat. As previously stated, the sides must be well glued to the chines and the risers.

made longer than their neat length in the boat so that they can extend through notches in the framing of the transoms cut to receive them. This makes their installation much simpler than the usual procedure.

After the stringers are in place and fastened, their ends are trimmed off flush with the outside of the transom framing, which is then covered with plywood, well glued and nailed. Next the side planks go on, and last, the bottom. All are well glued.

Because of the extreme rake of the bow transom as well as the considerable in-curving of the sides to meet it, there is a lot of beveling on both the sides and the bottom. The accompanying diagrams show both the inside and the outside and the amount of beveling required.

The recommended way is to lay out the shape of the inside face on a flat surface—a piece of heavy plywood will do—and make up the frame to fit these lines. After the halved joints have been glued and reinforced with plywood gussets according to the drawing, the beveling is done. The notches for the fore-and-aft stringers need not be cut until the transom frames are in place on the ladder frame, and so are not shown in the drawings.

The stern transom, unlike the bow transom, requires very little beveling, and since this can be done just as

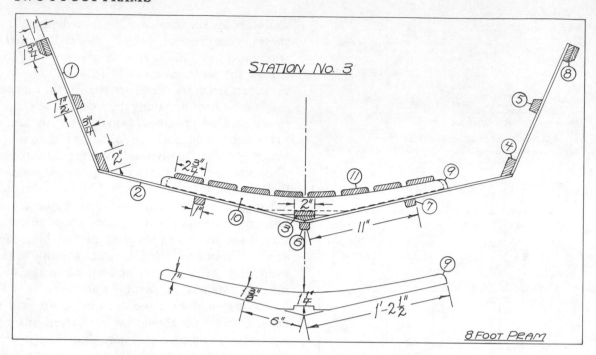

STATION No. 3

8 FOOT PRAM

The nails or screws that hold them in place until the glue cures are supplementary. Screws are not necessary, but if they are used, they should be ¾-inch number 8 bronze. One-inch number 12 bronze ring nails would be more than adequate. If their points break through the inside of the chine and riser strips, these are easily filed off. Longer nails might be used at the ends for fastening to the framing of the bow and stern transoms.

2. *Bottom planking:* These two panels are likewise ¼-inch or 5-mm first-quality marine plywood. They are brought to a tight edge-to-edge fit along the inner keel strip or keelson (see *3),* but should be slightly oversize so as to extend beyond the ends and sides about ⅛ inch, to be planed off flush with the outside after the glue has set. Fastenings are nails or screws, the same as those for the sides. It should be kept in mind that the outer plywood covering of the bow and stern transoms is put on with glue and screws or nails, like the sides, before the bottom panels go on.

3. *Internal keel or keelson:* This is made up from two strips of clear spruce, 2 inches wide and ½ inch thick, sprung in place over the molds with glue between the strips and held together until the glue has cured with clamps and a few temporary nails. The two strips bend more easily than a single strip of the combined thickness and hold their curved shape after the glue has set.

The recess cut into the molds for holding this member should be just deep enough so that when the keelson is planed to match the V of the bottom only the least possible amount of wood is removed in fairing. This is important. As much of the keel strip as possible should remain after planing, for strength and secure nailing of the bottom panels.

The keel strip will be made up longer than the boat so that its ends will project through the notches cut in the framing of the bow and stern transoms to receive it. After it has been bent in place, glued, and fastened with 2-inch number 10 screws, the ends are cut off flush with the transom framing, to be covered later with the outer facing of plywood, like the sides.

4. *Chine strips:* These are ¾-inch clear spruce and are 2 inches wide before being beveled to conform to the V of the bottom, after they have been bent into place around the forms. When they are so installed, they are fastened to the permanent frame that serves as a mold at station 2, and at either end to the bow and stern transoms. (The chine strips are notched, or let in, flush to these three members.) Fasten with 2-inch number 10 screws or the equivalent, and set in glue.

5. *Risers:* These full-length longitudinals are likewise clear spruce, ¾ inch thick and 1½ inches wide before beveling. The top edges are beveled so they will be level and horizontal athwartships. This is because

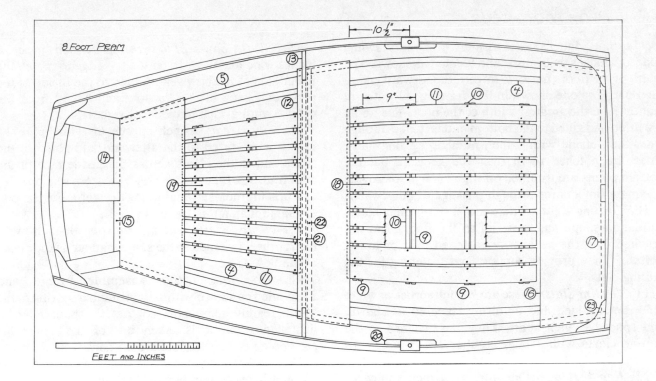

8 FOOT PRAM

FEET AND INCHES

the middle thwart and the end seats rest on the risers, and the end seats want to be glued to them. Like the chine strips, the risers are let in flush to both the sides of the permanent frame at station 2 and the transom framing at either end of the boat. The risers are likewise longer than the boat when installed, and are fastened, glued, cut off flush, and covered when the outer facing of plywood goes on.

6. *Outer keel strip:* This longitudinal is clear spruce, ¾ inch thick or deep by 1 inch wide. It is installed after the bottom plywood is on. Just enough is planed off the joint where the bottom panels come together on the keelson to seat the outer keel strip. It is bedded in glue and fastened with 1½-inch number 10 screws or with 1½-inch or 1¾-inch ring nails, after which the ends are cut off flush with the outside of the transoms.

If desired, it can be cut shorter to allow splicing in a small skeg tapering from ¾ inch deep at the splice to about 2½ inches at the stern. Such a skeg could improve directional stability for rowing. It should be fastened from the inside as well as from the outside. Inside fastenings, 2-inch or 2½-inch number 12 screws or the equivalent, are put in through the keelson. Such a skeg can be tapered and thinned to ⅝ inch on its bottom edge.

7. *Outside bottom stringers:* Full-length stringers of clear spruce, ¾ inch by 1 inch put on flat. It is

important that they run parallel with the outer keel strip. These are important structural members that help directional stability and also serve as rubbing strips that protect the plywood bottom. These are put on with glue and fastened through the bottom into the six internal floors and the frame at station 2 with 1½-inch number 10 screws or number 12 ring nails of the same length.

These bottom stringers cannot be put on, of course, until the boat has been planked and turned over and the internal floors installed. Extra fastenings between the floors, put in from the inside through the plywood bottom into the bottom stringers before the glue sets, would add stiffness and ensure a good fit for the glue. These fastenings could be either ¾-inch number 8 screws or 1-inch number 13 ring nails.

8. *Outwales:* The outwales are glued up from two full-length strips of clear spruce, ½ inch thick and 1¾ inches wide. The bottom edge of the outer strip is beveled as shown in the drawing. The outwales are put on after the boat has been planked and turned over. They are glued to the sides of the boat and are nailed through the plywood sides from the interior of the boat with two rows of 1-inch number 12 ring nails spaced about 6 inches apart. They are also fastened from the outside into the frame at station 2, and at the ends to the corner knees (23).

9. *Floors:* There are six internal floors made of ¾-

inch spruce, dimensioned as shown in the drawing, spaced 9 inches on centers, and located as shown. The width of the floors narrows toward the forward end of the boat. The one shown in the drawing is located at station 3, at the greatest width of the boat. The floors are fitted and glued to the bottom and fastened through from the outside with 1-inch number 12 ring nails. They are notched to fit over the keelson, but the bottom points are trimmed off high enough to provide adequate limbers for through passage of bilge water.

10. *Grating cleats:* There are seven grating cleats similar in shape and material to the floors, but not notched over the keelson or fastened to it or to the bottom. They provide support and fastening for the grating slats.

11. *Grating slats:* These are ½-inch spruce or white pine dimensioned and uniformly tapered as shown, and spaced ½ inch apart. They are fastened to the grating cleats with 1-inch number 12 ring nails as shown.

12. *Removable rowing thwart:* ¾-inch spruce or white pine, 9 inches wide and located as shown in the drawings. This thwart is not fastened in but is removable, being merely notched to fit over the sides of the frame at station 2, as in a Banks dory. It also rests on the risers and on the stiffener *(22)* fastened to the top of the plywood bulkhead *(21)*. This thwart is left loose for ready removal so that the boat may be lightened when it is taken out of the water.

13. *Frame at station 2:* This substantial bracing member located approximately amidships is reinforced by the plywood bulkhead *(21)* extending from side to side below the thwart *(12)* and stiffened by a spruce strip (see *22*) ¾ inch thick and 1½ inches wide.

14. *Bow seat:* Spruce or white pine, a foot in width and long enough for a snug fit across the bow end. This is glued and nailed to the risers and to the cleats across the inside face of the bow transom. In addition to serving as a seat, this member braces the bow end of the boat and strengthens it immensely.

15. *Cleats, bow seat to transom:* ¾-inch spruce, 2 inches wide and beveled on the top edge to match the under side of the bow seat. Glued to the inside of the plywood facing of the transom and nailed from the outside with 1-inch number 12 ring nails.

16. *Stern seat:* ¾-inch spruce or white pine 11 inches wide, fitted to the after end and glued to the risers and to the cleats across the inside face of the after transom. Like the bow seat, the stern seat doubles as a bracing member reinforcing the stern. Fastened in the same manner as the bow seat.

17. *Cleats, stern seat to transom:* ¾-inch-by-2-inch spruce, fastened in the same manner as the cleats at the bow *(15)*.

18. *After floor grating:* Assembled from *10* and *11*. Nailed as shown with 1-inch number 12 ring nails. Made readily removable so that the boat may be lightened when it is taken out of the water for cartopping or stowage aboard a yacht.

19. *Forward floor grating:* Same construction as *18*, and likewise removable from the boat.

20. *Cleats for mounting oarlock sockets:* ¾-inch spruce 2½ inches wide and 9 inches long, glued to the inside of the boat and through-fastened into the outwale with 1½-inch or 1¾-inch number 10 screws.

21. *Plywood bulkhead:* Quarter-inch plywood, scribed and fitted to the bottom and sides of the boat at station 2, coming to the height of the seat risers, and glued and nailed with 1-inch number 12 ring nails to the after face of the permanent frame *(13)*.

22. *Stiffener:* Glued to the after face of the plywood bulkhead at the same height as the risers, and nailed with 1-inch number 12 ring nails.

23. *Corner knee braces:* ¾-inch mahogany or oak, laid out with the grain running parallel to the hypotenuse of their triangular shape. Each of their two sides is fastened with two screws, one through the end from the inside into the wale, the other from the outside through the outwale into the knee, close to its corner.

6

FOUR CANOES

Recreational small craft have never been more popular or numerous than they are now on both our East and West coasts. Their increase in the past 10 years, which has been nothing less than phenomenal, is almost certain to continue, for very good reasons. In an era of mounting costs and restricted budgets, many are finding that it is not necessary to own a large and expensive vessel in order to experience much of the pleasure and excitement of yachting. Indeed, affordable smaller craft open up additional areas of boating pleasure.

This applies in particular to canoes and kayaks, whether they are used for white water, wilderness cruising, sailing, racing, or lazy relaxation on summer afternoons. And those who build and maintain their own canoes and kayaks, as increasing numbers are doing, find additional fulfillment in working with tools and materials, in using their hands and their brains, in building something that is both useful and beautiful.

The growing popularity of canoes is reminiscent of a similar involvement with canoes for sport and recreation in this country a century ago, but with at least one important difference. Few of the earlier canoes were built by the owners; construction then was left largely to professionals. Part of the difference today is the availability of modern plastic glues and fabric reinforcements. When these new materials are used in combination with strips and veneers of wood, acceptable and even superior canoes and kayaks can be produced in home workshops.

Construction methods may have changed radically, but canoe design—that is, hull shape—has been little improved if at all in the last hundred years, except in the case of a few highly specialized racing canoes. We have not been able to improve on the shapes that were once built at Peterborough (Ontario), or by J. Henry Rushton, W. P. Stephens, R. J. Douglas, E. M. White, H.N. Morris, and other late-19th-century builders whose names are less well known.

Unfortunately, builders who would like to reproduce these older models today are more often than not unable to find lines and offsets. The usual practice in the past was to build from molds, most of which have long since disappeared. Because lines and offsets were not used, they were not recorded, and in the rare instances when they were, they were hardly ever published.

Included in this chapter are lines and offsets for four of these earlier canoes, which are not to be found elsewhere, I believe. Two are typical early sailing canoes, both from obscure sources. The third is a Peterborough plank canoe built by the Canadian Canoe Company. It is primarily a paddling canoe, but it has been adapted successfully for sailing. The fourth is Rushton's Arkansaw Traveler, which by Rushton's own account was developed on Canadian (Peterborough) lines.

A PETERBOROUGH PLANK CANOE

The Indian birchbark canoe, whose form the Peterborough builders reproduced in planks and strips of wood with very little change, was developed and perfected as a workboat for transportation and the hunt, and so it remained and was built for unnumbered generations. It was not until shortly after 1850 at Peterborough, on the Otonabee River, that the Indian canoe was first adapted and successfully built for use as a pleasure craft.

According to Donald Cameron, in a paper read at the Peterborough Historical Society in 1975, it was sometime between 1850 and 1860 that John Stephenson of Ashburnham and Tom Gordon of Lakefield "led off in the building of plank-and-rib canoes." Stephenson's son Alfred told Cameron that his father, born in 1830, built the first canoe to replace the birchbark and the dugout and that it was a board canoe. The Gordon descendants agree that this may well have been the case, but claim that Tom Gordon "designed and manufactured for sale the first plank canoes."

These two builders may have been the first, but

William English of Peterborough, who started building in 1861, and Daniel Herald of Gore's Landing, Rice Lake, were not far behind. That all four of these Peterborough-area builders seem to have gotten started more or less simultaneously is an indication that the plank canoes must have been a success from the outset, and that they were in considerable demand almost as soon as they appeared.

They were, in fact, a radical departure in construction, the first ones requiring only three planks to fill out the side. Later, when wide boards of cedar and basswood became harder to get, the number of side planks was increased to four.

John Stephenson had previously run a planing mill. This would have been no later than the 1850s, and at that time such woodworking machinery was quite new. Without a means of producing a plentiful supply of cheap, wide boards of a uniform ¼-inch thickness, Peterborough plank canoes would have been out of the question. In casting about for new uses and an expanded market for the quantities of smooth planed lumber that his mill could produce, it was natural that Stephenson should come up with the idea of building wide-board canoes. The time was certainly right for replacements for the heavy log dugouts then in use and the Indian birch canoes that were in short supply.

The wide-board plank canoe is uniquely a Peterborough product, a boat that was never built commercially outside the area. Although these canoes were not copied—at least in their construction—they greatly influenced and may even have initiated the production of all-wood canoes, which flourished in the United States from roughly 1870 to shortly after 1900.

The construction of the wide-board all-wood canoe is relatively simple and straightforward, although how it was possible to cup the ¼-inch boards sufficiently to conform to the hard turns at the bilges without splitting the planks is a mystery to me. Some have claimed that the boards were softened and made pliable by sponging with hot water, but I have not yet tried it to see how this was done. In any case, the planks were clinch-nailed to bent ribs spaced 6 inches apart on centers. This was the rib spacing found on the remains of an old William English canoe.

Between the ribs, the plank seams are covered with sections of batten stock, which were also used for ribs in the William English canoe. There the ribs and battens are half-rounds of Canadian rock elm measuring a scant ¾ inch wide and ⅜ inch thick. This apparently was a uniformly produced mill product gotten out in quantity on a shaper. Clinch fastenings are slim, cut nails of bronze or hardened copper, ¾ inch long and stiff enough to drive through the hard rock elm without crippling.

As a boy, Albert English, Donald Cameron's informant, assisted his father in building plank canoes. This was perhaps around 1915 or slightly before. (Albert was born when his father was 69.) He vividly recalls his difficulties in bending the boards and pulling them into place in order to get them to conform to the curves of the sides so that they could be nailed.

It was probably due to such difficulties, as well as to the increasing shortage of clear, wide lumber, that wide-board construction was eventually replaced to a great extent by other methods, mostly variations of strip construction. Strip construction has much to recommend to amateur builders now.

There must have been a rapid evolution from the first wide-board plank canoes, but that evolution was never recorded and is now lost. Certainly the first models must have been much heavier and more crudely lined than the highly perfected hulls that have survived and come down to us as Peterborough canoes.

Whether the builders ever made use of lines is doubtful. From the canoes that still exist, and from what is to be seen in builders' catalogs and in photographs, it appears that there were no more than a few closely similar standard shapes. Apparently builders at the time had concluded that the optimum canoe shape for general recreational use had been attained.

Jack Hazzard of Washington, D.C., in his nineties and still active as a canoeist, purchased a new 16-foot William English all-wood canoe in 1920. In 1980, using this canoe as a plug, he glued up a paper replica that has since seen considerable use and proved quite successful. The paper replica is laid up with strips of a strong, brown kraft paper bonded together with a

Jack Hazzard sailing his William English Model 21 canoe, the same model shown in this engraving from an early catalog of the William English firm. Hazzard describes the rig on his 16-foot by 30-inch Blue Bonnet *as a "patched-up" affair of 60 square feet that sailed well but not too fast. The photo was taken in 1930.*

On the Potomac River, Jack Hazzard tries out the paper canoe he built in 1980 using his 1920 William English boat as a plug.

waterproof plastic adhesive. The result is both strong and very light. Sufficient rigidity is attained by internal bracing with wood strips. When an old canoe that has not lost its shape is available to serve as a plug, such construction would seem to have real possibilities for the home workshop.

Paper combines exceptional strength and toughness with exceptional light weight. At one time paper boats seemed to offer great promise in this country. For a brief period slightly more than a hundred years ago, paper racing shells by Waters, Balch and Company of Troy, New York, won most of the important races in college rowing. What was lacking then, and for a long time thereafter, was a reliable waterproof adhesive. Now that we have plastic resin glues that are completely and permanently waterproof, there is no reason why paper should not come into its own as a boatbuilding and canoe-building material.

A more conventional method of canoe construction, and the one principally used by Peterborough builders, is to start with a building form over which steamed ribs are bent. At first the Peterborough builders covered the ribs with wide strakes of planking—three, and then four, boards to the side. Wide boards were followed by longitudinal strips with ship-lap edges, although one of the Peterborough builders briefly tried a tongue-and-grooved strip, and another backed the seams between his wood strips with long strips of thin brass with edges that turned and clinched into the wood. In all cases the wood strips were nailed to the ribs with small nails, the points of which barely came through and were turned back into the rib.

Quite recently a new form of strip construction for canoes has developed. Ribs are omitted, strips are edge-glued together, and this shell-built hull is covered inside and out with a thin overlay of fiberglass. An extremely lightweight, handsome boat results. Practitioners of this method claim the boat is adequately strong, but I have yet to be convinced that ribs can be omitted with impunity. Although I have no knowledge of failure by any glued-strip canoe, I do know of a small sailboat so built that developed lengthwise splits in the sides when dropped a short distance into the water in launching.

The lines and offsets appearing here were taken from a canoe formerly owned by William B. Coolidge of Washington, D.C. Several years ago he donated the boat to the Mystic Seaport Museum, Mystic, Connecticut, and it is now in the small-craft collection there.

Small metal plates that serve as reinforcements on the outside of the sheer strakes, backing up the ends of the two thwarts, are stamped with the name of the Canadian Canoe Company, the builder. According to a booklet on sailing canoes published by the American Canoe Association in 1935, the most popular and fastest open canoes then available in stock models for adaptation to sailing were Model 16, built by the Canadian Canoe Company, Peterborough, Ontario, and Model 64, built by the Peterborough Canoe Company, Peterborough. "The two model numbers designate cedar canoes of rib-and-batten construction," the booklet explains, "but these manufacturers also furnish an identical model both in basswood rib and batten and in longitudinal cedar strip construction. Lengths of all models are 16 feet, beam 31 inches, depth amidships 12 inches and weight approximately 75 pounds." The dimensions cited correspond exactly

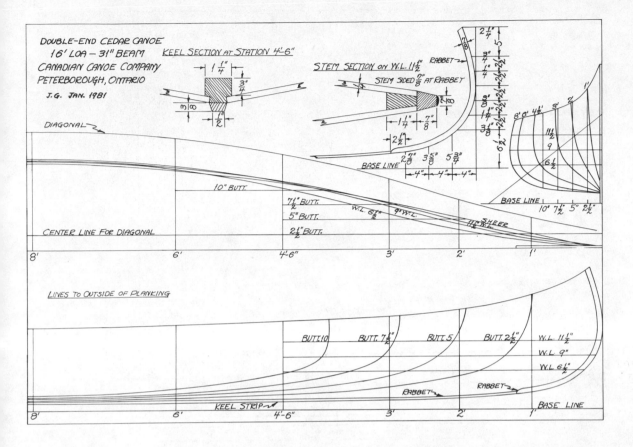

DOUBLE-END CEDAR CANOE
16' LOA — 31" BEAM
CANADIAN CANOE COMPANY
PETERBOROUGH, ONTARIO

J.G. JAN. 1981

	STATIONS	STEM	1'-0"	2'-0"	3'-0"	4'-6"	6'-0"	8'-0"
HEIGHTS ABOVE BASE LINE	SHEER	1-11-5	1-7-3	1-4-7	1-3-7	1-2-7	1-2-4	1-2-0
	RABBET	—	0-3-5	0-2-3	0-2-0	0-1-7	0-1-5	0-1-5
	BUTT. 2½"	—	1-7-3	0-5-6	0-3-6	0-2-4	0-2-0	0-1-7
	BUTT. 5"	—	—	1-1-2	0-5-6	0-3-2	0-2-3	0-2-0
	BUTT. 7½"	—	—	—	0-10-3	0-4-3	0-2-6	0-2-2
	BUTT. 10"	—	—	—	—	0-6-0	0-3-4	0-2-5
HALF-BREADTHS	SHEER	0-0-3⁺	0-2-4	0-5-2	0-7-7	0-11-2	1-1-3	1-2-5
	W.L. 11½"	0-0-3⁺	0-1-7	0-4-6	0-7-5	0-11-5	1-2-0	1-3-2
	W.L. 9"	0-0-3⁺	0-1-5	0-4-1	0-7-1	0-11-3	1-2-1	1-3-4
	W.L. 6½"	0-0-3⁺	0-1-1	0-3-0	0-5-6	0-10-3	1-1-5	1-3-1
	KEEL RAB.	0-0-3⁺	0-0-3⁺	0-0-3	0-0-3	0-0-3	0-0-3	0-0-3
	DIAGONAL	0-0-4	0-2-5	0-6-0	0-9-2	1-1-3	1-4-0	1-5-2

Left: *Measurements are given to the outside of the ¼-inch thick planking. The diagonal, which is shown in the lines drawing, is 15 inches above the baseline and 19 inches out on the baseline.* **Below:** *The Canadian Canoe Company boat donated to Mystic Seaport by William Coolidge. The lines and offsets presented here were taken off this canoe. (Mystic Seaport photo by Mary Anne Stets)*

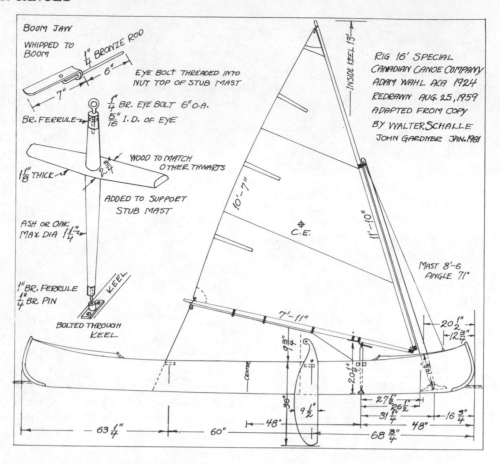

with those of the Coolidge canoe, which is also of cedar rib-and-batten construction, and this combination of evidence would seem definitely to establish it as a Canadian Canoe Company Model 16.

According to Walter Schalle of the American Canoe Association, it was for one of these Model 16 Canadian canoes with a modified length of 17 feet that the rig shown here was designed and built by Adam Wahl, an ACA member. Schalle believes it to be the fastest lateen rig ever raced in the ACA. (After 1913 the ACA established a "special" racing class of decked canoes that permitted lengths up to 17 feet.) During the early 1920s Wahl won 20 of 21 consecutive races; he finished second in the other, due to a broken mainsheet.

Wahl's Canadian Canoe Company 17-foot special had long decks, no seats, two thwarts, a cut-down keel, and an extra-wide gunwale. The advantages of its rig—in particular the simplicity and ease of handling—are obvious.

The outfit is so well balanced that the boat could at times be sailed without the steering paddle, directional control being maintained simply by moving the leeboard. Nevertheless, due to the location of the mast, the rig was not easy to install.

Sail plans for rigging these canoes have been published in various places. The American Canoe Association booklet "Sailing Canoes" (June 1, 1935) contains several with full details and specifications. Jack Hazzard, already mentioned as the owner of a William English Peterborough, wrote several articles in the 1930s for *Popular Science Monthly* and other publications, for canoeing enthusiasts interested in converting their stock-model paddling canoes for sailing. Others as well published such material about that time.

Most of the canoes converted to sail were the so-called rag canoes—the canvas-covered stock models built for paddling. But no lines of stock canoes were published for the would-be builder. There were various reasons for this.

First, the canoe companies had a proprietary interest in their models, and inasmuch as they were in the business of building canoes to sell, they were not about to provide lines for the use of home builders. Second, it would not have been ethical for anyone else to have taken off the lines of such canoes and circulated them while they were still being built commercially, even if this could have been done legally at the time. Finally, the work of taking off such lines, fairing them, and drawing them so that they could be used is considerable, and ordinarily it would not have paid anyone to do it. It was principally for these reasons that no hull lines or measured offsets for the cedar and basswood three- and four-plank Peterborough stock canoes of the 1920s and 1930s were published, as far as I have been able to discover.

But since then the companies that produced these canoes have gone out of business and disappeared, and after a half century or so their designs have passed into the public domain. There is no longer any reason why these designs should not be freely available to anyone wishing, and able, to use them.

J. HENRY RUSHTON'S ARKANSAW TRAVELER

No one of the old-time builders has fared better in the current revival of classic American small craft than J. Henry Rushton, whose first lightly built boat for wilderness travel was assembled in a Canton, New York, barn in 1873. Before his death in 1906, several thousand lightweight canoes and rowboats bearing the Rushton name were produced. The recognition now accorded Rushton by canoeists and frequenters of our lakes and inland waterways is fast reaching the degree of adulation paid by yachtsmen to the Herreshoffs of Bristol.

With the publication of Atwood Manley's *J. Henry Rushton and His Times in American Canoeing* in 1968 the Rushton revival was well on its way. Amateur builders have taken to reproducing his designs—for one, the diminutive clinker canoe Wee Lassie. Since the appearance of Manley's book, scores of Rushton canoes and boats have turned up, and others are coming to light all the time, from the most unlikely places. That many of the canoes require only minimal restoration before they are ready to go back in the water speaks well for Rushton's construction methods and the quality of his materials.

It was not enough to be a first-rate builder in the face of the intense competition that characterized the boatbuilding business in this country in the first quarter of the 19th century. To survive and prosper, one had to be an able businessman as well. Rushton was not lacking in this respect. In addition to facing the same American competition that forced into bankruptcy such concerns as the R.J. Douglas Company of Waukegan, Illinois, and H.V. Partelow and Company of Boston, Rushton had to compete with the builders in Peterborough, which was not far from the Rushton factory in Canton, New York. Tom Gordon, Herald and Hutchinson, William English, and James Z. Rogers (who operated the Ontario Canoe Company) were producing superior canoes and exporting them in increasing numbers to the United States.

In the 1880s Rushton moved to meet his Canadian competition head on by adding to his line a 15-foot-by-30-inch "Canadian-model" canoe obviously adapted from those built at Peterborough. There must have been a favorable response, for in his 1891 catalog he announced his "Canadian-model" canoes would now be available in five lengths, from 12 to 16 feet. His explanation to his customers reads as follows: "Believing our Canadian model a superior one for an open canoe for cruising and hunting, we have decided to build it in several lengths. The beam will be nearly the same in all. The construction will be *smooth skin* by our regular methods. Decks and seats as shown..., bent oak stems, ribs spaced 2 inches apart."

The crew of J. Henry Rushton's Canton, New York canoe factory sometime before 1893. Rushton is seated in the front row with papers in his hand. Nelson Brown, his foreman, stands at left in the second row. The Rushton factory was one of the best known in this period when canoeing was the rage.

Will Kip, an associate foreman in Rushton's canoe factory, stands in either a Ugo model or Arkansaw Traveler canoe (it is difficult to tell one from the other at this angle) while boating in company with Old Joe Ellsworth, Rushton's mentor. Old Joe is in a Rushton Princess. They are on the Little River near Canton, New York, about the late 1890s or earlier.

Although the construction of Rushton's Canadian-model canoes differed somewhat from their Peterborough counterparts, they were identical in shape, or nearly so, judging from lines published in Rushton's 1891 catalog. Although these lines are not dimensioned and not large enough to build from easily and accurately, they were skillfully drawn. They may have been the work of the Racine, Wisconsin, naval architect Fred W. Martin, mentioned by Rushton in his so-called *Book of Knowledge* as having drawn lines for him. Whoever the draftsman was, he must have been familiar with Peterborough canoes.

It could not have been long after the appearance of the 1891 catalog that Rushton gave Benjamin Kip, who was working for him at the time as a draftsman, directions for drawing lines for an especially fine canoe. This boat was to be part of the Rushton exhibit at the forthcoming Columbian Exposition, which was scheduled to open in Chicago in 1892 but was delayed until 1893 because of the financial panic of that year. This panic all but ruined Rushton, for he had badly overextended himself financially in preparing an exhibit that would outshine his competitors, both American and Canadian.

After the canoe was built it was discovered that the keel was slightly warped. Rushton rejected it, selling it to Kip for $10. This was Rushton's first Arkansaw Traveler. When the Kip estate was settled some years ago, the canoe was sold to the Wells family of Massena, New York. Following damage sustained in the second Rushton Memorial Canoe Race at Canton in 1963, Nathaniel Wells restored the canoe completely, and the family now use it and maintain it in tip-top shape. In commenting on this canoe to Atwood Manley, Nat Wells characterized it as "an extremely tippy number, like all Arkansaw Travelers."

How many Arkansaw Travelers were built, and what the demand was for them and for the other Canadian-model paddling canoes—the Ontario, the Igo, and the Ugo—in the difficult period following the Columbian Exposition, when the Canton business was barely able to keep its head above water, is not known. In the 1895 Rushton catalog the Arkansaw Traveler, listed under "Canadian Model Light Paddling Canoes," gets a full page. It was offered in four lengths, from 14 to 17 feet; in one grade, "A"; and four different styles of decking. Illustrations consisted of a profile view of a finished canoe and greatly reduced hull lines. It was described as follows:

These canoes are uniformly 18 inches deep bow and stern, and 10 inches amidships. The planking is ¼ inch

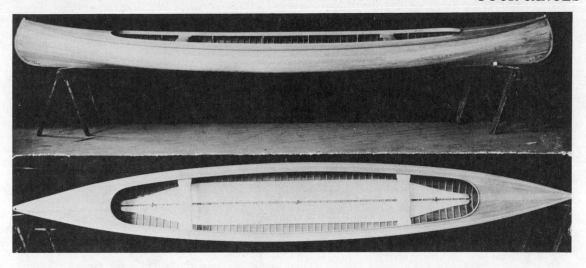

*This Arkansaw Traveler, photographed in the Rushton shop prior to 1916, had the "Style C" decking—
that is, 3 inches of deck all around, with a slight coaming. (Courtesy the Canton Library)*

thick and ribs are spaced about 2½ inches center to center. Gunwales are of the usual width, and the material and workmanship throughout are of the best.

The canoe is a modification of the well known Canadian canoe. It combines to a marked degree, fine lines, ease under paddle, safety, and stiffness. It is somewhat lighter than the Ugo canoe. It rivals the birch bark in weight and speed, and is more staunch, seaworthy and durable.

This is a canoe that requires some care in handling except from expert canoeists. It is not built like a racing shell, but at the same time is fast enough to be in a class with them.

This canoe is ordinarily finished with two thwarts instead of seats, as is shown. Average weights with

Style A decks are from 51 pounds to 65 pounds according to length.

In both the 1903 and 1904 catalogs the four Canadian-model paddling canoes are virtually unchanged, except that the weight of the Arkansaw Traveler is reduced to "40 pounds and upwards, according to size and style of decking," in 1903, and to "45 pounds and upwards" in 1904. In keeping with the changed format of these two catalogs, the hull lines of the Arkansaw Traveler are twice the size of previous representations, making them large enough, but just barely, to scale up to a workable size. This I have done, and the results are presented here. Of course, to

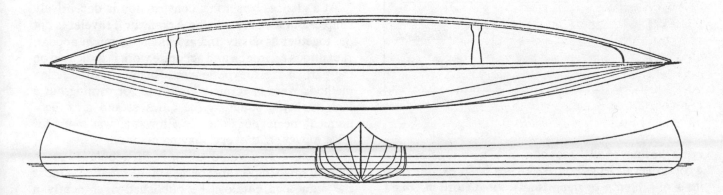

A drawing of the Arkansaw Traveler taken from the 1904 Rushton catalog.

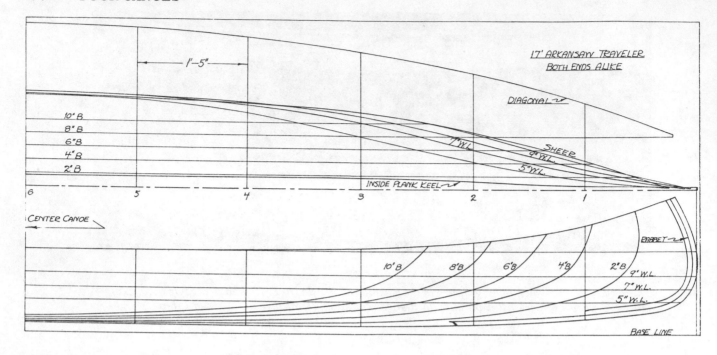

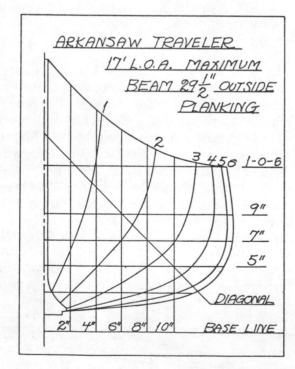

Scantling dimensions and construction details have been obtained from *Iola,* a Rushton canoe in Mystic Seaport Museum's small-craft collection. *Iola* has been identified as an Arkansaw Traveler, and is so listed in Bray's *Catalogue of Mystic Seaport Museum's Watercraft Collection,* although it was built without thwarts, and its dimensions differ slightly from those of the Arkansaw Traveler in the Rushton catalogs.

Iola is planked lapstrake but finished smooth, as the catalogs specify—a method by which Rushton achieved a superior result. The laps are planed to a feather edge, bedded with thick varnish, and fastened with very small tacks, Adirondack-guideboat fashion. Today, gluing might be easier and even more effective.

At a glance, Rushton's construction is deceptively simple. But a canoe like the Arkansaw Traveler is not put together as easily and as quickly as might appear. A cautious approach and accurate work is indicated on the part of the inexperienced. Rushton's production methods were exactingly contrived for turning out a high-quality product by the quickest and most economical means possible. No allowance was made for false moves, and every shaving counted.

For those who would follow in Rushton's footsteps there are two important sources of information. One is the numerous catalogs he published over nearly a quarter of a century. Unfortunately, very few have survived except for those in the library at the Adirondack Museum and those in the public library at

bring the lines of a 17-foot boat up to working size from a total overall length of 6½ inches is an exacting job involving plenty of opportunity for distortion. But I must say the lines faired out well in enlargement, which indicates they must have been accurately drawn in reduction.

OFFSETS 17' ARKANSAW TRAVELER								
	STATIONS	STEM	1	2	3	4	5	6
HALF-BREADTHS	SHEER	0-0-2	0-4-3	0-8-5	0-11-6	1-0-7	1-1-5	1-2-1
	W.L. 1-0-6	0-0-2	0-3-7	0-8-4	0-11-6	1-0-7	1-1-5	1-2-1
	W.L. 9"	0-0-2	0-3-0	0-7-2	0-11-0	1-1-1	1-2-1	1-2-4
	W.L. 7"	0-0-2	0-2-3	0-6-0	0-10-1	1-0-5	1-2-1	1-2-4
	W.L. 5"	0-0-2	0-1-4	0-4-1	0-8-0	0-11-3	1-1-3	1-1-7
	INSIDE KEEL	—	0-0-4	0-1-2	0-1-5	0-1-6	0-1-6	0-1-6
HEIGHTS ABOVE BASE LINE	SHEER	1-8-6	1-4-5	1-2-0	1-1-0	1-0-6	1-0-5	1-0-5
	INSIDE KEEL	—	0-3-0	0-2-2	0-2-0	0-2-0	0-2-0	0-2-0
	BEARDING AT KEEL	—	0-3-0	0-2-2	0-1-6	0-1-4	0-1-4	0-1-4
	2" BUTTOCK	SHEER 1-6-6	0-6-1	0-2-7	0-1-7	0-1-5	0-1-5	0-1-5
	4" BUTTOCK	SHEER 1-5-0	1-1-3	0-4-7	0-2-6	0-2-1	0-1-7	0-1-6
	6" BUTTOCK	SHEER 1-3-4	—	0-7-0	0-3-6	0-2-5	0-2-1	0-1-7
	8" BUTTOCK	SHEER 1-2-2	—	0-10-7	0-5-0	0-3-1	0-2-4	0-2-2
	10" BUTTOCK	SHEER 1-1-3	—	—	0-6-7	0-4-0	0-3-0	0-2-4
DIAGONAL		0-0-5	0-5-1	0-9-5	1-0-7	1-3-1	1-4-3	1-4-6

DIAGONAL UP 1'-3" ON CENTER LINE. OUT 6" ON 9" W.L.
AND 10" ON 5" W.L. KEEL PLANK 3/4" THICK OAK.
MEASUREMENTS IN FEET, INCHES, AND EIGHTHS.
MEASUREMENTS INSIDE PLANKING. STEM SIDED 1".
BOTH ENDS THE SAME. STATIONS 1'-5" APART.

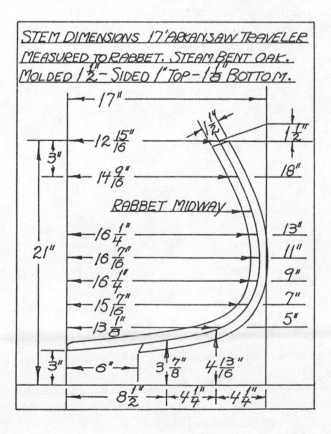

STEM DIMENSIONS 17' ARKANSAW TRAVELER
MEASURED TO RABBET. STEAM BENT OAK.
MOLDED 1½" – SIDED 1" TOP – 1⅛" BOTTOM.

Canton, New York. In 1983, however, William Crowley's *Rushton's Rowboats and Canoes*—a facsimile reprint of the 1903 catalog, supplemented by some fine photographs and related material—was published for the Adirondack Museum by International Marine Publishing Company. The other source is, of course, Manley's *Rushton and His Times in American Canoeing*.

These are the printed sources. I should point out, however, that the surviving Rushton boats themselves are a basic primary source not to be overlooked. Much is to be learned about their construction from direct examination, but much more could be learned if they could be taken apart piece by piece. Until the day when a wrecked survivor turns up, a boat too far gone for restoration and thus a candidate for dissection, we cannot be entirely sure just how some things were done. We don't know, for example, exactly how the Rushton keel rabbet was cut.

The construction process developed in the Rushton shop is taken up in detail in the appendixes of Manley's book. Not everything is explained here, but the great deal that is stands up remarkably well when checked against actual boats and the known building procedures of Rushton's contemporaries.

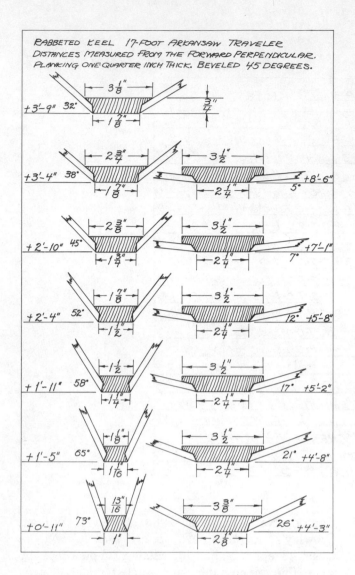

RABBETED KEEL 17-FOOT ARKANSAW TRAVELER
DISTANCES MEASURED FROM THE FORWARD PERPENDICULAR.
PLANKING ONE-QUARTER INCH THICK. BEVELED 45 DEGREES.

Manley tells us that Rushton's son, J.H. (Harry) Rushton, was still alive when Manley was writing his book. Harry had worked in his father's shop and had carried on the business for a time after the elder Rushton's death. He was thoroughly familiar with the details of the construction process and had a good memory. His account, included in Manley's book, is surprisingly complete and precise after a lapse of some years, although there are several things that should have a fuller explanation. I cannot recommend too strongly a thorough study of Harry Rushton's account, together with an attempt to visualize each step in the building procedure he describes.

Boats like the Arkansaw Traveler—in fact, all of Rushton's lightly planked cedar boats—were planked *bottom up*. The various sectional molds, made from a full-size laydown in the usual way, were attached at the proper heights and distances to what is called a *bed piece*. As far as I can determine from photos and from reading between the lines, this is what we now generally call a *building form,* which consists of a number of pieces instead of a single one.

Apparently this arrangement stood on the floor and supported the molds at a convenient height for working. Another way of supporting the molds during the planking process would be to use a ladder frame, directions for which are to be found in several places elsewhere in this book.

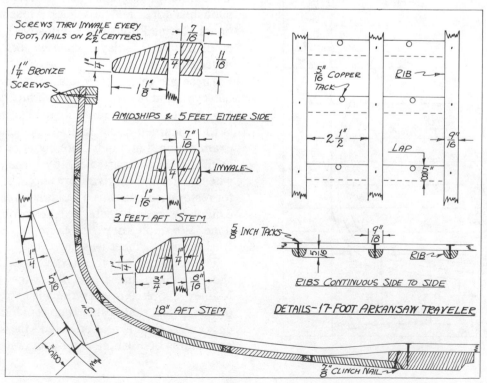

DETAILS—17-FOOT ARKANSAW TRAVELER

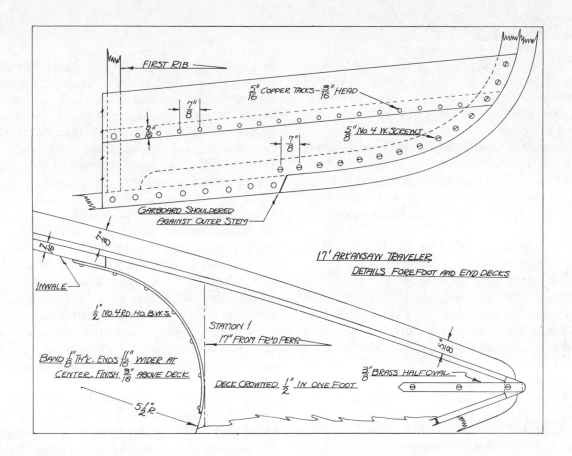

FIRST RIB

$\frac{5}{16}$" COPPER TACKS — $\frac{3}{16}$" HEAD

$\frac{7}{8}$"

$\frac{2}{16}$"

$\frac{5}{8}$" No 4 W. SCREWS

$\frac{7}{8}$"

GARBOARD SHOULDERED AGAINST OUTER STEM

17' ARKANSAW TRAVELER
DETAILS FOREFOOT AND END DECKS

INWALE

$\frac{1}{2}$" No. 4 RD. HD. B.WK.S

STATION 1
17" FROM FR'D PERP.

$\frac{3}{8}$" BRASS HALF OVAL

BAND $\frac{1}{8}$" TH'K. ENDS $\frac{11}{16}$" WIDER AT CENTER. FINISH $\frac{3}{16}$" ABOVE DECK

DECK CROWNED $\frac{1}{2}$" IN ONE FOOT

$5\frac{1}{2}$"R

How many molds were used, how far apart they were set, and just how they were positioned is not stated. For this particular Arkansaw Traveler, the molds could probably be set on the stations given in the lines plan, where they are shown to be 17 inches apart. However, it might be found expedient to change this mold spacing slightly so that the molds come exactly where ribs will be placed.

In that case, as planking proceeds an occasional long, thin, resin-coated nail with a large leather washer under the head can be driven through the planking lap into the mold. A few of these here and there will keep the planking tight against the molds as the planking operation proceeds. Later these nails are pulled, as they have to be when the planked-up "shell" is removed from the building form and turned right side up for ribbing. If the molds are positioned correctly, the holes left by these nails can be covered by the ribs and the holes themselves may be reused for rib fastenings.

This may seem like a lot of trouble, but when clinker planking is laid up over molds, it frequently tends to pull away as the strakes are put on. Unless there is some way to hold the planking tight against the molds until the "shell" is complete, the designed shape will be lost.

What Rushton did to prevent this is not explained. This method of using long, thin nails with large leather washers for easy pulling worked well for me when I built the 27-foot four-oared racing gig *General Lafayette,* which was clinker-planked with ¼-inch white cedar. I recommend the procedure highly.

Most, if not all, of Rushton's rowboats and planked cedar canoes had flat plank keels of ¾-inch thick red oak, and I believe I know why. It was not that white oak was not available. Rather, it was that white oak tends to twist and turn in small sections and to pull out of true. Well-seasoned red oak of good quality is much more stable and dependable in this respect.

I recall old-time boatbuilders referring to white oak as "too strong" for light keels and the like—the fastenings couldn't hold it. As just mentioned, Rushton rejected the first Arkansaw Traveler his firm built because a slight twist developed in the keel. Could it have been made of white oak?

As for lasting, it appears that select, well-cared-for red oak in small sections lasts adequately well, as attested by a good number of surviving Rushton boats. Their red oak keels are still sound after 70, 80, and even 90 years of use.

One thing not explained by Harry Rushton is just how the Rushton plank keel is rabbeted to receive the garboard plank. The tightness of the boat depends upon a good job here, and it is a tricky operation because the plank angle, or deadrise, changes continuously from nearly flat amidships to almost vertical at the ends of the boat.

The Adirondack guideboat avoids a keel rabbet entirely, its bottom being beveled like that of a dory. This allows the garboard to run down by, and its lower edge is planed off flat in line with the rest of the bottom surface. To protect this edge, one adds a thin, narrow, metal shoe.

This construction is feasible for the guideboat with its rather steep angle of deadrise amidships, but not for a boat like the Arkansaw Traveler, which has a flatter bottom and only about 5 degrees of deadrise amidships. The Rangeley Lakes boat has a similar problem. Here a plank keel is rabbeted centrally, but the rabbet dies out toward the ends, and the edge of the garboard is carried down by to be planed off flush with the bottom surface. In this case, however, a shoe is added that covers the bottom and the exposed edges of the garboard.

The Arkansaw Traveler has no shoe and shows a close seam the whole length between the bottom and the garboard plank. How this was done is not shown anywhere. It has been necessary to work out a method, and the one detailed in the accompanying drawing will result in construction that is tight and strong.

The procedure should not be too difficult, although it is admittedly a fussy operation to cut. Whether this is the way Rushton did it remains to be seen. The answer, as mentioned, will have to wait until we can take apart an old Rushton boat.

When the boat is set up for planking, the flat keel is fitted into the recesses cut in the molds to receive it. The keel is then forced down and secured one way or another so that it takes the slight fore-and-aft "rocker," or camber, that is required.

The inner stempieces, beveled to receive the ends of the planking, were first secured to the ends of the keel plank. The outer stempiece covers the ends of the planking, thus making a stem rabbet—or rather the cutting of a stem rabbet—unnecessary. This simplification saves both time and labor.

The same method is used in building the Rangeley Lakes boats and may have been borrowed from Rushton. Although it appears that the Rangeley Lakes boat was derived from New York State prototypes, this did not occur until after Rushton had begun to build using this method.

Harry Rushton states that the stems were steam-bent to shape over a form, two 1-inch strips at a time. One of these served as the inner stem, the other, the outer stem. The Arkansaw Traveler in the collection at Mystic Seaport Museum shows inner and outer stempieces molded ¾ inch rather than 1 inch (although they are sided 1 inch), and these are the dimensions I have given the stempieces for the 17-foot Arkansaw Traveler considered here.

Whether there would be any problem from so-called springback—a slight loss of shape when the bent pieces are removed from the mold—I do not know. If there were, what allowances Rushton might have made remain uncertain, but this is something that has to be taken into consideration.

Now that we have reliable waterproof glues, laminated stems are quite feasible for this boat. Where facilities for steam bending are not readily available, laminated stems might be the way to go. Certainly there would be no problem of springback with laminated stems.

The outer stem is fastened through the inner stem with several flathead wood screws. In this case 1¼-inch number 12 bronze screws would be about right. The addition of glue would greatly strengthen the joint and is recommended.

One of the most difficult operations in building this boat—more difficult than rabbeting the keel plank—is "backing out"—that is, hollowing the inside of the planking where needed so that it fits the sectional curves of the hull. These curves are fairly extreme at the turn of the bilge, in some cases requiring as much as 5/16 inch of backing or hollowing.

Thus, the planking used here would have to be over ½ inch thick to start with. Furthermore, the hollowing—as well as the corresponding rounding on the outside—must be exact, and must be done prior to fastening the plank in place.

Once the fastenings are in (particularly the tacks through the laps, put in both from the inside and the outside of the boat), no wood can be removed, since the fastenings lie on the surface. If the boat is to be varnished, only light sanding and removal of dents by sponging with hot water may take place after fastening.

The problems faced here, and the order of skill and careful workmanship required, are much the same as for the Adirondack guideboat. For that reason, some might decide to apply cold-molded techniques—or some of the other current forms of glued construction—to this hull form.

As it was, according to Harry Rushton, his father

A sampling of other Rushton
canoe models. **Top:** *The Huron
paddling canoe, a huskier model
than the Arkansaw Traveler.*
(Courtesy Canton Library)
Middle: *A sailing canoe owned
by Nathaniel Wells of Massena,
New York. S. Paul Rushton
(standing) and his brother, Roy
M., grandsons of the canoe build-
er, pose beside the boat at the
American Canoe Association's
Century Weekend Celebration in
Clayton, New York, in 1980.*
(Watertown Daily Times *photo*)
Bottom: *A canvas-covered cedar
canoe, the Indian Girl model.
This lovely classic was owned in
1982 by Ray Jenkins of Tupper
Lake, New York.*

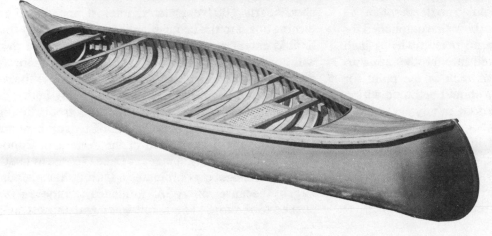

used a thick varnish in the laps that hardened very much like glue. Consequently, the laps sometimes had to be chiseled apart in repairing a boat. Thus, for all intents and purposes this varnish was a glue, although a glue inferior to what is available now.

Getting metal fastenings identical to those used by Rushton is probably not possible now, unless you happen to discover an old stock hidden away in some 19th-century storehouse or attic. This also applies to the extra slim tacks and small sizes of cut copper nails available to Rushton. The nails were used for clinching through the ribs; the tiny tacks went through the edges of the laps when boats were built smooth, as was the Arkansaw Traveler.

The cut nails used for fastening the garboard to the bottom plank are no problem. Annular, or ring, nails of an appropriate size would do very well for this. Small bronze screws (number 4, ⅝-inch) are readily available for plank ends, and very small screws might be substituted for clinch nails in fastening through the laps into the ribs, just as they are in fastening the laps of Adirondack guideboats.

Although the extra slim tacks used through the edges of the laps are no longer produced, the somewhat stouter and readily available ⁵⁄₁₆-inch copper tacks can be used instead if holes are made through the thin part of the lap to prevent splitting. Harry Rushton says that in the Rushton shop these fine tacks were driven through the white cedar laps without piercing for them beforehand.

For guideboats, however, holes through the thin lap edges were made with a very small pointed awl that was diamond-shaped and sharp on both edges. This was applied so as to cut *across* the fibers of the grain, thus avoiding any splitting. Eventually Lewis Grant replaced this awl with a small, high-speed drill.

When a drill is used, it should go no deeper than the thin side of the lap, leaving the thick side untouched for better holding. There is also no reason why ⅝-inch copper tacks could not be used through the laps into the ribs. This would leave ¹⁄₁₆ inch of the point for clinching. In this case the lap should be bored with a high-speed drill, as would be done in any case before ribbing started.

The ribbing process itself is explained by Harry Rushton. To what extent red, or rock, elm would be available for ribs, I cannot say. But as in the case of the stems, I believe good-quality white oak would be entirely adequate as a substitute.

AN R.J. DOUGLAS CRUISING CANOE

At a time when larger yachts are fast pricing themselves out of reach, the old-time sailing canoe has much to offer the adventurous sailor—as much, or more, in a small package than is to be found in many a larger and more costly yacht. It need not be expensive. It can be built and rigged in the home workshop, and there is an infinite variety, at least potentially, to meet every individual need or desire.

The thrills of racing competition have wide appeal, it is true, and the old sailing canoes are probably best remembered as racing canoes, but their potential for the more relaxed pleasures of cruising should be equally considered. Indeed, indications are that cruising canoes and canoes for afternoon sailing—in other words, canoes that are put to more relaxed and noncompetitive recreational uses—are showing the greater increase in popularity.

New building techniques and new building materials are making it possible for handy but relatively unskilled amateurs to construct designs that heretofore would have required a professional. And not a few, it should be said, find building their canoe as pleasurable and rewarding as sailing it.

The rise of the cedar sailing canoe in America in the final quarter of the 19th century was little short of meteoric, and its decline came with equal suddenness. As we look back across the years, it seems that the glorious days of varnished cedar and white sails had scarcely begun before they were finished.

Before the 1890s were over, the classic cedar canoe had toppled from its pinnacle and was swept aside by the surging competition of newly arrived bicycles, canvas canoes, gas marine engines, and larger yachts, followed by automobiles and a great deal more. But now, nearly 100 years later, interest appears to be turning again to the cedar-planked canoes, if only to a limited extent as yet. Whether a full-fledged revival will come remains to be seen, but here and there an occasional survivor from this bygone era is being restored, and scattered new ones are being built.

For the first 10 years or so after the introduction of canoe sailing into this country from England in about 1870, until the organization of the American Canoe Association and its first meet at Lake George in 1880, cruising canoes predominated. During the 1880s, largely because of ACA influence, canoe racing pushed to the fore. The result was highly specialized racing canoes that did not serve the broader recreational needs of the time. This shortcoming undoubtedly contributed to the decline of planked cedar and basswood canoes. Less costly and more adaptable means for satisfying those recreational needs appeared, notably canvas-covered canoes such as J. Henry Rushton's Indian Girl. It was the Indian Girl, more than anything else, that saved Rushton's business from near bankruptcy during the critical time following the financial panic of 1893.

Today the general-purpose cruising canoe has more appeal than the highly specialized racing canoe. In addition, it is not too difficult for amateur construction. Although opportunities for cruising with sail and paddle are considerably fewer than they were 100 years ago, there are still extensive waterways for the cruising canoe that are relatively uncrowded and uncontaminated. Puget Sound and much of the Great Lakes still offer spectacular opportunities for this type of boating.

In the fall of 1980 three men rowed a 17-foot Swampscott dory the more than 200 miles around Long Island. They took their time, stopping along the way to eat and sleep, and enjoyed themselves immensely—just the sort of cruise for which the right kind of sailing canoe is eminently suited. Such a canoe would also be suitable for an afternoon spin, an overnight trip, a weekend excursion, or perhaps even an extended voyage such as the one S. R. Stoddard completed in 1885 when he sailed his canoe, the *Atlantis,* from Glens Falls in upstate New York to the upper reaches of the Bay of Fundy. A news clipping that appeared while Stoddard was en route gives the flavor of this adventure:

AN ADVENTUROUS CRUISE—Mr. S.R. Stoddard of Glens Falls has begun his 2,000-mile trip in his canoe, the Atlantis. He left Glens Falls on

S.R. Stoddard's canoe, the Atlantis, *is shown at Delaney's Farm on Grindstone Island in the St. Lawrence River, circa 1884.*

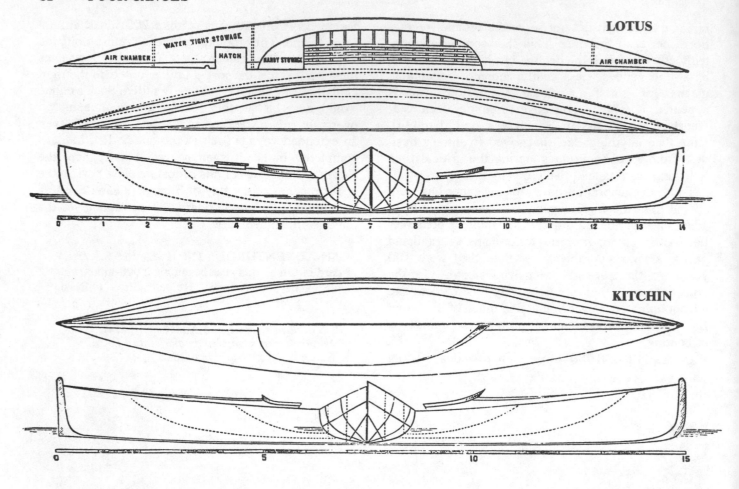

LOTUS

AIR CHAMBER   WATER TIGHT STOWAGE   HATCH   HANDY STOWAGE   AIR CHAMBER

0 1 2 3 4 5 6 7 8 9 10 11 12 13 14

KITCHIN

0   5   10   15

Four cedar-planked canoes from the 1887 R.J. Douglas catalog. The Lotus, 14 feet by 28 inches, is a much lighter canoe than Our Cruiser and was designed more for a paddler than a sailer. Kitchin, 15 feet by 26 inches with a depth of 8 inches and a weight of 50 pounds, was designed for A.W. Kitchin of Chicago, who won many paddling races with her in 1886. The Georgia D. is 15 feet by 31½ inches, with a depth amidships of 10 inches and a weight of 70 pounds. She was the largest size stocked by the R.J. Douglas Company. Note the small centerboard just forward of the rudder.

Tuesday, the 7th inst., and arrived in New York—at the Knickerbocker Club boathouse—Friday evening last. He will sail along the north shore of Long Island Sound to New Bedford, across Buzzards Bay to Woods Hole, through the Vineyard and Nantucket sounds to Chatham Roads, around Cape Cod, across to Plymouth, along the coast to Boston and north to St. John, across the Bay of Fundy to Arcadia, up the basin and river of Minas to Truro, up the Gulf of St. Lawrence to Montreal, through Lake Champlain and thence home. The canoe was built under the instructions of Mr. Stoddard, himself. It is 18 feet long, 3 feet wide, 18 inches deep, draws 8 inches of water, and carries two sails of a pattern of the owner's invention. Mr. Stoddard, though having no fears of his safety, is alive to the fact that his course will encounter the dangers of Point Judith, the long stretch of coast at Cape Cod, with the sweep of the Atlantic, the Bay of Fundy fogs and high tides, and the Gulf of St. Lawrence. He will be accompanied by Professor Charles Oblenis, who joined him at Albany on the trip down.

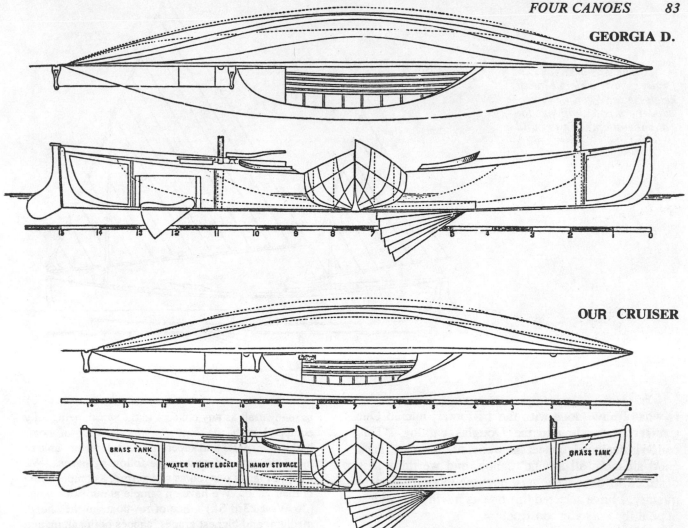

GEORGIA D.

OUR CRUISER

BRASS TANK

WATER TIGHT LOCKER   HANDY STOWAGE

BRASS TANK

Stoddard's *Atlantis* was somewhat larger than many of that period's canoes, as would be necessary to carry two travelers safely and with some degree of comfort on a long voyage across wide stretches of open ocean. The lines of Stoddard's canoe, built for him by Fletcher Joyner, former Adirondack guide and one of the leading canoe builders of his time, have not survived. This is unfortunately the case with many notable early canoes.

Nevertheless, considerable design data for these craft have survived, and await reclamation for use by today's builders. The best sources, of course, are the handful of sailing canoes from that period that still exist in museums and in the hands of private owners. As yet, however, the lines and details from most of these canoes have not been taken off, and to do so would present a lengthy, tedious, and exacting job at

best. Much work needs to be done to put this material in shape for builders to use.

There are a limited number of published plans, notably those by W.P. Stephens and the English designer Dixon Kemp. There is another source, which I have drawn upon here: the published lines and building information found in some of the catalogs of contemporary boatbuilding concerns.

The 14-foot cruising canoe presented here is one of four cedar-planked canoes offered in the 1887 catalog of R.J. Douglas and Company, Waukegan, Illinois. Three are sailing canoes; the fourth is a fast paddling canoe built for racing. Lines for the four canoes are reproduced in the catalog.

Although these lines are incomplete as given and much reduced in size, it is possible to supply what is missing and to enlarge them to a workable size, which

The sail plan for Our Cruiser shows a simple lateen ketch rig. The fanlike center-board poses a challenge for anyone attempting to build her today.

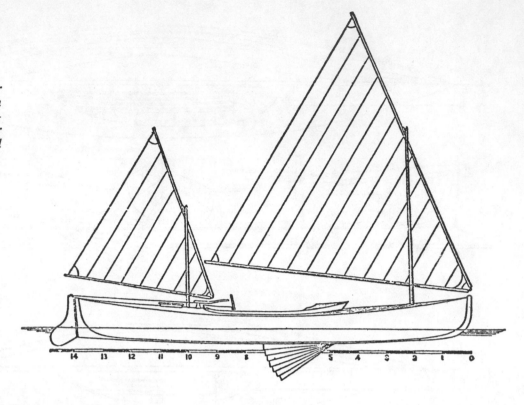

is what I have done with the 14-footer, named Our Cruiser. According to the Douglas catalog, "This canoe is designed to meet the wants of those desiring a good staunch 'all around' canoe, and we think it is destined to become a very popular model." Consequently, I have selected this one as having the widest appeal for amateur construction.

At the time this catalog was issued, the Douglas Company was certainly one of the largest builders of boats and canoes in this country. It also built all manner of pleasure craft for sail and steam up to 40 feet or thereabouts. Its 1887 catalog, which runs nearly 70 pages, is replete with illustrations, and its abundant commentary makes interesting and informative reading.

In 1888 Merwin, Hulbert and Company of New York City, billing itself as "Manufacturers of Fire-Arms and Ammunition and dealers in a most complete line of High-Grade Sporting and Athletic Goods," brought out a large, 56-page catalog devoted in great part to boats manufactured by Douglas. The following statement appears on the inside cover:

To The Boat Loving Public: Being the General Eastern Agents of R.J. Douglas Co., Waukegan, Illinois (probably the largest boatbuilding concern in this country, and who, in all probability turn out twice

as many craft as any concern in the world, being fully equipped with the best machinery, staff of boat-builders, experts and superintendents), we are able to make the prices found in the following pages....We carry, as far as our rooms will permit, a complete line of their goods. We have on sample at our salesrooms (26 West 23rd St.) a line of rowboats in the cheap, medium, and highest grades, canoes both sailing and paddling, shells and sail boats....We guarantee prompt delivery on rowboats and canoes; steam launches, sailboats, barges and shells are generally built to order.

Some idea of the amount of building carried on by R.J. Douglas and Company, as well as something of the firm's operating philosophy, may be gleaned from the remarks addressed "To The Boating Public" at the beginning of its 1887 catalog:

We are constantly securing the most expert men in the line of designers, draughtsmen, builders and finishers from all parts of the United States and Canada. We never "lay off" our builders in the fall, but pile up the stock, and at this writing have in stock 300 boats ranging from a 40 foot steam launch to a 10-pound canoe. We do not aim to make a cheap boat, i.e. without profit, nor put the price so low we have to

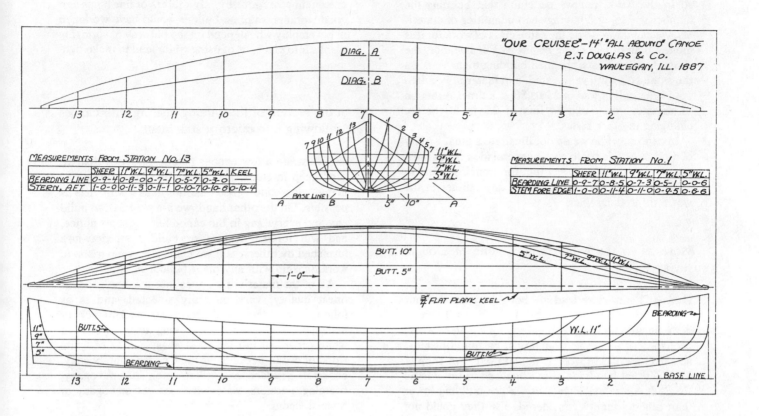

"OUR CRUISER"—14' "ALL AROUND" CANOE
R.J. DOUGLAS & Co.
WAUKEGAN, ILL. 1887

DIAG. A

DIAG. B

MEASUREMENTS FROM STATION No. 13

	SHEER	11" W.L.	9" W.L.	7" W.L.	5" W.L.	KEEL
BEARDING LINE	0-9-4	0-8-0	0-7-1	0-5-7	0-3-0	—
STERN, AFT	1-0-0	0-11-3	0-10-11	0-10-7	0-10-6	0-10-4

MEASUREMENTS FROM STATION No. 1

	SHEER	11" W.L.	9" W.L.	7" W.L.	5" W.L.
BEARDING LINE	0-9-7	0-8-5	0-7-3	0-5-1	0-0-6
STEM FORE EDGE	1-0-0	0-11-4	0-11-0	0-9-5	0-6-6

"OUR CRUISER", 14' CEDAR CANOE. R.J. DOUGLAS & Co, WAUKEGAN, ILL. 1887

	STATIONS	STEM	1	2	3	4	5	7	9	10	11	12	13	STERN
HEIGHTS	SHEER	1-8-4	1-6-6	1-4-6	1-3-0	1-1-4	1-0-5	1-0-0	1-0-6	1-1-4	1-2-2	1-3-4	1-5-2	1-6-5
	BEARDING L.	—	0-4-4	0-2-6	0-2-4	0-2-1	0-2-0	0-1-6	0-1-6	0-1-7	0-2-0	0-2-3	0-4-0	—
	OUTER KEEL	—	0-3-1	0-2-3	0-2-1	0-1-6	0-1-5	0-1-3	0-1-3	0-1-4	0-1-5	0-2-0	0-2-4	0-3-0
	BUTT. 5"	—	—	0-8-6	0-5-1	0-3-4	0-2-4	0-2-0	0-2-1	0-2-5	0-4-4	0-8-4	—	—
	BUTT. 10"	—	—	—	1-0-0	0-6-3	0-4-1	0-3-0	0-3-6	0-6-1	—	—	—	—
HALF-BREADTHS	SHEER	0-0-4	0-4-7	0-8-1	0-11-0	1-0-6	1-2-0	1-2-6	1-1-4	1-0-0	0-10-0	0-7-2	0-4-0	0-0-4
	W.L. 11"	0-0-4	0-3-0	0-6-3	0-9-6	1-0-2	1-1-6	1-2-6	1-1-3	0-11-5	0-9-1	0-6-2	0-2-7	0-0-4
	W.L. 9"	0-0-4	0-2-2	0-5-1	0-8-6	0-11-4	1-1-4	1-2-5	1-1-0	0-11-1	0-8-3	0-5-3	0-2-3	0-0-4
	W.L. 7"	0-0-4	0-1-4	0-3-6	0-7-1	0-10-3	1-0-6	1-2-1	1-0-3	0-10-3	0-7-2	0-4-1	0-1-5	0-0-4
	W.L. 5"	0-0-4	0-0-6	0-2-2	0-4-6	0-8-1	0-11-1	1-1-1	0-11-3	0-8-7	0-5-3	0-2-7	0-1-0	0-0-4
	FLAT KEEL	0-0-4	0-0-4	0-0-7	0-1-2	0-1-5	0-1-6	0-1-6	0-1-5	0-1-2	0-0-7	0-0-4	0-0-4	
	DIAGONAL A	0-0-5	0-4-3	0-8-0	0-11-1	1-1-5	1-3-6	1-5-1	1-3-3	1-1-3	0-10-6	0-7-7	0-4-2	0-0-5
	DIAGONAL B	0-0-5	0-2-0	0-4-2	0-6-1	0-7-5	0-8-6	0-9-5	0-9-3	0-8-3	0-6-4	0-4-5	0-2-3	0-0-5

MEASUREMENTS TO INSIDE OF PLANKING AT THE BEARDING OF STEM, STERN POST & KEEL IN FEET, INCHES, EIGHTHS. DIAGONAL "A" 1'-4" ABOVE BASE LINE, OUT 1'-9½" ON BASE LINE. DIAGONAL "B" 9" ABOVE BASE LINE, OUT 9½" ON THE BASE LINE.

slight the work, but we do claim that building the number we do, and buying such quantities of materials, we can afford to do the same class of work for less money than others doing business. For instance, the cheap hunting boats; the men building them work on the same boats the year round, and material is gotten out in the mill in lots of 25 to 50 at a time. Again on "Lakeside," we build in lots of 25 to 50 before changing to other styles.

In canoes, while we do not illustrate a great variety of models, we do try to give a general idea of our most popular ones, and will say that for model, workmanship, and material, we challenge any builder in the world to produce finer.

More as to the extent and volume of Douglas's business:

Our nails and white lead are bought by the ton; our iron by the car. Our wood work, as far as it can be done, is gotten out by machinery. Our pattern work, designing of all kinds, draughting, casting, finishing, and iron and brass work is done in our own shop....The fact that hundreds of our boats go to the Pacific Coast is alone evidence that we are building lower than others, quality considered, else they could not afford to pay freight for such a distance.

R.J. Douglas and Company used three planking methods for its various craft—clinker, carvel, and "ribband-carvel," the latter generally known today as batten-seam construction. Whereas some of the Canadian canoes built at Peterborough were planked ribband-carvel, Douglas canoes seem to have been planked clinker, like most canoes from the leading contemporary American builders such as Rushton, Joyner, and Ruggles. The clinker work carried out in the Douglas shop is described in part as follows:

We use machinery as far as it can be utilized, but this can only be done to a limited extent on clinker work, as all planks must be gotten out by hand, no two on a side being alike either in shape or bevel....Our hulls are all planked up to the wales before a rib is placed in them, and it is frequently the case that a boat is taken off the stocks in this shape (when some order comes in that is more urgent) and laid aside to be ribbed at our leisure. We merely mention this to show that a boat must be built to shape and not sprung, or it could not retain its shape. The consequence is, the planks have no strain on them, and the frame is put in only for strength, and can then therefore be much lighter than has been the custom in years gone by....In this era of fine boats and good workmanship, no builder would have workmen in his employ who depend on the old way of springing planks into place, or of using white lead to make tight joints.

In the section of the catalog dealing with canoes is the following introductory statement:

We illustrate a few canoes herein, of styles that we shall keep in stock, and have aimed to combine as many "all around" good qualities in as few models as possible. On the other hand, we are prepared to build any and everything in the canoe line on short notice, and will furnish designs or build from drawings furnished by others, and we challenge comparison in workmanship with any other builder in America....

All of the material that goes into a canoe is of the finest quality, very carefully selected, and is as follows: i.e. Stems and sternpost, hackmatack or mahogany, ribs white oak, planking the finest of clear white cedar, all full length strakes, carlins of white wood or cedar, decks of Spanish cedar or mahogany, backrests, rudder and tiller, etc., of mahogany, coaming, partners, wales, etc., also of mahogany or Spanish cedar.

All of our canoes illustrated herein are fastened with copper nails and burrs and riveted, and right here let us say that all work as light as ¼ inch should be fastened in this manner, since when the planks are beveled the edges are very thin, and a clinched nail is driven back halfway through this thin edge, in order to draw it tight, and is thus very liable to draw through and make a short-lived boat, while, on the other hand, a burr on the inside, well riveted, makes a thin, light boat as little liable to spring apart as one much heavier fastened with clinched nails.

It takes much more time to fasten a boat in this manner, but it is the only perfect way on very light work and would invariably be adopted for this class of work were it not for the extra expense attending it.

In conclusion, we will refer our readers to the official account of the meet of the W.C.A. (Western Canoe Association) at Ballast Island last year (see "Forest and Stream," Aug. 12, 1886), and they can be the judges as to whether we got our share of the prizes....In a report of the meet published in the Cincinnati "Commercial Gazette," the writer says: "The best paddling canoes were 40 pounds weight and built by R.J. Douglas & Co., Waukegan, Illinois. They were beauties and glided through the water without a ripple. The best setting sails were a pair of sprits on R.P. McCune's "Pretzel" Tippecanoe, measuring together about 120 feet, the largest amount of sail carried by any canoe at the meet." The above-mentioned sails were also made by us, and the same maker makes all of our canoe sails now.

Beyond what has been quoted, there is no additional building information that might apply to the construction of Our Cruiser. I suggest, however, that a serviceable hull could be built to the lines set forth here by the same methods, and with the use of the same scantlings, that we described for the Arkansaw Traveler.

Although Douglas has insisted, with some justification, that riveted fastenings are superior, Rushton's clinched tacks and small, cut copper nails have stood the tests of use and time and would be quicker and easier. But because small, cut copper nails for clinching are not now available, necessity dictates rivets. Not so for the small tacks used by Rushton on thin laps, and in this case I would definitely follow his practice.

The stem and sternpost for Our Cruiser had best be natural knee bends of hackmatack, if available. If not, properly made glued laminations could be substituted. The stem might be steam-bent oak, like that of the Arkansaw Traveler, although the molded width required by Our Cruiser is much greater. Obviously, the sternpost could not be steam-bent.

The same oak bottom board or keel used in the Arkansaw Traveler, made to the same dimensions and rabbeted in the same way, may be used in Our Cruiser. One thing presents a bit of a problem: Radix centerboards are no longer manufactured, and such a canoe as this really requires a folding centerboard of some sort. I expect, however, that as demand builds up someone will start making them again. In the meantime, I am sure the resourceful builder will be able to improvise a substitute.

A 13-FOOT ENGLISH CRUISING CANOE OF 1883

The career of the classic wooden sailing canoes in this country was spectacular but brief. They dominated the American boating scene for barely 20 years before plummeting from view. This period began about 1870 with William L. Alden's *Violetta*. Modeled on the *Nautilus*, which was designed in England by Warrington Baden-Powell, vice-commodore of the Royal Canoe Club, it was built for cruising the coastal waters surrounding Long Island by Everson of Williamsburg, New York. The peak was reached at the International Meet at Grindstone Island in the Saint Lawrence in the summer of 1886, when American sailing canoes soundly trounced their British rivals in the racing events. And before 1900 it was all over.

But during this relatively brief period a great deal of experimentation with hull shapes and sailing rigs went on, knowledge of the results of which could prove of great assistance to present-day canoeists. The two outstanding published sources are W.P. Stephens's *Canoe and Boat Building for Amateurs,* with its 50 plates of working drawings of lines, construction, and rigs, and the voluminous works and numerous editions of the British naval architect and yacht designer Dixon Kemp. The amount of detail recorded by Kemp is prodigious. Another rich source that will repay some patient digging is the back files of *Forest and Stream.* All of these sources are long out of print and scarce, but are to be found in most large research libraries.

There are other contemporary sources, less well known, such as the British sporting publication *The Field.* In 1883 *The Field* printed an account by C. Penrose of a 13-foot cruising canoe built by R.J. Turk, professional builder of boats, punts, and canoes, in his shop on the upper Thames at Kingston, a London suburb. The cruising canoe was then at the peak of its popularity in Great Britain and North America.

The British had first made it popular when John MacGregor toured the waterways of Europe in 1865 in his first Rob Roy. This canoe served not only as his trusty conveyance but as his kitchen and bedroom as well, despite its diminutive dimensions—LOA 14 feet, beam 25 inches, and depth amidships 11 inches. His published account fired the popular imagination, and four more Rob Roys followed, along with cruises in the Baltic and the Holy Land. The Royal Canoe Club of London dates from 1866, and the New York Canoe Club, modeled on it, was founded in 1871.

Famous contemporary cruising canoes included Baden-Powell's *Nautilus* and W.P. Stephens's *Jersey Blue.* Rushton built his first Rob Roy in 1876, and continued to supply a widespread demand for them into the 1880s.

Later on, shortly before sailing canoes in general were to suffer a decline, canoe racing was to overshadow cruising. But in 1883 canoe cruising still

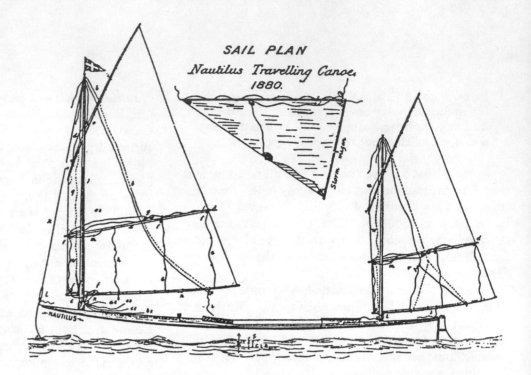

SAIL PLAN
Nautilus Travelling Canoe,
1880.

The "cruising and racing" sail plan of the Nautilus *as drawn by British naval architect Dixon Kemp for the 1886 edition of his* Manual of Yacht and Boat Sailing. *Her "travelling" sail plan featured a high-peaked, almost triangular mainsail that set on a short mast and could be stowed snugly and easily for paddling.*

held first place in popular interest and dominated boating sport.

The account in *The Field,* December 22, 1883, of the Kingston canoe launched and sailed in that year is reproduced here.

The following is a description of a cruising canoe which has been recently built by Mr. Turk of Kingston, for a member of the R.C.C., and is intended to combine, as far as possible, good cruising qualities with those demanded by the peculiar and somewhat unsatisfactory conditions of up-river sailing. She is the third canoe of an experimental series constructed in hopes of attaining these qualities; and it may be well, before proceeding to her description, to give some account of the objects aimed at.

The foremost requisite of a cruising canoe is that she should be capable of being carried easily by two men, without the necessity of dismantling, i.e., removal of gear, centerboards, etc. She should be capable of being carried to the water from the boathouse and launched at once without a lot of preparation. She must paddle fast and easily in a calm, sail well to windward and otherwise, and be dry and safe in broken water. She should have sufficient stability and size to render moving about on board, sleeping, and cooking &c., as safe, easy, and comfortable as possible, and finally, be well and simply fitted and rigged.

After a prolonged trial of several canoes built to the R.C.C. first class, these were condemned as insufficiently portable and generally too unhandy, and it was determined to experiment with a smaller and lighter craft.

With this view, a canoe was built in 1881 with a beam of 2 feet 6 inches and a length of 16 feet. The beam was thus limited, partly to assist in the reduction of weight, and partly to keep within the R.C.C. second class, in case any racing for that class should be instituted.

She was a great improvement on the first class boats in portability and in paddling, was fast under sail in anything like a true breeze, and remarkably dry and comfortable in rough water, very greatly surpassing the R.C.C. first class craft in this last respect. She was, however, hardly light enough for two men to portage. Weighing 120 pounds without her sails, or ballast, she could not sail her best at the weight of 150 pounds allowed by the R.C.C. second class; while the length which made her so good a sea boat also made her a trifle slow in the stays, which, though unimportant for below-bridge sailing, was found a fatal obstacle in the light, baffling airs of Kingston Reach.

In the following year a second canoe was built, in which the length was reduced to 14 feet and the beam to 2 feet 3 inches. She proved an entire success for paddling—so much so, that she was frequently launched for that purpose alone, and could be carried, with centerboard and gear complete, by two men, or even boys.

Her weight without centerboard, sails or gear, was 60 pounds. She performed very satisfactorily under sail, with the help of from 20 pounds to 40 pounds of ballast, when no luggage was carried; but her proportional length appeared to be too great for so light a boat to stay very rapidly or certainly without a steady breeze.

She was also inconveniently crank for cruising, as it required some steadiness to stand in her when light, and to move about on board.

The design (under consideration) has the beam of the first of these canoes, namely 2 feet 6 inches, which

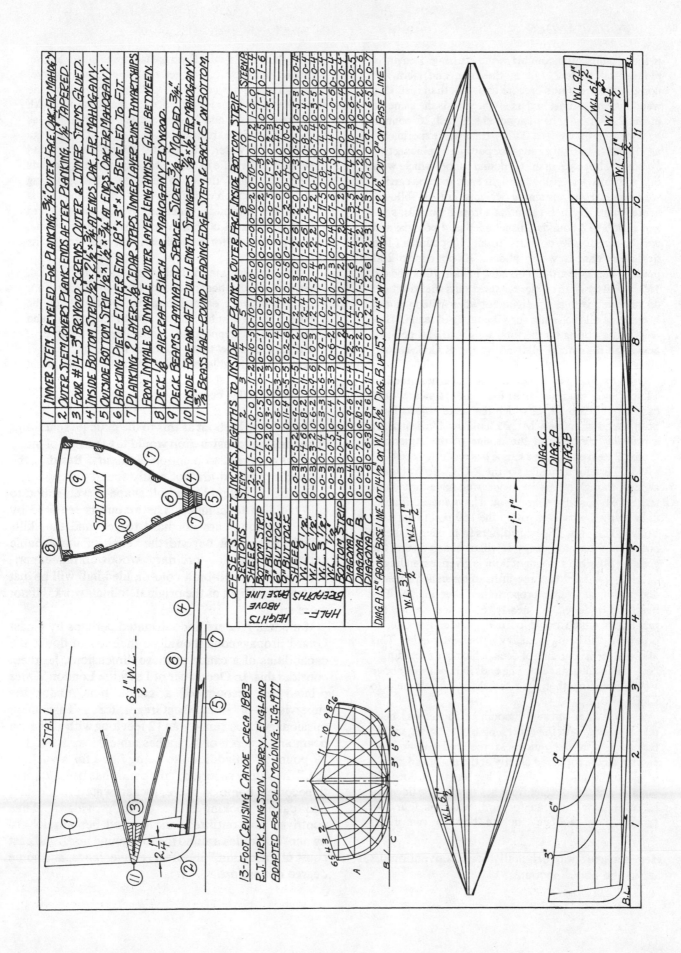

Construction notes:

1 INNER STEM. BEVELED FOR PLANKING. 3/4" OUTER FACE. OAK, FIR, MAHOGANY.
2 OUTER STEM. COVERS PLANK ENDS AFTER PLANKING. 1/4" TAPERED.
3 FOUR #14-3" BR/WOOD SCREWS. OUTER & INNER STEMS GLUED.
4 INSIDE BOTTOM STRIP 1/2 × 2 1/2 × 3/4 AT ENDS. OAK, FIR, MAHOGANY.
5 OUTSIDE BOTTOM STRIP 1/2 × 1 1/2 × 3/4 AT ENDS. OAK, FIR MAHOGANY.
6 BACKING PIECE EITHER END 18" × 3" × 1/2. BEVELED TO FIT.
7 PLANKING. 2 LAYERS 1/8 CEDAR STRIPS. INNER LAYER RUNS THWARTSHIPS. FROM INWALE TO INWALE. OUTER LAYER LENGTHWISE. GLUE BETWEEN.
8 DECK 1/8 AIRCRAFT BIRCH OR MAHOGANY PLYWOOD.
9 DECK BEAMS LAMINATED SPRUCE. SIDED 3/8. MOLDED 3/4.
10 INSIDE FORE-AND-AFT FULL-LENGTH STRINGERS 1/8 × 1/2 FIR MAHOGANY.
11 1/16 BRASS HALF-ROUND LEADING EDGE STEM & BACK 6" ON BOTTOM.

STATION 1

OFFSETS—FEET, INCHES, EIGHTHS TO INSIDE OF PLANK & OUTER FACE INSIDE BOTTOM STRIP

		SECTIONS	STEM	1	2	3	4	5	6	7	8	9	10	11	STERN P.
HEIGHTS ABOVE BASE LINE		SHEER	1-2-6	1-1-1	1-0-0	0-10-5	0-10-0	0-10-0	0-10-0	0-10-2	0-10-7	0-11-2	1-0-1	1-1-2	
		BOTTOM STRIP	0-2-0	0-0-5	0-0-0	0-0-2	0-1-0						0-0-5	1-0-1	1-1-6
		3" BUTTOCK		0-6-2	0-3-0	0-0-5	0-0-2	0-0-0	0-0-0	0-0-0	0-0-2	0-1-2	0-3-0	0-5-4	
		6" BUTTOCK			0-6-0	0-3-0	0-1-0	0-0-4	0-0-0	0-0-0	0-1-0	0-2-0	0-5-5		
HALF-BREADTHS		SHEER	0-0-3	0-0-5	0-2-0	0-6-0	0-11-5	1-2-4	1-3-0	1-2-6	1-0-5	0-7-0	0-2-0	0-0-4	
		W.L. 9 1/2"	0-0-3	0-0-5	0-2-0	0-8-2	1-1-7	1-2-4	1-2-6	1-2-4	1-0-0	0-4-7	0-0-4		
		W.L. 6 1/2"	0-0-3	0-0-3	0-3-2	0-9-6	1-1-0	1-2-2	1-2-3	1-2-2	0-11-2	0-4-5	0-0-4		
		W.L. 3 1/2"	0-0-3	0-1-4	0-5-5	0-9-7	1-0-1	1-1-3	1-1-5	1-0-4	0-8-4	0-3-0	0-0-6		
		W.L. 1 1/2"	0-0-3	0-2-6	0-7-2	0-9-3	0-10-5	0-11-0	0-11-3	0-9-5	0-6-2	0-2-4	0-0-6		
		BOTTOM STRIP	0-0-3	0-4-0	0-7-0	0-7-1	0-7-0	0-4-4	0-3-4	0-3-2	0-2-2	0-1-0	0-0-6		
		DIAGONAL A	0-0-4	0-5-0	0-11-5	1-3-5	1-4-6	1-5-0	1-5-2	1-4-2	1-2-0	0-7-2	0-0-5		
		DIAGONAL B	0-0-6	0-6-3	0-11-1	1-0-1	1-1-3	1-2-4	1-2-6	1-1-5	0-11-6	0-6-0	0-0-7		

STA. 1

6.1" W.L. 2 (sic)

13-FOOT CRUISING CANOE CIRCA 1863.
R.J. TURK, KINGSTON, SURREY, ENGLAND.
ADAPTED FOR COLD MOLDING. J.G. 1977

DIAG. A 15" ABOVE BASE LINE. OUT 14 1/2 OR W.L. 6 1/2. DIAG. B UP 15" OUT 14" ON B.L. DIAG. C UP 12 1/2" OUT 9" OY BASE LINE.

DIAG. C
DIAG. A
DIAG. B

W.L. 3 1/2"
W.L. 1 1/2"
W.L. 6 1/2"
W.L. 9 1/2"

1'-1"

B.L.

is found ample for comfort when cruising. Length is reduced to 13 feet, but as the stem and stern are upright, the reduction is more apparent than real. Her weight is 86 pounds, and as all the gear is the same as in the 2 foot 3 inches canoe, she is just 26 pounds heavier when complete. This weight was experimentally found to be light enough for portage by placing two 14 pound shot bags in the 60 pound canoe, which, with this addition, was still quite light enough to be carried with ease. Her remaining weights are as follows: centerboard, $\frac{3}{16}$ inch galvanized iron, 8 pounds; sails and paddle, 12 pounds; miscellaneous, 4 pounds; add weight of hull, 86 pounds—total 110 pounds. (The first-class canoes weigh about 170 pounds to 200 pounds; centerboard, 60 pounds; ballast, 70 pounds to 150 pounds.) With moderate-sized sails she will stand up very well with this weight; but when sailed without luggage, is all the better for 40 pounds of lead in shot bags, which bring up the total weight to 150 pounds, being the maximum allowed by the R.C.C. second class.

Only two canoes have hitherto been described in "The Field," and, as far as the writer is aware, only two have been built, in which the same objects have been aimed at; namely Mr. Baden-Powell's design for a cruising canoe...and the design of the American Jersey Blue from which a canoe has recently been built by Mr. Turk for a member of the R.C.C. Both of these canoes, though otherwise successful, have turned out rather heavy, and probably would have some difficulty in bringing themselves within the 150 pound limit for sailing. The present design differs from each of these, both in outline and fittings. It will be observed that the greatest possible amount of floor is given, extending in nearly a dead flat to three-fifths of the canoe's beam, and about the same proportion of her length. The depth is reduced to nearly 6 inches below the maximum which could be taken under the rule, in order to avoid being topheavy when lightly laden. This allows a great rounding of deck, which has accordingly been taken advantage of. The ends flare out well above water, and, together with the sheer, should help to keep her dry.

A somewhat unusual amount of rocker has been taken, which, with the short length of the craft, makes her stay with the quickness required for up-river sailing. Being rockered chiefly at the ends, and hardly at all in the middle 5 feet of her length, it does not greatly, if at all, detract from her speed. The lines are slightly fuller aft than forward, which is found to prevent any tendency in the bow to run under water.

Her construction originally was conventional, as noted in the *Field* account:

The planking is clinch-work [lapstrake], this having proved immensely stronger than the ribband carvel though not quite so pretty looking. Throughout the middle body, where the planks run nearly parallel with the keel, the "lands" [laps] are left full strength, as they offer little resistance to the boat's passage through the water, but greatly strengthen her, and perhaps add a trifle to initial stability, while at the ends they are fined down to nothing....The planking material is ¼ inch cedar with oak timbers; the keel is pine, the thickness required by the centerboard rendering a keel of this material sufficiently strong. Pine is also used for the deck carlines, on account of its lightness.

The timbers are ⅜ inch molded; ¾ inch sided, reduced at the head; spaced 13 inches with floor timbers between each throughout the middle of the boat. This gives sufficient strength to the boat to stand the strain of sleeping on board when hauled up, if ordinary care be taken to support the bilges. It is generally preferable, however, to let the boat lie afloat for sleeping, and she will be found to possess abundant stability for this purpose.

To build such a boat as this to the delicate scantlings of her original construction would tax the skill of many professionals, not to mention amateurs. Besides, the materials required are not easily found today.

On the other hand, the hull shape is well suited to cold-molding techniques. The materials required by these techniques are not hard to get, and the skills called for are not beyond the reach of the capable amateur possessing ordinary woodworking experience. And the well-built cold-molded hull will be just as strong and light as the original "clinch-work," if not more so.

If modern readers, indoctrinated perhaps by Coast Guard propaganda, should be inclined to doubt the capabilities of a canoe of these dimensions, let them consider this. In December of 1879 the London *Times* printed an account of a canoe built under the supervision of John MacGregor for a Tasmanian missionary. This canoe was 12 feet long with a 28-inch beam and a depth of 12 inches amidships; it weighed 79 pounds. "In addition to being fitted for a yacht at sea," the *Times* reported, "the canoe has been adapted to become a home on shore, locker, waterproof cabin, and patent cooking stove being provided." Thus contrived and outfitted, she carried her missionary owner "300 miles around the ironbound north and east coast of Tasmania," in safety, convenience, and some degree of comfort.

7

DOWN EAST WORKBOAT

The 18-foot outboard-powered workboat offered here is similar to a well-known type developed and used in eastern Maine. Formerly, boats like this one were built of wood in local boatshops along the coast of Washington County from Jonesport to Eastport, and to a lesser extent by the local fishermen for their own use.

The hull shape derives from the so-called double-wedge model and is basically the same as that of early inboard-motor speedboats at the beginning of this century. The high bow and sharp entrance form something like a wedge turned up on edge, and the stern resembles another wedge rotated a quarter of a turn to lie flat.

Both the Canadian Cape Island lobsterboat and the early Jonesport lobsterboat have the double-wedge hull, which combines good seakeeping ability with speed. If this 18-foot boat were doubled in size without

alteration of its lines or proportions, and if a solid deadwood, a sternpost, and a rudder were added, the result would be a classic Maine lobsterboat. There can be little doubt that the first outboard boats like this one were turned out by shops experienced in producing larger, wooden, inboard-powered lobsterboats. The resemblance is too close to be accidental.

In the summer of 1981 a Washington County reader of the *National Fisherman* asked if lines and details for building such outboard boats might be available somewhere. He had seen some of the older wooden boats of this type and liked them very much, but the local shops had stopped building them in favor of fiberglass. This reader wondered if the 18-footer's lines had ever been recorded, though he doubted that the local builders had worked from drawings.

I replied that although I did not have any such plans and did not know of any, I was not unfamiliar with the

Photographs and measurements of this old wooden craft were the basis of the plans presented in this chapter. Note her wedge-shaped bow, her foredeck, and the stout, well-braced transom cut down for an outboard motor. She is typical of the 18-foot workboats that originated in Washington County, Maine.

type. I also told him that if he could find a representative example to photograph and measure for some basic dimensions, and if he would send these measurements and a set of prints to me, I would work out lines and construction details. He complied, and so did I. The results are presented in this chapter.

Lines are given to the *inside* of the planking so that the molds can be made directly from them without having to deduct the plank thickness. Practically without exception, these boats were planked carvel, or smooth, yet there is no reason they couldn't be planked clinker, or lapstrake. In fact, this latter method has

certain constructional advantages that might commend it to some builders.

For a one-off carvel job, the boat should probably be set right side up. First, the "backbone" assembly of stem, keel, keel batten, and transom is positioned on the stocks, which are made high enough to give comfortable access to the bottom during planking. Next, the solid floors, correctly shaped from the full-size laydown of lines, are installed, and the molds are secured in place at their respective stations.

Ribbands are then run fore and aft on the outside of the molds from stem to transom on approximately the same lines that the planking will follow. These are temporarily fastened to molds with long wood screws and washers. The ribbands must be stout enough to support the steam-bent frames without giving when the frames are forced against them, and they should be spaced closely enough to allow the frames to take a fair bend, but no closer.

After this has been done, the boat is ready to plank. As the planking goes on, the ribbands are removed, one by one.

If many of these boats were to be built as stock items, it might be easier and faster to plank them upside down on a form—provided, of course, that there is a means for lifting the hull off the building form and righting it after planking is completed.

In building the planking form, the molds are cut down by an amount equal to the thickness of the ribbands plus the thickness of the frames. The ribbands are fastened to the molds, and the locations of the frames are marked on them. In framing out, as this is called, the hot frames taken from the steam box are bent around the *outside* of the ribbands and clamped to them until they have cooled and permanently taken the correct shape. The plank is fitted most efficiently while the hull is in a bottom-up position.

When it is time to lift the completed hull off the building form prior to turning it over, some provision must be made for collapsing the after molds sufficiently to clear the "tumblehome" at the stern. This generally can be done by making the after molds in two sections, which are held in place by easily removable screws.

Not only is it much easier to fit and fasten the plank when the hull is bottom up, but it is also easier to plane, smooth, and caulk the planked hull when it is in this position. But hulls that are at all large and heavy are not lifted and turned over easily and safely except with equipment and manpower not always available in small boatshops or one-man, backyard operations.

If this boat is to be planked clinker, the planks should be ½ inch thick instead of the ⅝ inch specified for the carvel hull. If one man is to do the job unassisted, it would be best to set the boat right side up. In this position he can, without help, rivet the lap fastenings as each strake goes on by holding on against the head of the rivet on the outside and peening it on the inside in one operation.

When a boat is built in this way, it is recommended that as the strakes go on they be temporarily secured to the molds. Ideal for this are long, thin, resin-coated nails that hold well in soft wood; thick leather washers

about ½ inch in diameter are placed under the heads. When these nails are driven in solidly, the washers apply firm pressure to the plank without marring it. When the time comes to draw the nails and remove the mold, the washers provide enough thickness to afford a good grip for the tongs or nail puller. The holes that are left can be used for fastening into the bent frames that replace the building molds.

When a clinker hull is planked bottom up, it is not necessary to rivet each lap separately as the planks are put on, provided the planks are accurately shaped and fitted and are temporarily nailed to the molds as just described. The lap nails are driven as planking proceeds, but no riveting need be done until all the planking is on and the boat has been turned over. Then one job can be made of it. This is the way planking is commonly done in the British Isles, and it certainly is the quickest and easiest way to accomplish what is at best a tedious operation. An assistant will be required to hold on against the heads of the nails on the outside of the hull.

A few words of warning: Nails or rivets driven through the laps should be bored for in advance. Holes must be exactly the right size, which can be determined beforehand by boring test holes in pieces of scrap wood at the bench. Lap nails should fit snugly.

Holes should be small enough so that the nail retains enough drawing power to pull the lap tight and hold it until it is riveted, but not so small as to run the slightest risk of splitting the lap. Holes may be drilled, or a brad awl of the right size may be used.

The end of the awl is beveled square across like a chisel and is applied *across* the run of the grain to sever its fibers. Meanwhile, the palm of the hand is used to apply pressure to the awl as it is briskly rotated from side to side. A quick, clean hole with no risk of splitting is the result. The knack is readily acquired, and for operations like this it is just as effective as drilling, if not more so.

The brad awl is one of those simple but truly effective, time-honored tools that for one reason or another have gone out of fashion. Unfortunately, those tools that have replaced them are generally more complicated and often less effective.

If riveting is to be delayed until the boat is turned over, it is of utmost importance that strakes be gotten out to the correct shape so that they do not have to be sprung edgewise for the laps to fit. Springing, or edge-setting, planks in this way is almost certain to cause

OUTBOARD WORKBOAT
18' LOA · 6'-4" BEAM · 2'-5" INSIDE DEPTH ADMIDSHIPS
EASTERN MAINE – PASSAMAQUODDY BAY

	STEM	STA. 1	STA. 2	STA. 3	STA. 4	STA. 5	STA. 6	STA. 7	TRAN.
18' OUTBOARD WORKBOAT									
HALF-BREADTHS									
SHEER	0-0-4	0-11-7	2-2-0	2-9-6	3-1-2	3-0-6	2-9-2	2-4-6	2-1-6
30" W.L.	0-0-4	0-8-4	1-11-7	2-8-6	3-1-1	3-0-7	2-9-5	2-5-1	2-1-7
24" W.L.	0-0-4	0-6-7	1-10-0	2-7-1	3-0-3	3-0-6	2-10-2	2-6-2	2-3-2
18" W.L.	0-0-4	0-5-1	1-7-5	2-4-5	2-10-4	2-11-6	2-9-6	2-7-0	2-4-2
12' W.L.	0-0-4	0-2-7	1-3-0	1-11-5	2-5-4	2-8-5	2-7-6	2-5-7	2-4-4
HEIGHTHS									
SHEER	4-3-2	3-11-0	3-5-4	3-1-4	2-11-0	2-9-1	2-7-6	2-7-2	2-6-5
BEARDING L.	—	0-7-6	0-0-6	0-0-6	0-0-6	0-0-6	0-0-6	0-0-6	0-0-6
BUTT. 10"	—	3-1-4	0-8-7	0-7-0	0-6-3	0-6-1	0-6-1	0-6-0	0-6-0
BUTT. 22"	—	—	2-0-0	0-11-0	0-8-2	0-7-2	0-6-6	0-6-5	0-6-4
BUTT. 28"	—	—	—	1-5-0	0-11-1	0-9-0	0-8-3	0-9-2	0-10-7
DIAGONAL A	0-1-6	1-3-0	2-8-1	3-2-0	3-4-3	3-5-3	3-6-1	3-6-3	3-6-4
DIAGONAL B	0-1-1	0-6-6	1-8-3	2-4-2	2-9-0	2-11-2	2-10-2	2-8-1	2-6-2

OFFSETS TO INSIDE 5/8 PLANKING. MEASURED FROM BASELINE IN FEET-INCHES-EIGHTHS.
DIAG. "A" UP 3'-6" ON CL-OUT 2'-4" ON BASELINE. DIAG. "B" UP 2' ON CL-OUT 3' ON 12" W.L.

them to gape at the laps. When this happens, the only way to ensure a tight boat is to complete the riveting as planking proceeds. Then it is still possible to get clamps on the laps to hold them together until they can be drawn tight and permanently secured by peening the rivets.

A tip for those with limited experience in getting out lapstrake planking: The closer the shape and width of the spiling batten to the plank to be spiled, the better. For greatest accuracy, the spiling batten should partially overlay the lap whose shape is to be taken.

Instead of copper rivets for the laps, nonferrous clinch nails can be used. They are quicker and perhaps easier to put in. However, in my experience, clinch nails do not hold as well as rivets for most jobs and are not as neat in appearance. Besides, the supply of suitable clinch nails is quite limited—more so at present than that of rivets.

Where there is sufficient thickness of wood for annular, or so-called ring, nails long enough to develop sufficient holding power, these can replace screws. Bronze wood screws have become so outrageously expensive that I refuse to recommend them. Hot-dipped galvanized wood screws, well coated with zinc (the only kind to consider), last fairly well but don't have much holding power in sizes under number 10 because of the buildup of zinc in the threads. Electroplated screws last little better than plain steel, and thus are quite worthless.

The relatively thin (⅜-inch) canoe-type frames originally used for this boat in eastern Maine and in the Canadian Maritimes now offer something of a fastening problem. The malleable old galvanized iron chisel-point clinch nails that were formerly used for this are no longer manufactured. Their wide, thin, sharp chisel points driven across the grain cut through the fibers much the same as a brad awl does and clinched over on the inside easily, neatly, and with good holding strength.

The 1½-inch copper clinch nail produced in Anacortes, Washington by Skookum Fastenings may be the best substitute fastening now available for the plank-to-frame fastenings in this boat, but I prefer rivets, even if they mean more work. The total plank-to-frame thickness of 1¼ inches is not enough for either annular nails or screws. For fastening the bottom planking to the 2½-inch oak floors, however, annular nails would be an excellent choice—say 1¾-inch or 2-inch number 11s. Likewise, number 10 or number 11 annular nails for the keel batten to keel and

number 9 or 10 for the floors through the keel batten into the keel are recommended.

These larger sizes should, of course, be bored for to prevent splitting. But care must be taken not to get the holes too large, especially in members that might be water-soaked at times, since the holding power of annular nails is greatly reduced in wet oak.

A word about mixing ferrous and nonferrous fastenings: I believe there is little danger of harmful galvanic action in this boat. Above the waterline any combination would be okay, but below the waterline, to forestall any possible trouble, the careful builder might want to avoid mixing.

Flat canoe frames are shown because that was the kind used in these boats, but there is no reason a builder could not substitute narrower, thicker frames if good bending stock were available. Probably the reason for these flat frames was the absence of such good bending species as white oak or Canadian rock elm in the region where the boats developed.

For carvel-planked boats, steam-bent frames might be sided 1 inch and molded ⅞ inch, although different builders might vary these dimensions somewhat. One advantage of these thicker frames, besides increased stiffness, would be that screws or annular nails could be used for plank fastenings. Eight-inch centers would be a normal frame spacing.

Of course, for clinker plank, frame sections would be smaller and spacing somewhat closer together. I should then want plank fastenings to be rivets, although clinched, plank-through-timber fastenings have sometimes proved quite adequate.

Much of the detail in the view at section 6 is self-explanatory and needs no comment. Note, however, the oak floors (3) that occur at each mold station. They provide a solid foundation for the wide, nearly flat bottom and good fastening for the bottom planking. These floors are cut back from the keel batten to provide 2-inch-wide limbers (6) on each side, allowing full-length drainage under the tightly planked bottom sole (9).

The middle plank (10) is removable to afford access for sponging out the bottom. The sides, inside, are sheathed tightly (11) as high as the risers (7), giving a large, tight, open working cockpit that extends as far forward as a watertight bulkhead under the after end of the bow deck. This bulkhead comes as high as the risers, leaving ample access between it and the deck to the underdeck stowage space.

The bow deck is copied from those shown in

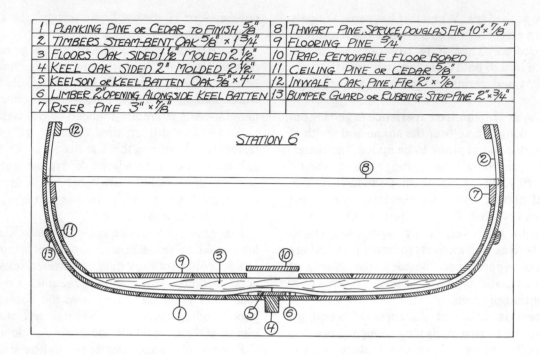

1	PLANKING PINE or CEDAR TO FINISH 5/8"	8	THWART PINE, SPRUCE, DOUGLAS FIR 10" x 7/8"
2	TIMBERS STEAM-BENT OAK 5/8" x 1 3/4"	9	FLOORING PINE 3/4"
3	FLOORS OAK SIDED 1 1/2" MOLDED 2 1/2"	10	TRAP, REMOVABLE FLOOR BOARD
4	KEEL OAK SIDED 2" MOLDED 2 1/2"	11	CEILING PINE or CEDAR 5/8"
5	KEELSON or KEEL BATTEN OAK 5/8" x 4"	12	INWALE OAK, PINE, FIR 2" x 7/8"
6	LIMBER 2" OPENING ALONGSIDE KEEL BATTEN	13	BUMPER GUARD or RUBBING STRIP PINE 2" x 3/4"
7	RISER PINE 3" x 7/8"		

STATION 6

photographs of typical down-east boats of this type. By comparative scaling we determined it to be approximately 5 feet 6 inches long and show it as such. These boats were often banging into heavy head seas, and such a deck, in combination with the high bow, kept a lot of loose water from coming aboard.

The photographs in my possession do not show any construction closing off the space under the deck, but I have included the watertight bulkhead because it seems to me that this would be a good storage area. A considerable amount of dry storage space for gear, clothing, and the like is thereby made available. Provision for locking it up ensures limited security for things left aboard while the owner is absent—including the motor.

It must be understood that anything more than limited security is impossible to guarantee. There is no way of turning a boat like this into Fort Knox. Determined thieves could even saw a hole in the side of the boat without too much difficulty, if the loot they were after seemed worth it. But this is an extreme scenario. What is important to guard against is the casual sneak thief who happens by when the owner isn't around. In this case, a padlock is ample deterrent.

A bulkhead located as specified also greatly braces and stiffens the hull to withstand the hard pounding

that boats like this must take when driven at high speed into a heavy chop.

The bulkhead is got out in identical halves from 1/2-inch plywood. It need not be marine grade. One-half-inch exterior fir, good on one side, will be quite adequate, since only the outside can be seen after it is in position. It fits tightly against the inside of the planking and the underside of the deck, and is scribed by using a template made up of thin pieces of wood; a spiling block takes off the exact shape. To seal it against leakage, it is well bedded all around—especially at the bottom—with an adhesive bedding compound such as Boatlife's Life Caulk or 3M's 5200, formulations that have good body and do not become brittle in curing. In addition, it should be well fastened to the heavy side frames, the deck beam, and the backing post. Number 11 or number 12 annular nails, galvanized wire nails, or galvanized boat nails, if any can be found, are all suitable for this. Number 12 hot-dipped galvanized wood screws could also be used.

The detailed drawing showing layout and construction of this bulkhead is keyed as follows:

14. *Plywood bulkhead:* Half-inch exterior fir, good on one side.

15. *Heavy backing timber:* Molded 1 1/4 inches but sided 1 3/4 inches, the same as the others. These are

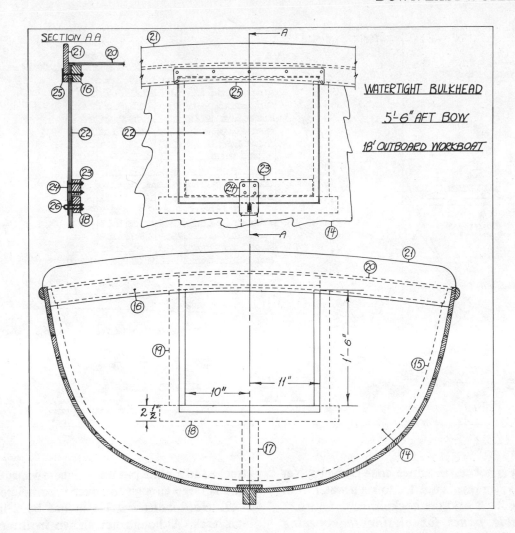

molded twice as thick as the other timbers to provide solid backing for the plywood bulkhead and to ensure secure nailing. They can be steam-bent in one piece if good bending stock is available, or they can be laminated from two ⅜-inch strips glued and nailed together after they are bent in place.

16. *Deck beam:* Molded 2¼ inches, sided 1½ inches. Oak, or glue-laminated to the required curvature from thin strips of Douglas fir or spruce. Crown is 2½ inches in a span of 5 feet. Epoxy-glued, laminated deck beams like this are lighter than oak, yet adequately strong. Still, they take longer to make than solid beams sawn to shape from oak plank.

To frame out this short deck, five more beams will be required for a spacing of 11 inches on centers. The same beam mold can be used for all. The ends of the beams will land on a section of clamp fastened to the timberheads and running forward to the stem.

17. *Backing post:* 2½ inches wide by 1½ inches thick. Oak, Douglas fir, spruce, or hard pine. White pine might be used, but it is rather soft for good nailing.

18 and 19. *Horizontal and vertical framing for the opening through the bulkhead:* Same as *17.*

20. *Exterior plywood, good on one side:* With deck beams sided 1½ inches and spaced 11 inches on centers, leaving 9½ inches unsupported space between beams, ⅜-inch ply is probably thick enough. One-half-inch ply would make a very solid deck, but the extra weight is probably not warranted.

21. *Deck coaming:* Oak or white ash, ¾-inch finished thickness. Molded width is 6 inches, cut to the same camber as the deck. It extends 3 inches above the surface of the deck and reaches slightly below where the deck beam comes behind the face of the bulkhead. Whether or not the boat photographed originally had

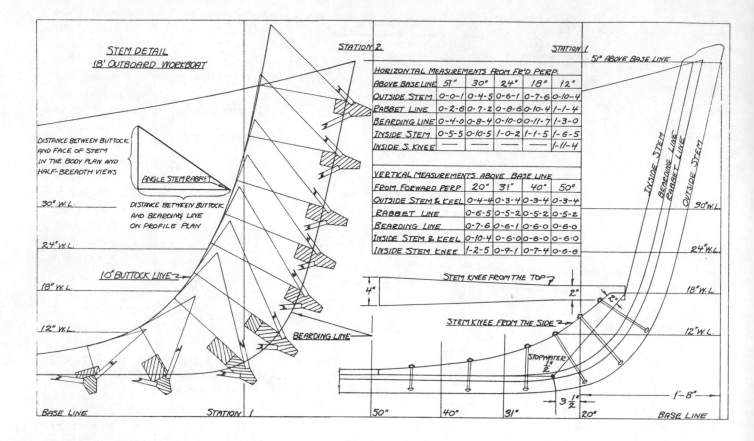

STEM DETAIL
18' OUTBOARD WORKBOAT

Horizontal Measurements from Fr'd Perp.					
Above Base Line	51"	30"	24"	18"	12"
Outside Stem	0-0-1	0-4-5	0-6-1	0-7-6	0-10-4
Rabbet Line	0-2-6	0-7-2	0-8-6	0-10-4	1-1-4
Bearding Line	0-4-0	0-8-4	0-10-0	0-11-7	1-3-0
Inside Stem	0-5-5	0-10-5	1-0-2	1-1-5	1-6-5
Inside S. Knee					1-11-4

Vertical Measurements Above Base Line				
From Forward Perp	20"	31"	40"	50"
Outside Stem & Keel	0-4-4	0-3-4	0-3-4	0-3-4
Rabbet Line	0-6-5	0-5-2	0-5-2	0-5-2
Bearding Line	0-7-6	0-6-1	0-6-0	0-6-0
Inside Stem & Keel	0-10-4	0-6-0	0-8-0	0-6-0
Inside Stem Knee	1-2-5	0-9-1	0-7-4	0-6-8

such a coaming is not certain since none is shown. Yet it is not unlikely, for one is needed to keep water from draining off the deck into the cockpit.

22. *Removable panel for closing the opening through the bulkhead:* Half-inch plywood.

23. *Backing piece:* 2½ inches wide by 1½ inches thick. Oak, Douglas fir, or spruce. This stiffens the panel and provides secure bolting for the hasp plate.

24. *Hasp plate:* Stainless-steel plate 3 inches by 5½ inches fastened by four ¼-inch bolts.

25. *Reinforcement plate:* Stainless-steel plate 2 feet long by 2½ inches wide, fastened through the coaming, bulkhead, and deck beam with seven ¼-inch-diameter bolts. This plate reinforces the coaming where the coaming covers the pocket into which the upper end of the removable panel fits when it is in place and the opening through the bulkhead is closed. Without this reinforcing plate the closure would be less secure, since the coaming could be split away more easily.

26. *Hasp staple:* This should be hardened if possible. Although shown through-bolted, it could be attached to a plate put on with screws, since the hasp plate is large enough to cover it completely.

27. *Half-oval trim:* 1½ inches by 2 inches by 1 inch. Oak. Although not shown in the photos, this should run the full length of the boat for appearance.

The primary consideration in the construction of the transom is sturdiness. Because the transom receives the full thrust of the motor, and because there is no telling how large a motor some might decide to use, the transom should be built extra strong, with a large safety factor.

My first choice would be oak, 1⅜ inches or 1½ inches thick. Hard pine or old-growth, rift-sawn, first-quality Douglas fir could also be used. Spruce is not suitable here because it rots too easily when exposed to the weather.

Two or three widths of plank will have to be joined together, since a single plank of the width required cannot be obtained. If it is made up of three planks, the strongest way to piece them together would be to drift them with ⅜-inch galvanized rod into the middle section from both the top and the bottom. It would not be necessary to drive the rods all the way through. A two-piece transom could be doweled together with short lengths of ⅜-inch galvanized rod.

Another way to make up the transom would be to use pine reinforced on the inner face with oak fashion pieces 3 inches wide and 1 inch thick, sawn to shape, epoxy-glued and screwed around the edge with number 12 or number 14 hot-dipped galvanized screws 2¼ inches long. The pine could also be fastened into the oak through the outside with number 10 or number 11 annular nails. To favor the grain, these fashion pieces should be got out in several short lengths, which are merely butted when they are fastened on. In nailing on the planking, it may be necessary to bore these fashion pieces so that they can take the plank fastenings.

Heavy quarter knees at the sheer are required, and these must be securely fastened through the inwale, timberheads, and sheer plank. Likewise, the stout central knee bracing to the keelson is needed. This knee should be bolted through keel and keelson.

One of the photos on page 92 shows the transom cut down, apparently for a motor with a 15-inch shaft. For rough-water use, a motor with a 20-inch shaft would be preferred by some. In that case, less of the transom would have to be cut away. In choosing an arrangement for mounting the outboard motor, it is recommended that the over-the-stern dry well specified by the Outboard Marine Corporation be considered. I show it in a diagram for the 20-foot garvey discussed in Chapter 12.

The stem and the stem knee should be laid out full size from the profile view, and templates of thin wood (¼ inch would be about right) should be made to fit the full-size lines exactly. The rabbet line and the bearding line are marked on the stem pattern, and holes about ³/₃₂ inch in diameter are bored about 2 inches to 3

inches apart through both the rabbet line and the bearding line for their full length. Prick marks can then be made through these holes on either side of the 2-inch-thick oak stempiece, and through these marks, using a narrow, flexible batten, both the bearding line and the rabbet line can be drawn. These lines are sufficient guide for cutting the stem rabbet; a small rectangular block of the ⅜-inch planking stock can be used for a gauge.

Whereas the stem can be sawn out from an ordinary straight piece of 2-inch-thick oak plank, the stem knee is best got out of 4-inch-thick stock, and if the grain is curved to correspond somewhat to the curve of the knee, so much the stronger and better. If only 2-inch stock is available, 1-inch-thick pieces can be glued on each side to give the 4-inch width needed at the after end for the back rabbet. In addition to gluing, these scabs should be well nailed.

Bolts are ⅜-inch galvanized, located as shown. It might be preferable to fasten the stem and stem knee together first, before bolting them onto the keel. If the stem and stem knee are first glued together and allowed to cure, it will be easier to bore for the bolts with less chance of slippage.

One ½-inch dry-pine stopwater, put in exactly as shown, will suffice. It should be cut off flush with the inside of the rabbet so that caulking can be driven tightly against it on either side.

Also shown is a method for getting the angles for cutting the stem rabbet, given the bearding line and a closely adjacent buttock line in the profile view. For accurate results the buttock-line plane should be fairly close to the center plane of the hull, especially if there is much curvature in the planking lines toward the bow. Here, the distance is 9 inches from the buttock to the face of the stem, 10 inches to the centerline of the hull.

· 8 ·

Yacht Tenders

THE LAWLEY TENDER

When sailing yachts were at their zenith, which is to say during the couple of decades just prior to World War I and for a brief period afterward, two great building yards stood head and shoulders above all the rest in this country—Herreshoff's in Bristol, Rhode Island, and George Lawley and Son on the Neponset River just over the Boston line in Massachusetts. Both yards went out when the large yachts went out. The difference is that the Herreshoff yard is still green in our memory, largely because of the popular writings of L. Francis Herreshoff, whereas Lawley's, lacking a chronicler, is now largely forgotten.

Much of the Lawley story will never be told now, and a pity it is, for there was much worth telling. But most of those who were there are gone, and most of the fine yachts built there are gone as well.

Old-time yachtsmen still around will tell you that

Lawley yachts were unexcelled for finish in a day when finish was important and there was money to pay for it. And in no division or department of the Lawley yard were standards of finish and the quality of workmanship maintained more strictly than in the boatshop.

The man responsible for this was a canny, hard-bitten Scot who had learned his trade and learned it well on the banks of the Clyde. John Harvey was his name and he ran a tight ship. He held sway over the boatshop like a feudal lord over his fiefdom, and it has been said that even the management of the yard hesitated to venture across the threshold of John Harvey's shop without first asking his permission.

Woe to a new man who had the temerity to claim to be a first-class boatbuilder. John Harvey had to humble him and make him regret his brashness. Men who had worked for Harvey 10 and 15 years still had to come to him to have the shape of a thwart knee or

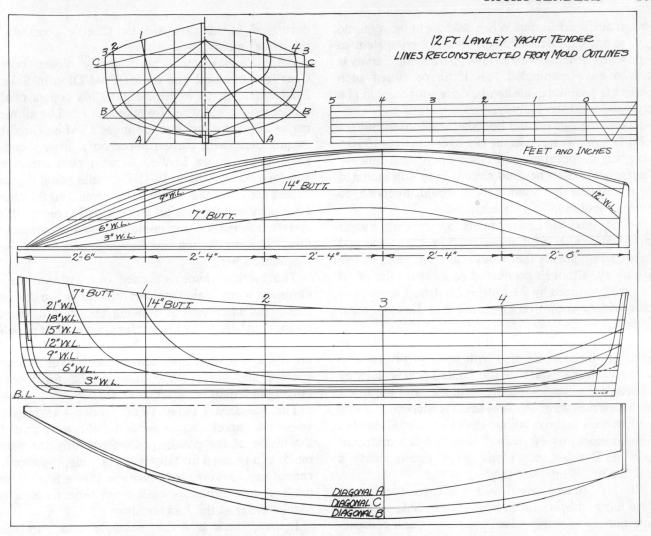

12 FT. LAWLEY YACHT TENDER
LINES RECONSTRUCTED FROM MOLD OUTLINES

FEET AND INCHES

OFFSETS 12' LAWLEY TENDER. FEET, INCHES, EIGHTHS		STEM-KEEL	STA. 1	STA. 2	STA. 3	STA. 4	TRAN.
HEIGHTS	SHEER	2-4-5	2-0-4	1-10-0	1-8-5	1-9-3	2-0-4
	BEARDING	2-4-4	0-1-4	0-1-4	0-1-4	0-1-4	0-7-3
	7" BUTT.	——	0-6-0	0-2-7	0-2-4	0-4-1	1-0-2
	14" BUTT.	——	1-8-7	0-5-1	0-4-1	0-6-6	1-4-0
HALF-BREADTHS	W.L. 3"	0-0-6	0-3-1	0-7-4	0-9-5	0-4-0	——
	W.L. 6"	0-0-6	0-7-1	1-3-5	1-6-7	1-0-0	——
	W.L. 9"	0-0-6	0-9-5	1-6-6	1-9-5	1-6-4	0-2-1
	W.L. 12"	0-0-6	0-11-3	1-8-0	1-10-6	1-8-7	0-6-5
	W.L. 15"	0-0-6	1-0-5	1-8-5	1-11-1	1-9-5	1-0-6
	W.L. 18"	0-0-6	1-1-5	1-9-2	1-11-3	1-9-5	1-3-2
	W.L. 21"	0-0-6	1-2-2	1-9-4	——	——	1-3-3
	SHEER	0-0-6	1-2-7	1-9-5	1-11-3	1-9-2	1-2-4
	DIAG. A.	0-0-7	1-2-5	1-10-0	2-0-1	1-10-1	1-3-7
	DIAG. B.	0-1-0	1-3-6	2-0-1	2-2-5	2-0-1	1-3-6
	DIAG. C.	0-1-3	1-3-7	1-8-3	1-9-1	1-6-5	0-11-0

DIAG. A UP 21" ABOVE BASE LINE. OUT 14" ON B.L. DIAG. B UP 24½" ABOVE B.L. OUT 24" ON 6" W.L. DIAG C UP 24½" ABOVE B.L. OUT 26" ON 18" W.L. KEEL AND STERN POST SIDED 1⅜" breasthook marked out. When asked why he required this, and if experienced help were not competent to cope with such relatively simple operations, Harvey is said to have responded that if he permitted such matters to pass out of his hands, there soon wouldn't be any need for John Harvey.

In looking out for the boatshop he looked out for John Harvey as well. In his old age—the late 1930s, when the corporation had come upon hard times—contracts for launches and similar craft still included the stipulation that John Harvey would supervise, so great a reputation had he acquired.

In its heyday the Lawley boatshop sent forth a great variety of smaller craft, including power launches and some sailing yachts that would be considered of fair size today, although accounted small then. But of all the craft produced by the Lawley boatshop, none were more widely known or esteemed than Lawley yacht tenders.

In and around Boston and Marblehead in the days when Marblehead claimed with some justification to be the yachting capital of the United States, Lawley tenders were considered the ultimate, and the finest yachts carried them. Perhaps these tenders did not tow quite as well as those built to the celebrated Columbia lifeboat model by Herreshoff, but that is a matter of opinion. Besides, not many large yachts made a practice of towing their tenders.

Lawley tenders rowed well and carried well, and were fair and beautiful to look upon. Looks were not unimportant in a day when ostentation and conspicuous consumption were a not inconsiderable part of the yachting scene.

One of the hands who worked in the Lawley boatshop for many years, and who got along very well with John Harvey, no doubt in part because he posed no threat of any sort to Harvey's position, was Charles (Charlie) Chandler, a native of Barbados and a fine boatbuilder. During the long term of his employment in the boatshop at Lawley's, Charlie worked on and built many tenders, and at one time or another he went to the trouble of tracing the outlines of the molds for his own use. The construction of these tenders was standardized and embodied in a set of molds used and kept in the shop. You may be sure they were well guarded, and it is most unlikely that John Harvey would knowingly have permitted their removal in outline from the boatshop.

It is doubtful if the original molds still exist. Once a shop is shut down for good, molds and patterns are frequently thrown out, burned, or otherwise lost or destroyed. In this case, at least, Charlie's outlines of the tender molds have survived.

After Lawley's was permanently closed down, Charlie worked off and on for Fred Dion in Salem, Massachusetts, to whom he gave his copies of the tender molds, and when I worked for Fred he allowed me to copy the outlines for myself. After carefully tracing them with carbon paper on a large sheet of heavy brown paper, I rolled them up, put them away, and forgot about them. In 1977, while going through papers and plans that had been accumulating for years, I dug out the mold outlines and decided to record them and the information they contained in more permanent form. The results are the drawings and dimensions reproduced here.

The section shapes checked out with surprising closeness when I laid them out full size on the drafting table, and later on the drawing board. The tender considered here is the 12-foot length, the most popular and widely used size. Note, however, that the molds are marked so that they can be used, with different spacing and some slight adjustments, for tenders ranging in length from 10 to 14 feet.

The standard Lawley yacht tender was planked smooth or carvel, and the section molds were given to the inside of the planking. Consequently the same molds can be used for lapstrake planking, if desired. I cannot say for sure, but I assume that a few clinker tenders were probably built from time to time on special order at the Lawley shop.

In fact, there is a fine example of a varnished lapstrake mahogany and cedar tender of unknown origin in the small-craft collection at the Mystic Seaport Museum. It gives every indication of having been built from Lawley molds, now that I have compared it with the mold outlines shown here.

Note that the molds include those for the stem, the apron, the slightly curved forward end of the keel strip (which is otherwise perfectly straight and uniform in molded thickness and siding), the triangular section of deadwood, and the sternpost. No mold is required for the keel batten strip, which rests on top of the keel and provides back rabbet for the garboards. This backbone, together with the section molds and the transom, was all that was required for setting up the boat for planking. This was the Whitehall method previously developed for building the working Whitehalls, from which fancy American yacht tenders originated. I have a set of Whitehall molds, identical in all respects except the dimensions, that were used in the Partelow shop in Boston in the 1880s.

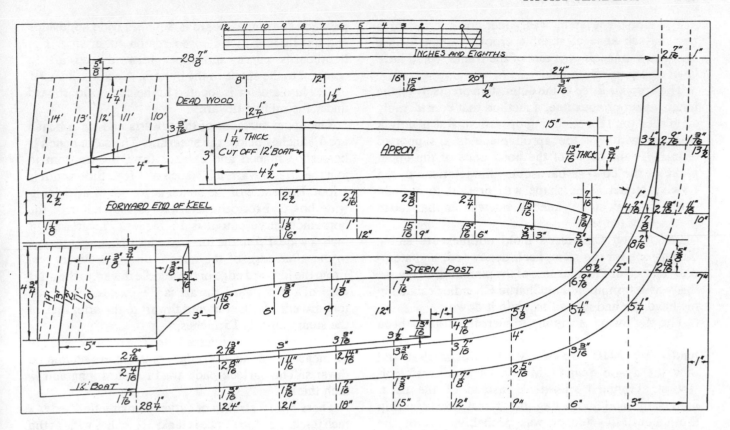

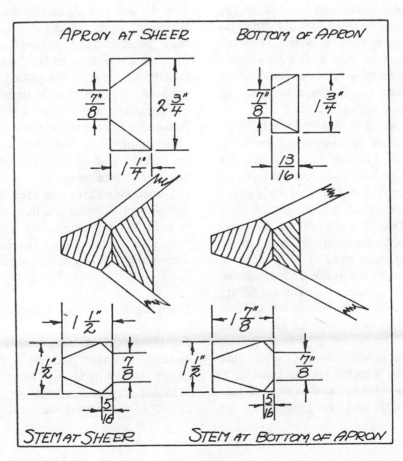

The one-piece stem was generally got out of a hackmatack knee of suitable crook. Except for the mahogany transom, the rest of the frame would have been seasoned white oak.

The apron is fitted to the outer stem precisely on the inner rabbet or apex line, a method that considerably simplifies the rabbet-cutting operation. But mainly it was the width of the apron piece that supported fullness in the curve of the hood ends of the upper plank at the bow—a handsome characteristic of the Lawley tender. This shape was present to a slight extent in the Boston Whitehall, but was emphasized in the Lawley tender.

Lacking on Chandler's mold outlines are siding dimensions for the stem, keel, deadwood, and sternpost, as well as the thickness of the planking. Of course this was information that Charlie Chandler carried in his head; he had no call to write it down.

The following scantling dimensions have been obtained from a 12-foot carvel-planked Lawley yacht tender, hull 1710, supposedly built around 1920 and now in Mystic Seaport Museum's small-craft collection. Trimmed with teak instead of the usual mahogany and exhibiting the finest workmanship throughout, this tender was probably part of the matching outfit for some large Lawley-built luxury yacht. Bronze lifting rings fore and aft indicate that this tender was intended to be carried on board. The cast-bronze thwart knees, quarter knees, and breasthook are not found in early Lawley tenders, but became standard equipment after the Lawleys reached the pinnacle of their building career.

Overall length is 12 feet 2 inches and the beam, 4 feet 3 inches. The keel, stem, deadwood, and sternpost are oak, sided 1½ inches. The keel batten is oak, 2⅞ inches wide and ⅜ inch thick. Inwales are oak having a horizontal width of 1 inch, tapered to ⅞ inch at the ends, and a vertical thickness of ¾ inch. The apron is oak and has 3 inches of width of after face at the sheer height and 1½ inches of fore-and-aft thickness to the inner rabbet line at the stem head. The timbers, of steam-bent oak, are ⅝ inch wide and ½ inch in molded thickness, are spaced 7 inches on centers, and are continuous from side to side. The transom is teak, ¾ inch in finished thickness. The stern bench and thwarts are teak, ¾ inch thick. The seat riser is teak, ⅝ inch thick and 1¾ inches wide, tapering to 1 inch wide at the bow end. Floorboards are ¾ inch thick and fitted tight. They are screwed down to frames and to several floor strips across the garboards and keel batten, and are

painted. The center board is 8 inches wide amidships and has three 4-inch floorboards on either side. The floorboards curve and taper forward and aft to conform to the shape of the bottom. A sponge hole 5½ inches in diameter is located in the center floorboard under the middle thwart.

The upper surfaces of the thwarts and stern bench are 6⅞ inches below the sheerline. The stern bench is horseshoe-shaped and extends from the transom to join the after thwart, a distance of 4 feet. Side width is 1 foot. Each side of the bench is got out of a 15-inch-wide board. From the transom to the center of the horseshoe-curve cutout is 16 inches. Thwarts are 8 inches wide. From the forward edge of the after thwart to the after edge of the middle thwart is 28 inches. From the forward edge of the middle thwart to the after edge of the forward thwart is 27 inches. From the forward edge of the forward thwart to the after face of the stem apron is 15 inches.

There are two rowing stations. The oarlock pins are 12 inches aft of the after edges of the after and middle thwarts. The oarlock pads are 11 inches long and ⅝ inch thick.

There are 10 strakes of carvel planking finished ⁷⁄₁₆ inch thick. The top strake is teak, 3¼ inches wide at the bow, 4¼ inches wide amidships, and 3⅛ inches wide at the stern. Plank widths on the stem, except for the sheer plank and the garboard, are from 2⅛ inches to 2¼ inches. The bow end of the garboard is kept low so that the top edge of the garboard, viewed in place on the boat, appears straight or nearly so. The width of the garboard amidships is 4¾ inches. Planks are fastened with copper nails and riveted. Nails are small, about number 18, English standard wire gauge; burrs are about ⁹⁄₁₆ inch OD. The planks below the sheer plank are white cedar.

The outside sheer trim takes a standard cotton rope bumper and is hollowed from teak strips 1⁵⁄₁₆ inches wide by ⁹⁄₁₆ inch thick. The circular hollow is ¾ inch wide and ¼ inch deep. The center posts under the three thwarts are turned from 1-inch square stock.

Planking the Lawley Tender Carvel

For those familiar with clinker construction it would certainly be easier and less work to build the 12-foot Lawley tender lapstrake rather than to plank it carvel. Whether to plank clinker or carvel depends on a variety of considerations, some of which are discussed

This clinker-planked yacht tender is representative in its lines and interior layout of the fine 12-foot tenders built by Lawley and by Charles Lawton.

in connection with the Lawton tender, which is presented in the second part of this chapter. Some prefer the appearance of varnished carvel planking, and some claim that a boat so planked rows more easily, but this is a matter of opinion. The clinker boat is definitely stronger and will stand more hard use.

The novice who elects to build carvel will be well advised to adopt the procedure and order of work generally followed in commercial shops. He can start out by making molds for the four stations shown in the lines plan, and by making the transom. Next the pieces that form the backbone—the stem, apron, keel, deadwood, and sternpost—are got out and assembled with the transom. Bevels and rabbet are cut and stopwaters put in preparatory to setting up. This is done right side up on stocks, and high enough off the ground for convenience in fairing and planking the bottom. There are at least two good reasons for building right side up: One, it greatly facilitates bending in the timbers; two, it enables one person alone to do the riveting, although a helper who can hold the bucking iron makes things much easier.

In setting up, the molds must be centered, leveled, plumbed, and securely braced and shored. The transom is horned for perfect thwartships alignment. Substantial sheer battens running from stem to stern directly above the sheerline not only assist in fairing but help hold everything in place. At the bow these battens are fastened to untrimmed extensions of the apron and stem, which will be cut back later to their finished lengths. At the stern, temporary pieces rise above the inside face of the transom on either side to meet the sheer battens. Of course the molds are also made to extend high enough above the sheerline to take fastenings from the sheer battens.

The setting-up process is not complete until the molds have been thoroughly checked for perfect fairness throughout by fairing battens applied in various positions. These battens must run fair while touching all underlying mold surfaces at the same time. If high spots are found they are trimmed, and any low spots are brought up by shimming. When molds are carefully and accurately made, very little fairing is required.

Before the ribbands go on it is advisable to line out the planking, clearly marking the plank widths on the molds, stem, and transom. It will be a great help if the widths and lining can be taken off a scale half-model previously prepared—standard procedure for anyone building a particular type of boat for the first time.

Ribbands follow the lining operation. No ribbands are needed at the sheer, since sheer battens are already in place. Nor is a ribband needed in the garboard location. Ribbands should be about 1½ to 1¾ inches wide and ¾ to $^{13}/_{16}$ inch thick, and on the stiff side rather than being too limber. They should be straight-grained and without defects. They must bend fair, and they go on in one continuous length. If the upper ribbands are too stiff for the fullness in this tender's topsides at the bow—an especially handsome characteristic of the Lawley tender—their ends may be split with the bandsaw the necessary distance back, so that they can take the required curve. The ribbands line with the planking, and there is one for each plank, less the sheer plank and the garboard, as I have explained. Long flathead wood screws with washers under their heads fasten the ribbands to the molds.

Before the timbers go in, the garboards can be fitted and fastened in place. Their forward ends will need to be steamed or soaked in boiling water. Having the garboards in place helps when the timbers are bent in. The garboards are screwed to the stem and transom and riveted to the keel batten. Long, slim wood screws with washers under the heads secure the garboards to the molds temporarily. Later these screws are removed and the holes plugged.

Before the timbers are put in the steam box they are sanded and their inside faces are rounded very slightly. Also, the spacing of the timbers is clearly marked on the inside of the ribbands. Except for two or three pairs of timbers at the bow and a couple at the stern, the timbers run continuously from sheerline to sheerline. For best results, two persons are needed for bending in the timbers, one on either side of the boat. The timbers, hot and flexible from the steam box, are forced down inside the ribbands so that they lie on their station marks, and at the same time they are twisted as much as necessary to make them lie flat against the ribbands. This gives the correct bevels for attaching the planking. After the hot timbers have been clamped (not too tightly) to the sheer batten, their ends are tapped with a hammer. This drives the timbers down for a snug touching fit against all the ribbands. After that a nail is driven into the sheer batten through the timber head to secure the timber, and the clamp is removed.

With the garboards already in place, the second strake to go on will be the sheerstrake, directly under the sheer batten. As planking proceeds, the ribbands are removed one at a time and replaced with the corresponding plank; work proceeds from the garboard up and from the sheer down. Each plank is fastened in place as it is fitted. The last plank to go on, the so-called shutter, comes just above the turn of the bilge, where there is little or no twist or sny to worry about. When tapped into place, a properly prepared shutter should go in like a stopper into a bottle. Where plank edges need beveling, both meeting edges are beveled equally. The final operation before planks are hung on the boat is to burnish their edges by hard rubbing with a polished round of hardwood; this will compress their edges slightly. Later, when the planks take up moisture, these edges will swell back, tightening the planking immensely. Each plank as it goes on should be set up against the plank next to it as tightly as can be managed. A pair of chain clamps will be of great help for this. A boat of this sort, properly planked, will require caulking only in the garboard seam next to the keel and at the hood ends of the planking in the stem rabbet. When the boat is varnished, the planking seams can hardly be detected.

Once this tender is planked, no further special directions apply. Construction can be completed as for any other well-built small boat. The interior of the Lawley 12-footer is treated essentially the same as that of the Lawton 10-footer, which is detailed in the pages that follow.

THE LAWTON 10-FOOT TENDER

The first part of this chapter originally appeared in the *National Fisherman* in September 1977, and the response to it surprised me. I had expected interest, but not quite to the extent that developed. Several readers wrote that they had Lawley tenders that they would gladly permit me to inspect and measure. A Long Island man offered his for sale. A reader in Maine had worked as a young man in the Lawley boatshop helping Gus Deveau. There was also a letter from a yachtsman who remembered Lawley tenders from his boyhood, when they were numerous on Massachusetts Bay—particularly the 12-footer, "a splendid boat, easy towing and easy rowing, carvel planked, with a plumb stem and graceful sheer, the classic cutter of an earlier era when men of note were transported about their business in style."

Because of this interest, I decided to put into print for the first time the lines of a not dissimilar boat, the Lawton 10-foot tender, rechecked and redrawn for the occasion. These lines had been in my possession for over 30 years, awaiting disposition, and I felt it was high time they saw the light of day. Thus, they were published, together with explanatory and descriptive comments, in the January 1978 issue of *National Fisherman*, and are reprinted here.

I obtained the lines for the 10-foot tender from the builder, Charles Lawton, a man renowned for his fine tenders and whose reputation as a superlative craftsman is still green in Marblehead, Massachusetts. They came into my possession when Charlie and I were working together at the James F. Graves Beacon Street yard in Marblehead during World War II.

At that time Charlie, who was approaching 90 and had been working at the boatbuilding trade for close to 70 years, specialized in building these tenders. Except for legs that were a bit stiff, Charlie was still going strong and still turned out a good day's work with the best of them.

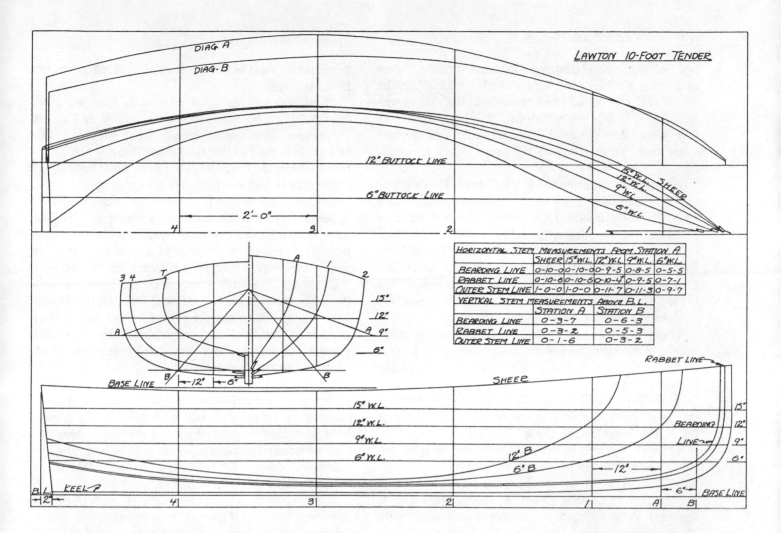

LAWTON 10-FOOT TENDER

HORIZONTAL STEM MEASUREMENTS FROM STATION A	SHEER	15"W.L.	12"W.L.	9"W.L.	6"W.L.
BEARDING LINE	0-10-0	0-10-0	0-9-5	0-8-5	0-5-5
RABBET LINE	0-10-6	0-10-6	0-10-4	0-9-5	0-7-1
OUTER STEM LINE	1-0-0	1-0-0	0-11-7	0-11-3	0-9-7

VERTICAL STEM MEASUREMENTS ABOVE B.L.	STATION A	STATION B
BEARDING LINE	0-3-7	0-6-3
RABBET LINE	0-3-2	0-5-3
OUTER STEM LINE	0-1-6	0-3-2

10-FOOT LAWTON TENDER – OFFSETS, FEET, INCHES, EIGHTHS	STATIONS	STEM	A	1	2	3	4	TRAN.
HEIGHTS	SHEER	1-10-7	1-9-6	1-8-6	1-7-0	1-6-1	1-6-2	1-7-0
	BEARDING	—	0-3-7	0-2-5	0-2-0	0-1-7	0-2-6	0-5-5
	RABBET	—	0-3-2	0-2-1	0-1-5	0-1-4	0-2-3	0-5-2
	KEEL	—	0-1-6	0-1-0	0-0-4	0-0-4	0-0-4	0-0-4
	BUTT. 6"	—	1-0-2	0-6-2	0-2-5	0-2-1	0-3-3	0-7-2
	BUTT. 12"	—	—	1-1-0	0-3-5	0-2-6	0-4-5	0-9-5
HALF-BREADTHS	SHEER	0-0-5	0-8-3	1-2-1	1-8-3	1-9-7	1-8-2	1-2-2
	15" W.L.	0-0-5	0-7-2	1-1-0	1-8-0	1-10-1	1-8-3	1-2-7
	12" W.L.	0-0-5	0-5-7	0-11-4	1-7-3	1-10-0	1-8-0	1-2-1
	9" W.L.	0-0-5	0-4-0	0-9-0	1-6-2	1-9-1	1-6-5	0-11-0
	6" W.L.	0-0-5	0-1-7	0-5-4	1-4-1	1-7-4	1-3-4	0-1-4
	RABBET	0-0-5	0-0-5	0-0-5	0-0-5	0-0-5	0-0-5	0-0-5
DIAGONALS	DIAGONAL A	—	0-7-4	1-0-5	1-8-0	1-10-5	1-8-4	1-3-0
	DIAGONAL B	—	0-8-1	1-0-0	1-5-6	1-6-6	1-4-6	1-0-1

LINES INSIDE PLANKING–OUTSIDE TRANSOM. HEIGHTS ABOVE B.L.

PLANKING 3/8". STEM AND KEEL SIDED 1 1/4".

DIAGONAL A. UP 17", OUT 22" ON 9" WATER LINE.

DIAGONAL B. UP 17", OUT 12" ON 3" WATER LINE.

These lines and offsets show a rounder, more cut-back forefoot than does the Lawton 10-foot tender donated to the Mystic Seaport in 1980, as will be discussed in the text. The tender from which the lines were taken more than 30 years ago may have been a slightly modified custom model, but the only change appears to have been in the stem.

Charlie and I got along well together. I made a point of lending a hand whenever he needed it for such jobs as bucking rivets and chasing stock in the mill downstairs, and Charlie appreciated it. Helping Charlie was a privilege and the kind of opportunity that doesn't come twice, and you may be sure I made the most of it.

When Charlie retired at 90, following the death of his wife, and went back to spend his declining years with his family in Saint John, New Brunswick, he left a sheaf of plans and drawings with me. I still have a box of boat molds that he used when he worked for Partelow in the canoe factory at Riverside on the Charles River in the 1890s. His shop notebook for recording special dimensions and directions for custom work started about that time.

The 10-foot tender was possibly his most popular boat and the one most in demand at the time I knew him. Even though yachting in Marblehead had begun to decline, there was still enough call for these tenders to keep Charlie busy most of the time in his corner at the head of the boatshop stairs; an occasional dory or other craft took up the slack.

Years afterward, following Charlie's departure to Saint John, Graves produced a fiberglass version of what purported to be the Lawton tender—taken, I presume, from Charlie's building molds remaining at the yard. What changes, if any, were made to facilitate the molding process I cannot say, though such changes often are made.

That some changes may have been made is suggested by reports coming to me that the performance of the glass tenders, at least the first ones, was inferior to that of Charlie's wooden ones. It was claimed that the glass boats were not as stable, possibly in part because of the excessive weight of the glass in the topsides.

The design of this tender is a critical one that will not tolerate much variation in the established lines. A slight departure here or there, though it might not be apparent to the unpracticed eye, could spoil the performance or at least damage it appreciably.

In a point-by-point comparison with Lawley tenders, those built by Lawton stack up favorably in all respects. Both have had their ardent proponents.

The perfected yacht tender of 60 years ago was the outgrowth of rigorous competition, a boat that excelled in both performance and appearance. Cost was not an overriding consideration. Yachtsmen were willing and able to pay for quality, and therefore workmanship did not suffer from drastic efforts to cut building costs.

These tenders had to row and tow well, be moderately good seaboats, carry heavy loads, yet shine like a piece of fine furniture. They not only had to be light in weight so that they would handle easily and row well, but they had to appear light, since delicacy of construction was aesthetically important.

Indeed, in one respect the heavy emphasis placed on appearance dictated a delicacy of scantlings that had an adverse effect on the lasting qualities of the tenders. Bent-oak timbers were shaved down so small—in some cases barely ½ inch by ⅜ inch in cross section— that almost invariably they broke much sooner than they should have. There are few old tenders that do not have cracked or broken timbers or frames, which have often been "sistered" and sometimes replaced. But the planking of such tenders, if not everything else apart from the frames, has lasted well.

The lines given here are drawn to the inside of the planking, so that either a carvel or clinker boat may be constructed on molds made from them. For a clinker boat with plank ¼ inch thick, however, the bearding line would need some readjustment. The bearding line shown is drawn for planking ⅜ inch thick, the recommended thickness for a carvel boat.

Building with clinker planking is easier, in my opinion, especially if the boat is to be varnished. Tight-seam carvel planking finished bright requires absolute precision of planking fit, but with clinker planking, some slight adjustment in the fit of the laps is possible without being obvious or apparent. Consequently, the same exacting precision is not required.

Clinker planking does not have to be hollowed or "backed out" on the inside to fit the round of the molds, and can be finished flat and sanded at the bench. Carvel planking, on the other hand, must be "backed out" precisely to fit the hull curves. After it is fitted and fastened in place, it must be planed and sanded to perfect curvature and smoothness without planing away the countersunk recesses for the rivet heads, which must be filled with facing tinted to match the color of the varnished hull.

Prior to 1980 I had few details to offer for the building of this tender. I could have worked out scantlings to go with the lines, but although they probably would have come very close, they would not have constituted the genuine article as built by Lawton—so I refrained. This is where things stood when, in the summer of 1980, a letter arrived from a yachtsman in Argentina who was seeking plans for a classic yacht tender. Donald M. Street, author of *The Ocean-Going Yacht,* had suggested that I might be able to supply them.

My correspondent informed me that he was considering extensive cruising in South American waters and needed a good boat—he'd had his fill of rubber dinghies and other modern substitutes. Having a tender built in Argentina offered no problem as far as skilled boatbuilders and materials were concerned, but he needed working plans to go by. So far, he had not been able to locate any that would do. Could I help?

My first thought was, "This is easy," but when I began to cast about for detailed drawings of wooden tenders I realized what a dearth of specific building information for such boats there actually is. Lines and offsets for tenders are not lacking, but lines and offsets are only the skeleton—to be fleshed out in building the boat. Until very recently, this was done by the boatbuilder in the boatshop according to trade practice, and little or none of it was written down anywhere. Building details remained largely in the boatbuilder's head and hands, but also, to a considerable extent, in various molds and patterns evolved by rule of thumb and passed directly from boatbuilder to boatbuilder, from shop to shop, and from one generation to the next.

Apart from the fact that the boatbuilding trade as formerly practiced had no real need for published manuals, the principal obstacle to getting the necessary information onto the printed page was the difficulties involved in recording uniquely curved shapes on a reduced scale in such a way that they could later be enlarged and precisely reproduced.

Lines and offsets are relatively easy to record, but this method, developed by naval architects to record the hull shape of large, carvel-built vessels, was not applied to boatbuilding until well along in the last century, and then only partially. Getting small-craft hull shapes from patterns—once the builder had the patterns—was quicker, easier, and just as accurate as getting the shapes from a laydown of lines.

For that reason boatbuilders were generally reluctant to switch from patterns, and some have continued to depend on them to this day. For instance, experienced builders of Adirondack guideboats—which are unexcelled by any small-craft type anywhere in fine workmanship, finish, and sweetness of line—produced their boats entirely from inherited molds and patterns whose origins have never been traced completely.

Charles Lawton not only built his famed yacht tenders largely from molds, but also turned out various other boats by the same method. He once told me that as a young man back in the 1890s (when he was working at the Partelow canoe factory) he was able to produce Saint Lawrence River skiffs at the rate of one per working week of 56 hours. He managed to complete a boat, except for painting, in this short time only because he had patterns or molds for every part.

In the summer of 1980, by happy coincidence, a 10-foot Lawton tender was donated to Mystic Seaport Museum's small-craft collection by Ray Burns, Jr., of Marblehead. This clinker tender had served the *Grenadier,* a 59-foot-10-inch-LOA auxiliary schooner yacht designed by John G. Alden and constructed in 1931 by the Lawley yard.

Built for Henry A. Morss, Jr., and Sherman Morss, the *Grenadier* was subsequently owned by John A. Magoon and then by George E. McQuesten. Her owners were prominent in Marblehead yachting circles. And it was from McQuesten that Burns acquired the tender.

Whether this is the *Grenadier*'s original tender from 1931 is not altogether clear, but it most probably is. The boat shows wear, although she has retained her shape perfectly. There are no broken frames, split planks, or failing joints, in spite of the extremely light scantlings characteristic of Lawton's tenders.

One thing is immediately obvious in comparing the profile shape of this tender with the lines in this chapter. The two stems are not quite the same. The curve of the forefoot in the lines on page 107 is rounder, fuller, and cut back more. It also rises somewhat higher. How this came about I cannot say. Perhaps the boat from which the lines were taken years ago was a custom job. But in other respects the lines of the two boats appear to correspond closely.

When Lawton retired from boatbuilding, he gave me a box of much-used boat molds, which, as I mentioned, I still have. Included are stem patterns for a number of different boats: Whitehalls, a Saint Lawrence River skiff, his Adirondack, and his 10-foot tender. In order to compare the shape of the *Grenadier* tender's stem with Lawton's molds, I carefully took off the lines of the former from the boat. The takeoff and the molds checked precisely. There can be no doubt that the stem of the *Grenadier*'s tender was built from these molds.

The shape of the rounded, cut-back forefoot in the lines in this chapter has some resemblance to the

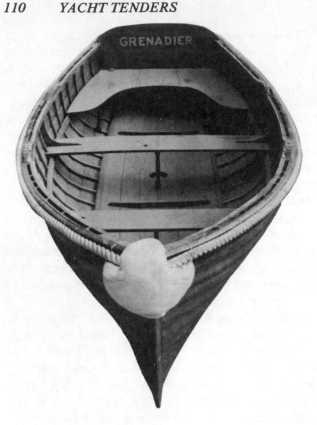

Formerly tender to the 60-foot auxiliary schooner Grenadier, *this classic 10-foot Lawton boat was donated to the Mystic Seaport Museum's small-craft collection in 1980. Note the curve of the forefoot, sharper than that shown in the lines on page 107.*

forefoot shape of Herreshoff tenders built after the so-called Columbia lifeboat model, although it is less extreme. The upper stem has less rake than that of the Herreshoff model. According to L. Francis Herreshoff, his tenders towed better behind a yacht and did not tend to dart and yaw as much as the Lawley model with its straighter stem and deeper, more sharply curved forefoot, which was of Whitehall derivation.

The *Grenadier*'s tender is much closer in this respect to the Lawley/Whitehall model. To the best of my knowledge, however, no one has ever accused a Lawton tender of misbehaving in the wake of a yacht.

Although varying in size, rake, and curvature, all of the stem patterns Lawton gave me are for composite stems and are laid out in the same way. They are contrived for the assembly of a curved stem and forefoot from three pieces that are easily and economically cut from ordinary straight-grained oak plank.

Natural crooks of hackmatack or oak with the shape grown in are, of course, ideal for stems. These, however, are hard to come by, are expensive, and require much labor to shape and fit. A well-made pieced-up stem is amply strong and lasting, just as

handsome when finished, and much cheaper and easier to make. Rabbeting for the hood ends of the planking is greatly facilitated in the pieced-up stem because the joint between the apron and the outer stem falls on the apex line of the rabbet.

The three essential parts of this stem assembly are the main, or outer, stempiece; the apron; and the stem knee, joining the first two to the straight strip that forms the keel. By making the apron from a separate piece, one can easily make it wide enough to give ample back-rabbet support to the curving ends of the topside planking. Generally there was also a rabbet mold for marking the curves of the rabbet and bearding lines at the turn.

The stem shapes are not difficult. It would be easy to duplicate them exactly by carefully tracing around them on a thin board and cutting to the line. But when it comes to recording these shapes in print on a reduced scale, the job is not quite as simple or easy. And a high order of accuracy here is critical.

I believe an accurate duplication can be made from the accompanying diagrams. Should this appear at first glance to be something of a puzzle, requiring some patience and study, that is to be expected. All the needed information is here. Enlargement to blueprint

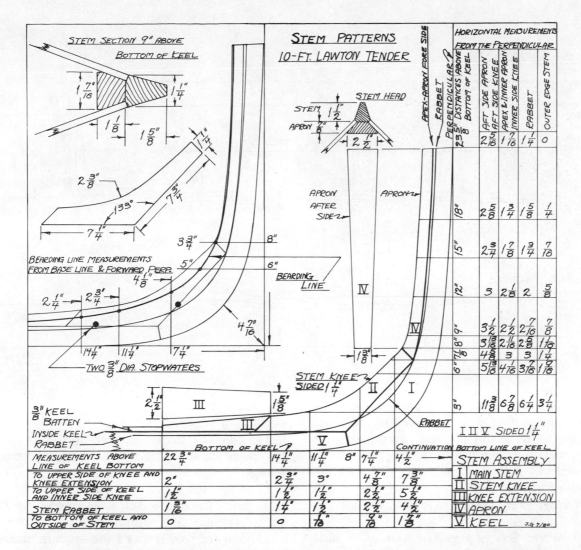

STEM PATTERNS
10-FT. LAWTON TENDER

STEM ASSEMBLY

I	MAIN STEM
II	STEM KNEE
III	KNEE EXTENSION
IV	APRON
V	KEEL

Stem patterns for the standard Lawton 10-foot tender. This stem shape with its more sharply curved forefoot could very easily be substituted for that of the lines given in this chapter when the full-size laydown is made.

size will not help. There may be a simpler and more direct way of presenting these data, but I have not found it.

Although the two stems are distinctly different, comparatively little adjustment would be required in the lines on page 107 if the stem shape of the *Grenadier* tender were substituted for the one shown there. This could be accomplished with no trouble at all when the necessary full-size laydown is made.

The amount of detail in this small and comparatively simple boat is all but staggering when it comes to getting down in print every precise detail required for duplicating it exactly, something no commercial boatbuilder would ever bother to do. Just how much detail there is will become clear from an examination of the sectional view through the boat at station 3, its widest part, as shown in the accompanying diagram.

1. *Frames:* White oak, ½ inch square, 6 inches on centers. Except for the two at the bow, the frames are continuous from gunwale to gunwale. The two bow frames are in two pieces joined across the stem-knee extension by small floors, and are canted slightly to conform to the curve of the sides at the bow, spreading at the top to about 7 inches on centers.

2. *Planking:* Ten strakes 5/16 inch thick, northern white cedar, except for the mahogany sheerstrake. Lapped ⅜ inch. Laps copper-riveted every 2 inches. Widths of planks, including laps, measured at each station: garboard, 4¾ inches; broad, 3¾ inches; number 3, 3¾ inches; numbers 5, 6, and 7, 2¾ inches; numbers 8 and 9, 2⅝ inches; sheerstrake, 3¾ inches.

3. *Inwale:* Oak, sided ¾ inch, molded 1 inch. Inside face rounded very slightly for appearance.

4. *Middle thwart:* Mahogany, 8 inches wide, ¾

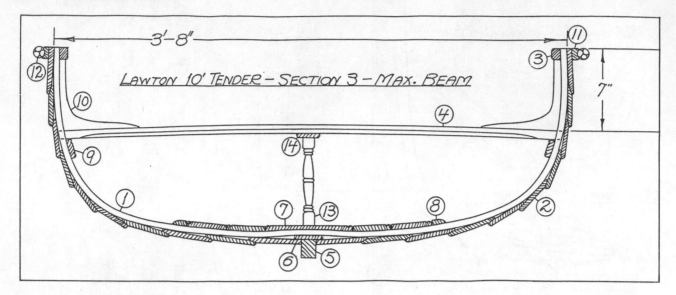

inch thick. Notched tight at the ends around two timbers and fitted snugly to the sides of the boat. Screwed to the riser and plugged. Sprung upward about ⅜ inch at the center by a supporting post. Under edges chamfered half the thickness of thwart for appearance of lightness.

5. *Keel strip:* Oak, sided 1¼ inches, molded 1½ inches.

6. *Keel batten:* Oak, 2⅛ inches wide by ⅜ inch thick.

7. *Bottom ceiling:* Cedar, ⅜ inch thick thinned to ¼ inch at ends to help twist. Outboard edges beaded a shallow 3/16 inch. Middle strip is 7¾ inches wide, tapering toward the ends. Hollowed slightly underneath to correspond to the upcurve of the frames above the keel batten. Outside strips, two on either side, are 3¼ inches and 3½ inches wide. Screwed to every other frame, but not plugged.

8. *Mahogany trim strips:* Slightly thicker and shaped as shown.

9. *Seat risers:* Mahogany, 1½ inches by ½ inch (or a hair less). One-eighth-inch bead top and bottom. Risers run full length of frames. Fastened to each frame with a number 8 screw. Not plugged.

10. *Thwart knees:* Hackmatack, fitted tight to inside of planking and joggled around lap lands. Knees rise with a tight fit behind the inwale to come flush with the top of the sheer plank. Rivet-fastened through sheer plank and inwale. Knees are ⅝ inch thick, 7 inches long on the foot, and fastened to the thwart with three screws. Molded approximately 2 inches through

the widest part of the throat. Outer edges rounded slightly for appearance.

11. *Outwale strip:* One-inch-by-¾-inch oak, hollowed and shaped to take 1-inch-diameter cotton-rope bumper.

12. *One-inch cotton-rope bumper:* Sewed on with linen thread through ⅛-inch holes bored every 2 feet in outwale strip, top to bottom.

13. *Turned post:* From 1-inch-square mahogany.

14. *Socketed block:* One-half inch thick; secures post.

Anyone attempting to build this tender will be well advised to approach the job as a puzzle, for in some respects it is just that, and therein lies not a little of its appeal to the amateur builder looking for new worlds to conquer. Taking risks and resolving uncertainties add zest and incentive.

Building such a boat is no mere act of turning down so many nuts on so many bolts, or something equally cut and dried. Rather, it is an open-ended process from start to finish, one that makes exacting demands on the builder's judgment, eye, and aesthetic instincts.

There is simply no practical way to provide in printed words and diagrams the complete directions for the harmonious blending of all the subtle curves that enter into the fabric of this diminutive vessel. Here, deviating as much as the thickness of one thin shaving in a critical place is equivalent to singing out of tune or striking the wrong note on the piano.

After many years of publishing how-to directions for

Interior views of the Grenadier's *tender show the light scantlings and fine detail that make it a difficult boat to build.*

boatbuilding, I have found that a certain number of readers always write back asking for blueprints, even though they would be of little help and would contain nothing not already provided. Except for their size and color, there is nothing special about blueprints, nothing magical. Generally what is needed is close and careful study, plus some judicious extrapolation when gaps appear, as they inevitably will.

The two detailed drawings to be discussed next cover construction thoroughly from amidships aft. They are keyed, as above, both for easy reference and to avoid cluttering the drawings with notes and dimensions.

First, it would seem appropriate to make some general observations on materials and fastenings. Five different lumber species were used for this boat: cedar, oak, hackmatack, mahogany, and pine. For planking, northern white cedar was the preferred wood, and because the boat was finished bright, absolutely clear cedar boards were required—lumber that was free of knots, sapwood, or other imperfections.

Cedar of this quality was not easily obtained in Lawton's time, and it is all but unobtainable now. This is what J. Henry Rushton had to say about such wood in his 1904 catalog:

> Do not confound our white cedar, which grows only in the most northern states and Canada, with the white

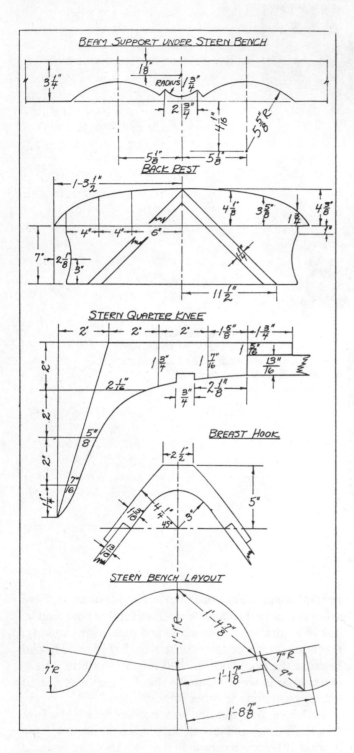

cedar of New Jersey and Virginia. The former is the lightest known wood of this or any country that is suitable for planks for small craft. One cubic foot, air seasoned (not kiln dried), weighs but 18 pounds, while the white cedar of New Jersey and Virginia weighs 28 pounds.

The northern cedar is soft, tough and durable. You can give it a vast amount of hard usage with but little injury, and time makes but little impression on it, as I have known cedar planking in a boat to be sound and perfect after 20 years' constant use every summer, and having such shelter during winters as may be found in a woods camp.

Thus, northern cedar is the preferred planking material for the Lawton tender, but it is not essential. Southern cedar—or juniper, as it is also known—is quite acceptable, even though it is slightly heavier and more prone to splitting. Lacking cedar, one may substitute other species as a last resort.

For ribs or timbers, inwales, keel, keel batten, outwale, sternpost, stem, apron, and stem knee, oak was used. For the keel, a piece of dense, close-grained red oak was sometimes preferred to white oak because of a tendency of the latter species to warp and twist in larger sections, thus pulling the boat out of shape. Builders characterized such oak as being too "strong." But for the steam-bent ribs or timbers, only the choicest white oak bending stock was considered. This was stripped from the butt logs of young, fast-growing trees cut close to the ground.

Only perfectly clear, straight-grained wood was selected. The wider the annual rings and the denser and heavier the wood, the better. With half an hour to an hour of boiling (or wet, low-pressure steam), such white-oak timbers can be tied in knots.

The timbers in the Mystic Seaport Museum's Lawton tender, only ½ inch square in section, must have been of the choicest select white oak, for despite the age of the boat, not one is cracked or broken. These days, prime white oak for timbers could be difficult or impossible to secure, necessitating substitutes that would need to be increased somewhat in section to ensure adequate strength. If bending stock of any sort is unobtainable, it would be possible to use glued-up, laminated ribs or timbers—if these were properly made.

Breasthook, thwart, and stern quarter knees in this boat are natural-crook hackmatack. Seasoned apple-limb crooks would make a handsome substitute, and were preferred by the old-time builders when they could get them. As a last resort, glued laminations would serve.

The mahogany used in the boat is high-grade Honduras with close, dense grain and rich, dark color. The stern transom, backrest, backrest cleats, stern bench, thwarts, supporting posts, risers, stretchers, oarlock pads, and sole trim or edging strips were all made from it. Pine was used for the end cleat under the bench and for the supporting crossbeam.

The screws originally used were brass, since this is what was obtainable when the boat was built. But bronze is far superior and should be used today.

Copper rivets through the laps and timbers are spaced on 2-inch centers. Precise spacing of the fasteners is critical for appearance in first-class work.

A cut nail of copper—parallel-sided one way and wedged-shaped the other—with a blunt, square end was used, but these are not generally available today. The square end punched through the hot oak timbers without the splitting that sometimes results when sharply pointed nails are not bored for first.

Boats were planked right side up, which permitted the builder to rivet the laps without assistance as the planking was put on strake by strake. After the planking was completed, holes for riveting the timbers were carefully located and bored in the laps, and the points of the nails were inserted. These were driven as the hot timbers were bent in. Set up in this manner, timbering could be carried out as a one-man operation.

Today, nails for riveting the laps should not be too large. A number 13 copper-wire nail and a number 14 burr will be about right. The burr should fit tightly, both to hug the nail and to hold it in place for riveting after it is driven down with the burr set.

A sloppy fit is no good. The larger, dished, European-type roves are unacceptable for this job because they produce a heavy, clumsy appearance.

Nailheads should lie flat and flush with the surface of the planking in varnished work. If necessary, they can be brushed with a flat file in finishing. Care must be taken in hammering to avoid denting the soft cedar, although sponging the wood afterward with boiling water will bring the dents back if they are not too deep.

Larger nails—number 12s or even number 11s—are required for riveting in the inwales, breasthook, and knees. Screws should be large enough, but not

oversize: ⅞-inch number 8s through the hood ends of the planking into the oak stem; 1¼-inch number 8s through the after ends of the planking into the mahogany transom; 1½-inch number 10s through the thwarts and stern bench into the risers and supporting cleats; ¾-inch number 6s through the sole into timbers; number 10s from the stretchers through the sole into the timbers; 1¼-inch number 10s through the keel batten into the keel; and number 10s through the stern transom into the sternpost, although number 12s could be used here.

Wherever the wood is thick enough to hold plugs without undue reduction of strength, screw fastenings in a bright boat should be plugged.

The following references are keyed to the accompanying diagrams.

15. *Mahogany posts supporting thwarts and stern bench:* Turned from 1-inch square stock. Delicate appearance desirable.

16. *Stern bench:* Mahogany, ¾ inch thick. Cut to curve as diagramed. Under edge chamfered as shown for appearance of lightness. The outside is brought flush with the inner surfaces of the timbers without notching around them as is done with the ends of the center and forward thwarts. Screw fastenings plugged.

17. *Beam supporting stern bench:* Lower edge cut to ornamental shape as shown. Pine, 3¼ inches by ¾ inch.

18. *Cleat strip supporting ends of stern bench:* Screwed to inner face of stern transom. Pine, 2 inches by ¾ inch.

19. *Stern transom:* Mahogany of ¾-inch finished thickness. Shape developed from the lines. Screw-fastened to the sternpost and plugged.

20. *Sternpost:* Oak, sided 1¼ inches. Fastened to keel with two ¼-inch bronze drifts.

21. *Stern quarter knees:* Hackmatack, sided 1 inch and molded as diagramed.

22. *Cleats to hold bottom of backrest:* Mahogany, fastened with number 8 screws and not plugged.

23. *Oarlock pads:* Mahogany, ¾ inch thick and beveled as shown. Space underneath, between inwale and planking, filled with solid reinforcement from timber to timber. Note that the ends are slightly curved for appearance.

24. *Oarlock sockets:* Set in flush with the top of the pads.

25. *Stretchers (foot braces):* Located 22 inches aft of the rowing thwarts' after edges. Mahogany, sided ¾

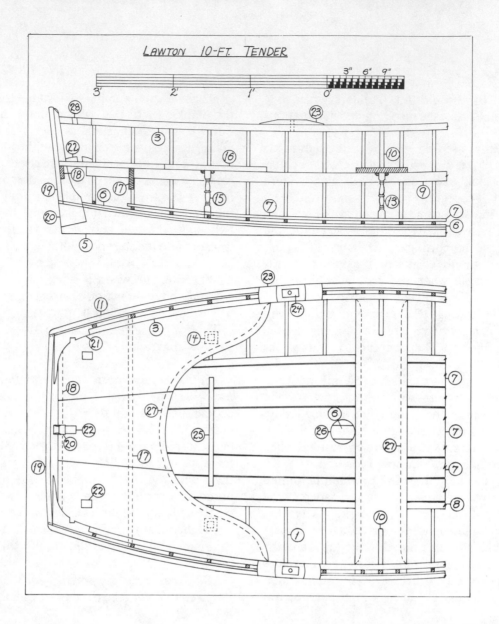

Lawton 10-Ft. Tender

inch, 1 inch high. Tapered and rounded at the ends. Screw fastenings plugged.

26. A 3½-inch-diameter hole cut through the sole for sponging out the bottom.

27. *Edges of the rowing thwarts and the stern bench:* Chamfered underneath to one-half full thickness and a 1-inch width for appearance of lightness.

28. Notches in stern quarter knees for backrest.

29. *Backrest:* Mahogany, ¾ inch, shaped as diagramed. Reinforcing strips on the back, held with oval-headed wood screws.

Planking widths are measured on the outside of the boat, minus the width of the ⅜-inch laps, except at the sheer. Widths on the stem: garboard (8½ inches back from extreme tip), 3½ inches; number 2, 2¼ inches; number 3, 2¼ inches; number 4, 2 inches; number 5,

1¾ inches; number 6, 1¹³/₁₆ inches; number 7, 1⁹/₁₆ inches; number 8, 1½ inches; number 10, 2⅜ inches.

Planking widths on outside of planking, minus laps, measured amidships: garboard, 3⅝ inches; number 2, 3⅝ inches; number 3, 3⅝ inches; number 4, 3¼ inches; number 5, 2¾ inches; number 6, 2⅞ inches; number 7, 2¾ inches; number 8, 2⅝ inches; number 9, 2⅝ inches; number 10, 3¾ inches.

Planking widths on outside of planking, minus laps, measured on the stern transom: garboard, 3¼ inches; number 2, 3¹/₁₆ inches; number 3, 2¹/₁₆ inches; number 4, 2⁷/₁₆ inches; number 5, 2⁵/₁₆ inches; number 6, 2¼ inches; number 7, 1⅞ inches; number 8, 2 inches; number 9, 1¹³/₁₆ inches; number 10, 2½ inches.

These planking widths need not be followed precisely. Some slight adjustments may be necessary to secure fair planking lines. As a general rule for clinker planking, plank widths narrow as side curve increases, so that the laps may be closed.

9

SEA BRIGHT SKIFF

One of our most distinctive small fishing boats is the Jersey sea skiff, or Sea Bright skiff, as it is also called. It takes its name from the area where it originated: Sea Bright, New Jersey, on the southern half of the barrier beach that constitutes the Sandy Hook peninsula, just across the bay and south from New York City.

The surrounding waters have always been known for their abundance of fish. But it was not until the mid 1840s that a local fishing industry sprang up there and fishermen took up part-time residence in shacks and tents among the sand dunes of the barrier beach during the fishing season, which lasted from May through November.

In 1868, according to one account, "fifty-five men and boys—all fishermen..." were living at Nauvoo, as Sea Bright was first called. Twenty years later, due to the active demand for fresh fish from the expanding population of New York City, the Sea Bright fishery was flourishing. A guidebook printed in 1889 estimated that there were 250 boats with crews of two men each based at Sea Bright. The average "fare" of fish per day per boat was 150 pounds, making an aggregate daily total of 37,500 pounds, or 4,575,000 pounds from June 1 to October 1—by no means an insignificant part of burgeoning Manhattan's diet, even when these numbers are substantially discounted. "Sea Bright," the guidebook continued, "has been a fishing center for about fifty years. The population is a mixed one, nearly all nationalities being represented, among them Scandinavians and Negroes being prominent."

Fishing in small boats off exposed beaches where considerable surf is frequently encountered requires a special kind of boat. It must be burdensome yet buoyant, with ample "lift" and sheer at either end. Flat

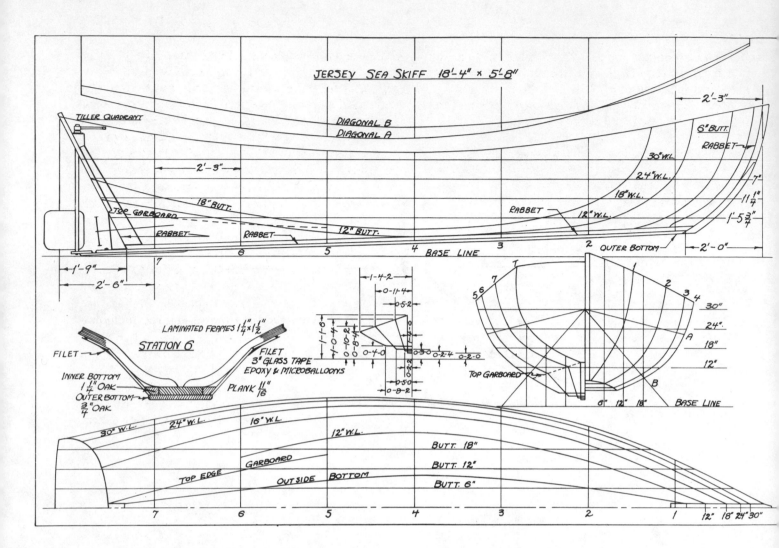

JERSEY SEA SKIFF 18'-4" x 5'-8"		STEM	1	2	3	4	5	6	7	T
HEIGHTS	SHEER	3-11-4	3-6-0	3-1-0	2-10-0	2-8-4	2-9-0	2-10-6	3-2-0	3-7-2
	OUTSIDE BOTTOM	0-8-1	0-8-0	0-7-0	0-5-6	0-5-0	0-4-0	0-3-1	0-2-5	0-2-0
	BUTT. 6"		1-1-6	0-7-0	0-5-6	0-5-0	0-4-0	0-7-7	1-0-5	1-3-4
	BUTT. 12"		2-1-6	0-10-3	0-7-0	0-5-6	0-6-1	0-10-3	1-3-0	1-7-1
	BUTT. 18"			1-4-1	0-10-3	0-8-6	0-9-6	1-1-4	1-6-4	2-1-2
HALF-BREADTHS	SHEER	0-1-2	1-3-0	2-1-1	2-7-0	2-9-6	2-10-0	2-8-0	2-3-6	1-9-2
	OUTSIDE BOTTOM	0-1-2	0-1-6	0-6-0	0-9-0	0-10-0	0-8-3	0-5-2	0-2-3	0-1-4
	W.L. 12"	0-1-2	0-4-7	1-2-1	1-8-5	1-11-0	1-9-3	1-3-2	0-5-1	0-1-4
	W.L. 18"	0-1-2	0-8-5	1-7-3	2-2-2	2-4-6	2-3-5	2-0-2	1-5-4	0-10-3
	W.L. 24"	0-1-2	0-11-3	1-10-1	2-4-7	2-7-4	2-7-0	2-4-4	1-11-2	1-5-1
	W.L. 30"	0-1-2	1-1-2	2-0-0	2-6-4	2-9-3	2-9-1	2-6-7	2-1-7	1-8-3
	DIAGONAL A	0-1-3	1-0-6	1-11-0	2-5-2	2-7-6	2-7-2	2-4-7	2-0-1	1-6-7
	DIAGONAL B	0-2-0	1-2-2	1-10-7	2-2-6	2-4-1	2-3-1	1-11-6	1-7-4	1-3-7
DIAGONAL A 2'-6" ABOVE BASE LINE. OUT 2'-0" ON 24" W.L. DIAG. B 2'-6" ABOVE B.L.										
OUT 2'-2" ON B.L. OFFSETS MEASURED IN FEET, INCHES & EIGHTHS TO OUTSIDE OF PLANKING										

floors are required for the loaded craft to take the beach and to remain upright when the swells recede, leaving it high and dry.

The 1889 guidebook offers this description of the boats in use at Sea Bright at that time:

> Their fishing boats are fourteen and one-half and fifteen feet long, designed for two men, although there is a one-man boat of thirteen feet....The boats are all made by builders in the vicinity and cost eighty-five dollars. The frame is cedar, and the sheathing of oak [*sic*], with coppered keels. Each boat weighs about three hundred pounds and is easily handled by two men....The boat is rigged with jib and mainsail, and if there is any wind the fishermen sail out to the grounds. The boat is then anchored and the sails wrapped around the mast, which is unshipped.
>
> There are no ropes except the main and jib sheets, and no steering apparatus, the course being made by an oar. A primitive and simple centerboard, which is taken out when necessary, is dropped when the boat is sailed. The fishing grounds are by no means limited, and the fishermen go from one to fifteen miles away, as they deem best.

I believe whoever wrote this was not a boatbuilder. Surely, the frame was oak and the "sheathing"—that is, planking—was cedar.

A fuller and more informed description of these early boats is to be found in Peter J. Guthorn's *The Sea Bright Skiff and Other Jersey Shore Boats* Rutgers University Press, 1971. Guthorn makes the early skiffs about 15 feet long with a 5-foot beam and a U-shaped transom raked about 30 degrees.

Below the transom, the wide after ends of the garboards are twisted so that they stand vertically in order to fasten against the sternpost. This produces what has been called a *reverse chine*, which runs for several feet forward of the stern before gradually dying out toward the midsection in the normal rounded curve of the side.

Instead of a solid skeg or deadwood aft, the space between the after ends of the two garboards is hollow. Sometimes called a *hollow skeg*, this space is a feature that later facilitated the installation of the inboard engine. In the old skiffs, Guthorn states, the width of the plank bottom, which took the place of a keel, was commonly one-third the beam of the boat, although this was not always adhered to.

In the beginning, these boats were frequently referred to as dories. In fact, in shape and construction there was little difference at first between these Jersey shore boats and contemporary New England dories and wherries. The Maine salmon wherry, surviving down to the present time, has the same reverse chine and "planked-up," or hollow, skeg. There can be no doubt that all three of these 19th-century fishing work boats—Jersey beach skiffs, New England wherries, and dories—originated from a common source: the 18th-century Colonial bateau, developed for military use during the French and Indian Wars, when thousands were built.

When the gasoline engine became available around 1900, it was immediately adopted by fishermen along the Jersey shore, and the Sea Bright skiff underwent a marked change. In general, the shape and construction remained much the same, but power skiffs were considerably enlarged, and the sailing rig, including the centerboard, was discarded.

In August 1915, *The Rudder* published lines and a construction plan by Roger M. Haddock for a motorized skiff. These were taken from some skiffs then being built by Huff Brothers, Pleasure Bay, Long Branch, New Jersey. The following descriptive item accompanied the drawings:

> All along the coast of New Jersey, with a few on the Long Island shore and others extending well down the Atlantic Coast, where landings have been made on the sandy beaches, may be found the New Jersey or Sea Bright skiff. It is a boat better adapted to the use of fishermen in those particular localities than the dory or even the Norwegian pram, which it somewhat resembles. Their usual length is from 18 to 30 feet, with a flat floor slightly curving. Before the advent of the gasoline engine, they were equipped with single sprit sails or with a sail and small jib and, with a centerboard pretty well forward, would work to windward in very rough water and half a gale. In landing on the beach with fares of fish in a heavy swell, it is an unusual thing for a boat to get away from the willing hands of those who rush down into the surf to haul her out above the wash or reach of the next swell. Being very full aft, they are burdensome and lift with a sea.
>
> In no class of working boats has the gasoline engine been so willingly received as in the New Jersey skiffs. As usually installed, the flywheel is protected by a circular casing and the engine itself is covered by a removable hatch. The shaft runs low; a two-bladed wheel is used and so fastened that the blades are athwartship when the engine is on low center. When

landing on the beach the wheel is protected by being out of the way as much as possible. Engines of 2½ h.p. are used for the smaller sizes and for the larger, rarely over 5½ or 6 h.p.

The boat for which lines and offsets are printed in this chapter is very similar to this Long Branch boat, but it is not the same. Rather, it was built some years later and used in Great South Bay off the south shore of Long Island. Its length of 18 feet is at the lower end of the 18-to-30-foot range mentioned in *The Rudder*.

It would not be difficult to enlarge this boat, if so desired. In fact, it would be quite easy. The simplest way would be to cut the hull at station 4 and insert 2 or 3 extra feet between the two portions. The two end portions would not be disturbed or changed in the slightest. No fairing of the lines would be required.

Another way, which would require some fairing and a bit more manipulation of the lines, would be to enlarge the flat plank bottom by both lengthening and widening it, but retaining the same curved outline. The stem, transom, and sectional shapes at the various stations would not be changed, except perhaps to deepen the hull by 1, 2, or even 3 inches in the case of a much larger boat.

The lines given here are to the outside of the planking, although these skiffs were almost always clinker-planked. In clinker planking it is usual to give the offset measurements to the *inside* of the planking so that it will not be necessary to deduct the planking thickness when making the molds.

In a workboat like this the difference is not significant, as it would be in a racing yacht. Although the offsets here are to the outside, nothing would be gained by deducting the plank thickness, either for clinker or carvel planking.

All in all, because of its hull shape this is a relatively simple boat to plank, with the exception, perhaps, of the reverse chine at the after end of the garboard. There are various ways of handling this reverse chine, but I am suggesting that the seam between the garboard and the plank above be treated as a carvel seam; that it be beveled to fit tight; that it be covered with a 3-inch width of glass tape set in epoxy; and that it be finished smooth with a filet of epoxy and microballoons put on as a thick paste. This is simple and easy to do, and it makes a very strong, permanently tight joint in this critical place.

Above this the planking could be carvel, but not thinner than 1¹⁄₁₆ inch, finished in order to hold the caulking. Conventional lapstrake planking probably would be easier and better. This could be done with ½-inch plywood, with the curved strakes gotten out of regular 8-foot panels and the short sections spliced to give the required lengths.

Splices are scarfed 12 times the thickness of the planking stock—in this case, 6 inches long for ½-inch plywood. Planed to make a tight fit and glued with epoxy, such splices are just as strong as the original ply, and if the required curves are laid out carefully on the 4-by-8-foot panels there is little waste. Considering the high cost and the difficulty of obtaining good-quality sawn lumber for planking stock, marine plywood used in this way could be the best and cheapest approach.

If good white-oak bending stock for timbers is available, such framing is certainly to be considered. A good framing job of steam-bent oak can hardly be improved upon. In some cases, however, suitable oak is simply not to be had. Should this be the case, I suggest making up laminated frames from thin strips of spruce glued with epoxy. Such laminated frames were used for the Herreshoff rowing boat built at Mystic Seaport in the spring of 1980, and the process is fully described in Chapter 1 of this book.

The process is not difficult, and the frames so made have proved more than satisfactory in every respect. There are several advantages. The frames can be made exactly to the required shape. There is no "pullback." Set up on the flat plank bottom, they take the place of molds, and the planking is fastened directly to them as it is put on. No ribbands, no fairing, nothing of that sort is needed.

Further, spruce is stiff and extremely strong for its weight. It also holds fastenings quite well—much better than pine, for instance. And because it is light in weight, a larger section can be used to get the equivalent strength of oak frames, without adding undue weight in the topsides. Finally, the numerous glue lines separating the thin laminates go a long way to prevent absorption of water, obviating much of the danger of rot.

The stem is like a dory stem: It is not rabbeted but rather is made up of an inner and an outer part. The latter consists of two pieces sawn out of straight-grained plank and scarfed together when they are put on, after the boat has been planked and the ends of the planking faired off to the curve of the inner stem. The inner stem can be sawn out of ordinary plank, but it could also be laminated like the frames.

The inner bottom is 1¼-inch oak, nearly straight fore and aft, with only a hint of rockered curve in the bow end. Somewhat more than 20 inches wide amidships, it will require two, and possibly three, planks pieced together. The edges are beveled to conform to the angle of the garboards, which cover them and are nailed to them, exactly as in dory construction. The projecting bottom edges of the garboard are planed off flat to conform to the underside of the bottom plank.

After this surface has been well painted with antifouling paint, and coated with bedding as well, the outer bottom of ¾-inch oak is put on with screws, which enable it to be removed easily should replacement because of beach wear become necessary. A layer of Irish felt between the inner and outer bottoms would not be a bad idea.

As shown, this boat is suitable for the installation of a small inboard engine. The hull has been given enough draft to get the propeller underwater even when the boat runs light, yet the propeller and rudder do not project below the bottom to interfere with beaching. This boat can be run up on a beach, will sit upright, and can be easily hauled up with rollers; no cradle is needed.

The engine will be located well aft under a small engine box and behind a thwart-high, watertight bulkhead. Although no fuel tank is drawn, it might best be located under the short section of deck forward. Narrow waterways and low coamings will run along the sides of the boat. Tiller lines leading from the rudder quadrant aft will run underneath to a small wheel or stick located against the coaming on the port side amidships.

Considerable room would be lost by the addition of a centerboard trunk. Because of that, if a sailing version is desired, some may want to lengthen the boat by 2 or 3 feet, as already suggested. There should be no hesitation in doing this, since it is easily accomplished and a better seaboat—as well as one of greater capacity—will result.

For an engine I have chosen a small diesel, in accordance with popular trends of the day. There are several makes now being distributed, any of which would be suitable. Some owners prefer one make, some another, but as far as I can determine, no brand has demonstrated overwhelming superiority.

I finally picked the smallest Yanmar, the 1GM 7.5 h.p. model. It is compact and light (dry weight 154.5 pounds), it is moderately priced as diesels go, and

Yanmar parts and service are widely available, an important consideration. I might have settled instead on a Norwegian Sabb, a fine engine of long-recognized superiority. For a time I toyed with the idea of installing an old-fashioned one- or two-cylinder make-and-break or jump-spark gasoline marine engine. But I gave that up when I found that engines of this type with power equivalent to the diesels were much larger and at least twice as heavy; that they require oversized propellers, which might present problems in a boat intended for easy beaching; and that they cost approximately as much. The safety of diesel over gasoline also influenced my choice.

Finally, let me repeat: One is not necessarily tied to Yanmar. Any of a number of similar small diesels could be installed with a minimum of alteration.

The closed engine compartment has several features that bear mentioning, since these are generally not found in small powerboats. This compartment is closed off from the rest of the boat by a ½-inch-thick plywood bulkhead extending from side to side and fastened to the bent-oak frames 11 inches forward of station 6. This bulkhead makes the compartment watertight up to the top of the sill of the slide opening. No water from the central portion of the boat can flow aft past this bulkhead into the after one-third (nearly) of the hull.

Ample (which is not to say generous) access to the engine is provided by a hatch opening through the bulkhead and deck that closes with a standard yacht-type "slide." When the slide is shut and the drop boards or closure boards are in place, the engine compartment is completely enclosed—and therefore impervious to the weather—and it can be locked. Having under lock and key the engine and such gear as one wishes to keep aboard the boat is increasingly desirable today because of the thievery and vandalism now plaguing the waterfront. I do not claim that access could not be gained with an ax or sledgehammer, but under ordinary circumstances security is assured.

If a tight bulkhead were to be raised forward just under the overhang of the deck and as high as the thwarts or slightly higher, all loose water taken over the side in heavy weather would be confined to the central portion of the boat for convenient bailing; at the same time it would be restrained in some measure from surging back and forth as the boat pitched. I have not shown this bulkhead in the drawings, but it is well worth considering. It would not be difficult to install,

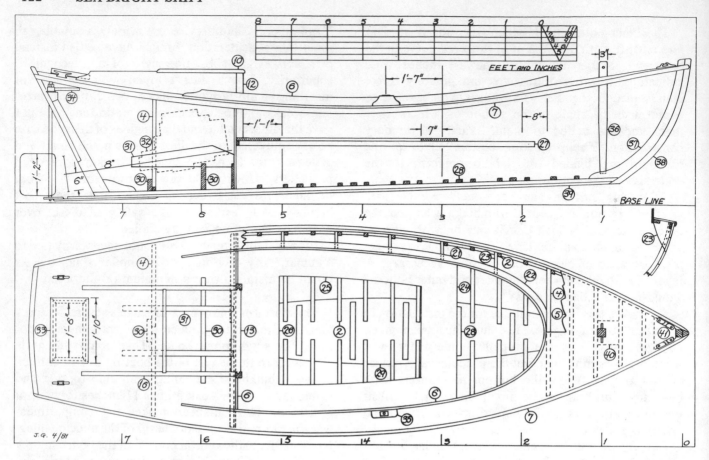

would provide dry storage under the deck in the peak, and would not be in the way.

Every aspect of boatbuilding has been hit hard by inflation, but none worse than fastenings. I like bronze wood screws, but their price, especially in small lots and at retail, is so ridiculous that I no longer consider them a possibility. In many places bronze annular (ring) nails are an acceptable substitute for bronze screws. They don't come cheaply, but they are still substantially less expensive than screws. My experience has been that their holding power diminishes markedly in water-soaked oak and probably in all thoroughly saturated wood. This suggests that wire size should be generous and that when bored for, holes should be no larger than is needed to prevent splitting. In soft wood, frequently, no preboring at all is needed.

If this boat is carvel-planked with $^{11}/_{16}$-inch finished plank thickness on 1¼-inch oak frames, I suggest that 1½-inch number 8 bronze ring nails be used, set below the surface deep enough to putty, although 1¾-inch nails could be used without breaking through the inside

of the frames. Certainly longer number 8s can be driven through the lower edge of the garboards into the inner oak bottom—2½ inches would be about right. If the hull is clinker-planked, copper rivets would be needed between the frames for the laps, with ring nails into the frames and bottom. A limited offering of copper clinch nails is now on the market.

Clinch nails are not as neat as rivets, nor do they have quite the same holding power as well-peened rivets, but they serve adequately for some construction. Unfortunately, copper has nearly attained precious-metal status, and how long we can continue to put it into boats if its price keeps rising is something to consider.

Old-fashioned hot-dipped galvanized iron or steel fastenings generously coated with honest-to-goodness zinc are not to be sneezed at, if they can still be found. The electroplated stuff covered with a wash a few molecules thick is worthless, despite being pretty to look at.

This is a small boat that will be out of the water, and therefore partly dried out some of the time. In addition,

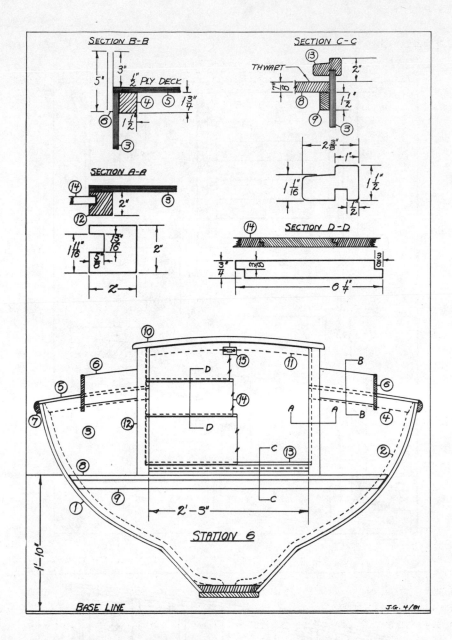

SECTION B-B

SECTION C-C

THWART

SECTION A-A

SECTION D-D

STATION 6

2'-3"

1'-10"

BASE LINE

J.G. 4/81

there won't be all kinds of electrical equipment sending currents through the structure. Both factors should keep electrolysis from being a problem. Thus, I see no danger in a judicious combination of ferrous and nonferrous fastenings. Surely it is all right to use galvanized fastenings above the waterline, in the interior, and wherever the structure does not become thoroughly soaked. In fresh water, galvanized fastenings can be used throughout.

Glue is a great adjunct to metal fastenings, sharing much of the load with them and greatly strengthening the hull. Where it can be applied to joints and meeting surfaces, I highly recommend it—either a standard epoxy formulation or Aerolite 306 urea-formaldehyde. Avoid quick-setting epoxies. Too often they do not give the builder time enough to make desirable adjustments and to do the job properly.

The following numbered explanations correspond to numbers on the drawings:

1. *Planking:* Carvel, $^{11}/_{16}$ inch thick, finished. Northern white pine, white cedar, juniper, cypress, Douglas fir, or Port Orford cedar. Fastened with number 8 bronze ring nails. Alternate planking: Clinker, $^9/_{16}$ inch thick if sawn lumber and ½ inch thick if plywood.

2. *Frames:* Steam-bent oak, 1¼ inches by 1⅜ inches. The lower ends can be split a short way with a saw to facilitate their taking the sharp bend required to land on the bottom. Alternate: Glued laminated frames, 1¼ inches by 1½ inches. Spruce or Douglas fir.

3. *Plywood bulkhead:* Half-inch marine-grade fir plywood.

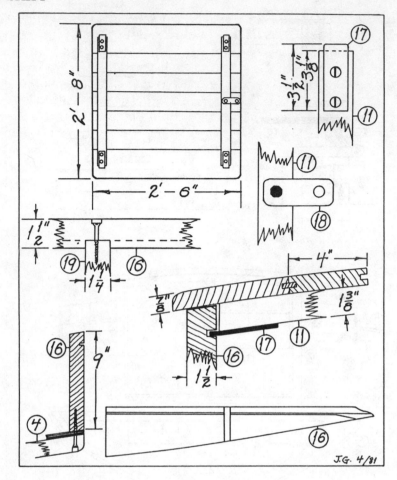

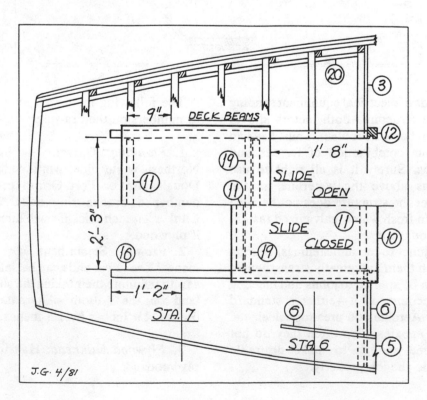

4. *Deck beams:* Oak, molded 1¾ inches, sided 1½ inches. Can be laminated spruce or Douglas fir. Camber: Rise amidships approximately 6 inches in 6 feet.

5. *Deck:* Half-inch marine-grade fir plywood. Ring-nail fastened.

6. *Coaming:* Steam-bent oak, finished ½ inch by 5 inches. Can be glue-laminated to shape using several thin layers of mahogany.

7. *Half-oval trim:* Oak, ¾ inch thick, 1¾ inches wide amidships tapering to 1⅜ inches at the ends.

8. *Thwarts and side benches:* White pine, ⅞ inch to ¹⁵/₁₆ inch thick.

9. *Thwart beam:* Pine, 1½ inches by ⅞ inch, nailed and glued to plywood bulkhead.

10. *Slide:* Top, mahogany or pine, ⅞ inch thick. Inside strips, 4 inches wide. Outside strips, 5 inches. Splined as diagramed, fitted tight, and glued. Screwed to slide beams. Holes plugged. Pine painted; mahogany can be bright.

11. *Slide beams:* Oak, 1⅜ inches molded, 1¾ inches sided. Camber: 1½-inch rise in 3 feet.

12. *Stiles for bulkhead opening:* Oak, 2 inches by 2 inches. Grooved as diagramed to take ends of drop, or closure, boards.

13. *Sill or stool:* Oak, shaped as diagramed and fitted tight at the ends to prevent leakage. Ends left long on inside to bulkhead to fasten to it for extra support.

14. *Drop, or closure, boards:* Pine or mahogany as diagramed. Should slip easily up and down in the stile grooves or channels without being sloppy. Edges are rabbeted as diagramed to shed rainwater when closed.

15. *Lock plate:* ⅛-inch brass as diagramed. Holed to receive brass padlock hasp when the slide cover is closed.

16. *Slide runners:* Oak, 1½ inches thick and shaped as diagramed. Must fit the deck perfectly; glued to deck and securely fastened from the inside through both decking and deck beams. First, the deck beams are installed full length across the boat. Next, the plywood deck covering is put on except for the aperture under the slide, but without cutting the deck beams extending across this aperture. These are not cut out until the runners are in place, fitted, and fastened.

17. *Brass end pieces:* ³/₁₆-inch flat brass, 3½ inches long by 1½ inches wide, fastened to the ends of the slide beams with two 1-inch number 10 or number 12 wood screws. These end pieces slide in the grooves in the inside face of the runners, holding the slide on.

They should slip easily without being sloppy. Both the fore and aft slide beams have them. To remove the slide, remove the end pieces on the forward beam. Push the slide cover back as far as it will go, lifting it enough to clear the slide end beam between the runners. The grooves in the runners are widened at the ends to permit this. You can then slip off and remove the slide cover without unscrewing the brass end pieces on the after slide beam.

18. *Padlock hasp:* ³/₁₆-inch flat brass or hardened stainless. Pivots on its bolt into the forward slide beam.

19. *Slide end beam:* Oak. Ends are let into the runners as the beam is screwed and glued to the plywood deck for a watertight fit. Otherwise there will be leakage at the after end of the slide. There are small limbers through the runners for drainage just aft of this end beam.

20. *Clamp:* Oak, ⅞ inch by 1½ inches. Nailed to the frames to support the ends of the deck beams at the fore and aft ends of the boat.

21. *Sheer filler pieces:* Pine, ⅞ inch by 2 inches. Fitted between the timberheads from the after bulkhead to the first forward deck beam. Nailed and glued to the inside of the sheer plank. These provide support for the edge of the side decking, which is glued and nailed to them.

22. *Coaming backup:* Pine, ⅞ inch by 2 inches. This can be in short lengths sawn to shape and spliced together. Must fit tight against the coaming, to which it is glued and nailed. Supports the coaming and also the edge of the decking, to which it is glued and nailed. Tight fit for watertightness.

23. *Side-decking supports:* Two thicknesses of ½-inch plywood decking (scraps) glued together. Ten inches long on the frames, to which they are glued and nailed. Notched as diagramed to take the coaming backup (see *22*).

24. *Forward thwart:* ⅞- to ¹⁵/₁₆-inch pine, 1 foot wide, located as diagramed. One foot ten inches above baseline.

25. *Side bench:* Pine, same thickness as thwarts and securely cleated to them on the underside. Supported on the outboard edge by the thwart riser (see *27*).

26. *After thwart:* ⅞- to ¹⁵/₁₆-inch pine, 1 foot 2 inches wide, 1 foot 10 inches above baseline. Glued to thwart beam (see *9*) and to plywood bulkhead for watertight fit.

27. *Thwart riser:* Pine, ⅞ inch by 1¾ inches. Nailed to the frames.

28. *Bottom cross cleats:* Oak, 1½ inches by 2

inches. Nailed to the bottom and positioned as diagramed. One foot six inches on centers the full length of the bottom.

29. *Inside bottom:* Oak, 1¼ inches thick, three boards wide.

30. *Floors under engine beds:* Oak, 1½ inches thick.

31. *Engine beds:* Oak, 2 inches thick.

32. *Engine:* Yanmar 1GM 7.5 h.p. marine diesel.

33. *After hatch:* Pine throughout. Keep as low as possible. Maximum height need not be more than 1¾ inches overall. Provides access to rudder quadrant and space aft of engine. Must be watertight and have secure closure.

34. *Rudder quadrant:* Ten inches/twelve inches.

35. *Rowlock base:* Slightly higher than the coaming, as shown.

36. *Forward bitt:* Oak, 3 inches square, tapering below the deck to 2 inches where it lets into the base of the stem; ½-inch bronze pin, 6 inches long.

37. *Inner stem:* Oak, sided 2½ inches and molded as dimensioned in the lines plan at the beginning of this chapter. Could be scaled with sufficient accuracy from the profile view printed herewith. Since the outer stem is put on after planking, as in dory construction, no rabbeting is required. Can be sawn from a straight plank, but one with some shape or curve is better.

38. *Outer stem:* Oak, in two pieces as diagramed. Should fit perfectly against the inner stem and the hood ends of the planking. To be glued and spiked in place.

39. *Outer bottom:* Oak, ¾ inch to ⅞ inch thick. Seams should overlap seams in inner bottom. Nailed in place with a nonhardening, antifouling bottom compound between the two layers. This acts as a shoe to take the wear from landing on beaches. Easily renewed when worn. Nails should have substantial heads to facilitate pulling.

40. *Blocking for bitt:* Oak, ⅞ inch. Fits tightly between deck beams and is glued to underside of deck.

41. *Breasthook block:* Oak, thick enough (1¼ inches to 1½ inches) to give solid fastening for the bow chocks. Glued to underside of deck.

The drawing on page 122 showing a profile and plan view of the construction should be accurate enough to scale. A more detailed dimensioning of the engine installation, rudder, steering layout, and so forth is provided below.

The sectional view at station 6, showing the after bulkhead, slide, and entrance into the engine compartment, was drawn before I decided to move the bulkhead forward one frame, or approximately 10 inches. The dimensional changes were so slight that I did not consider it necessary to redraw the sectional view.

One of the drawings on the opposite page shows a simple arrangement for steering, one much used formerly for small-displacement launches; the other gives sectional views through the hull in the way of the engine bed. These sectional views are intended to be self-explanatory. It may be worth mentioning, however, that while the engine-bed stringers *(31)* are let into the solid floor *(30)* at station 6, 10 inches forward of station 7 these stringers are notched to fit *over* the bent frames *(2)* without cutting into them.

In determining the height and the slope of the engine-bed stringers, I had to take a number of competing requirements into account and make adjustments to satisfy them all. If the boat is to be gotten on and off the beach easily, the propeller should not extend below the line of the bottom. Yet the wheel must be submerged when in operation, and the deeper the better.

Although the specification sheet the manufacturer furnished for the engine puts the maximum installation angle at 15 degrees, the American distributor recommends a 12-degree maximum. Here I have been able to keep it down to 8 degrees to provide for variations in the angle of trim under special or emergency operating conditions. Because of the sea skiff's hollow garboards at the after end of the engine-bed stringers, these stringers cannot be placed as close to the bottom as would be possible if there were more width here.

A number 2 10-inch standard wheel mounted on the port side as shown should be ample for easy steering. The bent tiller arm will drop the steering cable enough to clear the deck beams. Either a turnbuckle or a tension spring introduced at some convenient place in the steering-cable circuit is needed to take up any slack and to keep the cable taut. The bent tiller arm shown here replacing the tiller quadrant, as first detailed, is simpler, is easier to obtain and rig, and will work just as well, if not better.

The construction drawings presented earlier in this chapter do not show a fuel tank. The logical location would be forward under the foredeck. Depending on the shape and size of the tank selected, it might be necessary to replace the bitt *(36)* with a large deck

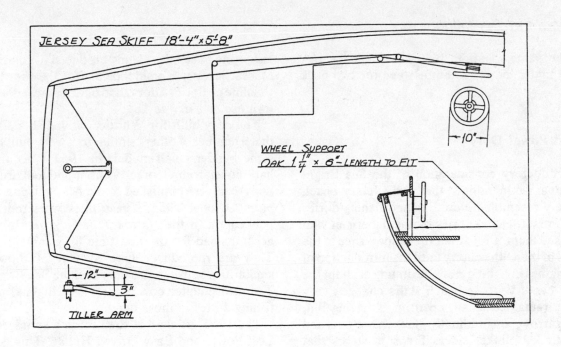

JERSEY SEA SKIFF 18'-4" x 5'-8"

WHEEL SUPPORT
OAK 1¼" x 6"—LENGTH TO FIT

10"

12"

3"

TILLER ARM

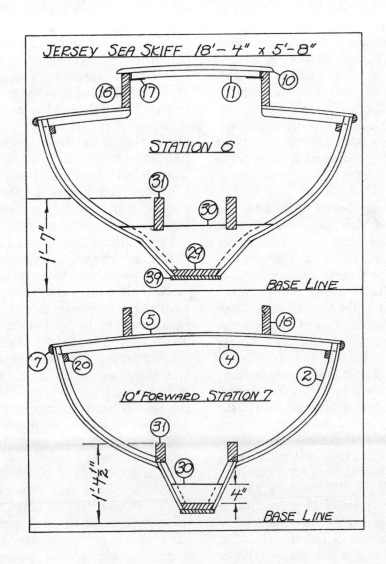

JERSEY SEA SKIFF 18'-4" x 5'-8"

16 17 11 10

STATION 6

31

30

29

39

1'-7"

BASE LINE

5 16

7 20 4 2

10" FORWARD STATION 7

31

30

1'-4½"

4"

BASE LINE

cleat in the same location, bolted through the oak block *(40)* under the deck and between the two deck beams.

Hammond Power Dory

In our introductory consideration of the Sea Bright skiff's origins, we mentioned that early Jersey beach skiffs closely resembled New England fishing dories and were, in fact, called dories by the fishermen who built and used them. From their first appearance in the early years of the 19th century until the introduction of gasoline engines in fishing craft, beginning at about the end of the century, these beach skiffs changed very little. They remained small, open boats having flat, relatively narrow, longitudinally planked bottoms and slightly rounded clinker sides. Transom sterns that narrowed toward the bottom made them virtually double-ended on the water.

But motors brought rapid and radical change. Skiffs got wider and bigger in a hurry, and some of them, it must be admitted, suffered in appearance, although from the standpoint of utility and seakeeping ability they proved more than adequate. Despite the clumsy appearance of some of these early power conversions, others were more expertly modeled, earning excellent reputations both as working boats and as dependable pleasure craft, a reputation the type retains to this day.

What happened to Jersey beach skiffs after the gasoline engine appeared also happened to New England fishing dories, except that early power dories were far more numerous and more widely used. Between 1900 and 1920 or thereabout, thousands of these power dories were to be found throughout the Northeast and as far west as the Great Lakes. They were easily the most numerous class of small power-boats then in use. Quantity builders such as Emmons in Swampscott, Toppan in Boston, and the Atlantic Company, makers of the Gurnet Dory, in Amesbury, Massachusetts, advertised widely. Other well-known builders, such as Chamberlain in Marblehead and the Cape Cod Dory Company in Wareham, catered more to local demand. There were also many small shops turning out the new craft on a limited custom basis.

One such builder was Jesse Hammond of Danversport, Massachusetts, who in 1904 built a 28-foot power dory in his Endicott Street shop for George Whittier of the same town. This dory, said to be capable of 9 m.p.h., was considered a "speedboat" at the time, being equipped with a 6 h.p. two-cylinder two-cycle Essex gas engine produced in nearby Lynn, Massachusetts. Hammond, one of the first to put a gasoline engine in a dory, had built a power dory for his own use as early as 1899.

The dory built for Whittier proved so satisfactory that a number of others similar to it were built from the same builder's half-model. In 1951 I acquired this half-model from George Whittier and took from it the lines that were published in the *Maine Coast Fisherman*, October 1955. These lines were redrawn for publication in the *National Fisherman*, July 1981, accompanied for the first time by a table of offsets. They are reproduced here by way of showing the similarities between this dory and the Sea Bright skiff. The next chapter covers the New England powered fishing dories in more depth.

The 1955 article was the first in a series on "Low Cost Power and Easy Driven Hulls." This dory was offered therein as a boat having an easily driven hull form that for its size was exceptionally economical of power as long as no attempt was made to exceed the optimum hull-length speed for a displacement hull.

This is an exceptionally easy hull to plank: There are no difficult shapes or bends of any sort. As I stated in the 1955 article, "The model shows specialized development of dory design. The round sides, the very narrow bottom and the hollow sections aft are unusual (in classic dory hulls). Whittier recalled that the hull was planked lapstrake and dory fashion, but with more numerous and narrower planks than is usual in smaller, typical dories—a departure necessitated by the size and shape of the hull."

This hull could be planked carvel just as well as clinker, as some might prefer to do. Cape Cod dories built at Wareham were planked thus. In general configuration, this Hammond power-dory hull is not too dissimilar to the smaller Jersey beach skiff that we have been considering. In fact, the same construction details worked out for the beach skiff could easily be adapted for the Hammond power dory. At the same time there would be wide latitude for individual preference in such matters as stem construction—for example, whether to stay with the classic two-part dory stem or choose a rabbeted stem instead. Likewise, a rabbeted sternpost with some exposed deadwood would be an alternative to covering the sternpost with the hood ends of the planking, dory fashion.

Because of the easy lines of the Hammond hull, boats built from the half-model can be made shorter or longer by as much as several feet without altering the basic shape and performance of the hull—simply decrease or increase the spacing between the central

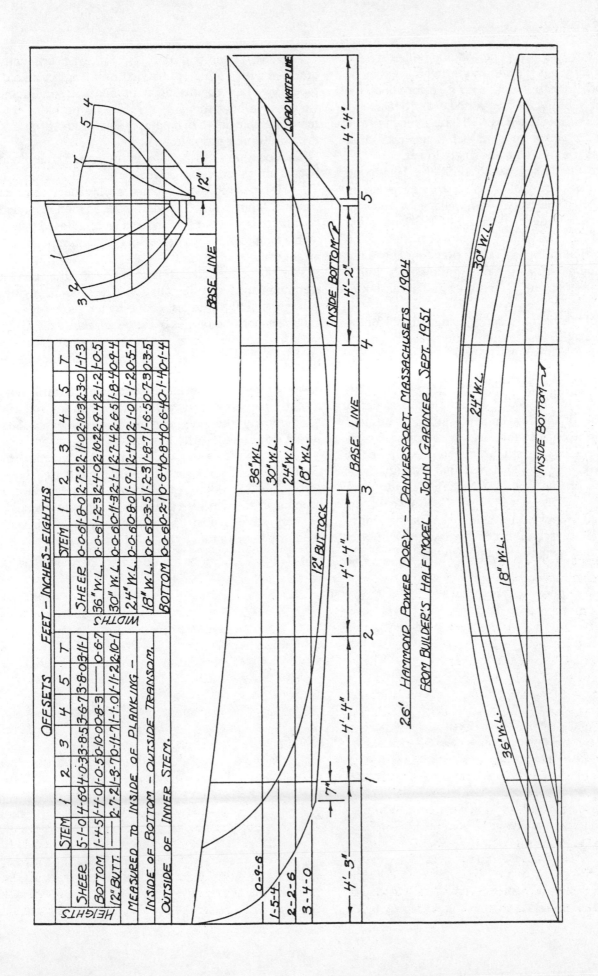

26' HAMMOND POWER DORY – DANVERSPORT, MASSACHUSETS 1904

FROM BUILDER'S HALF MODEL. JOHN GARDNER SEPT. 1951

molds. The bow and stern ends should be left strictly alone. Thus, although the half-model, which was made on a scale of 1 inch to 1 foot, is for a 26-foot boat, the boat built for Whittier, as mentioned, was 28 feet long. One 24 feet long might just as well have been built and would have proved a good model, I am confident, although less roomy and somewhat slower.

Much like the Jersey beach skiff, the Hammond power dory has deep, hollow garboards at the stern. This helps keep displacement low, making for excellent seakeeping performance. Because of the long, slim, easy lines of the Hammond hull, however, there is no abrupt transition in the lay of the planking above the hollow garboards aft, as there is in the beach skiff— one of the reasons the Hammond hull is easier to plank.

A principal reason for selecting a small diesel for the 18-foot beach skiff was its small, compact size and its comparatively light weight: only 154.5 pounds dry, with an overall length of 20.75 inches; height, 19.09 inches; and width, 16.14 inches. As I mentioned above, for the beach skiff, I had first considered installing one of the low-horsepower, slow-turning, old-type marine engines that originally powered such boats. Such engines are still produced in Nova Scotia and used by Canadian fishermen. The Atlantic two-cycle marine engine from Lunenburg Foundry and Engineering in Lunenburg, Nova Scotia comes to mind. Instead I decided on a lighter, faster-turning, modern small diesel in order to save weight and because it turns a smaller-diameter wheel.

For the Hammond dory, which was originally powered with a 6 h.p., old-style Essex engine, an old-type Canadian engine might be considered. Engine weight in a boat this size presents no problem, and there is ample depth of displacement for an 18-inch or even a 20-inch propeller.

The location of the engine in the larger Hammond boat is not as critical as it is in the 18-foot beach skiff. There is much more latitude for varying the placement to suit different interior arrangements. In the Hammond boat there is plenty of room for a small, closed cuddy with a couple of berths and even rudimentary cooking arrangements.

The 18-foot beach skiff is about as small as can be recommended for the installation of an inboard engine. A larger hull provides less economy but more options, and the superior qualities of the beach skiff's displacement hull become more apparent with some increase in size. As the need for fuel economy becomes more insistent, some people are certain to return to old-type, easily driven displacement hulls, which until very recently had almost passed from the boating scene.

Practically the only commercial builder of Sea Bright power skiffs who has managed to survive and who is still building in wood is Charles Hankins, 504 Grand Central Avenue, Box 7, Lavallette, New Jersey 08735. Although Hankins has adapted the beach skiff to meet his customers' demand for speed, he can still furnish the old-type, easily driven, economy beach craft.

· 10 ·

BOSTON FISHING POWER DORIES

At the beginning of this century, Boston was the largest fishing port in the United States. The city's fishing activity centered at T Wharf, where, according to an account in the *Fishing Gazette* of December 5, 1908, the local fleet of some 200 motorized Swampscott-model fishing dories tied up. Ranging in length from under 20 feet to nearly 30 feet, these dories were manned by hardy Sicilian fishermen, two and three men to a boat.

The Spartan requirements of power-dory fishing at the time tested both men and boats. An account of the risks and daily round of grinding toil was vividly reported in the *Gazette*:

Hard, constant usage is the lot of the Boston motorboat fishing fleet. Nothing but a screeching gale keeps them in port. Starting out at daybreak or before, the boats go down the north and south approaches a distance of 15 or 20 miles and set trawls for cod or haddock.

They are exposed to the full force of the Atlantic, and nothing but a reliable outfit has any right to take the chance they willingly accept. Returning to the pier after 2 P.M., the catch is sold, and the crews begin to bait trawls for the next set. That completed, they go to their homes for a little sleep or turn in on the boats.

During the flounder season, the trips are nearer home and the danger is not so great. For downright endurance, the torching of herring in the fall months tests motors most brutally. For 10 or 12 hours at a stretch, the machines are kept running, sometimes throttled to the slowest speed, then opened wide and as quickly shut down again, according to the movements of the schools of fish.

During the latter half of the 19th century, Boston's expanding immigrant populations of Irish and Italians

Above: *This photo taken in 1913 or 1914 shows the Sicilian powered fishing dory fleet at the head of South Dock, T Wharf, in Boston. (The Henry D. Fisher Collection, Mystic Seaport Museum)*
Opposite: *Another view of the "mosquito fleet." The fishermen are baiting their trawls. (Courtesy of The Society for the Preservation of New England Antiquities)*

required large quantities of fish. Fish was a large part of their traditional diet and was then both plentiful and cheap. Close by, abundant stocks of food fishes still frequented the waters of Massachusetts Bay.

For a time, the local fisheries that supplied the Boston market were dominated by Irish fishermen in their Paddy boats, sailing craft similar to the "hookers" they had been accustomed to in the old country. But toward the end of the century, as the new waves of Italian immigrants arrived, the Paddy boats succumbed to competition from Sicilian fishermen who, in the beginning, were not averse to rowing 15 to 20 miles a day in all kinds of weather.

These Sicilians adopted the round-sided Swampscott dory, developed in the town of that name on Boston's North Shore, and found these boats admirably suited to their needs. Eminently seaworthy and able, Swampscott dories both rowed and sailed well, could carry heavy loads, stood up to hard use, and were relatively cheap.

When the wind permitted, the fishermen sailed their dories; when it did not, oars came into play. Still, these craft were too dependent on the vagaries of the weather. Sometimes they did not make it back to port in time to command top prices for their fish, and in hot weather the lack of ice meant that the catch was not always in the best condition when boats finally did reach port.

Yachtsmen adopted the new gasoline motors first, and fishermen followed suit soon after. The changeover from sail was completed in a surprisingly brief time. Sails vanished from the Boston fishing fleet practically overnight. How this came about is described so well in the *Fishing Gazette* that I shall not presume to improve upon its narrative:

The first out-and-out motor fishing boat in Boston was a Swampscott dory fitted with a centerboard. It was a fast sailer and carried a crew of two men. Its owners got becalmed one day with a catch of cod and

haddock, which spoiled on their hands when the market was high. As they tossed and pitched in the doldrums down by Boston light, a little motorcraft slipped by and was soon out of sight in the direction of the city wharves.

The occupant of the motor-propelled boat was a yachtsman with moorings at South Boston. Within a day or two, he was hunted up by the fishermen, who sought all manner of information about his motor, its make and cost, which was cheerfully given, and the fishermen were filled brimful of helpful suggestions before they quitted the club float. The fishing dory was taken to a yard in East Boston, and a four-horsepower, two-cycle motor of the make-and-break type soon followed it.

The boatbuilder was somewhat at a loss to decide how best to install the motor, but he finally spiked a block of wood to the transom, bolted a skeg to the dory bottom, so as to give the propeller plenty of room, bored the shaft-hole at what he believed to be the proper pitch, and then fashioned oak foundations on which to lag the engine.

Considerable squinting was needed before the motor could be got in line with the shaft, and lots of shim pieces of wood were tucked under the base of the machine to get a fit. Finally, when everything was

declared to be right, and the exhaust pipe had been extended from a crude muffler through the side of the boat, the fishermen paid their bill of about $15, and the innovation was christened with Scotch as it splashed into the dock.

The older of the boat's owners grabbed the crank and essayed to start the motor. It didn't respond at first, so he got on his knees in front of it and began to spin the fly wheel with both hands. Suddenly it started and broke his wrist with the kick.

That modernized dory remained in the dock several weeks before an "expert" explained that it was the man's fault that he got hurt. He said the fisherman was altogether too reckless and ought not to have got on his knees to start a motor. He explained to the men the proper way to do the trick, got the engine running in fine form, gave a party of fishermen a spin down to the Graves, and from that day, makers of reliable gasoline motors have done a splendid business in supplying the Boston demand, and boats without number have been transformed from sail to motor in the same yard where the first craft discarded sail for an up-to-date pusher.

When the first motor fisherman got well into the harness, her owners' wives began to appear on the street in new dresses and wore smiles of contentment while promenading the North End of Boston, where

Old photographs of the dories at T Wharf give an idea of what the open cockpit (top) and decked-over (bottom) dories looked like from the outside; interior arrangements must be reconstructed from the few sources available. (The Henry D. Fisher Collection, Mystic Seaport Museum)

the Sicilians have their homes. The boat was a wonder in the way of earning money. She made two trips, sometimes three, while the sailboats were getting their fares to market.

A bigger success on a small scale never appeared in the harbor. It was no use for the old-fashioned craft to compete with the new-fangled boat. The immediate rush for motors sent manufacturers to their wits' end to keep up with the orders, and the same engine (Mianus) is in vogue today in larger sizes and with correspondingly more power.

Another contemporary publication, the *Nautical Gazette*, shows in its March 1, 1906 issue a photograph along with a lines plan and construction plan for a Camden Anchor–Rockland Machine Company power dory. The boat illustrated was 25 feet long and

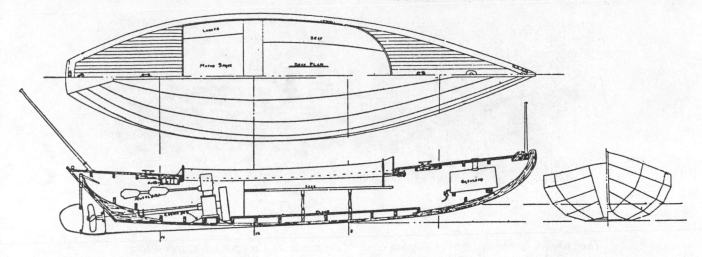

The Nautical Gazette *of March 1, 1906 featured this 25-footer, ruggedly built of pine over oak by Camden Anchor–Rockland Machine Company of Maine.*

had a beam of 6 feet. A 4½ h.p. single-cylinder three-port Knox engine (manufactured in Camden, Maine) produced a speed of about 8 m.p.h.

The claim was made that as far as seaworthiness goes, these dories had no superiors. The *Nautical Gazette* explains:

> These boats are designed to withstand the severe weather they are subjected to on the bleak coast of Maine during the winter season. The keel, ribs, sternpost, stem, bottom board and engine foundation are made of native oak; planking, native pine, 1¼" [*sic*] thick; galvanized iron fastenings; deck, pine with oak frame; coaming, oak; fender rail, oak; decked over fore and aft to take in tank, muffler and batteries; bulkheads are of pine with doors fore and aft; ribs, steam-bent oak, 1" square, 10" on centers; fittings, galvanized iron. Many of these boats are finished with winch heads, which are driven by means of sprocket chains and are used for dragging scallops and hauling lobster pots.

Of course, dory planking 1¼ inches thick is out of the question. This has to be an error. The maximum plank thickness for a dory of this size would be ⅝ inch. Fore-and-aft bulkheads with doors indicate closed storage compartments under the decks at either end, yet the motor, lacking any covered engine box or compartment, seems to have been quite open and exposed.

This was an early installation. Quite soon after, the larger, powered fishing dories had closed engine compartments built into the stern. These were bulk-headed off from the rest of the boat and had a low trunk that rose above the stern deck, to which it was fastened. Entrance was through a companionway topped by a sliding hatch cover.

On the T Wharf 30-footers, the steering wheel was mounted on the inside of the engine-compartment bulkhead, and the helmsman stood inside the companionway with the slide pushed back to steer. His body filled the narrow companionway opening and served to keep out loose water in bad weather. Within reach was the pump, which would discharge a barrel of water in a few minutes, according to a 1912 *Power Boating* report.

The engine compartments varied considerably in size and arrangement, depending on the builder and the length of the dory. The accompanying illustration of a 30-foot Toppan fishing dory shows a large engine compartment built into the stern. Judging from photographs of T Wharf fishing dories as well as from contemporary descriptions, this one closely resembles the engine compartments favored by Boston's Sicilian dory fishermen. In fact, it is more than likely that a number of the dories then fishing out of T Wharf were Toppan-built.

According to its 40-page catalog for 1906, the Toppan Boat Manufacturing Company, "designers and builders of high-grade power dories, whaleboat launches, trunk cabin cruisers and special boats built

This 30-foot dory built by the Toppan Boat Manufacturing Company features a large engine compartment built into the stern, a configuration favored by Boston's Sicilian dory fishermen. (Courtesy Mystic Seaport Museum)

to order,'' had its factory, wharf, yard, and storehouse at Charlestown and its office and showrooms at 9 Haverhill Street, Boston, three doors from Haymarket Square. In 1906 Toppan was an established and successful company in a period of expansion and growth. Although it has long since been out of business, its dories are not forgotten. A fine example of one of the company's smaller power dories was displayed in 1982 at Boston's Museum of Transportation after having been restored by the museum's Skills Shop.

What the Toppan catalog had to say about its line of power dories was probably no great exaggeration:

These well-known boats need no description here. No better sea boat can be built.

We have shipped our boats to nearly every country in Europe, and our export trade is still growing. The same can be said in regard to our home market: still growing. The reader must surely know there is a reason, and if you are thinking of purchasing and want a good reliable outfit at a popular price, kindly read the testimonials at the end, and you will then see WHY the Toppan boats are in such demand.

The many pages of testimonials, all dated 1906, were submitted from all over the United States. There were also letters from Vienna; Genoa, Italy; and Quebec. The one from Canada reads:

Gentlemen: The 20-foot Toppan dory launch has given first-class satisfaction in every respect. The boat is a first-class sea boat and has both speed and carrying capacity. The 3 h.p. Toppan engine gave fine results, and as I had *never even seen* a gasoline engine, let alone run one, I was more than pleased. Batteries troubled some, but when I put on a magneto, everything was fine. I have got nearly eight miles per hour. If you want to refer anyone to me, do so, and I will be more than glad to speak a good word. Yours truly, E.B. Blackwell, Manicouagan, P.Q., Saguenray Co., Canada.

The demand for the new power dories that had greatly expanded Toppan's business in Boston also made itself felt in Swampscott, where E. Gerry Emmons was the largest dory builder at that time. Boats from the Emmons factory were shipped to all regions of this country and to many other parts of the world. The Emmons Company had gotten into power boats early, marketing its own gasoline engines in 1, 2½, 5, and 6 h.p. sizes, and could well have been the first firm to install a gasoline engine in a dory.

A fisherman's power dory built by Emmons is shown here, reproduced from the company's catalog, which described the boat as

our 20-foot overall lobster and fishing dory, 5-foot beam, 21 inches deep. Has oak bottom, hardwood frame, pine planking, five strakes on a side, galvanized fastenings throughout, house and slide over motor, three cross seats, grating in bottom of boat, rudder and yoke, centerboard if wanted.

Boat is painted two good coats inside and out. Fitted with a 2½ h.p. Emmons motor, plain wheel and shaft, copper tank in bow, brass deck-plate in deck and tank, brass feed-pipe to motor, batteries, spark, coil,

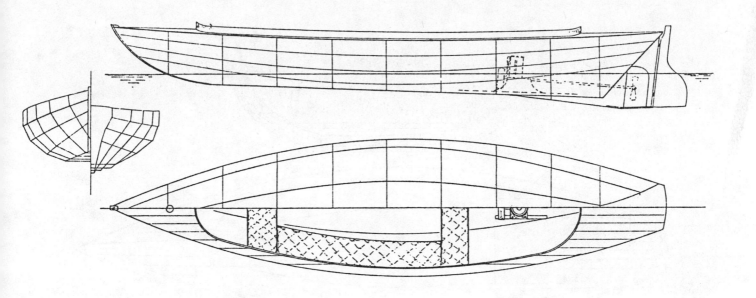

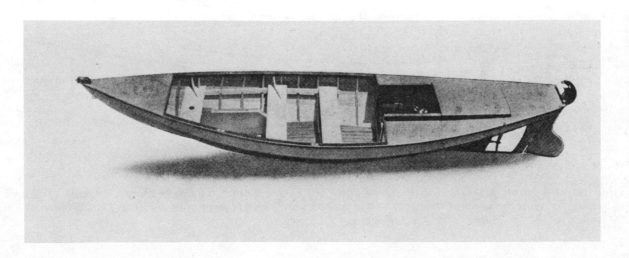

The popularity of power dories in Boston carried over to Swampscott. There, E. Gerry Emmons built boats like this 20-footer. The lines appeared in an early 1900 issue of The Rudder magazine, and the photograph was printed in an Emmons catalog of the time. Fitted with a 2½ h.p. motor, the dory sold for $275.

muffler, etc., steering wheel, oars and rowlocks. Price, $275.

One thing to be noted here is that the engine compartment for this 20-foot dory, unlike that of the 30-foot Toppan model, is not topped by a trunk. The companionway slide is attached directly to the stern deck. Undoubtedly this is because a raised trunk aft in this 20-foot dory would be out of proportion to the rest of the boat.

Although Emmons produced a variety of other boats, both large and small, dories were the foundation and mainstay of his business. Pages 17–19 of the catalog (circa 1905) contain a historical sketch of the origins and development of the Swampscott dory. Several paragraphs apply to the new power dories, especially those for inshore fishermen:

The use of the dory for general purposes has greatly increased within the last decade, and with the

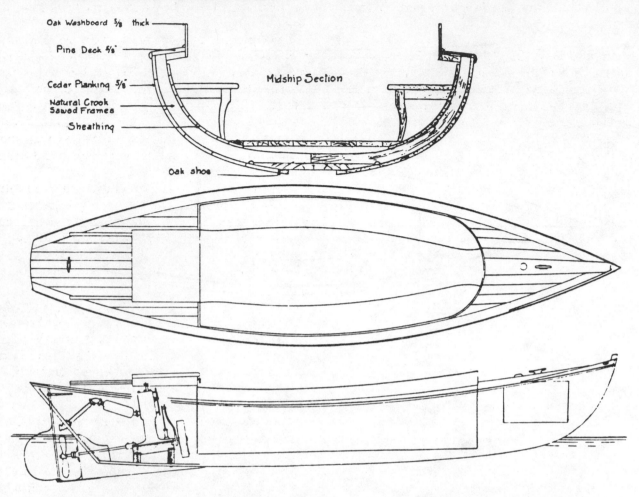

This 20-footer with carvel planking was designed and built by the Cape Cod Power Dory Company of Wareham, Massachusetts. The construction plan here appeared in the February 25, 1911 issue of Motor Boat. *The engine was a single-cylinder two-cycle 3½ h.p. Palmer or a 4 h.p. Ferro motor.*

marvelous growth of the manufacture of small power boats, the experiment was made of harnessing the dory with other than manpower. Even before this, the demand began to grow for a light dory for rowing and sailing, with more attention paid to comfortable fittings than in the fisherman's model, and the 16-foot and 18-foot dory, fitted with a leg-o-mutton sail, speedily became a favorite for pleasure boating.

But with the fitting of these dories—of all the models mentioned—with small gasoline engines, their pleasure-giving qualities and usefulness were greatly increased.

Shore fishermen began to look at them with interest, and now not a few of the Swampscott and other home toilers go out to their nets or lobster pots without the weariness of an "ash breeze," but instead may be seen of a summer morning standing erect with yoke lines in hand, scudding rapidly from one buoy to another, like veritable sea kings guiding their chargers.

Similar to the Emmons 20-foot power fishing dory is a 20-footer by the Cape Cod Power Dory Company of Wareham, Massachusetts. A construction plan for this craft was published in *Motor Boat*, February 25, 1911. Beam was 5 feet 6 inches. The engine was a single-cylinder two-cycle 3½ h.p. Palmer or a 4 h.p. Ferro motor.

As can be seen, this dory is carvel-planked rather than being lapped or clinker-built. Toppan also carried carvel-planked dories for those who preferred a boat with smooth planking, but these cost slightly more. Some fishermen believed smooth-planked dories lasted better and were tighter because they could be caulked. One of these early, smooth-planked 20-foot Cape Cod dories has survived more than a half century of service at Pine Island Camps in Belgrade Lakes, Maine, and is now preserved in the small-craft collection at Mystic Seaport Museum, Mystic, Connecticut.

The success of the Italian fishermen in Boston waters contributed directly to the early demise of the dory fleet. As soon as they acquired sufficient resources and could raise the required capital, they moved on in the expanding economy to larger vessels that could operate in more distant waters. Their catches became bigger and so did their profits.

In little more than 20 years, the power dory was obsolete as a working fishing boat and all but forgotten. But today, with the growing number of people considering small-scale fishing as a possible source of supplemental income, interest in the Swampscott dory is reviving. These boats appear to have most of the features and qualities that the small-scale fisherman requires.

None of the original dories have survived, and no detailed drawings of their construction details have ever been discovered. But we do have enough information about these dories, gleaned from a variety of sources, to be able to reproduce them fairly accurately.

We know almost exactly what these dories were like on the outside. What is less certain is just how they were built on the inside. How were the fish holds made? Did some have self-bailing cockpits? Did they have watertight bulkheads, and if so, where were they located? What were the cuddies like on the inside?

Few, if any, of these dories seem to have been exactly alike in all details. Their interior arrangements were constructed to suit their owners. I will try to make these arrangements consistent with what we do know and convenient for the duties this dory traditionally performed.

The lines shown here are typical Swampscott-dory lines, of which numerous authenticated examples exist. They are for a 28-foot-8-inch dory, the largest used by the Italian fishermen. I have given the keel a fair amount of drag at the stern to gain necessary depth for a slow-turning propeller of ample size.

The frames also serve as building molds; for this 28-foot-8-inch dory, they would be 30 inches apart. A smaller boat could be built by simply decreasing the frame spacing. The lower limit would be 24-inch spacing, which would give an approximate overall length of 24 feet. A 26-foot dory could be built by eliminating one frame spacing amidships but keeping the rest intact. If a reduction of this kind were made,

the lines should be refaired by laying them down full size.

Swampscott dories were relatively inexpensive at the beginning of this century. They were clinker-built of the cheap white-pine boards that were then abundantly available in long lengths and extra-wide widths. Clinker construction is much quicker and requires far less labor than carvel planking. Today, white-pine lumber is even more expensive than some mahogany, and not to be had at any price in the wide widths of former times.

Nevertheless, marine plywood is an acceptable substitute. I have specified ½-inch marine fir. The strakes can be made of standard 8-foot and 10-foot panels in sections and spliced together when applied to the boat. Working in this manner (coupled with some planning and foresight) would virtually eliminate any waste of planking material.

The splices are made with 6-inch-long scarfs and put together with epoxy glue and nails. The 1½-inch-wide planking laps are also epoxy-glued, which produces a hull of great rigidity and strength. Plank splices are spaced to fall on the frames as shown in the diagram and are staggered to separate them as much as possible.

The details for splicing the planking are shown in the drawings and should be studied carefully until everything is clear and fully understood. A two-part clamp with a through bolt used for pulling the scarfed surfaces together until the glue hardens makes the splice as strong as the original uncut plywood itself.

Both the inside and outside pieces of this clamp are made of hardwood. A ⅜-inch carriage bolt is driven through a slightly smaller hole in the inside piece so that it fits tightly. A slightly larger hole through the splice allows the bolt to slip through easily. The hole in the outside part of the clamp should also be slightly larger for easy assembly.

A few turns with the wrench after the washer and nut are in place will apply sufficient pressure to bring the scarfed surfaces of the splice together and in firm contact. A tight pine plug fills the hole through the splice when the bolt is removed.

The surface of the scarf should be planed almost to a feather edge, but not quite, leaving an edge thickness of 1/32 inch or a hair less. A sharp smoothing plane is desirable for removing the bulk of the wood on the scarf surfaces. These surfaces should be finished and brought smooth and fair with a low-angle block plane.

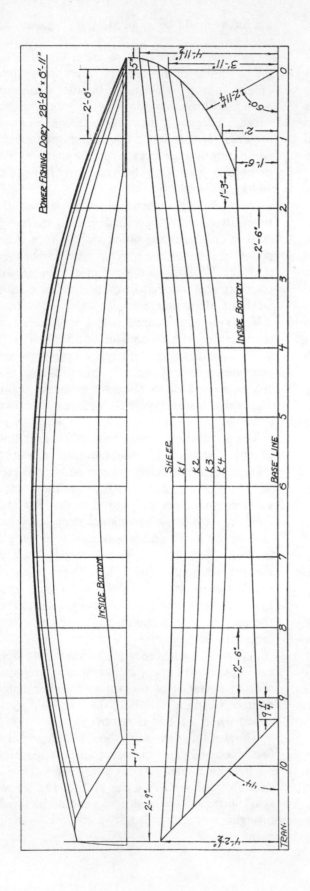

Power Fishing Dory 28'-8" × 6'-11"

Sheer
K1
K2
K3
K4

Base Line

Inside Bottom

Inside Bottom

Tran.

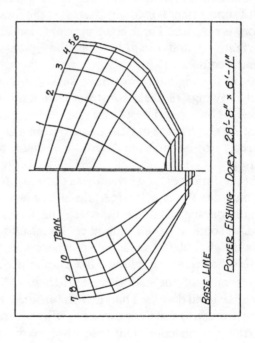

Base Line

Power Fishing Dory 28'-8" × 6'-11"

	STATIONS	STEM	1	2	3	4	5	6	7	8	9	10	TRANSOM
HEIGHTS	SHEER	4-11-7	4-8-1	4-5-0	4-2-1	3-11-6	3-10-1	3-9-1	3-9-0	3-9-5	3-10-6	4-0-3	4-2-4
	KNUCKLE 1	4-8-0	4-3-6	4-0-1	3-8-5	3-6-1	3-4-3	3-3-6	3-3-5	3-4-3	3-6-0	3-8-0	3-10-1
	KNUCKLE 2	4-3-4	3-11-0	3-6-6	3-2-5	2-11-7	2-10-1	2-9-3	2-9-4	2-10-6	3-0-5	3-3-2	3-5-3
	KNUCKLE 3	3-11-0	3-6-1	3-1-4	2-9-1	2-6-1	2-4-1	2-3-5	2-3-7	2-5-0	2-7-3	2-10-2	3-0-3
	KNUCKLE 4	3-5-5	3-1-4	2-8-7	2-4-4	2-1-4	1-11-4	1-10-4	1-10-5	2-0-1	2-2-5	2-6-1	2-7-7
	BOTTOM	1-6-3	2-0-0	1-5-4	1-3-7	1-2-5	1-1-4	1-0-3	0-11-3	0-10-3	0-9-2	1-7-4	0-8-3
HALF-BREADTHS	SHEER	0-0-4	1-2-3	2-0-4	2-8-0	3-1-2	3-4-1	3-5-1	3-4-5	3-2-4	2-10-3	2-4-7	1-9-5
	KNUCKLE 1	0-0-4	1-1-7	2-0-0	2-7-5	3-0-6	3-3-5	3-4-5	3-4-1	3-1-7	2-9-7	2-4-5	1-10-6
	KNUCKLE 2	0-0-4	1-0-6	1-10-4	2-6-1	2-11-2	3-2-0	3-3-2	3-2-7	3-0-5	2-8-5	2-3-1	1-10-3
	KNUCKLE 3	0-0-4	0-10-4	1-8-0	2-3-5	2-8-5	2-11-3	3-0-3	3-0-1	2-10-1	2-6-0	2-0-2	1-8-1
	KNUCKLE 4	0-0-4	0-8-1	1-4-7	2-0-0	2-4-3	2-7-1	2-8-3	2-8-3	2-6-1	2-2-1	1-8-5	1-5-4
	BOTTOM	0-0-4	0-0-4	0-4-1	0-8-4	0-11-1	1-0-3	1-0-0	0-10-5	0-8-0	0-4-2	0-9-2	0-2-0

OFFSETS POWER FISHING DORY 28'-8" x 6'-11"

MEASUREMENTS IN FEET, INCHES AND EIGHTHS INCHES. HEIGHTS MEASURED ABOVE BASE LINE.

MEASUREMENTS TAKEN INSIDE PLANKING - INSIDE BOTTOM - OUTSIDE TRANSOM - OUTSIDE TRUE OR INSIDE STEM.

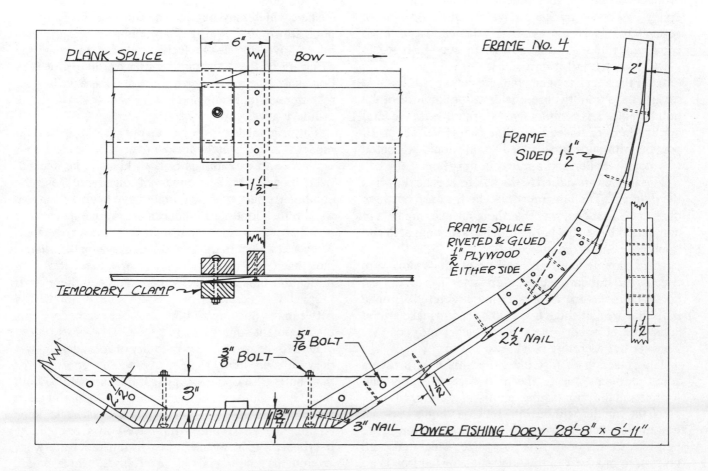

PLANK SPLICE

BOW →

FRAME No. 4

2"

FRAME SIDED 1½"

FRAME SPLICE RIVETED & GLUED ½" PLYWOOD EITHER SIDE

1½"

TEMPORARY CLAMP →

2½" NAIL

1½"

5/16" BOLT

3/8" BOLT

3"

2/20

1½"

3" NAIL

POWER FISHING DORY 28'-8" x 6'-11"

It is absolutely essential that both planes be as sharp as possible and in the best working order. Failure to make proper wood scarfs is due almost invariably to planes that are dull, set incorrectly, or used improperly—sometimes all three.

With seven strakes on a side, three or four splices in each strake, and two scarfs in each splice, almost 100 scarf surfaces have to be cut. This represents a lot of planing, but is not nearly the job that planing the outside of a carvel-planked boat of equal size would be. It might save time to make up a simple jig and cut these scarfs with a router.

Despite the scarfs and laps that have to be planed and fitted, this plywood lapstrake construction is one of the quickest and easiest methods I know. Furthermore, plywood is available almost everywhere, whereas other kinds of planking material frequently are not.

Plywood takes glue readily, and when the splices and laps are properly glued, a tight, superstrong product results. I recommend Chem-Tech's T-88 epoxy adhesive thickened with Cab-O-Sil, or an equivalent thixotropic agent. Mix them into a pastelike consistency that is stiff enough to stay in place in vertical joints until it hardens.

After the boat has been planked and the glue has had several days to fully cure, the dried-out interior of the hull should be completely saturated with several applications of linseed oil that is thinned about 20 percent with mineral spirits. The oil should be heated in a double boiler and applied boiling hot.

The strakes are nailed to the oak frames as shown in the diagram. The laps must also be fastened between the frames in such a way that their surfaces are held in contact until the glue hardens. The fastenings also add reinforcement to the glue.

In the past, galvanized chisel-point clinch nails were used as the standard glueless lap fastenings for dories, but these nails are no longer manufactured. Bronze nails that are soft enough to clinch readily make a good substitute. Copper rivets are neater and possibly stronger but are more trouble to put in.

The selection of fastenings for this boat presents some problems due to the high cost of copper and bronze and the poor lasting quality of galvanized steel. Here the builder will have to make a choice between how much money he wants to spend and how long a life he plans for his boat. The galvanized-steel nails and bolts used in a boat of this kind (galvanized iron is no longer available) can be expected to last reasonably well for about 10 years, providing no special electrolysis problems develop. Because this boat will have an engine and some electrical installations, attention must be given to this possibility.

If the builder decides to use galvanized bolts, he might want to make the boat sturdier by increasing the size of the floor-through-bottom bolts to ½ inch in diameter and the floor-through-frame bolts to ⅜ inch in diameter.

Copper and bronze fastenings throughout should last almost indefinitely. However, the extra cost of nonferrous fastenings will be considerable.

Construction details and interior arrangements for a motorized dory such as this must be based on our best judgment from the few sources available. As stated above, none of the Italian dories have survived. No original construction plans were ever drawn, or at least none have come to light so far. About all we have are a couple of descriptive accounts by journalists, the one in the *Fishing Gazette,* December 1908, and one in *Power Boating,* April 1912. We can also refer to various photographs, especially those of Henry D. Fisher, which may be seen in Andrew W. German's book *Down on T Wharf.* These photographs are most informative and leave little doubt as to what the exteriors of these fishing dories were like. But they don't show the interior arrangements. Here we have to rely more on judgment and experience—even on plain, ordinary guesswork.

The original dory type had an open cockpit; the later model was completely decked over. The photographs we have show examples of both kinds. The decked-over model has a number of disadvantages, the combined effect of which might have been a deterrent to its wide adoption. Full decks are more expensive to build, requiring additional materials and extra labor. They add weight to the topsides, increasing the roll in a hull that tends to move a lot in any case. It is also difficult to make full decks tight and keep them so. If rainwater is admitted, it gets trapped in joints and between the decking and the deck beams, becoming a highly potent source of rot.

Due to the increased possibility of rot, decked-over dory hulls are likely to have appreciably shorter lives than hulls with open cockpits. If decks could be built flush, it would be much easier to make them tight, but some sort of low bulkheads are necessary to keep equipment, gear, and what-have-you from sliding overboard. This would mean fitting the waterways around the upper ends of the frames, which would serve as stanchions. Joggling the waterways to fit snugly around the frames is tricky, precise work.

These joints would then have to be caulked tight or "pined,"—that is, fitted with dry pine wedges driven tight. Furthermore, some scuppers of some sort would be required to allow any water that came aboard to drain quickly.

No hint remains of just how this was originally accomplished, but the simple construction shown in the drawing would work. Waterways of 1-inch-by-8-inch pine are fitted snugly against the inside of the top strake, just above its lap with the plank below.

The top strake is also thicker, $^{13}/_{16}$ inch, for needed extra strength. A strand of cotton wicking set in thick oil paint (white lead if you can get it) is laid in the seam where the two planks come together. Three-inch galvanized wire nails spaced 4 inches apart are driven (from the outside) through the top strake into the waterways.

Scuppers measuring 1 inch high by 12 inches long are centered between the frames in each bay. The openings are cut through the top strake, level with the surface of the waterways.

The decked-over boats must have been less comfortable and not as convenient to work from as the older model with the open cockpit. The 1908 description from the *Fishing Gazette* specifies "a hatch amidships with a watertight, standing room forward, where the crew hauls trawls."

This seems to indicate a tight well of some sort forward, open at the top and large enough for two men to work from (most of the boats carried crews of two men). Without a cover, such a well, as distinguished from a hatch, would be bound to take on water in heavy and breaking seas, putting the boat down by the head and even endangering stability. It's possible the well was self-bailing, in which case it would need to have draining scuppers and perhaps be floored over above the load waterline.

In the accompanying drawing of a fully decked dory, I show a second covered hatch forward that opens into the fish hold below. The hold extends back to the watertight bulkhead at station 7, which separates the engine compartment and cuddy from the rest of the boat. The fish hold is tightly floored over on top of the frame floors with removable traps down the center, and it is tightly sheathed against the frames about two-thirds of the way up the sides.

Water taken in through the hatches is cleared by means of a large hand pump located just forward of the bulkhead at station 7. One of the crew can operate it by standing just inside the cuddy and engine compartment and reaching through the slide entrance. In 1912,

Power Boating described such a pump as "the galvanized barrel kind with spout and a wooden handle on either a wood or metal rod....The handle of the pump is within convenient reach of the man who steers and who operates the engine, and will discharge a barrel of water in a few minutes, taking care of a bad leak or deluge that gets below."

Large hatch covers can get in the way when they are taken off the hatches. To make them easier to stow they can be hinged in the middle with large piano hinges, which permits them to be folded to half their full size. Hinged in this way, covers will not be completely watertight. But what little water drips through, while intolerable in a yacht, is inconsequential here.

The open model I have drawn shows nothing distinctive or unusual. The cockpit is floored over, and the sides are sheathed partway up in the manner described for the decked model. From the bulkhead at station 7, the cockpit extends to station 2, where it is bulkheaded off partway up. This provides easily accessible dry stowage space under the foredeck.

The rather high coaming of steam-bent oak stands 6 inches above the narrow side decks or waterways. This is not so high as to make working difficult but is still high enough to keep out a lot of loose water. A canvas spray hood could be easily fitted, as could a snap-on canvas cover to keep rainwater out of the cockpit when the boat is lying at mooring. The pumping arrangement would be the same as for the decked model.

The combination cuddy and engine compartment is identical for both models. It provides dry shelter for both the engine installation and the two- or three-man crew. Extending as far forward as station 7, this section occupies approximately one-third of the overall length of the boat. It could be set back a foot or even more to give additional room in the cockpit or fish hold. Nonetheless, the frame at station 7 is convenient for locating the bulkhead, and ample room in the cuddy has much to commend it.

The cuddy trunk shown here rises 14 inches above the deck at its forward end, with the top crowned 2 inches or 3 inches. The forward end of the slide extends 6 inches above that, sloping back to 3 inches. This does not afford much space below, but there is plenty for sitting headroom above the low seats on either side of the boat, just aft of the bulkhead and abreast of the slide entrance.

The engine is set as far aft as efficient operation will permit, with skeleton transoms built on either side. These serve as low benches or berths with open-access

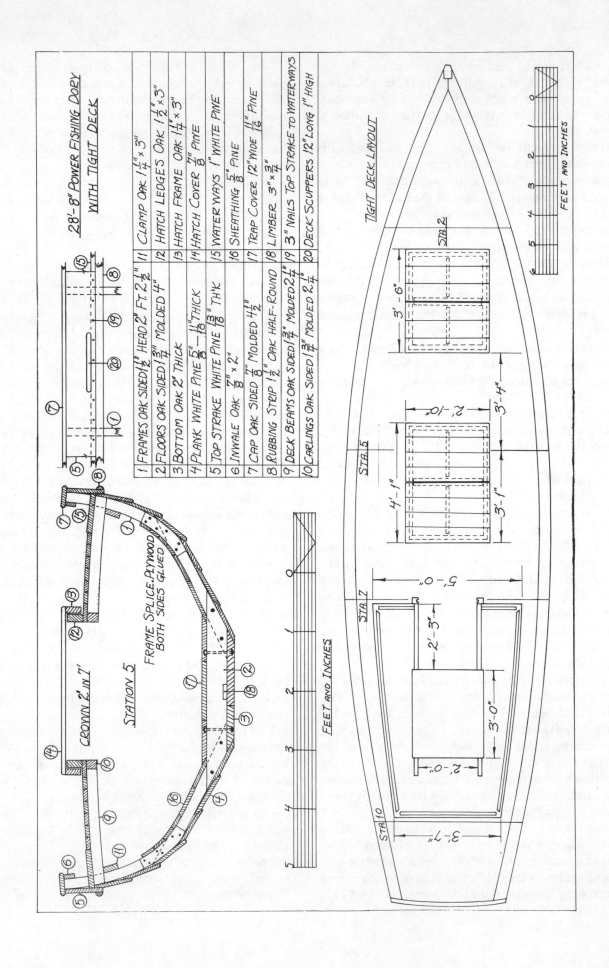

28'-8" POWER FISHING DORY WITH TIGHT DECK

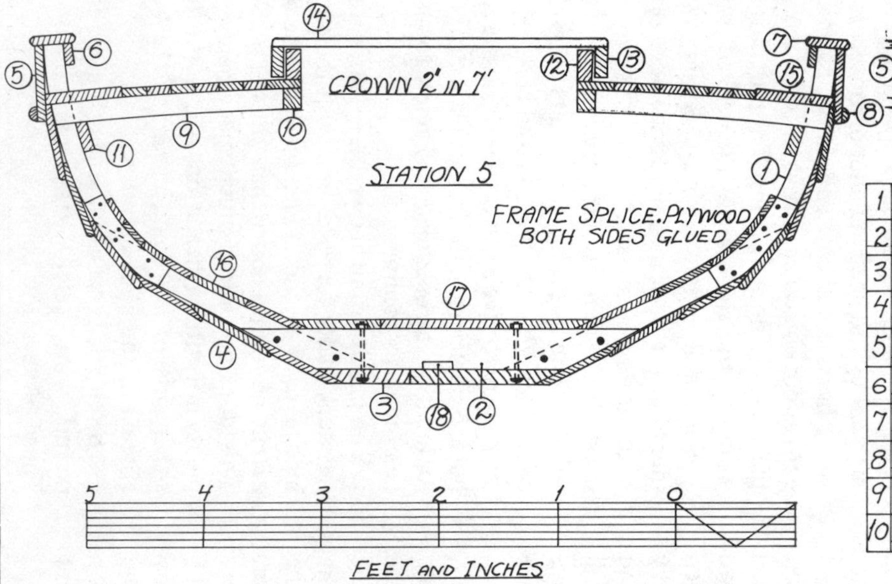

CROWN 2" IN 7'
STATION 5
FRAME SPLICE. PLYWOOD BOTH SIDES GLUED
5 4 3 2 1 0
FEET AND INCHES

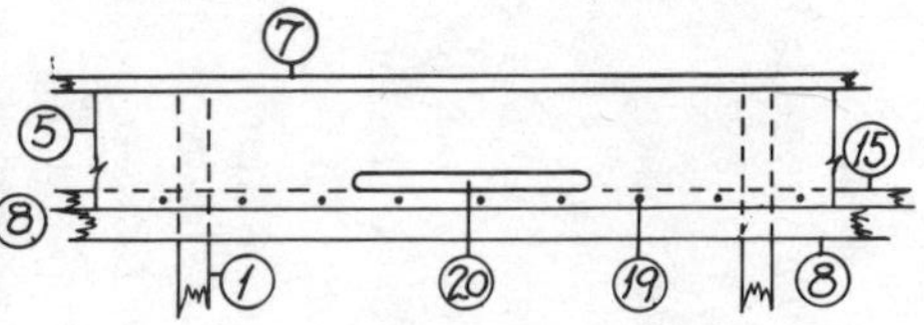

1	FRAMES OAK SIDED $1\frac{1}{2}$" HEAD 2" FT. $2\frac{1}{2}$"	11	CLAMP OAK $1\frac{1}{4}$" × 3"
2	FLOORS OAK SIDED $1\frac{3}{4}$" MOLDED 4"	12	HATCH LEDGES OAK $1\frac{1}{2}$" × 3"
3	BOTTOM OAK 2" THICK	13	HATCH FRAME OAK $1\frac{1}{4}$" × 3"
4	PLANK WHITE PINE $\frac{5}{8}$"—$\frac{11}{16}$" THICK	14	HATCH COVER $\frac{7}{8}$" PINE
5	TOP STRAKE WHITE PINE $\frac{13}{16}$" TH'K	15	WATER WAYS 1" WHITE PINE
6	INWALE OAK $\frac{7}{8}$" × 2"	16	SHEATHING $\frac{5}{8}$" PINE
7	CAP OAK SIDED $\frac{7}{8}$" MOLDED $4\frac{1}{2}$"	17	TRAP COVER 12" WIDE $\frac{11}{16}$" PINE
8	RUBBING STRIP $1\frac{1}{2}$" OAK HALF-ROUND	18	LIMBER 3" × $\frac{3}{4}$"
9	DECK BEAMS OAK SIDED $1\frac{3}{4}$" MOLDED $2\frac{1}{4}$"	19	3" NAILS TOP STRAKE TO WATERWAYS
10	CARLINGS OAK SIDED $1\frac{3}{4}$" MOLDED $2\frac{1}{4}$"	20	DECK SCUPPERS 12" LONG 1" HIGH

TIGHT DECK LAYOUT

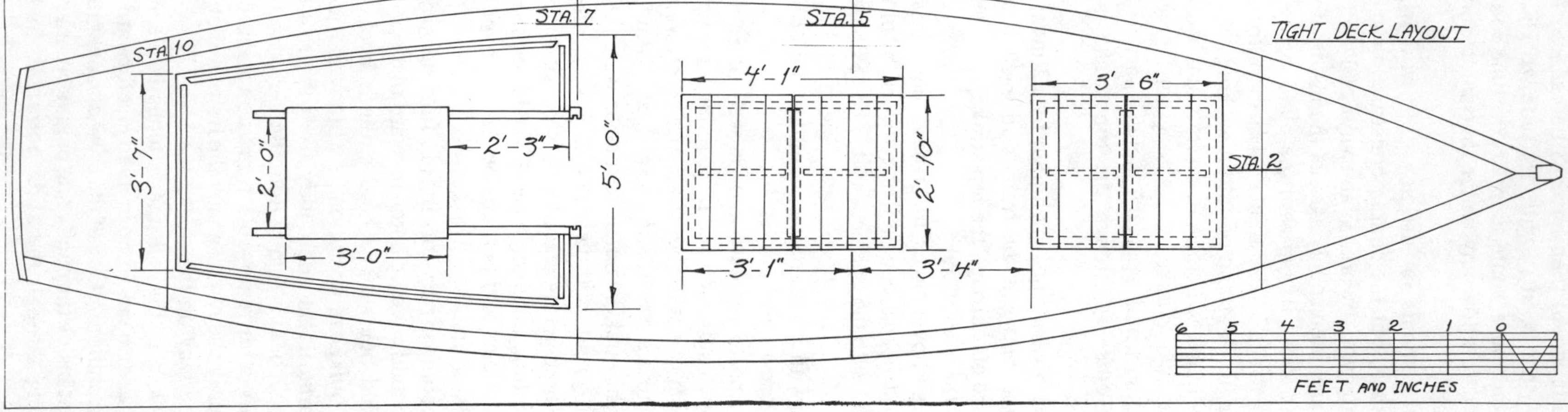

STA. 10
STA. 7
STA. 5
STA. 2
3'-7"
2'-0"
2'-3"
3'-0"
5'-0"
4'-1"
2'-10"
3'-1"
3'-4"
3'-6"
6 5 4 3 2 1 0
FEET AND INCHES

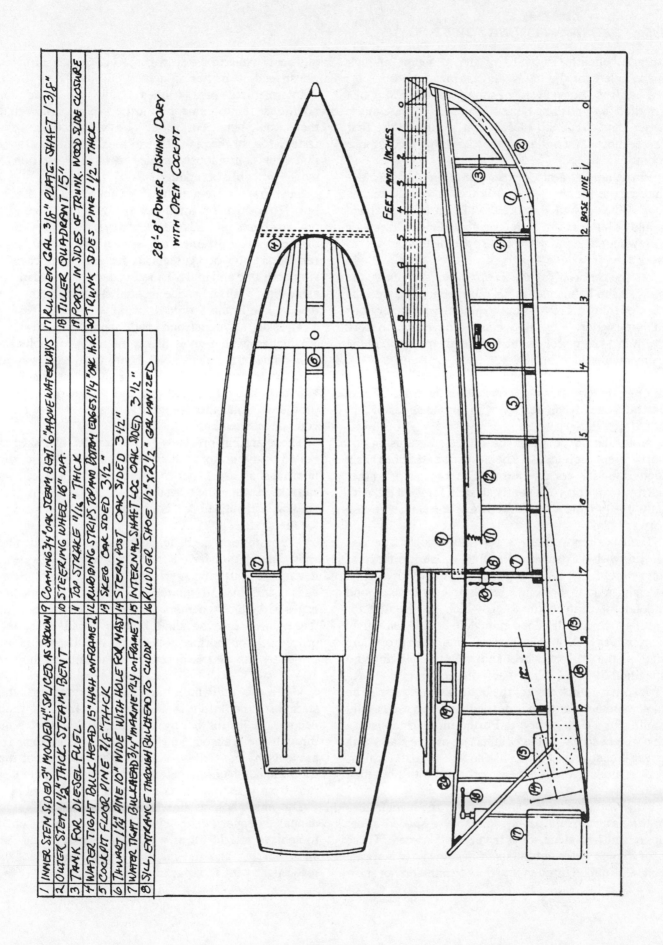

28'-8" POWER FISHING DORY
WITH OPEN COCKPIT

1	INNER STEM SIDED 3" MOLDED 4" SPLICED AS SHOWN
2	OUTER STEM 1½" THICK. STEAM BENT
3	TANK FOR DIESEL FUEL
4	WATER TIGHT BULKHEAD 15" HIGH ON FRAME 2
5	COCKPIT FLOOR PINE ⅞" THICK
6	THWART 1¼" PINE 10" WIDE WITH HOLE FOR MAST
7	WATER TIGHT BULKHEAD ¾" MARINE PLY ON FRAME 7
8	SILL, ENTRANCE THROUGH BULKHEAD TO CUDDY
9	COAMING ¾" OAK STEAM BENT. 6" ABOVE WATERWAYS
10	STEERING WHEEL 16" DIA.
11	TOP STRAKE ¹¹⁄₁₆" THICK
12	RUBBING STRIPS TOP AND BOTTOM EDGES 1¼" OAK H.R.
13	SKEG OAK SIDED 3½"
14	STERN POST OAK SIDED 3½"
15	INTERNAL SHAFT LOG OAK SIDED 3½"
16	RUDDER SHOE ½" X 2½" GALVANIZED
17	RUDDER GAL. ⅜" PLATE. SHAFT 1⅜"
18	TILLER QUADRANT 15"
19	PORTS IN SIDES OF TRUNK. WOOD SIDE CLOSURE
20	TRUNK SIDES PINE 1½" THICK

FEET AND INCHES

BASE LINE

storage beneath. Forward of the transoms enough space is left for the low seats just mentioned.

The first heavy, slow-turning gasoline engines installed in the fishing dories 75 years ago were much larger than the small diesels that would be the first choice now. Accordingly, they took up much more room.

For example, a modern 22 h.p. Sabb diesel (more than ample for these boats) is only about 40 inches long. When installed, more than 2 feet of clear space would be left forward of the engine—plenty of room for a crewman to stand at the slide opening to steer and to work the pump.

As the reporter for the *Fishing Gazette* put it, the body of the helmsman in his oilskins pressed into the slide opening makes this cubbyhole almost impervious to flying water. When both hands are required to work the pump, the wheel can be held by the pressure of the helmsman's thigh or hip.

Ventilation is obtained from square holes cut through the two sides and the end of the trunk. These can be closed when desired with simple slides of thin board.

Note should be taken of several features of the dory's construction, these being identical in both basic models under consideration. The bottom is rather narrow for a dory; it is nearly straight fore and aft, with only the slightest bit of upward curvature in the forward end.

If the bottom were made perfectly straight from end to end, without camber, the effect on performance, if any, would not be enough to matter. With such a straight, narrow bottom it is possible to have a good amount of drag in the keel, which is essential for getting the propeller deep enough to be fully effective. This is especially so with large-diameter propellers such as the 24-inch wheel shown in the drawing and specified for the 22 h.p. Sabb diesel.

Two-inch-thick oak for the bottom might seem to be larger and heavier than is needed, but it provides solid nailing for a tight garboard. Furthermore, establishing this weight so low in the boat has a positive stabilizing effect. Because the bottom has no fore-and-aft camber, it does not have to be bent and can be thicker than usual.

As reported in the *Fishing Gazette,* the sawn frames in the early Boston power dories were spaced 3 feet apart and had steam-bent frames in between. These bent frames were continuous from gunwale to gunwale and were nailed through into the bottom. I do not show

any bent frames in the drawings, since the sawn frames are spaced 30 inches on center.

Intermediate bent frames could be added for additional reinforcement if desired, but I doubt that they would be necessary. The substantial, well-fastened lapstrake planking and the internal sheathing that runs continuously from station 7 to station 2 would probably be enough.

Sawn frames are got out of ordinary straight stock, but if live-edge or flitch-sawn lumber is used, the builder should take advantage of any natural curvature in the planks. Frames are spliced as shown, and reinforcing plywood gussets are fastened on each side with both glue and nails. The stem can be spliced in the same way, with the splice located as indicated by the dashed line in the profile drawing.

The skeg, sternpost, and inside shaft log are all sided 3½ inches, which gives plenty of room for bolts on either side of the shaft hole. There is an easy way to bore the shaft hole and to get it right. First, the stern assembly should be laid out and drawn full size in profile so that molds can be made of the three component members.

These are cut precisely to the molds. The skeg is bolted to the bottom before setting up. Likewise, the internal shaft log, fastened to the transom, serves as a stern knee when the transom is set up. The sternpost goes on last, but before it is fastened in place it is bored for the shaft.

This is done on the bench with the post laid flat. The shaft line is transferred from the mold to the post, having previously been lifted from the laydown. Both ends of this line are squared down across the opposite edges of the block; centers are then marked on each of these lines, and the shaft hole is bored using the procedure for boring holes for shaft-log drifts or through bolts that is described in detail in Chapter 12.

When the shaft hole has been bored through the sternpost, the latter is fastened in place. It then becomes a jig for boring the rest of the shaft hole through the transom and the interior shaft log. To prevent any possibility of leaks at the bottom of the transom, a ⅝-inch-diameter pine stopwater is put in. It runs from side to side, as indicated in the drawing.

The shaft hole is lined with either lead pipe or annealed copper tubing. These are swelled at the ends to achieve a tight fit, as well as to properly seat the stern bearing and the inside stuffing box, which is made tight with flax packing.

11

MATINICUS PEAPOD

The design for this 15-foot Matinicus peapod was based on a photograph taken at Matinicus Island in 1954 by Jerry McCarty, at that time editor of the old *Maine Coast Fisherman*. To a boatbuilder like myself who had made a close study of peapod lines, the overall shape and proportions of the fisherman's heavily built working pod were clearly revealed in the broadside view the photograph provided. The challenge of working out actual dimensions together with lines and offsets for a closely similar pod without straying beyond the limits imposed by the photograph was one I could hardly resist. The result was well received at the time by *Maine Coast Fisherman* readers. Several of the pods were built and got good reports. But then the pod faded into obscurity, so to speak, not to return to the public eye for nearly 20 years.

In 1973 Harold Kimber, a retired master boat-builder who for many years had operated a boatyard on the River Brue in Somerset, England, was invited to deliver the principal address at Mystic Seaport Museum's annual Small Craft Workshop. Afterward he was invited by Lance Lee, the director of The Apprenticeshop—which at that time was located in Bath, Maine—to come to Bath for a month to demonstrate clinker boatbuilding. Kimber was pleased to accept, and several different boats were considered for demonstration purposes, among them the Matinicus pod. Kimber liked the pod, and that was the one he finally selected.

This choice proved to have been well considered. The boat so built met every expectation, becoming the prototype of a stock model that The Apprenticeshop still continues to build for its customers. Although this pod was designed as a rowboat, since the lobster fishermen generally rowed their pods while tending

Above: *This photograph of a peapod taken in 1954 at Matinicus Island, Maine, served as the basis for the design in this chapter. (Jerry McCarty photo)* **Right:** *Boatbuilders at The Apprenticeshop, now located in Rockport, Maine, put the finishing touches on another 15-foot Matinicus pod. (Neal Parent photo)*

An Apprenticeshop-built Matinicus peapod with sailing rig. (David Lyman photo)

their traps, some of the pods built at The Apprentice-shop have been fitted with a spritsail and rudder and have been found to sail quite well for their type of boat. As long as the proportions and construction of the basic hull are not tampered with unduly, builders might experiment with a variety of simple rigs if they should be so inclined.

For amateurs with some boatbuilding experience or the equivalent, it would not be forbiddingly difficult to substitute a flat plank keel—say, 7 inches wide amidships, tapering to 2 inches wide at the ends, and 1¾ to 2 inches thick—for the beam keel of the original

design. By mortising a slot in this plank keel, it would be easy to install a centerboard should the builder desire a thoroughgoing conversion to sail. In fact, numbers of working pods did have plank keels of this sort, although not for the purpose of installing centerboards. Most working pods were not fitted with centerboards, for a simple reason: If someone in a boat such as this is in a hurry to make a destination to windward, he can often make better progress rowing dead for it than he can tacking back and forth under sail.

The accompanying drawings contain the essential

Another view of a Matinicus peapod built by the Apprenticeshop. This 15-footer is suitable for amateur construction. (Steve McAllister photo)

information required for building. What follows here is largely suggestions for procedures applying specifically to the building of this boat. Some basic boatbuilding experience—including some knowledge of the materials, the tools, and such essentials as laying down lines, steam bending, and lapstrake planking—is assumed.

Since the ends of this pod are exactly alike, the full-size laydown of lines need include only one half of the hull plus an additional station for assistance in fairing. One 4-by-10-foot panel of plywood is all that is needed. Molds are made for all stations except station 1. In other words, two station 2 molds, two station 3s, two station 4s, and one station 5 are made.

The keel, keel batten, two stem assemblies, and the molds are set up at a convenient height for working.

Two stout sawhorses will serve nicely. Stems and molds are plumbed, leveled, and secured in place with braces, shores, and stay-lathes. It is a good idea to secure the molds to the keel batten with short sections of angle iron bored for screws. When this is done, planking lines are marked on the molds. These lines locate the top inside edges of the eight clinker planks. The dimensions given for locating the planking lines are close, but a final trueing with a fair lining batten will be required. Such a batten, preferably of our native Eastern white pine, should be about 1½ inches by ⅜ inch in section, free of knots or other defects, and longer than the boat. This batten is tacked on the marks and then adjusted as required until it sights fair and true throughout, after which the marks are redrawn as necessary. Before the planking lines are

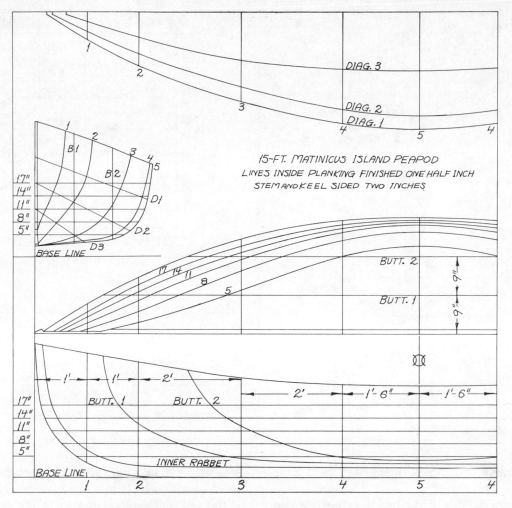

15-FT. MATINICUS ISLAND PEAPOD
LINES INSIDE PLANKING FINISHED ONE HALF INCH
STEM AND KEEL SIDED TWO INCHES

15-FOOT MATINICUS ISLAND PEAPOD							
	STATIONS	STEM	1	2	3	4	5
HEIGHTS	SHEER	2-7-5	2-5-0	2-2-5	1-11-2	1-9-5	1-9-3
	18" BUTTOCK	0-0-0	0-0-0	0-0-0	1-0-1	0-4-7	0-4-0
	9" BUTTOCK	0-0-0	0-0-0	1-0-6	0-4-3	0-3-2	0-3-1
	BEARDING LINE	0-0-0	0-6-4	0-2-5	0-2-4	0-2-4	0-2-4
HALF-BREADTHS	SHEER	0-1-0	0-6-7	1-1-2	1-10-0	2-2-3	2-3-3
	17" W.L.	0-1-0	0-5-0	0-11-4	1-8-2	2-1-3	2-2-5
	14" W.L.	0-1-0	0-3-6	0-9-7	1-6-7	2-0-5	2-2-1
	11" W.L.	0-1-0	0-2-4	0-7-6	1-5-2	1-11-5	2-1-2
	8" W.L.	0-1-0	0-1-2	0-5-2	0-2-5	1-9-6	1-11-6
	5" W.L.	0-1-0	0-0-0	0-2-5	0-10-1	1-6-1	1-8-3
	BEARDING LINE	0-1-0	0-1-0	0-1-0	0-1-0	0-1-0	0-1-0
DIAGONALS	DIAGONAL 1	0-1-1	0-6-5	1-0-6	1-9-0	2-2-2	2-3-5
	DIAGONAL 2	0-1-1	0-4-4	0-9-7	1-5-5	1-10-7	2-0-4
	DIAGONAL 3	0-1-2	0-2-2	0-6-0	0-11-3	1-1-5	1-1-6
	DIAG. 1 UP 23" OUT 24" ON W.L. 14". DIAG. 2 UP 17"						
	OUT 24" ON W.L. 5". DIAG 3 UP 11" OUT 9" ON W.L. 5".						
	LINES INSIDE PLANK IN FEET-INCHES-EIGHTHS. HEIGHTS ABOVE BASE L.						

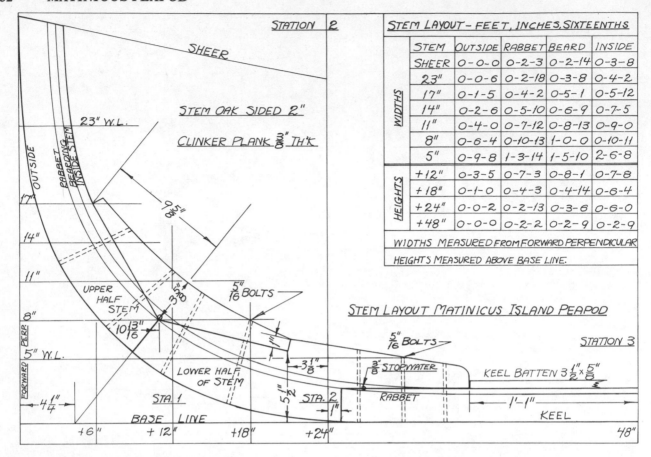

STATION 2

SHEER

STEM OAK SIDED 2"

CLINKER PLANK 3/8" TH'K

23" W.L.

17" OUTSIDE

RABBET BEARDING INSIDE STEM

14"

11"

8"

5" W.L.

FORWARD PERP.

OAK 5"

UPPER HALF STEM

LOWER HALF OF STEM

5/16 BOLTS

2/16

3/16

10 13/16

STA. 1

BASE LINE

4 1/4"

+6" +12" +18" +24"

3 1/8"

5 1/2"

STA. 2

5/16 BOLTS

STATION 3

3/8 STOPWATER

RABBET

KEEL BATTEN 3 1/2" × 5/8"

1'-1"

KEEL

48"

STEM LAYOUT – FEET, INCHES, SIXTEENTHS				
	STEM	OUTSIDE	RABBET	BEARD	INSIDE
WIDTHS	SHEER	0-0-0	0-2-3	0-2-14	0-3-8
	23"	0-0-6	0-2-18	0-3-8	0-4-2
	17"	0-1-5	0-4-2	0-5-1	0-5-12
	14"	0-2-6	0-5-10	0-6-9	0-7-5
	11"	0-4-0	0-7-12	0-8-13	0-9-0
	8"	0-6-4	0-10-13	1-0-0	0-10-11
	5"	0-9-8	1-3-14	1-5-10	2-6-8
HEIGHTS	+12"	0-3-5	0-7-3	0-8-1	0-7-8
	+18"	0-1-0	0-4-3	0-4-14	0-6-4
	+24"	0-0-2	0-2-13	0-3-6	0-6-0
	+48"	0-0-0	0-2-2	0-2-9	0-2-9

WIDTHS MEASURED FROM FORWARD PERPENDICULAR

HEIGHTS MEASURED ABOVE BASE LINE.

STEM LAYOUT MATINICUS ISLAND PEAPOD

marked, of course, the molds themselves must have been tested for fairness.

Ribbands are now installed along the sheerline and the planking lines. These ribbands should be about 1¾ to 2 inches wide and 1⅛ to 1¼ inches thick, and should run the full length of the boat. They must be free of knots and weakening defects in order to bend fair. They are generally fastened to the molds using number 12 or 14 bright steel screws 2½ to 3 inches long with small washers under the heads. Ribbands can be fir, spruce, or pine and may be spliced if necessary, as long as they bend fair.

When the ribbands are in place, the location and spacing of the timbers are marked on the inside. Timbers are preferably of select white oak, free of weakening defects, air dried or still green but not kiln dried, 1 inch wide by 9/16 inch thick. Spaced 7½ to 8 inches on centers, they should be laid out to miss as many of the molds as possible. If possible they should be long enough to reach from gunwale to gunwale. When steaming has made them soft, they are bent in place as marked. By twisting them with a wrench applied to the timberheads and by driving down on the

ends with a maul after they have been hauled against the ribbands with clamps, the hot timbers are made to lie flat and touching against the inside of the ribbands throughout. To hold the timbers in place after the clamps are removed, the builder may nail through from the inside of each still-hot timber into the ribbands using long, slim, resin-coated nails with thick leather disks under the heads. These leather disks serve to apply pressure and to facilitate pulling the nails when the time comes. They are dinked out of scrap leather with a hollow punch about half an inch in diameter. The nails are removed as planking proceeds. Another method for securing the timbers to the ribbands is with twists of soft, strong wire. A pair of small "vise grips" is ideal for tightening these twists.

The boat could be planked upright. A particular advantage of this method is that riveting can be done plank by plank as the planking proceeds, and one person can do the whole operation himself, bucking the rivets on the outside while he peens them on the inside. The principal disadvantage of planking upright is that it is awkward and difficult to fit the bottom planks.

If the boat is planked in the bottom-up position, on

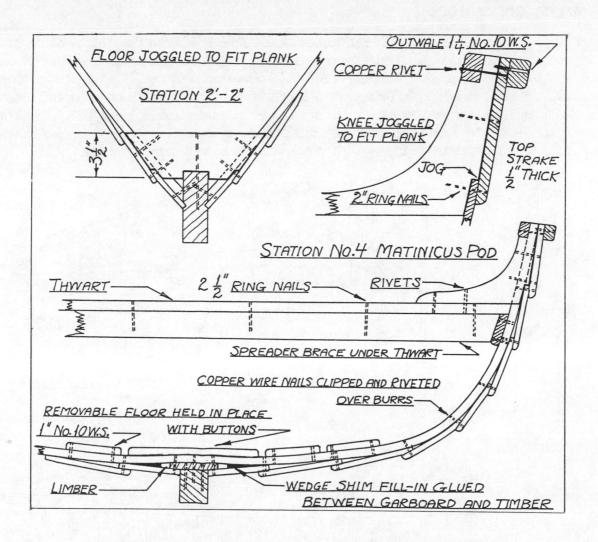

FLOOR JOGGLED TO FIT PLANK

STATION 2'-2"

3½"

OUTWALE 1¼ No.10 W.S.

COPPER RIVET

KNEE JOGGLED TO FIT PLANK

JOG

TOP STRAKE ½" THICK

2" RING NAILS

STATION No.4 MATINICUS POD

THWART

2½" RING NAILS

RIVETS

SPREADER BRACE UNDER THWART

COPPER WIRE NAILS CLIPPED AND RIVETED OVER BURRS

REMOVABLE FLOOR HELD IN PLACE WITH BUTTONS

1" No.10 W.S.

LIMBER

WEDGE SHIM FILL-IN GLUED BETWEEN GARBOARD AND TIMBER

PLANKING WIDTHS 15' MATINICUS PEAPOD						
STATION	STEM	1	2	3	4	5
SHEER	3 3/8	3 7/8	4 1/4	4 1/2	4 7/8	5 1/8
2	2 3/4	3	3 1/4	3 1/2	4 1/8	4 1/4
3	2 3/4	3	3 1/8	3 3/4	4	4 1/8
4	2 3/4	2 7/8	3 1/8	3 1/4	3 1/2	3 7/8
5	3	3	3	3 1/2	4 1/4	4 3/8
6	3	3 1/4	3 3/4	4 1/2	5 3/8	5 3/4
7	3 3/8	3 1/4	3 3/4	5	5 5/8	5 3/4
GARBOARD		1 5/8	3 1/2	4 1/4	4 3/4	5

PLANK LINES TOP INSIDE EDGE OF PLANKING
ADD WIDTH OF LAP 7/8" TO ALL PLANK EXCEPT
GARBOARD. WIDTHS WILL VARY SLIGHTLY.
FAIR WITH LINING BATTEN. W. PINE 5/16" x 1 3/8".

① KEEL OAK, SIDED 2", MOLDED 2½". ② KEEL BATTEN, OAK 3¾" WIDE ½" THICK. ③ TIMBERS, WHITE OAK STEAM BENT 1" × 9/16" THICK, CONTINOUS FROM RAIL TO RAIL EXCEPT LAST THREE TIMBERS AT THE ENDS. ④ SEAT RISERS PINE 2½" WIDE 5/8" THICK, TAPERED AT ENDS. ⑤ THWARTS 10" WIDE 7/8" THICK. ⑥ SPREADER CLEATS PINE 2½" × 7/8" TO FIT TIGHT BETWEEN THE SEAT RISERS. FASTEN THROUGH THWARTS AND BENCHES. ⑦ END BENCHES PINE 3/4" OR 7/8" THICK. ⑧ INWALE OAK 1⅛" × 3/4" THICK TAPERED TO 1" AT ENDS. ⑨ BREASTHOOK OAK, HACKMATACK, APPLE, GROWN SHAPES OR 2 PIECES PINNED AND GLUED TOGETHER. ⑩ SEAT KNEES OAK, HACK, APPLE, GROWN BENDS OR LAMINATIONS SIDED 1". 8-INCH FOOT. ⑪ OARLOCK PADS 7/8" OAK ⑫ FLOOR BOARDS 5/8" PINE. MIDDLE BOARD REMOVABLE FOR CLEANING. SIDE BOARDS SCREWED TO THE TIMBERS.

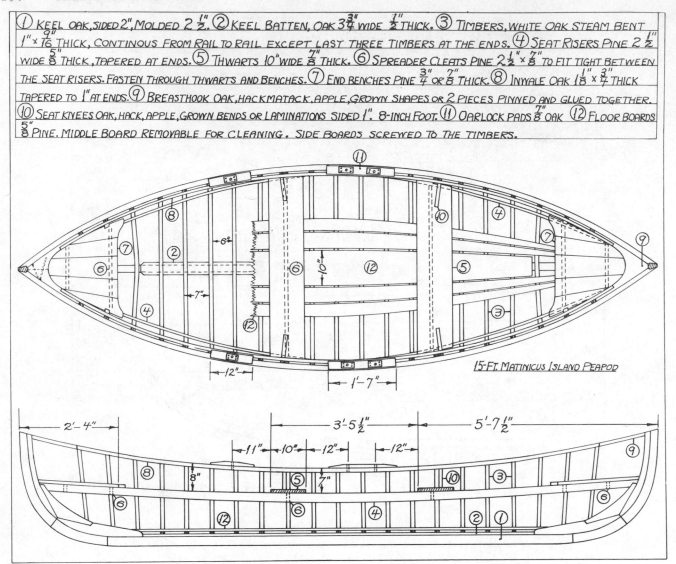

15-FT. MATINICUS ISLAND PEAPOD

the other hand, the garboards and broads will go on much more easily, but peening the rivets must generally be postponed until the planks are all on and the boat has been turned over. Then, although one operation can be made of the riveting, two persons are required to do it, one on the outside holding on and a second on the inside peening the rivets.

A variation of the upside-down method is sometimes used in production shops when building a stock model in quantity. The combined thickness of the ribbands and timbers is deducted from the molds before the ribbands are fastened in place, and the timbers are bent around the *outside* of the ribbands, permitting the planking to be fastened directly to the timbers as it is put on. When the planking operation

has been completed and the planked-up hull is lifted off, the form remains intact, ready to receive the timbers for another boat. This is an efficient method when a number of identical boats are built, but it would not pay to construct such a form for a single boat. Neither is it recommended when the plank fastenings are rivets rather than screws.

As an alternate method for planking a clinker hull, if only one boat is to be built, I'd like to suggest a combination of the right-side up and upside-down methods. After the timbers have been bent in and well secured to the inside of the ribbands with wire twists or leathered nails or both, the boat is turned over and the garboards and the next two planks above are fitted and fastened in place. The boat is then turned right side up

Though not a Matinicus pod, this boat being built at Mystic Seaport shows the standard peapod construction. The ribbands are on and planking is about to begin. (Mystic Seaport photo by Lester D. Olin)

A good interior shot showing the typical peapod seating arrangement.

One example of the many good peapods built by amateurs from the plans for a 14-footer in Building Classic Small Craft, Volume I. Construction methods are similar to those for the 15-footer offered here.

again. Whatever riveting is required for the planks already on is completed, and the remainder of the planking is fitted and fastened. This permits the builder to do whatever riveting is required for the upper plank without assistance. The bucking iron can be held against the rivet heads on the outside by pressure from some part of the builder's body—leg, side, or the like—while the burr is driven on from the inside and the rivet is snipped and peened.

In planking the topsides the ribbands are left in place as long as possible, removing them one by one as necessary to fit the planks. It will be easier to put in the seat riser, whose top edge is 7 inches below the sheer, before the topsides are closed in. In this way it will be possible to clamp it in place before fastening, by reaching through from the outside.

The following information supplements the accompanying drawings.

Stem and keel, white oak, sided 2 inches. Keel batten, white oak, 3¾ inches by ⅝ inch. Clinker planking, ⅜ inch thick, of cedar, white pine, or marine plywood. Timbers, steam-bent select white oak, continuous gunwale to gunwale, 1 inch by ⁹⁄₁₆ inch. Inwales and outwales, 1⅛ inches by ¾ inch, tapered slightly at the ends. Seat riser, pine, 2½ inches by ⅝ inch. Thwarts, 10 inches by ⅞ inch, pine or Douglas fir. Thwart knees and breasthooks, grown crooks if possible; can also be glued laminates.

Fastenings through laps into timbers, screws or copper rivets. Screws, number 8, 1-inch or 1¼-inch bronze. Plank to stems, keel batten, and timberheads, number 8, ⅞-inch bronze screws. If rivets are used, cut copper nails would be first choice, but since cut nails are now largely unobtainable, copper wire nails are an acceptable substitute. Through laps and timbers, use 2-inch copper wire nails snipped to the correct length for riveting after burrs tight enough to draw have been driven on with a burr set. Through laps between frames, use two 1⅛-inch copper wire nails spaced equally, snipped and riveted, with burrs set down tightly enough to draw. Through wales, planking, and timberheads, use 2½-inch copper wire nails riveted over burrs.

12

TWO GARVEYS

TWENTY-TWO-FOOT-FIVE-INCH WORKING GARVEY

Of all our native working craft, the type that occupies the bottom place on the totem pole in popular esteem must be the scow. Indeed, for many, *scow* is the lowest name they know for a boat. Although their scorn may be justified in some instances, it definitely does not apply to the many worthy, and even shapely, flat-bottomed, square-ended workboats that come within the generic classification of scow.

One such scow subtype that can hold its head high in any company of working craft—that is, when well built and properly designed—is the garvey, at home in shallow coastal waters from New Jersey to the lower Chesapeake. There is good evidence that the first New Jersey garvey was built about 250 years ago at West Creek by one Gervais Pharo, whose name in corrupted

form has passed down to us as the name of the workboat type he introduced.

Of course he did not originate the type. Flat-bottomed, square-ended scows of various shapes and sizes had been in use in Europe for many centuries before their appearance in the New World. As utilitarian craft they had much to commend them. Their simple construction made them relatively easy and inexpensive to build. Good carrying capacity was combined with shoal draft. Their wide, flat bottoms provided stable working platforms. And before conversion to power with the addition of skegs and deadwood, they beached easily and sat securely upright when grounded out.

On the debit side, the unmodified scow form is not suited to the open sea, although when properly designed and equipped with engines, some derivative scow forms have done quite well in rough water. One

157

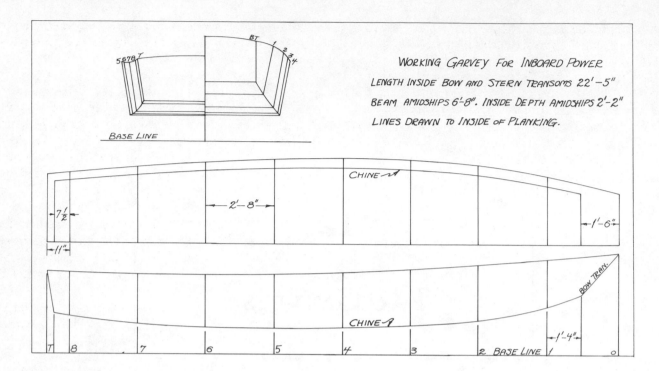

WORKING GARVEY FOR INBOARD POWER
LENGTH INSIDE BOW AND STERN TRANSOMS 22'-5"
BEAM AMIDSHIPS 6'-8". INSIDE DEPTH AMIDSHIPS 2'-2"
LINES DRAWN TO INSIDE OF PLANKING.

OFFSETS 22' GARVEY				
STATIONS	HEIGHTS		WIDTHS	
	BOTTOM	SHEER	BOTTOM	SHEER
BT	2-4-2	3-11-6	2-0-0	2-0-0
1	1-10-3	3-8-7	2-3-3	2-7-7
2	1-4-1	3-6-2	2-8-1	3-0-7
3	1-1-4	3-3-6	2-10-4	3-3-1
4	1-0-4	3-2-1	2-11-2	3-4-0
5	1-0-1	3-1-2	2-11-1	3-3-2
6	1-0-5	3-0-6	2-10-0	3-2-1
7	1-1-7	3-1-1	2-8-1	2-11-5
8	1-5-3	3-2-0	2-5-1	2-8-7
T	1-6-7	3-2-4	2-4-4	2-7-5

such type was the Hickman Sea Sled, very popular and quite widely used for a time just prior to the Great Depression as a high-speed pleasure craft. The Sea Sled was not particularly easy to build because of its modified, inverted V bottom, which also lessened internal capacity to such an extent that the Sea Sled was of little use as a workboat.

Following the Sea Sled, a variety of less extreme modifications of the scow equipped with power and designed for speed have been tried with varying success, including a number of tunnel-stern garveys. By far the most popular modification of the powered scow for pleasure use is the Boston Whaler.

As long as gasoline was plentiful and cheap, powered scows, including garveys, were developed for speed, as were most other types. Needless to say, this has changed. Many small-craft fishermen are now finding that economy of operation is paramount, and that the fast, energy-intensive boat is something they can do without. As long as it is not necessary to commute great distances to offshore fishing grounds or race to a distant market with the catch, speed is proving a costly and unneeded luxury. The garvey, which formerly was modified by flattening and straightening its run aft to give it planing speed, is easily returned to slower, more economical operation by restoring some of the original bottom rocker and cutting down on horsepower. That is what we have attempted to do with the working garvey considered here.

In working out the following design for a 22-foot garvey fishing launch to be powered with a 12 h.p. Spanish Sole diesel, I have drawn quite heavily on a 26-foot New Jersey fishing garvey taken off by Howard I. Chapelle at Tuckerton, New Jersey, in 1925. This design was presented in Chapelle's "Some American Fishing Launches," a paper given at the first Food and Agriculture Organization (FAO) International Fishing Boat Congress in 1953 at Paris and Miami, and later included in the published proceedings of the congress, *Fishing Boats of the World*, Vol. 1.

Very few plans for working garveys have been published other than the two in Chapelle's paper—the one mentioned and a highly distinctive Virginia trap boat of 29 feet. Chapelle had a high opinion of the working garvey, which he thought compared favorably with another of his favorite workboat types, the New Haven sharpie, which is also cross-planked on the bottom.

One advantage the garvey had was greater working capacity in a given length. Chapelle promoted the type whenever he could, encouraging its adoption by fishermen. He felt that its good qualities had been largely overlooked outside the limited area on the East Coast where it first appeared, and that it deserved to be more widely known and adopted.

I am told that the garvey I have drawn upon in working out the details for the one shown here was powered with an old four-cylinder automobile engine and ran about nine knots with the throttle two-thirds open. My shortened adaptation, which has a somewhat more rockered bottom and a 12 h.p. diesel, is expected to run very economically at a maximum speed of six or seven knots. I am suggesting the Spanish Sole diesel manufactured in Barcelona and distributed in this country by Beacon Plastic and Metal Products, 50 Park Avenue, New York, New York 10016.

What appeals to me in particular about the Sole is its light weight and compact size—only 189 pounds with electric start, and approximately 2½ feet long by 22 inches high by 19 inches wide—and its good record in the Spanish fisheries for more than 25 years, where for some time fuel economy has been even more urgent than it is here at present. There may be other small diesels that would perform very well in this boat, in particular the Norwegian Sabb, but I do feel the Sole, hardly known in this country up to now, deserves special consideration.

While I have used the 26-foot New Jersey garvey drawn by Chapelle as a model and as a control, so to speak, I have made the boat shown here 4 feet shorter, increased the curve of the bottom rocker at the stern slightly, and raised the height of the sheer by 4 inches. In his construction view, Chapelle did not show any bottom floors, any lengthwise stringers inside the cross-planked bottom, or any internal flooring for the working cockpit. I have added all three.

Cross floors at every frame station are bolted to the side frames with two 5/16-inch galvanized carriage bolts. In addition the chine is bolted through the bottom of each side frame. To further reinforce the cross-planked bottom, three stringers running fore and aft are let in flush with the bottom of the cross floors. This makes an exceptionally strong internal framing, and permits the use of ½-inch plywood panels for the side planking.

The 3½-inch-high cross floors support a tight sole or flooring of ¾-inch pine for the working cockpit, which is slightly more than 9 feet long by 5 feet wide. Sheathing on the sides and low, tight bulkheads at either end provide an enclosed working space, keeping dirt and water out of the bilge to a considerable extent. The center board is removable, permitting the removal of whatever water collects in the bilge. Limbers drain to the low point amidships.

The drawings reproduced herewith were plotted accurately to scale, and even in reduced size will yield reliable approximate dimensions by careful scaling. Where it has seemed that special explanation might be helpful, there are numbers keyed to the comments listed below. Altogether there should be enough information to provide a pretty good idea of how to construct this boat.

1. *Frames:* Oak. Spaced 16 inches on centers. Sided 1⅛ inches, molded 3½ inches at the bottom, tapering to 2 inches at the top. If Douglas fir is substituted for oak, siding should be 1¼ inches.

2. *Floors:* Oak. Sided 1⅛ inches, molded 3½ inches. Douglas fir, sided 1¼ inches. But see *28, 29,* and *52.*

3. *Sides:* Fir plywood, ½ inch to ⅝ inch thick. Marine grade or, if you are fortunate enough to find it, superior-quality exterior without internal voids. Put on as continuous panels. Can also be carvel-planked

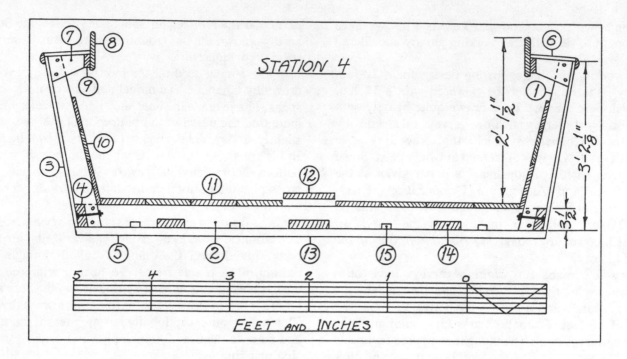

with white pine, Douglas fir, Port Orford cedar, or equivalent finished ¾ inch thick.

4. *Chines:* Oak. Sided 1½ inches, molded 3½ inches. Sawn to the required curve, and got out in two lengths in order to minimize the width of stock needed to give the required curve.

5. *Bottom cross planking:* Northern white pine, Douglas fir, juniper, or Port Orford cedar, 1⅛ inches thick. Planks put on no wider than 6 inches; 5 inches preferable. Nailed with 3½-inch galvanized nails. Cross planks wedged tight on inside. Outside caulking seams ⅛ inch to 3/16 inch wide. Driven cotton caulking payed with red-lead primer and puttied with non-hardening bottom-seam compound. No synthetic-rubber caulk.

6. *Side decking and end decking:* Half-inch fir plywood.

7. *Deck gussets:* Oak or Douglas fir. Sided 1⅛ inches and bolted to the top of the frames with two 5/16-inch carriage bolts.

8. *Coamings:* Oak. Three-quarters inch by 6 inches.

9. *Backing strip:* Oak or Douglas fir. Three-quarters inch by 2 inches.

10. *Side sheathing:* Pine or fir. Five-eighths inch thick.

11. *Cockpit floor:* Pine or fir. Three-quarters inch

thick and 7 to 8 inches wide tongue-and-grooved except for the removable 8-inch center board.

12. *Removable center strip:* Gives access to the bilge for bailing.

13. *Middle stringer:* Oak. One and an eighth inches thick, 7 inches wide.

14. *Side stringers:* Oak. One and an eighth inches thick, 4 inches wide. In two pieces with open joint amidships to provide a limber so the bottom can drain to the center. Fastened together with a butt block on top over the open joint.

15. *Limbers in cross floors:* 1½ inches long by ¾ inch high.

16. *Engine box:* Removable flat cover. One side hinged to fold down part way to give convenient access to the engine. Watertight when closed.

17. *After bulkhead:* Seven inches above the cockpit floor.

18. *Forward bulkhead:* Same as *17.*

19. *Fuel tank:* Six gallons or larger.

20. *Filler cap.*

21. *Chine splice:* Located well forward to minimize the amount of curve in the forward section.

22. *Thwart:* Pine or fir. Twelve inches wide; ⅞ inch thick, or thicker. Eight inches below top of coaming.

23. *Sternpost:* Oak. Sided 3 inches, molded 6

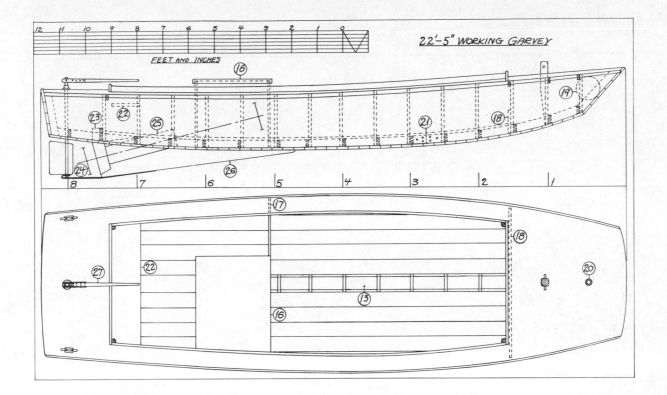

FEET AND INCHES

inches. Extends up into the interior of the boat and bolts to a 6-inch-wide cross floor. This ensures that the deadwood cannot easily be wracked sidewise should the boat ground out hard. The sternpost should be laid out with the run of the grain so as to avoid cross grain as much as possible.

24. *Propeller:* Thirteen-inch-by-eleven-inch three-bladed wheel.

25. *Split shaft log for 1-inch shaft:* Sided 3½ inches and 8 inches when bolted together.

26. *Deadwood:* Oak. Sided 3½ inches.

27. *Tiller:* Pinned to the 1¼-inch rudder stock with a single ⅜-inch bolt, allowing the tiller to be raised and lowered easily.

For the most part, the construction of the 22-foot-5-inch working garvey is relatively simple, straight-forward boatbuilding, well within the capabilities of a nonprofessional who has some mechanical experience and a fair amount of woodworking skill.

Scantlings are fairly heavy, befitting a workboat, and construction is on the rugged side, because this is not a speedboat and hull weight is not a critical factor. This gives the builder more leeway and makes the job quite a bit easier.

One of the things that requires some special attention and study is the engine installation. Another is fitting together the deadwood–shaft log–sternpost

assembly and attaching it to the cross-planked flat bottom.

For a workboat that stands some chance of being beached on occasion, the deadwood must be solidly attached. Otherwise there is a good chance of its being sprung to one side or the other, throwing the engine out of line, should the boat ground out hard. One measure taken to prevent this is to have the sternpost extend up into the boat and bolted to an extra-heavy cross floor (*29* in the accompanying drawings).

I have specified a split shaft log because it is not overly difficult to make with tools ordinarily available to the nonprofessional; the equipment needed to bore a solid shaft log of this size might be difficult to obtain. I have specified a heavy, 3½-inch siding for the shaft log and deadwood to make boring the ⅜-inch holes for the through bolts on either side of the shaft hole less critical.

The semicircular grooves in the two halves of the split log that form the shaft hole can be roughed out on an ordinary circular saw and finished with a gouge. A rounded molding plane with a blade an inch or so wide, if one can be had, will help.

The slots for the splines on either side of the shaft hole are also cut on the circular saw. The splines themselves should be dry white pine. They should fit snugly and be bedded in red-lead primer—not the synthetic nonlead substitute now being sold, but

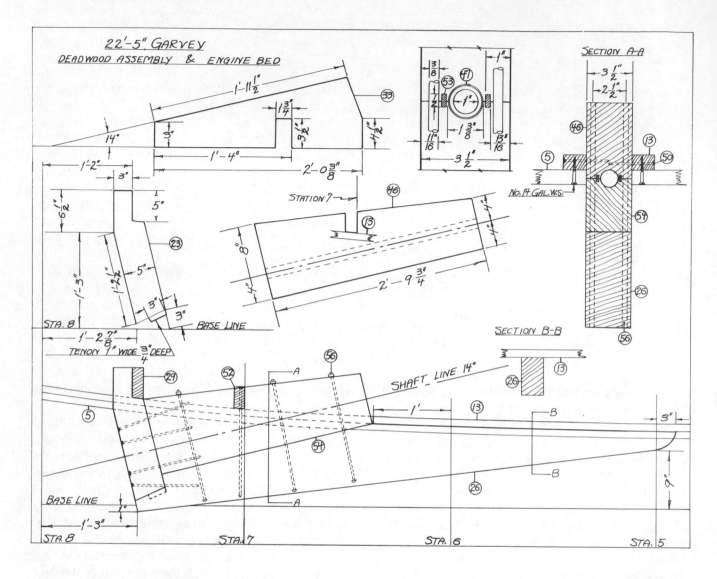

genuine red lead, the real McCoy. In fact, the whole bottom should be primed with red lead, especially the caulked seams of the cross-planked bottom. The cotton caulking, after it has been driven tight, should be thoroughly saturated with red lead for a lasting job.

Even though this is a simple, flat-bottomed workboat, it should be laid down full size before construction starts. This is particularly recommended for the nonprofessional, first-time builder. Not only will such a laydown make the work much easier, saving time in the long run, but without it the inexperienced builder is likely to find himself completely at sea as he gets into the job. Even if some initial study is required, it will be time well spent.

From this laydown, molds can be lifted for the several pieces that form the deadwood–shaft log–sternpost assembly. These molds are best made of ¼-inch plywood and should fit together precisely. With the molds as patterns, the pieces for this assembly are got out of 3½-inch oak. If this is done accurately, not only will these pieces fit together exactly, but the assembly will also fit into place in the hull structure.

It is best to drill for the bolts that will hold this assembly together before the shaft hole is put in. The location of these bolt holes is important, and drilling them is one of the most critical operations in the construction of this boat. If any of these long bolt holes deviate by even a small fraction of an inch, it will mess things up thoroughly.

Fortunately, there is a simple but reliable method

for drilling such holes accurately and safely. I have not seen it described in any of the boatbuilding books, although it may have been. In any case, it should be more widely known and used.

The several pieces to be bolted or drifted together are fitted together on a bench or some other flat, level surface at a height above the floor convenient for working. Then straight lines representing the centers of the drifts or bolts to be put in are marked across the upper surface of the assembly, which must be smooth and flat. The pieces are then separated so that the lines marked across their upper surfaces can be squared down across the edges on either side.

Next, an adjustable combination square is set to the required distance in from the upper surface to the bolts, and with the square as a gauge, this distance is squared down from the upper surface across each of the bolt lines, as marked on both edges. The intersections where these lines cross represent the precise centers of the bolt holes to be bored. Note that all measurements on the edges *must* be taken *only* from the upper surface.

Using a carpenter's spurred auger the size of the bolt holes to be bored, start shallow holes on both edges *exactly* on the centers that have been marked—¼ inch is deep enough, but no deeper. To bore the holes through from side to side, you can use either a long drill bit or a "barefoot" ship auger. The latter is best for this purpose. These are often extended by having a length of drill rod welded onto them. For holes ⅜ inch in diameter, most electric drills with ⅜-inch chucks will do, although one of moderate speed is to be preferred.

The procedure for drilling the bolt holes is as follows. The piece to be bored is clamped to the bench, its marked side up. A short straightedge of 1-inch pine board (or something similar) is laid across the upper surface exactly along the line marking the center of the hole to be bored. It is then temporarily tacked in place with a couple of small nails to prevent it from accidentally shifting.

One end of the straightedge should extend 8 to 10 inches, or thereabouts, beyond the piece and toward the drill. The operator inserts the point of the drill bit or auger into the shallow hole that's already been started and lines up his drill precisely with the edge of the straightedge in preparation for boring. This is readily done by sighting.

At the same time, an assistant, standing some distance to the side and at right angles, directs the operator to raise or lower his machine until the long shank of the drill is exactly parallel to the overhanging end of the straightedge. As drilling proceeds, the assistant watches closely to see that the drill shank remains parallel and is not raised or lowered in the slightest.

Drilling proceeds in this manner until the bit is *halfway* through the piece, but no more. The bit is then withdrawn, and drilling is started from the other side, following the same procedure as before. If care has been taken, the second hole will meet the first head-on in the center of the piece. If not, it will at least be so close that passing the drill through once from side to side will clear the hole, permitting the bolt or drift to be driven easily.

When all of the pieces have been drilled separately in this manner, they are reassembled—use the lines on the upper surface to realign them—and then clamped together so they cannot shift out of position while the bolts are being driven. A couple of strips of board nailed temporarily across the upper surface will serve for this. All the holes should line up, although it is just as well to pass the long drill bit through them before the bolts are driven.

This is a thoroughly tested procedure that cannot fail if care is taken and directions are strictly followed. I have used it for years in my boatbuilding classes, where it has been amply demonstrated that no experience or particular skill is required to do it successfully. It is the most trustworthy method I know for boring long holes through assemblies of several separate members in preparation for through bolting. This is particularly true when tolerances are critical— for example, when there is a double risk of the hole running off and either breaking through into the shaft hole or coming out through the side of the deadwood. This method is simpler, quicker, and easier than rigging a special boring jig, except possibly on a production job, and it's more accurate and dependable than any improvised jig I have ever seen.

Of course, a drill bit of the right size is essential, but that is another story. To make sure that the bit or auger you choose is neither too large nor too small, you should bore some test holes in the same timber before you proceed.

The boat is turned upside down for framing and planking. The bottom cross floors bolted to the side frames serve as molds, all except the floor at station 7 *(52 in the drawings)*, which is best fitted and installed after the deadwood assembly is in place and the boat

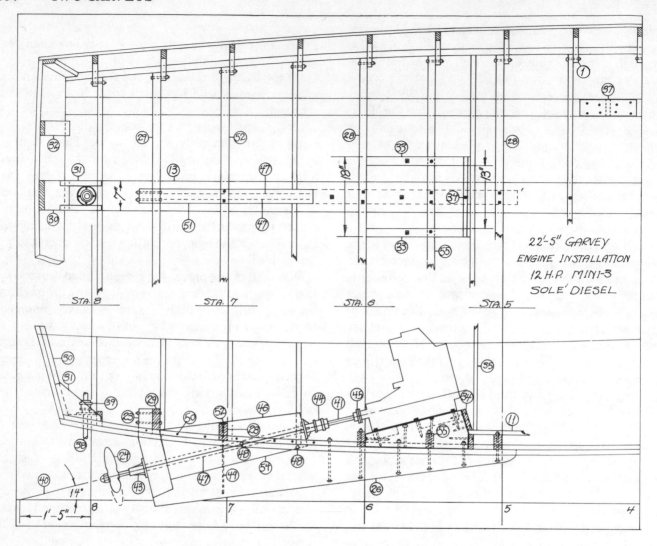

22'-5" GARVEY
ENGINE INSTALLATION
12 H.P. MINI-3
SOLE' DIESEL

has been turned back over. The recess in the upper half of the shaft log is not cut to receive this floor until it is fitted. The plan shows this floor fastened to the deadwood assembly with drift bolts on either side of the shaft hole.

These bolts could be through bolts whose holes were bored at the same time as those for the bolts through the deadwood assembly. This might be the better way of installing this floor. Holes through the floor *(52)* that connect with the already bored holes through the shaft log and deadwood should not be difficult to locate, and in doing it this way there would be no chance of hitting the shaft hole or breaking out through the side.

The engine beds are put in after the boat is turned over, when it will be most convenient to fit them over the bottom floor midway between stations 5 and 6

(55). They should be fastened to this cross floor with drift pins.

Lead pipe used to be the standard material for making watertight shaft-log liners, but it is often difficult to obtain today, so soft copper tubing may be substituted.

By carefully hammering well-greased turned and tapered wooden plugs of different sizes into the lead pipe, it is expanded so that it fits the ends of the shaft hole tightly. After being bedded with white lead, it is flanged over and nailed with copper tacks in the shallow recess cut for it to give a flat seat for the stern bearing. Soft copper tubing can also be expanded and flanged over in much the same way. To soften copper by annealing, bring it to a red heat and quench in cold water. It's just the opposite of steel in this respect.

The two stopwaters *(48)* shown for the deadwood

assembly are essential if the boat is not to leak. Obviously, the one in the way of the shaft hole cannot go all the way through and must be installed in two short pieces cut to the exact length before they are driven. They are located so the caulking in the seam at the ends of the short cross plank will make up tightly against them. Stopwaters should be made of dry soft pine or the equivalent.

Bore a hole the right size through a piece of oak board. Relieve the sharp edge of the hole on the upper side and apply grease. Plane or turn the stopwater to a diameter slightly larger than required. Drive it through the hole in the oak board with a heavy hammer or top maul. This will size the stopwater and compress it. When moisture strikes it, it will swell and become very tight.

Bottom boards are nailed to the chines and the cross floors with 3-inch galvanized wire nails, since cut boat nails probably are not available. The heads should be well set in for puttying. The bottom boards are fastened to the bottom stringers with 2-inch number 14 galvanized wood screws.

Construction Details

The following construction details relate to the numbered elements in the accompanying drawings.

28. The siding of these two oak cross floors is increased to 1¾ inches, molded 3½ inches, to beef up the bottom structure for support of the shaft log, deadwood, and engine beds.

29. *Oak cross floor:* Molded 6 inches, sided 1¾ inches. Supports the end of the sternpost, which projects through the bottom and is bolted to it with two ⅜-inch galvanized carriage bolts. This is a structural member of critical importance, carrying much of the weight of the shaft log and deadwood in addition to preventing the deadwood from being loosened and knocked sidewise should the boat accidentally strike an obstruction or ground out on a hard beach.

30. *Transom center frame:* Oak, sided 1⅛ inches and molded 7 inches to match the width of the middle bottom stringer *(13)*.

31. *Two knees:* Oak, sided 1⅛ inches and rising 7 inches against the transom center frame.

32. *Intermediate transom frames:* Oak. Sided 1⅛ inches, molded 4 inches.

33. *Engine beds:* Oak, sided 2½ inches. See dimensioned drawing for molded shape.

34. *Cross brace:* Oak, forward end of the engine beds. Sided 1⅛ inches. Fastened with 4½-inch galvanized wire spikes.

35. *Forward end of the engine box:* Pine, sided ¾ inch to ⅞ inch.

37. Limber through side stringers to drain to the center of the boat. Cut to leave a 1-inch gap between the ends of the two parts of the stringer. Joined with an overlapping block of the same material on top and fastened with 2-inch number 14 galvanized wood screws.

38. *Rudder stock:* One-inch diameter.

40. *Shaft line:* Fourteen degrees with the baseline and load waterline. This is well within the specified maximum installation angle of 20 degrees for the Sole diesel.

41. *Propeller shaft:* One-inch diameter. Propeller: Three blades, 14 inches by 11 inches.

43. Stern bearing.

44. *Inside stuffing box:* Flax packing.

45. Shaft coupling.

46. *Shaft log:* Upper half, oak, sided 3½ inches. See dimensioned profile layout for split shaft log.

47. *Shaft-hole liner:* Lead pipe or soft copper tubing, 1¼ inches inside diameter.

48. *Stopwaters:* ¾-inch soft dry pine. Located where the shaft line and the bottom of the split shaft log cross the caulking seam of the bottom planking.

49. *Drift bolts:* ⅜-inch galvanized drift rod driven through the floor at station 7 into the deadwood on each side of the shaft hole. Replacement by through bolts is optional.

50. Galvanized wire nails 3½ inches long spaced 5 to 7 inches through sides of the middle stringer into the sternpost–shaft log–deadwood assembly.

51. Three-and-a-half-inch cutout through the 7-inch middle stringer to admit the deadwood assembly.

52. *Floor aft of station 7:* Dimensions increased from 3½ inches molded height to 4½ inches.

53. *Shaft-log splines:* ³⁄₁₆-inch by ½-inch dry white pine set in red lead.

54. Lower half of split shaft log.

56. Three-eighths-inch galvanized bolts.

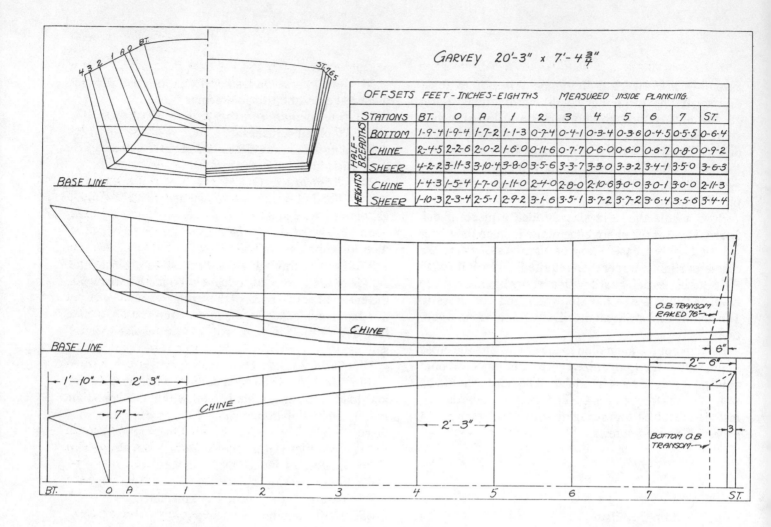

Garvey 20'-3" x 7'-4¾"

STATIONS		BT.	0	A	1	2	3	4	5	6	7	ST.
OFFSETS FEET-INCHES-EIGHTHS MEASURED INSIDE PLANKING.												
HALF-BREADTHS	Bottom	1-9-4	1-9-4	1-7-2	1-1-3	0-7-4	0-4-1	0-3-4	0-3-6	0-4-5	0-5-5	0-6-4
	Chine	2-4-5	2-2-6	2-0-2	1-6-0	0-11-6	0-7-7	0-6-0	0-6-0	0-6-7	0-8-0	0-9-2
	Sheer	4-2-2	3-11-3	3-10-4	3-8-0	3-5-6	3-3-7	3-3-0	3-3-2	3-4-1	3-5-0	3-6-3
HEIGHTS	Chine	1-4-3	1-5-4	1-7-0	1-11-0	2-4-0	2-8-0	2-10-6	3-0-0	3-0-1	3-0-0	2-11-3
	Sheer	1-10-3	2-3-4	2-5-1	2-9-2	3-1-6	3-5-1	3-7-2	3-7-2	3-6-4	3-5-6	3-4-4

TWENTY-FOOT GARVEY

In designing this boat I have attempted to produce something that builders keep asking for every so often. Combined in this single vessel are as many as possible of the various features and characteristics specified by them for a workboat of small or moderate size.

Heading the list of requirements are the following: The boat has to be one that can be easily constructed without special boatbuilding skills or knowledge, which is to say one that is well within the capabilities of anyone with elementary carpentry experience and proficiency. Materials must be relatively inexpensive, although nothing is really cheap today, and readily available. So, instead of hard-to-get boatbuilding lumber, all that is required is standard construction lumber obtainable at most well-stocked retail outlets.

The materials list is short. Standard 2-inch Douglas-fir or hard-pine joists, net thickness about 1½ inches, serve for framing throughout. One-inch boards (net ¾ inch thick) of northern white pine, southern hard pine, or Douglas fir in narrow or medium random widths will be used for the foundation of fore-and-aft stringers that underlie the ⅜-inch fir or hard-pine plywood covering the bottom, sides, and decks, and for the cockpit floor and side sheathing. For fastenings, hot-dipped galvanized wire nails in several lengths and epoxy glue will be used. Little else is required for constructing the bare hull, exclusive of the painting and the usual fittings to be added in equipping the boat for service.

After a lot of thought, we picked the garvey as the type of hull that would best meet the majority of our listed requirements. Twenty feet seems to be a popular and useful length, although this hull could easily be stretched out several feet or shortened to 18 feet.

The pram bow and the slight V forward should handle moderate seas without pounding the way a dead flat bottom would. Naturally this garvey will not prove as seaworthy as a boat like the St. Pierre dory, and is not recommended for offshore fishing in the stormy North Atlantic. Yet I am confident that it will be adequate for coastwise fishing under reasonable weather conditions. This hull has extra carrying capacity, can handle heavy loads, and provides a stable working platform. Although this hull is more or less a typical garvey hull, its construction is distinctly different, having been simplified to an extent not seen before, yet without any sacrifice of strength.

Power is supplied by an outboard motor. Much working room is saved by using an outboard instead of an inboard engine, and because there is no need for either shaft log or rudder there are significant savings of materials and labor.

A bare minimum of woodworking hand tools will suffice. All that are absolutely essential are two handsaws (a rip and a crosscut), a nail hammer, a plane (preferably a jack plane), a rule, a carpenter's square, a bevel square, and a couple of 6-inch C-clamps. A chisel would be handy but is not essential. Of course, an electric handsaw will speed up the operation greatly, and it might pay to get one if the time factor is important and power is available. And naturally a well-equipped woodworking shop will be even better.

Because the boat is a garvey, there is no stem or keel to rabbet. There are no difficult planking bends, no steam-bent frames or steam bending of any sort. No full-size laydown of lines is required, since dimensions and beveling for the frames that serve as molds are diagramed here.

It is recommended that the boat be set bottom up for planking on a ladder frame.

The pieces that make up the frame assemblies—that is, the side futtocks (*1* in the accompanying diagrams) and the bottom cross floors (*2*)—are cut out of 2-inch fir joists (1½ inches thick, net) as diagramed, and are beveled at the bench before they are put together. Beveling is much easier when the pieces are separated.

All the bevels are "under" bevels, as illustrated in the diagram. This requires that frames from station 5 forward be set on the forward side of the station lines with their beveled edges sloping forward, and that frames from station 6 aft be set on the after side of the station lines with their beveled edges sloping aft.

The exceptions are the transoms, which are set *inside* the ends. These are beveled "standing"—the opposite of under beveling. This requires that they be

framed larger than the finished dimensions on the outside, to provide enough wood for beveling. See the diagram for the bow transom.

After beveling, the frames are assembled with plywood gussets applied to both sides of the chine knuckle. These are put on with epoxy glue and 1¾-inch galvanized nails spaced as shown.

It is recommended that the outline of the frame be accurately marked out on a flat, smooth surface—bench top, worktable, or floor. In assembling a frame, its pieces are laid out in conformity with this outline, beveled side up, and the gussets fastened on. Then the frame assembly can be turned over and the gussets put on the other side. When this has been done, triangular pieces of 1½-inch fir joist, previously marked and cut to shape, are inserted with glue into the two pockets on the inside of the frame assembly and are nailed through the gussets. The ends of these pieces are also nailed into the frame. Finally a cross spall for the ladder-frame setup is temporarily nailed in place. Double-headed staging nails work well for this as well as for setting up the ladder frame.

For this boat, the top edge of the cross spalls should be exactly 3 feet above the baseline. When the outline of each frame is laid out prior to assembly, it will be easy to locate the top of the cross spall 3 feet above the baseline.

In addition to the frames, assemblies of the bow and stern transoms must be made before the boat can be set up for planking. Both of these transom assemblies consist of internal framing of fir joist 1½ inches thick covered on the outer side with ⅜-inch plywood that holds them together and fastened with glue and galvanized nails. After the bottom and sides are planked, the projecting ends of the stringers and the plywood covering them are trimmed flush with the surface of the transoms, and an outer layer of plywood is put on with nails and glue, covering all. Finally the raw edge of this final layer of plywood on the ends is covered with fiberglass tape set in epoxy.

What is most distinctive and different about the construction is the planking, which is done in two layers. First is an under layer of fore-and-aft stringers ¾ inch thick nailed directly to the frames. These are covered by an outer layer of ⅜-inch plywood, which is nailed through into the frames as well as being nailed and glued to the stringers. There is only a minimum of fitting since many of the stringers are perfectly straight, as can be seen in the diagram of the bottom. Those shown are 5½-inch boards, but they could just

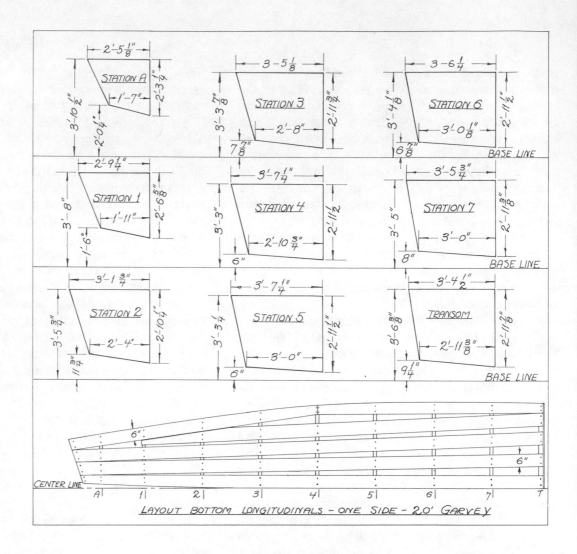

Above and opposite: *Dimensions and bevels as originally drawn for the frames and transoms of the 20-foot garvey. The stern transom rake was subsequently changed to conform to Outboard Marine Corporation recommendations (see page 172); if this modified rake is adopted by the builder, slight changes to the stern transom dimensions and bottom bevel shown here will be necessary.*

as well be narrower or wider, depending on what is conveniently available.

It should be noted that the middle stringers show a bit of curve at the forward end due to the deadrise of the V bottom. This will require some trimming to bring the two middle stringers together in a touching fit on the centerline, as well as some slight beveling of their inner edges on account of the V. Because of its curve, the outside stringer is made of two lengths spliced together.

All the longitudinal stringers in this 20-foot boat will most likely need to be spliced together from two or more shorter pieces. Joints in adjoining stringers

should be well staggered—that is, separated as much as possible. Joints may be butted on the frames provided they are well nailed, but short scarfs would be better, glued and nailed through into the frames. In any case, these bottom stringers are to be well nailed into the bottom cross frames with 2½-inch hot-dipped galvanized wire nails.

No time need be lost in measuring these longitudinals exactly to length. Any excess is allowed to project beyond the face of the transoms. It will be sawed off flush in one operation prior to adding the outer facing of plywood to the transom.

The recommended order of work in planking the

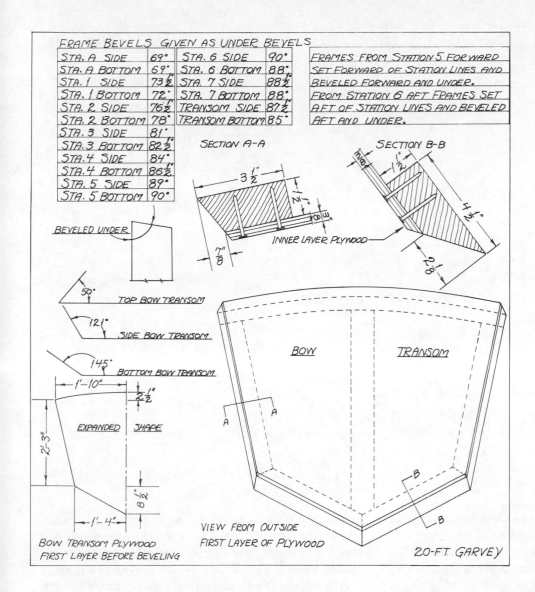

FRAME BEVELS GIVEN AS UNDER BEVELS

STA. A SIDE	69°	STA. 6 SIDE	90°
STA. A BOTTOM	69°	STA. 6 BOTTOM	88°
STA. 1 SIDE	73½°	STA. 7 SIDE	88½°
STA. 1 BOTTOM	72°	STA. 7 BOTTOM	88°
STA. 2 SIDE	76½°	TRANSOM SIDE	87½°
STA. 2 BOTTOM	78°	TRANSOM BOTTOM	85°
STA. 3 SIDE	81°		
STA. 3 BOTTOM	82½°		
STA. 4 SIDE	84°		
STA. 4 BOTTOM	86½°		
STA. 5 SIDE	89°		
STA. 5 BOTTOM	90°		

FRAMES FROM STATION 5 FORWARD SET FORWARD OF STATION LINES AND BEVELED FORWARD AND UNDER. FROM STATION 6 AFT FRAMES SET AFT OF STATION LINES AND BEVELED AFT AND UNDER.

SECTION A-A

SECTION B-B

INNER LAYER PLYWOOD

BEVELED UNDER

TOP BOW TRANSOM

SIDE BOW TRANSOM

BOTTOM BOW TRANSOM

EXPANDED SHAPE

BOW TRANSOM PLYWOOD FIRST LAYER BEFORE BEVELING

BOW   TRANSOM

VIEW FROM OUTSIDE FIRST LAYER OF PLYWOOD

20-FT. GARVEY

sides and the bottom is as follows: After the frames have been set up on the ladder frame and checked for alignment and fairness, as well as plumbed, the side stringers are nailed on. Next, the side stringers that follow the chine are trimmed to conform to the curvature of the bottom, so that the outside bottom stringers will cover their edges in a close fit. Third, the bottom stringers are nailed on, and the outside stringers that extend over the edges of the bottom side stringers are trimmed and planed to conform to the curvature of the sides.

The ⅜-inch plywood that covers the sides can now be put on. On each side there are two lengthwise panels that butt on the center of the middle side stringer. These side panels are glued with epoxy to the stringers underneath, nailed through them into the frames with galvanized wire nails, and nailed into the stringers between the frames with large wire ring nails 1 inch long and spaced about 2 inches apart.

If we assume that the plywood panels for planking this 20-foot boat will be got out of standard 8-foot sheets, two splices in each panel will be required. These splices can be made either off or on the boat. They should be 8 to 12 times as long as the plywood is thick, and glued with epoxy. For detailed directions for splicing plywood, see Chapter 13.

Exact fits in installing these plywood panels are not required, which makes the job a lot easier. If the panels do not butt together perfectly on the underlying stringers, the open seams may be filled with epoxy and microballoons, or epoxy and fine sawdust, to be sanded smooth upon hardening. Of course, an effort should be made to keep any seam openings reasonably small. When the lower side panel is put on, it can be a

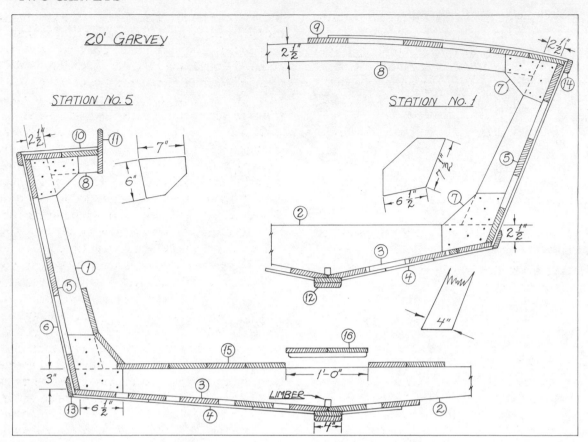

little wider than necessary, to be trimmed and planed fair with the bottom after the glue has hardened.

The plywood covering the bottom is installed in the same way. The diagram shows three lengthwise plywood panels on each half of the bottom. Two on each side would probably conform to the slight twist of this veed bottom without any difficulty. The number and width of the plywood panels on both sides and the bottom and the location of the stringers underneath can be varied considerably for economical utilization of materials available. A little attention given to planning in this regard can yield significant savings in materials.

Because the bottom plywood goes on last, the raw edge of the outside panels should be covered with fiberglass tape set in epoxy. This is covered in turn by the chine strip *(13)*, which is glued and nailed in place. This makes a strong, lasting, perfectly waterproof joint along the chine.

Fiberglass tape and epoxy are also applied under the laminated keel *(12)*, but first the raised V at the center of the bottom must be planed flat for a width of 4

inches to seat the keel strips. The first of these is nailed on over the strip of fiberglass tape before the epoxy has cured. The top strip is also put on with epoxy glue and should be well nailed with 3-inch galvanized nails.

A word about galvanized wire nails: These are the easiest and cheapest of all fastenings. No bolts, drifts, or screws are required. They are good for at least 10 years, by which time the boat should have paid for itself several times over and a new one is in order.

The following are keyed to numbers in the accompanying diagrams:

1. *Side frames:* 1½-inch fir or hard-pine joist.
2. *Frame bottoms:* 1½-inch fir or hard-pine joist.
3. *Bottom stringers:* One-inch boards (net ¾ inch), pine or fir.
4. *Bottom panels:* ⅜-inch fir or hard-pine plywood.
5. *Side stringers:* Same as bottom stringers.
6. Plywood side panels.
7. *Frame gussets:* ⅜-inch or ½-inch fir or hard-pine plywood.
8. *Deck beams:* 1½-inch fir or hard-pine joist.

9. *Deck stringers:* Same as side and bottom stringers.

10. *Plywood decking:* Same as bottom and side panels.

11. *Coaming:* Six inches by ¾ inch, pine or fir.

12. Two strips of ¾-inch pine or fir, 4 inches wide.

13. *Outside chine strip:* Pine or fir, 3 inches by ⅝ inch.

14. *Sheer trim:* Pine or fir, 2 inches by ¾ inch.

15. *Flooring:* Pine or fir, ¾ inch thick.

16. *Trap:* Same material as the flooring.

People who build their own boats are prone to making changes in the original plans. To discourage this tendency, designers often warn that if changes are made, they will not be responsible for the results. More often than not, this is no deterrent. Builders go right ahead with alterations according to their own ideas, sometimes with happy results, sometimes not.

The lesson is clear. Boats designed for amateur construction should be able to tolerate some alterations, because they are going to be made anyway. The ideal is a hull of proven lines and simple, straightforward construction with plenty of options left open to the individual builder. And this is what I have aimed for with this garvey—a general-purpose workboat hull with which there is considerable leeway for adaptation to a variety of needs.

The lines show a hull that is quite high-sided. When the boat carries no payload but only the motor, a couple of occupants, and miscellaneous equipment, the freeboard amidships will be about 26 inches, and the distance from the cockpit floor to the top of the coaming 32 inches. If this seems too high-sided, it would be the simplest thing in the world to lower the sheer by several inches. Merely subtract the desired amount while laying out the frame molds. No other alterations in the hull design would be required.

On the other hand, some will find the ample freeboard desirable if heavy loads are to be carried, a task for which the boat is well adapted. By raising the cockpit floor several inches and making it watertight, one could make the cockpit self-bailing, which is highly desirable for some fishing operations. And for extra-heavy loading, the scuppers could always be closed.

If a larger boat is needed, it would be easy to stretch this one out by inserting one or two additional frames amidships, setting them at the same frame spacing (27

inches) as the rest. This would not affect the ends of the hull, and no other alterations or adjustments would be needed. The hull could even be shortened, but caution is indicated here, for too much off the length could adversely affect performance. In shortening the boat, as in lengthening it, the excess should be removed amidships and the ends left alone.

Although the boat shown here is powered with an outboard motor, the hull is well suited for a small inboard engine. It would not be difficult to make the changes and additions that such an engine would require, though a considerable amount of extra work, as well as some extra expense, would be involved. But I see no design difficulties in adding a skeg, shaft log, rudder, engine beds, and engine box.

Where low or moderate working speeds would be satisfactory, any one of several small, light diesels now on the market would fill the bill nicely. A good example is the Sole, favored by Spanish fishermen and recommended for the 22-foot-5-inch garvey. This engine's comparatively low fuel consumption would soon cancel out the initial cost of conversion to inboard power, but the engine would never achieve anything approaching the speeds possible with large outboard motors.

If an outboard is to be used, there is much to say for the dry well recommended by the Outboard Marine Corporation for 1982 Evinrude and Johnson motors. Both companies make heavy-duty commercial motors that would be well suited to this boat; their 55, 40, and 25 h.p. models would all be appropriate. The size and dimensions of the well for the 20-foot garvey were adapted from five detailed sheets (numbers 21–25) obtainable from the Outboard Marine Corporation, 3145 Central Avenue, Waukegan, Illinois 60085. Although the diagrams for the well are fully dimensioned and explained here, it would be helpful to get these five sheets, which include instructions for a remote-control installation and arrangements for steering that I have not touched on here.

To conform to Outboard Marine's specifications, the angle of the transom is 14 degrees from the vertical, or 76 degrees from the horizontal. Note that the shaft length of the motor is 20 inches.

The motor mount *(17)* is a 2-inch-by-12-inch (1½-inch-by-11½-inch net) Douglas-fir plank built into the transom framing as shown in the diagram, which gives a view from the inside showing how it is made up. The mount could also be oak, if it were available.

In assembling the transom, the two side frames *(1),*

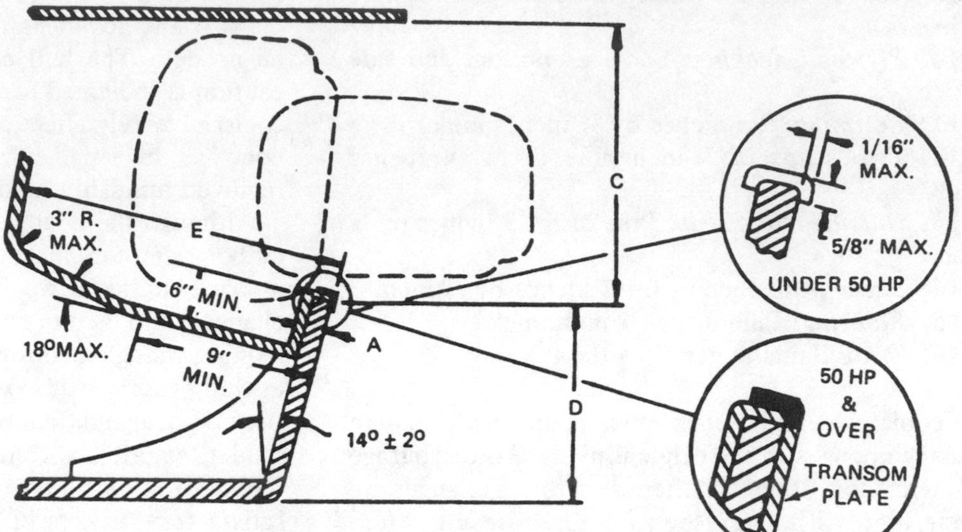

3" R. MAX.

E

6" MIN.

18°MAX.   9" MIN.

14° ± 2°

A

C

D

1/16" MAX.

5/8" MAX.

UNDER 50 HP

50 HP & OVER

TRANSOM PLATE

NOTE:

If transom cap strip is used, and extends beyond the transom more than 1/16", make a plate the thickness the cap extends beyond transom to bring transom surface flush for engine mounting. The transom plate should be made to conform to transom mounting bolt pattern shown on Sheet 22. This will allow the engine to be raised and lowered on transom without interference with stern brackets of engine.

MOTOR HORSEPOWER	"A" THICKNESS		"C" COVER HEIGHT	"D" TRANSOM HEIGHT (VERTICAL)	"E" ✕ CUTOUT LENGTH MINIMUM
	MINIMUM	MAXIMUM			
UNDER 5-1/2	1-1/4"	1-3/4"	19-1/2"	15 ± 1/2 OR 20 ± 1/2	15"
5-1/2 TO 15	1-3/8"	1-3/4"	22-1/2"	15 ± 1/2 OR 20 ± 1/2	15"
16 TO 61	1-3/8"	2"	29"	15 ± 1/2 OR 20 ± 1/2	21"
62 TO 85	1-5/8"	2-3/8"	32-1/2"	20 ± 1/2 OR 25 ± 1/2	22"
86 TO 149	1-5/8"	2-3/4"	32-1/2"	20 ± 1/2 OR 25 ± 1/2	22"
150 & OVER	1-5/8"	2-3/4"	32-1/2"	20 ± 1/2 OR 25 ± 1/2	26"

✕ "E" DIMENSIONS PROVIDE CLEARANCE FOR OMC OUTBOARD ENGINES.

The dry well design recommended by the Outboard Marine Corporation for its 1982 outboards.

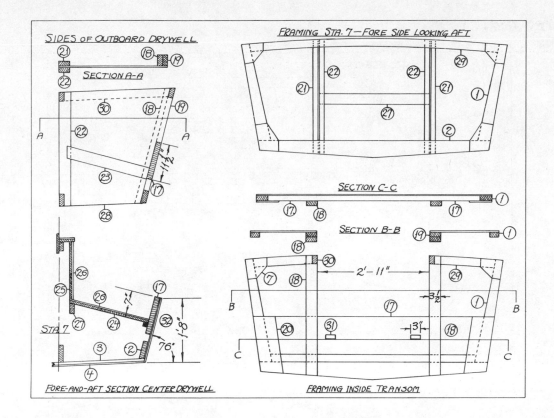

SIDES OF OUTBOARD DRYWELL

SECTION A-A

FRAMING STA. 7—FORE SIDE LOOKING AFT

SECTION C-C

SECTION B-B

FORE-AND-AFT SECTION CENTER DRYWELL

FRAMING INSIDE TRANSOM

the bottom frame *(2)*, the short lengths of deck beam *(29)*, the motor mount *(17)*, and two upright filler pieces *(19)* are laid out to correspond with an outline of the transom drawn on some smooth, flat surface. Gussets *(7* and *20)* are glued on with epoxy and are well nailed with 1¾-inch galvanized nails.

Small, temporary gussets of plywood scrap are also tacked on to hold the two upright filler pieces *(19)* in place between *17* and *29*. The framing can now be turned over to receive its first outside layer of ⅜-inch plywood, which is put on with glue and nailed.

The framing is then inverted, and the two upright framing pieces *(18)* are bolted in place with ⅜-inch galvanized carriage bolts—one through the deck beam *(29)*, two through the filler piece *(19)*, two through the motor mount *(17)*, and one through the frame bottom *(2)*. This greatly reinforces the motor mount, which is the only place in this hull where bolts are called for. A bit stock and bit would also be useful in making the two freeing ports *(31)* through the motor mount.

After the sides and bottom are planked, the transom is covered with its second, outer layer of ⅜-inch plywood. This is glued to the inner layer and along the edges.

Before this is done, the spaces at the transom between the bottom and side stringers must be solidly plugged with ¾-inch strips of stringer stock, which are

glued in place with epoxy. Otherwise, there may be leakage here. I cannot stress enough the necessity of having a tight seal along the bottom edge and sides of the transom.

The plywood sides of the well extend forward to station 7, which is framed in the usual way but with the addition of two uprights *(21)* that receive the well sides. These uprights are lengths of 2 x 4 (net 1½ x 3½) whose ends are halved over the frame bottom and the deck beam and spiked to them. The framing diagram for station 7 shows *22* and *27* in place, but these do not go on until after the sides are installed.

The addition of the carlin *(30)*, which is halved into the upper end of *18*, completes the backing for the plywood side. No backing piece is required at the bottom. After the plywood side panel has been accurately scribed and cut to fit, it is set in place and nailed to the backing pieces.

Now the upright *(22)*, notched to halve over the deck beam *(29)* and the frame bottom *(2)* and to take the end of the bottom support *(23)*, is fitted and spiked to the deck beam and frame bottom and into the backing post *(21)*.

The bottom of the dry well is supported by *23* and *27*. The former is spiked to *18* and is let into *22*. It is glued to the plywood side and well nailed through from the back of the plywood. The bottom of the well *(24)*

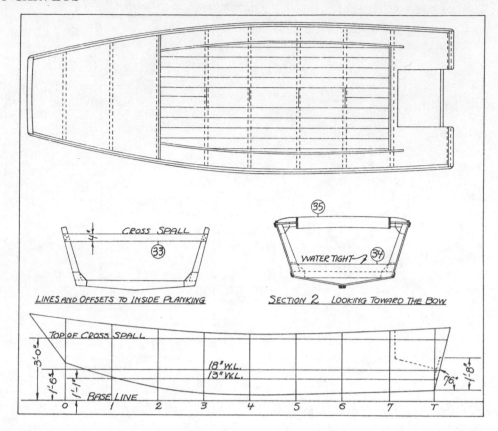

LINES AND OFFSETS TO INSIDE PLANKING

SECTION 2   LOOKING TOWARD THE BOW

consists of two layers, the first an under layer of 1-inch pine boards (net thickness ¾ inch). These run crosswise and are well nailed at the ends into *23*.

The outer layer of ⅜-inch plywood is glued and nailed to the under layer. In gluing around the edges care must be taken to prevent any possibility of a leak. Any water that managed to seep in between the two layers would almost certainly cause rot. The back of the well—actually its forward side—is made the same way as the bottom.

How the interior of the hull is finished out will depend on the needs and preferences of the builder or owner, so here we shall do hardly more than mention some general considerations in working out the interior arrangements.

The narrow side decks are important structural members that brace and stiffen the sides of the hull when there is a large, open cockpit. The forward deck, which we show coming back as far as station 2, also braces the hull, keeps out a lot of water, and provides dry storage space when combined with the watertight sill *(34)* that keeps water from surging forward from the cockpit. Because of its under layer of 1-inch pine

stringers fore and aft, the deck will be stiff enough without putting deck beams closer than the frame stations shown.

A self-bailing cockpit is a good idea. It keeps rainwater out of the bilge, and it makes for a clean boat, since it is easy to flush out any dirt that may find its way into the cockpit. And, as mentioned, the scuppers can always be plugged.

The following information will be useful in determining the height of a self-bailing cockpit. The weight of the boat when finished, provided it is built to the scantlings specified here, should be about 2,600 pounds, plus 600 pounds for the outboard motor, two occupants, and incidentals—or about 3,200 pounds total. On the waterline 13 inches above the baseline, displacement is approximately 3,200 pounds. At the waterline 18 inches above the baseline, displacement increases to 5,700 pounds.

It might be convenient to have one or more temporary cross thwarts, dory fashion. They would straddle the side frames and rest on a seat riser, added here especially for this purpose but also serving to brace the side. These removable thwarts would brace

A 20-foot garvey built in 1983 from the plans presented here. The builder, Warren Hatfield of Norfolk, Virginia, uses the boat for crabbing in lower Chesapeake Bay. A 60 h.p. Johnson outboard with a medium-power prop gives him a cruising speed of 12 to 15 m.p.h. and a top speed of about 20 m.p.h. Hatfield, an experienced builder, reported no problems in the construction, and he is impressed with the boat's strength. "One should loft the profile of the bow transom and the next three frames and include the ladder-frame building ways," he says. "That way a jig can be made with the correct angle to hold the bow in the proper position."

the sides too, but could be easily taken out and stowed when an open, unobstructed cockpit is desired.

A word of caution about turning the hull right side up after planking has been completed: This should not be attempted without plenty of help, and the procedure must be well thought out. This is fairly heavy construction for the home shop, and injury could result from carelessness. With the cross spalls in place on each frame to brace the sides, there is little chance of damage when the boat is rolled over.

Specifications for components are as follows. The numbers are keyed to the accompanying diagrams.

17. *Motor mount:* Two-inch (1½-inch net) Douglas fir or oak, 11½ inches wide.

18. *Framing for plywood sides of the motor well:* Two-inch-by-four-inch (net 1½-inch-by-3½-inch) fir or oak, bolted through deck beam, motor mount, filler piece, and frame bottom with ⅜-inch galvanized bolts.

19. *Upright filler piece between motor mount and deck beam and under the side framing piece:* Two-inch-by-four-inch fir or oak.

20. *Transom frame gusset:* ⅜-inch plywood, large enough to tie together side frame, motor mount, and frame bottom.

21. *Upright backing piece for plywood side of the motor well:* Two-inch-by-four-inch (net 1½-inch-by-3½-inch) fir or oak, halved at the ends to fit over frame bottom and deck beam and spiked to them.

22. *Upright to support the back of the motor well:* Two-inch-by-four-inch fir or oak, identical to *21* but

fitted and fastened in place after the plywood side of the well is in place. Spiked through into *21*.

23. *Support for the bottom of the motor well:* Two-inch-by-four-inch fir or oak. Installed after the plywood side is put on and glued and nailed to it. Let into *22* as shown and spiked to *18*.

24. *Under layer, bottom of well:* One-inch (net ¾-inch) pine boards laid crosswise.

25. *Under layer, back of motor well:* One-inch (net ¾-inch) pine boards.

26. *Liner, bottom of motor well:* ⅜-inch plywood. Glue around the edges to make completely tight. Leakage here will cause rot.

27. *Support for back of well:* Two-inch-by-four-inch fir spiked to *22*.

28. *Sides of well:* ⅜-inch plywood glued to *18, 21,* and *30*.

29. *Deck beams:* Molded 2½ inches, sided 1½ inches. Fir or oak. Camber 2 inches to 3 inches in 7 feet.

30. *Carlin:* Backs plywood sides of the motor well. Halved into *18*.

31. *Freeing ports:* Three inches by 1½ inches, to drain bottom of motor well.

32. *Outer layer of ⅜-inch plywood covering the outside of the transom:* Glued to the inner layer and along the bottom and sides. Nailed.

33. *Temporary cross spall:* One-inch pine or fir, 4 inches wide or wider.

34. *Watertight sill to keep water out of the storage space under the foredeck:* One-inch pine or fir 8 inches wide.

35. *Coaming, fore end:* Six inches wide.

13

CLAMMING SKIFF

In the spring of 1982 I received an inquiry about clamming skiffs from a coastal town in the western end of Maine's Washington County. Considerable commercial clam digging is done in that area, and outboard skiffs are required to bring the clams ashore from the distant flats and remote coves of the deeply indented coast.

The boats now in use, according to my informant, are mostly home-built. They are heavy, crudely constructed, flat-bottomed skiffs that are wet and pound badly in a chop. They are about 16 feet in length, which is about as large as they can be for convenient transportation in a pickup truck, and are commonly powered with 35 h.p. outboards.

In casting about for ideas for an improved skiff, my correspondent had come across a 14-foot-4½-inch outboard flatiron that I designed for the *Maine Coast Fisherman* nearly 30 years ago. It was later included in my *Dory Book*. He was impressed with the favorable report of a Great Lakes fisherman who had built one, and he felt the model might be worth adapting as a clamming skiff for use in Washington County.

The fact that this boat was constructed of plywood suggested that it might be built considerably lighter than some of the clamming skiffs now in use, a highly desirable feature when one must drag a boat off and onto distant stretches of flats or lift it on and off a truck. How would it be, he inquired, if the boat were to be enlarged by about 10 percent, bringing it up to 16 feet in length?

There is no reason this could not be done. But as I considered how these clamming skiffs are used, and the shortcomings described by my informant, it seemed to me that more was needed here than simply an enlargement of the old outboard flatiron, which is, after all, a more or less typical down-east flatiron except for its plywood construction. It would be

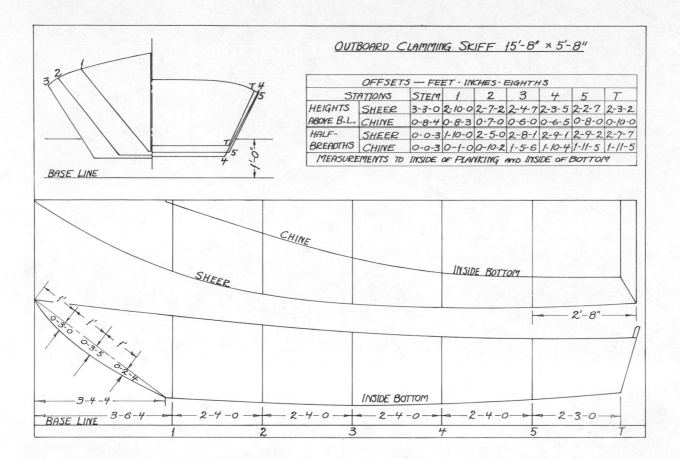

OUTBOARD CLAMMING SKIFF 15'-8" × 5'-8"

	STATIONS	STEM	1	2	3	4	5	T
OFFSETS — FEET · INCHES · EIGHTHS								
HEIGHTS ABOVE B.L.	SHEER	3-3-0	2-10-0	2-7-2	2-4-7	2-3-5	2-2-7	2-3-2
	CHINE	0-8-4	0-8-3	0-7-0	0-6-0	0-6-5	0-8-0	0-10-0
HALF-BREADTHS	SHEER	0-0-3	1-10-0	2-5-0	2-8-1	2-9-1	2-9-2	2-7-7
	CHINE	0-0-3	0-1-0	0-10-2	1-5-6	1-10-4	1-11-5	1-11-5
MEASUREMENTS TO INSIDE OF PLANKING AND INSIDE OF BOTTOM								

considerably lighter than a plank-built flatiron, but its wide, flat bottom would still pound in a chop, I fear, and it would be wet.

Certainly a wide, flat bottom aft was needed for carrying a heavy load, for supporting the outboard motor, for allowing a shoal draft, and for sitting upright on the flats. But couldn't the boat be made sharp forward so that it would have a soft entrance, and couldn't it be made with enough depth and flare at the bow to keep it dry? The result of some preliminary sketching and the construction of a scale half-model in soft, dry pine can be seen in the lines drawing reproduced here.

The long, raking stem coming all the way back to station or section 1, which is a sharp, widely flaring V, will give a soft, easy entrance with plenty of lift to keep the bow from dropping too low. A short length of bow deck extending back about 4 feet, together with a low, watertight bulkhead about a foot high under the after end, will keep the bow dry and provide a convenient storage space out of the weather. This will be fully detailed below.

The bottom has been widened aft, as has the whole after part of the boat, for greater capacity. Instead of making the bottom absolutely straight and flat fore and aft, a small amount of rocker—about 3 inches—has been added, but not enough to give much difficulty in shallow water. Six inches of level displacement figures to nearly 1,000 pounds; three more inches give an additional 700 pounds. How the boat trims will depend, of course, on how it is loaded.

Twenty-five horsepower is ample power, possibly more than ample. Certainly the boat could do with less. If the stern should show any tendency to squat, this could be offset by moving the load forward.

For lightness, fir plywood, ⅜ inch thick, has been retained for the sides. Three 4-by-8-foot panels will be required.

Each side will be spliced up from three sections: two full-length 8-foot sections and a small piece to finish out the tip of the bow. The two after sections (one for either side) can be got out of a single panel, as shown in the diagram. The bow sections will each require a panel, and there should be enough left over for frame gussets, for the low bulkhead under the forward deck, and for other small pieces.

Superior-quality exterior grade can be used if it is free from internal voids, thin veneers, and excessive patching. Otherwise, marine quality would be worth the extra cost. One alternative might be to sheathe

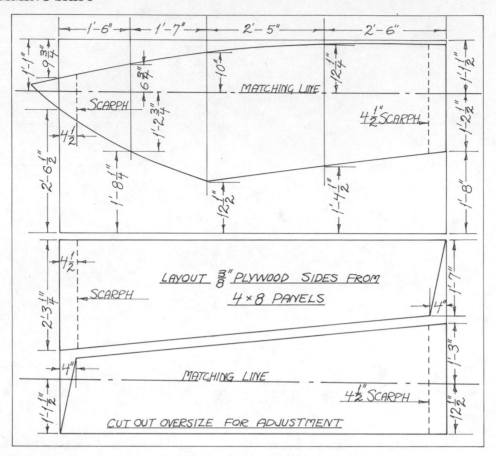

ordinary exterior-grade plywood with a covering of fiberglass or Vectra.

Splices should be epoxy-glued. They are not difficult to make, and the method for doing so will be fully explained below. Epoxy adhesive will also be needed for gluing the chine strips to the plywood sides, as well as for the outwales and the frame gussets. If used economically, one quart will probably be sufficient for the whole job. For the parts listed, epoxy, in my opinion, is absolutely essential for good results.

The shape of the plywood sides was obtained by taking a thin poster-board template from the scale half-model. It should be quite accurate. However, the pieces should be cut oversize to allow for some variation and adjustment. They are easily trimmed when they are fitted on the boat.

The "matching line" shown on the separate sections should run perfectly straight for the entire length of the side when its sections are scarfed together. This is to ensure correct alignment when scarfing. Otherwise, the glued-up side might not fit.

Instead of using plywood for the bottom, I show cross planking heavy enough to take the hard use a working skiff gets. With fore-and-aft bottom stringers inside and out, through-nailed for added stiffness, inside gratings, which would be required with a plywood bottom, will not be needed.

Cross planking can be native pine or cedar, and it is not difficult to put on. A cross-planked bottom will weigh more than one of plywood, but not a great deal more if inside gratings are omitted. Considering the abuse this workboat must take, a little added weight can be tolerated.

This will not be a lightweight boat, but I believe it will weigh considerably less than some of the clamming boats now in use. After all, if a workboat is to withstand the conditions these clamming skiffs must endure, they cannot be built too lightly.

The shape of this skiff makes it an easy boat to build—easier, in fact, than it may appear at first glance. The plywood side wraps around the frames with no hard bends whatsoever, as became apparent when the shape of the plywood side was duplicated

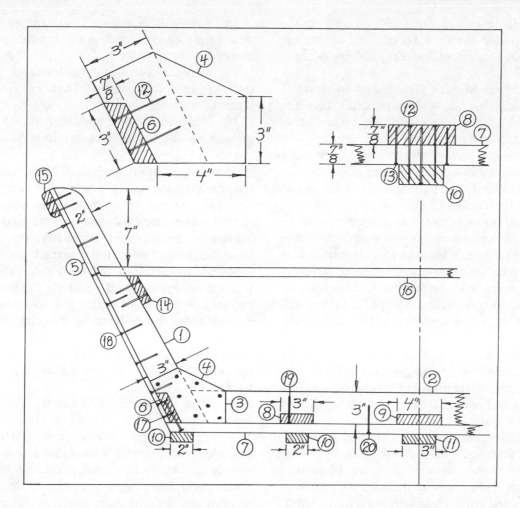

with poster board. Likewise, the chine strips have no bend to speak of.

The stem has such a slight curve that it can be cut out in one piece from a straight length of plank. Besides the plywood, lumber is pine, fir, and possibly cedar for the bottom, all from boards planed ⅞ inch thick. Oak can be used for the frames, chine strips, and fore-and-aft stringers, but it is not necessary and should not be used if weight is a primary consideration. If need be, every part except the plywood sides and the stem can be got out of white-pine boards planed to a finished thickness of ⅞ inch.

Fastenings are, for the most part, hot-dipped galvanized nails. If galvanized nails of this size and type are not available, ring nails, where specified, can be stainless or bronze without danger of electrolysis. Galvanized fastenings will last long enough, and then some, if they are hot-dipped with a generous coating of zinc. Electroplated fastenings are worthless.

The only place screws might be used to advantage is for fastening the plywood side to the chine strip. If ring nails of the right size cannot be obtained, 1-inch number 12 galvanized wood screws on 7- to 8-inch centers, staggered, should be used here to supplement and reinforce the glue joint.

The sectional diagram for frame 4 is keyed as follows:

1. *Side frames:* Molded 2 inches at the top, 3 inches at the bottom. White pine, oak, or Douglas fir, ⅞ inch thick.

2. *Bottom frames:* Molded 3 inches. White pine, oak, or Douglas fir, ⅞ inch thick.

3. *Frame gussets:* Fir plywood, ⅜ inch, both sides of frame. Assembled with epoxy glue and 1¼-inch number 11 or number 12 ring nails.

4. *Triangular filler piece between the two gussets:* Glued and nailed in place.

5. *Sides:* Fir plywood, ⅜ inch. Marine grade preferable; superior-quality exterior without internal voids, thin veneers, or excessive patching permissible.

6. *Chine strips:* Molded 3¼ inches to bevel 3 inches, sided ⅞ inch. Oak, white pine, or Douglas fir. Let into frames and fastened with two 2½-inch hot-dipped galvanized wire nails.

7. *Cross-planked bottom:* Plank ⅞ inch thick and 4 inches to 6 inches wide—and no wider. Cedar, white pine, or Douglas fir. Fitted tight inside; outside seams open ⅛ inch for caulking. Driven cotton caulking payed with red-lead primer and puttied with non-hardening seam compound. Bottom boards nailed to chine strips with 3-inch hot-dipped galvanized wire nails. Nailed to inside fore-and-aft bottom stringers with 1½-inch number 11 or number 12 ring nails.

8. *Inside bottom stringers:* Molded 3 inches and sided ⅞ inch. Oak, white pine, or Douglas fir. Cut into bottom frames and fastened with 2½-inch hot-dipped galvanized wire nails.

9. *Inside center bottom stringer:* Molded 4 inches, sided ⅞ inch. Oak, white pine, or Douglas fir. Cut into bottom frames and fastened with 2½-inch hot-dipped galvanized wire nails.

10. *Outside bottom stringers:* Molded 2 inches, sided ⅞ inch, fastened with 2½-inch nails.

11. *Outside center bottom stringer:* Molded 3 inches, sided ⅞ inch, fastened with 2½-inch nails.

12. *Hot-dipped galvanized wire nails, 2½ inches:* Must be hot-dipped; electroplated nails are worthless.

13. *Ring nails:* Number 11 or number 12 1½ inches.

14. *Seat riser:* Molded 3 inches before beveling, sided ⅞ inch. Oak, white pine, or Douglas fir. Fastened with 2½-inch hot-dipped galvanized wire nails.

15. *Outwale:* Molded 2½ inches amidships and aft. Tapers to 1¾ inches at the stemhead. Oak, white pine, or Douglas fir. Fastened into the frames with 2½-inch hot-dipped galvanized wire nails. Glued to the plywood sides and fastened through from the inside of the plywood with 1¼-inch ring nails, number 11 or number 12.

16. *Thwarts:* Ten inches wide, ⅞ inch thick. White pine or Douglas fir. Ends cut to straddle the frames like a dory thwart, for ready removal if desired.

17. *Ring nails:* 1 inch, number 11 or number 12, through ⅜-inch plywood side to chine strip, spaced 4 to 5 inches apart and staggered.

18. Two-inch hot-dipped galvanized wire nails through plywood sides into side frames every 3 to 4 inches.

19. Two-and-a-half-inch galvanized wire nails through inside fore-and-aft bottom stringers into bottom frames.

20. Three-inch hot-dipped galvanized wire nails through cross-planked bottom into bottom frames.

This is only a lowly work skiff. Nevertheless, a lot of thought has gone into its design, and every consideration has been given to making its construction as simple, straightforward, and easy as possible.

Despite its apparent simplicity, the dimensions must be maintained, the planned order of work followed, and accurate fits achieved, if the boat is to perform acceptably and stand up to the hard usage required of it. I'm not saying that this design and the recommended procedures for building it cannot be improved, but I must warn that unadvised and ill-considered changes here and there, even when they appear to be minor ones, could do much to spoil the boat.

Although the particular craft we are considering here is intended for use as a clamming skiff in Washington County, Maine, the construction and basic form are adaptable for other simple craft for a variety of uses. Built with considerably more bottom rocker, and fitted with a centerboard, rudder, and suitable rig, flat-bottomed boats of this general type will give a smart sail in semisheltered waters, although they are not suitable for venturing very far offshore in the open sea.

Small flats like this with the construction simplified still further make good, light tenders, shore-front workboats, and, because of their durability and great initial stability, good boats for children to play in on smooth water. Moreover, boats of this type make an excellent first boat for amateur builders. And they are comparatively inexpensive to build, to the extent that anything is inexpensive today.

No modern power tools are required, and in a pinch, a few basic hand tools can be made to do. The minimum kit would include a handsaw, chisel, plane, spokeshave, carpenter's square, level, chalkline, nail hammer, screwdriver, putty knife, and a pair of 6-inch C-clamps. Fastenings throughout can be hot-dipped galvanized common nails with the possible addition of some shorter galvanized ring nails of fairly stout gauge.

As previously mentioned, lumber can be limited to

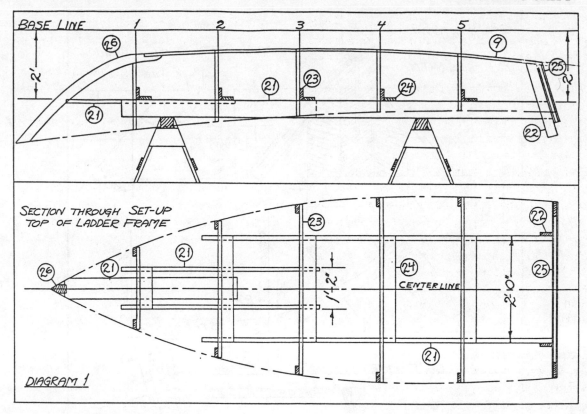

DIAGRAM 1

⅜-inch plywood and ⅞-inch softwood boards. It is best to use marine-grade plywood, despite the expense, since ordinary exterior grade is so inferior today, with thin outer veneers and internal voids, that much of it is not worth putting into a boat. Boards may be northern white pine, Douglas fir, loblolly pine, or cypress. Western red cedar, redwood, northern white cedar, and juniper are too soft to hold nails well, except for bottom planking. Scantlings have been worked out so that boards of only one thickness—⅞ inch—are required. This permits the lumber to be purchased in one lot and planed at the mill at one time.

One thing we have that old-time builders didn't have is epoxy glue. I'm sure they would have used it had it been available. There are many formulations. My first choice is Chem-Tech, my second, Cold-Cure. Both are widely advertised in boating publications. I do not care for WEST System epoxy because I find it sets too quickly to give me unhurried working time, because it is too thin, and because I am concerned about the effect of the hardener on my health. These same considerations apply also to a number of other epoxy formulations. Cold-Cure, by the way, has a strong odor that I distrust.

Epoxy is used throughout the skiff. The stem assembly is glued with it, as is the false, or outer, stem if it is laminated rather than steam-bent. The plywood frame gussets and the transom assembly are also epoxied, and the resin is used for scarfing the plywood sides and for gluing them to the stem, chines, and outwales. If used economically, one quart should do the job.

Once the boat has been set up it is more than half built, with only the preglued sides to be put on and the bottom cross-planked, caulked, and painted before the boat is turned over and the interior finished. Finishing involves little more than adding thwarts, oarlocks, and outwales, unless it is decided to add a short deck forward with a short, tight bulkhead under the forward end to keep the bilge water out of the bow.

Preparatory to setting up, however, a ladder-frame foundation and several subassemblies are built. These include the laminated inner stem; the outer stem, if it is to be glue-laminated from several thin strips; the five frame assemblies that also serve as molds, but remain in the boat; the full-length plywood sides scarfed together from three shorter pieces; and the glued-up composite transom. In addition, the middle bottom stringer should be cut out and fastened to the inner stem before the boat is set up. By fitting this into the

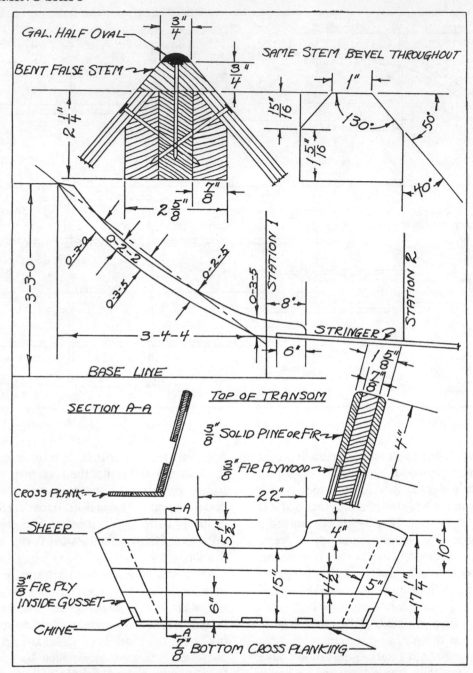

recesses cut for it in the bottoms of the frame molds one can check their alignment before securing them in place.

The inner stem is built up in three layers of ⅞-inch-thick boards, each layer consisting of two pieces whose lengths vary so that the joints can be well staggered when they are glued and nailed together. Nails must be located where they will not interfere with the beveling. Don't cut pieces to the exact width

and shape before gluing. Instead leave a little extra wood for trimming to the exact shape after the glue has set.

The stem is beveled ahead of time for the plywood planking with the same bevel throughout, as shown in the diagram, and the lower end is notched for the middle bottom stringer. A glued-up softwood stem is plenty strong for this, since much of the strength of the bow derives from the full-width plywood sides glued and nailed to the stem. The outer stem adds further strength. This can be bent oak, steamed or boiled, but if it is glue-laminated from thin strips, these can be bent around the inner stem, which is used as a gluing form.

The five three-piece frame assemblies are held together at the lower corners with plywood gussets on either side, glued on and nailed with 1¼-inch nails. Frame assemblies are beveled, and are notched to receive the chines and the bottom stringers.

Temporary cross spalls, 4 inches wide, are screwed on the *after* side of the frames. These are located with their upper edges (their lower edges when the frames are bottom up on the ladder frame) exactly 2 feet from the baseline, as shown on the lines drawing. These cross spalls must be exactly level as well; special care is required because the accuracy of the setup and the final shape of the boat depend on them.

In setting up, the frame molds are all placed on the forward side of the station lines and spaced according to the lines drawing, with the cross spalls aft of the station lines and the ladder-frame cleats aft of the cross spalls. The sides of frame 5 require no beveling at all. The rest are all beveled forward. The amount of beveling will be diagramed below. So little beveling is required on the bottoms of the frames that this is easily taken care of with a few passes of the plane after the boat has been set up and the bottom members are being faired for the bottom cross planking.

Glue-scarfing the plywood sides is done quite easily if the following procedure is followed. Scarfs are laid out 4½ inches wide, or 12 times the thickness of the plywood. With a sharp plane and some care, the scarf bevels can be accurately planed. The outer edge of the scarf surface should be brought to something less than a feather edge, leaving it a scant 1/32 inch. The excess is easily sanded flat after the glue has set. The scarf surface should be perfectly flat but roughened somewhat with coarse sandpaper or a fine wood rasp so that a thin coating of epoxy glue may be retained in the joint. This is essential if the joint is to hold.

Since the width of ply to be glued is slightly more than 28 inches, two 30-inch lengths of 2-inch-by-6-inch fir construction lumber, the same lumber used for the ladder-frame stringer (actual dimensions 5½ inches by 1½ inches), will be required for a press. Plane one flat side of each to a slightly convex camber, not more than ⅛ inch of convex curve. Place one of these on the floor, cambered side up. Cover with waxed paper. Lay on this the scarfed end of one of the

pieces of plywood, scarfed surface up. Spread with a liberal coating of glue and cover with the scarfed end of the other, or mating, piece of plywood. Tack with a fine brad at each end to prevent the glue joint from slipping or shifting.

Cover with waxed paper, and directly over this place the other 2-by-6, cambered face down. Midway between the ends, a 3-inch two-headed staging nail is driven through the plywood and into the 2-by-6 underneath. (Later, when the nail is pulled through, the plywood is easily plugged.) Two more nails are put in, one on each side of the center nail and about 8 inches distant from it. These are set down hard. If staging nails are not to be had, ordinary nails can be substituted with a piece of leather under the head to make them easy to pull later.

Finally, the cambered crosspieces are pulled together tightly with a C-clamp at either end. If this procedure is followed step by step, a perfect splice should result.

One warning: It is easy for the two pieces of plywood to get out of alignment during gluing so that the side will not fit. One precaution against this already mentioned is to cut the plywood a bit large for exact trimming later. The most reliable is to make use of a "matching line," as shown above in the diagram of plank shape. When the splice is set up and after the glue has been applied, the matching line across both pieces should be checked with a chalkline or long straightedge to see that it runs perfectly straight. If it does not, it should be adjusted as necessary so that it does, before final clamping.

The ladder-frame setup has proved to be the easiest way of making an accurate form for building boats planked bottom up. The one diagramed here calls for stringers of 2-inch-by-6-inch fir construction lumber as the principal members of the platform. It hardly needs saying that these stringers must be perfectly straight.

The frame spacing is laid out on the two longer pieces, and cross cleats 2 feet long, 4 inches wide, and ⅞ inch thick are located ⅞ inch aft of the frame stations and nailed solidly in place. Since all of the frames bevel forward, they are set with their after sides on the frame stations and with the cross spalls aft of the frame stations. This brings the latter snugly against the cross cleats.

It is understood, of course, that the stringers must run parallel to each other with the cross cleats square to them. Short stringers spaced 14 inches apart

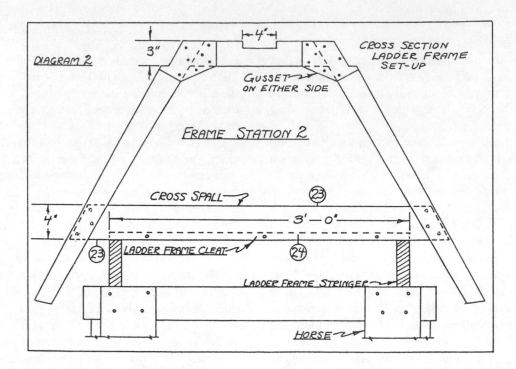

continue forward as the boat narrows. Finally, there is only the single plank that fits against the stem.

When the ladder-frame foundation is complete, a chalkline is stretched from end to end down the center, and a centerline is snapped. On this line the frame molds are located when they are set up according to the centerlines marked on their cross spalls.

The transom assembly is in three layers put together with glue and 1¼-inch nails. An internal core of ⅞-inch boards pieced together as shown in the diagram is held together by a partial covering inside with ⅜-inch plywood so that it can be set up on the building form. The outer covering of ⅜-inch plywood is not glued on until after the chines and the fore-and-aft bottom stringers have been fitted, nailed in place, and trimmed flush with the inner core.

This procedure makes the installation of these fore-and-aft members much easier and faster than if they had to be cut exactly to length to fit *inside* the transom. This way they start out a little long, their fore ends are fitted and pushed up tight, and what remains sticking out beyond the transom at the after end is sawed off flush to permit the outer covering of plywood to be glued on.

The exposed edges of the plywood at the top of the transom could be something of a problem. The only way to deal with this would be to saturate the edges with an oil-based paint to prevent the absorption of water as well as to harden the wood. Another method might be to bind with fiberglass tape set in epoxy.

Probably the best way is to stop the plywood about 4 inches below the top of the transom, replacing it with ⅜-inch-thick pieces of the same wood as the inner core, which are glued in place with epoxy as diagramed.

The diagrams illustrating the construction details just discussed are keyed as follows:

21. *Ladder-frame stringers:* Two-inch-by-six-inch fir.
22. *Transom support:* Two-inch-by-four-inch fir.
23. *Frame-mold cross spall:* ⅞ inch by 4 inches.
24. *Ladder-frame cross cleat:* ⅞ inch by 4 inches by 2 feet.
25. Transom.
26. Inner stem.

The side frames can be beveled at the bench before the frame assemblies are made. Frame bevels do not change over the length of the frames.

Frame 5 requires no beveling, and the bevels on the other frames are all cut sloping forward. However, the transom is beveled aft. That is, its after face finishes smaller than its inboard, or forward, face. Very little beveling is required on the bottoms of the frames, and this need not be done until the frames are set up on the ladder frame and the bottoms, chines, and edges of the plywood sides are faired to receive the bottom planking.

After the outer plywood facing of the transom has

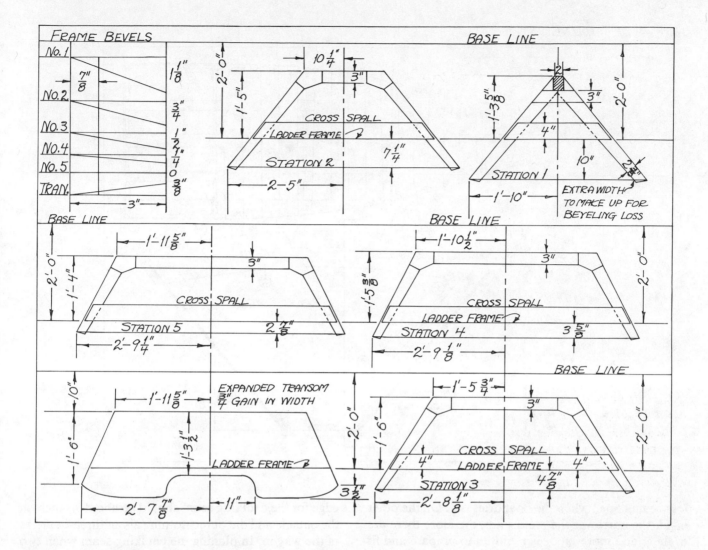

been put on with epoxy glue and well nailed with number 11 or number 12 1½-inch ring nails, the plywood sides go on, having been spliced full length as previously described. The sides must be well glued to the chines and nailed with plenty of 1-inch number 11 or number 12 wire ring nails. Nails should be spaced closely enough to ensure that the sides are brought in contact with the glue-covered chine surface throughout for an optimum gluing job.

The sides should also be glued to the ends of the transom and fastened with 2-inch galvanized nails. Glue is also used on the stem, and 2-inch galvanized common nails are adequate for fastening the sides to both the stem and the side frames.

When the sides are on and the glue has set, the bottom framing, including the fore-and-aft stringers, and the chines with the plywood sides attached are ready to be faired to receive the bottom planking. For this a piece of straight, flat board somewhat longer than the maximum width of the bottom is used as a

straightedge. The upper surfaces of the various members upon which the bottom planking will rest are planed so that they are perfectly fair and true. The straightedge should touch them all wherever it is placed in an athwartships position. The bottom planking throughout must touch frame bottoms, stringers, chines, and the bottom edges of the plywood sides.

Putting on the cross-planked bottom is not quite as simple an operation as it might appear, which is to say there is a definite procedure to follow and standards of workmanship to be met. Accurate fits are essential. Planks must be neither too wide nor too narrow. Widths from about 4 inches to 6 inches will be about right. Planks that are too wide will shrink excessively when they dry out, which will cause the seams to open up too much. Likewise, there is the danger of planks buckling when they swell.

The seams between the planks are essentially expansion joints, and the more seams there are, the

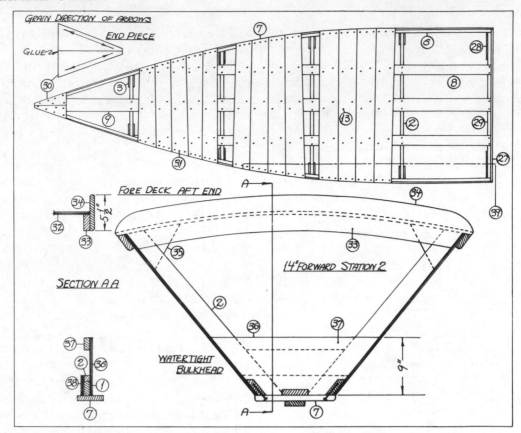

less seams open when the boat dries out. On the other hand, the narrower the planks are, the more there are of them and more labor is required to prepare and fit and, later, to caulk them. Besides, narrow planks are not as stiff, and if they are too narrow the ends may not nail securely.

There is one other thing to be taken into account. Slash-sawn boards—that is, boards cut from the side of the log—tend to cup toward the outside of the tree when they dry out and as they age. Thus, slash-sawn boards—boards most frequently used for bottom planking—should be put on the boat with the outside, or bark side, inside so that they will cup toward the inside of the boat, giving a smoother bottom with less drag. The wider the bottom planking used, the more important this consideration becomes.

When the bottom planking is fitted, the edges on the inside should be tight and touching for about the first one-quarter of plank thickness before beveling for the caulking seam starts. Caulking seams should be about ⅛ inch wide on the outside for each inch of plank thickness. Thus, for this boat with bottom planking ⅞ inch thick, the amount of bevel to be planed off each

edge for the caulking seam should be about ⅟₁₆ inch on the outside and die out to nothing about three-quarters of the way in. In planing the caulking seam when two planks come together, it is better to take wood off both planks equally rather than all off one.

These are general rules whose observation is likely to vary somewhat in practice. One thing may be depended on, however: Seams that are wider on the inside than on the outside will not hold caulking.

Planking starts at the stern with one of the wider planks securely nailed into the chines, transom, and bottom stringers. For nailing the plank ends to the chines, use 2½-inch 8-penny hot-dipped galvanized common nails spaced 2 to 2½ inches apart. If the chines are soft white pine, 3-inch 10-penny nails may make a more solid job. The second plank and those following are clamped in turn to the bottom stringers with a couple of C-clamps so that they are held down flat while being hauled up tight with a pipe clamp or door clamp against the plank previously fastened in place.

Lacking such a clamp, the builder can drive the plank up tight with just enough tension on the C-clamps to hold it snugly until it is nailed. A short piece of board should be used to pound against in order not to mar the edge of the plank.

After four or five planks are on and fastened, a space the width of a single plank is left vacant before the next plank is put on, and the planking operation is resumed as before. Observe that in the diagram this empty space tapers—that is, it is somewhat narrower at one end than the other. The plank that is later got out to fill it will be made to exactly the same taper but longer, and will be driven in place like a long wedge. There will be several of these wedge-shaped filler pieces the length of the bottom. They are all put in at the same time and set up together. The combined effect is to greatly tighten the bottom.

Note that the end piece at the bow runs fore and aft instead of athwartships and is made up of two lengthwise halves glued together, the grain on the outside running parallel with the outside of the boat. This brings the short grain inside where it is well supported. Left outside, the short grain could easily be split where the sides are nailed into the chine. Preparing the end piece in this manner may mean a little more work, but it makes for a much more dependable job.

After the bottom is planked, the plank ends are trimmed flush and are planed so that they fair with the sides. The seams are caulked with cotton set down tightly, but not tightly enough to strain the planks or break their edges.

The bottom edges of the plywood sides are beveled slightly before planking starts to provide a caulking seam after the bottom planking is in place. This must also be caulked. The tails of cotton driven into the ends of the bottom seams are brought all the way down and tucked into the seam between the bottom and the side planking. No opening anywhere that might cause a leak can be overlooked.

After the cotton is set in tightly it is saturated with a thin oil-based paint or primer. Red-lead primer is by far the best there is for this, but it must be thin enough to penetrate thoroughly. Several applications may be required for the best results. When the cotton has dried, the seams are filled with an elastic, nonhardening bottom-seam compound.

Before the boat is turned right side up, the bottom rub strips (that is, the outside bottom stringers) are nailed on, as previously diagramed; 2½-inch 8-penny hot-dipped galvanized common nails are used for this. If they are driven on a slight slant, they will hold better,

and the heads can be set in ⅛ inch or so without danger of the points coming through inside.

The drawing on page 179 shows rub strips 2 inches wide that follow the outside edges of the bottom. These strips, bent on to conform to the curve of the sides, would go on without difficulty and would protect the ends of the bottom planking, but they would drag water behind their curved inside edges, making the boat harder to move and slowing it down somewhat. Bottom rub strips offer the least resistance to forward movement when their inside edges are straight and parallel to the fore-and-aft centerline of the boat. Such a rub strip for protecting the outside bottom edges of this boat is shown by the broken line, *39,* in the accompanying planking diagram. It extends only 6½ feet from the stern, but is nearly 6 inches wide at its widest part.

When the rub strips are on and the bottom has been given a priming coat, the nails through the cross spalls into the ladder-frame cross cleats can be drawn to allow the boat to be turned right side up. But before the cross spalls are removed from the frames, the outwales are put on. They are glued to the plywood sides and well nailed from the inside through the plywood with 1-inch number 11 or number 12 ring nails to ensure snug contact throughout the glue joint. The outwales are nailed with 2½-inch 8-penny hot-dipped galvanized common nails to the stem, frames, and transom.

With the outwales in place and fastened, the cross spalls are removed so that the side stringers, serving as seat risers, may be sprung in and nailed, which further stiffens the sides. But if this boat is to have a watertight bulkhead and foredeck, these should probably go in first.

The diagram shows that the bulkhead under the after end of the short foredeck is located 14 inches forward of station 2. It could just as well be at station 2 if more covered space forward is desired.

The frame for the bulkhead, including the after deck beam, is assembled first, with the plywood gussets and bottom strip on the forward side to hold it together. After being beveled and fitted, the frame assembly is set up in place and fastened through the sides and bottom.

The width of plywood that forms the watertight bulkhead or barrier is scribed and cut for a tight fit all around and is fastened in with plenty of nonhardening bedding compound to ensure that there will be no leaks. Deck beams located 14 inches on centers are cut to length with appropriate end bevels to fit tight against the sides at the sheer. They are nailed through the sides into the outwales.

The plywood deck is bent on and nailed to the deck beams and to the outwales over which its edges extend. If the edges of the deck are glued to the top edges of the outwales, the result will be tighter and stronger. The deck can be put on in two lengthwise halves, the seam down the middle supported underneath by blocks between the deck beams.

Outside, the seam is covered by a strip tapered for appearance. This is similar to the construction found on Adirondack guideboats and Saint Lawrence skiffs. The forward coaming, shaped as diagramed, is put on last.

A decked-over section at the bow sealed off at the bottom with a low barrier of watertight bulkhead not only provides dry storage space for clothing, lunches, and the like, but also strengthens and stiffens the sides of the boat.

At each frame station, removable thwarts like dory thwarts are fitted. When in place, these thwarts rest on the seat risers with their ends slotted to fit around the side frames. When in place they brace the sides, but they are easily removed when this is desirable.

A stern bench a foot or so wide braces the transom and the stern and is solidly nailed to cleats on the transom and to the ends of the seat risers. Quarter knees at the sheer level fasten through the sides and outwales, as well as through the transom, further bracing the stern. These knees are about 9 inches or 10 inches either way and are laid out so as to avoid short, weak grain.

Oarlocks are located 12 inches aft of the after edge of the thwart at station 3. If the thwart is 9 inches wide and centered on frame 3, that would bring the oarlock pins 16½ inches aft of station 3. Some might want to install another pair of oarlock sockets the same distance aft of station 2 so that the boat could be rowed from either of these two thwarts, depending on the loading or the weather. Pads for the oarlock sockets are located inside the topsides at the sheer and are fastened into the outwales.

No floorboards are needed. Limbers should be cut through the bottoms of the frames to enable the bilge to drain fore and aft. A final consideration: If oak is conveniently available, it might be well to use it for side frames. And if soft pine is used for this, it might not be a bad idea to increase the sided thickness of the side frames.

Construction details just discussed are keyed to the diagrams as follows:

30. *Bow end piece, bottom planking:* Glued up from two lengthwise halves, cut out so that the lengthwise grain runs parallel with the outside.

31. *Two-and-a-half-inch 8-penny hot-dipped galvanized common nails:* Ends of bottom planking to chine strip. Three-inch nails can be used in soft pine.

32. *Deck:* ⅜-inch-thick fir plywood. Marine plywood if possible.

33. *Deck beams:* Molded width 2½ inches, sided thickness ⅞ inch, crown 3-inch rise in 5 feet.

34. *Forward coaming:* Pine or fir ¾ inch thick.

35. *Gusset, deck beam, and frame:* ⅜-inch fir plywood.

36. *Bulkhead:* ⅜-inch fir plywood.

37. *Bulkhead stiffener:* Pine or fir, molded 2 inches, sided thickness ⅞ inch.

38. *Three-eighths-inch plywood strip:* Ties side frames to frame bottom.

39. *Bottom rub strip:* Inner edge parallel to the fore-and-aft centerline of the boat.

Sequel

I like to get feedback from builders of my designs, whether favorable or not, although I must admit to preferring the former sort. Except for such feedback I might never know if the boats performed as intended, or if they did not, in what way they fell short and to what extent. It is just not possible to build and test a prototype for every new design before it is published, although that would be the way to go if economics permitted. Thus, it is never possible to predict with complete certainty just how a new design will turn out in all respects, regardless of how closely known design characteristics successful in other configurations may have been taken into account. For these reasons I paid particular attention to a letter from Paul Rainey, a West Virginia builder of the down-east clamming skiff who followed the above plans and directions when they were first published in the *National Fisherman.* The letter follows.

West Virginia may seem a strange place to build a Downeast clam skiff, but I built your plan as published in May, June and July, 1982. My 15th boat and my third to build. Lots of fun and the plans were excellent.

Started construction on July 4th and launched on September 12th. I added strip planked decking around the sheer for trim as well as for strength.

Paul Rainey's skiff as originally built and with the center console installed later.

Now I have some running problems. With all possible adjustments on my 25 h.p. outboard and all loading arrangements she still porpoises at any more power than just enough to get on plane, and with the engine in any position except the most outboard, she sprays water up the transom. After numerous tests, I have taken out all the cross seats and am installing a center console with steering controls, etc., to get me out of the stern. I did not want to do this because I wanted simplicity. It also bothers me that I am losing cross bracing. But I can't see forward for safety with such a high-running bow. I am hoping to correct this problem with most weight concentrated in the center. I have considered trim tabs, wedges and extended planking. I would appreciate any advice.

From the photographs that accompanied Rainey's letter it was clear the builder knew what he was about. They showed a shapely hull attractively finished and fitted out. There can be no doubt that the skiff was well built, and built as designed.

There was no mention in the letter of pounding in a chop or taking water over the bow. From this it can be concluded that the sharp entrance and the long raking stem took care of what are often serious faults in heavily built flat-bottomed skiffs. But apparently the boat did squat by the stern under the conditions of loading to which it had been subjected, and then there was the "porpoising" complaint. How to account for this? Could the 3 inches of rocker built into the bottom be responsible to any significant extent for these undesired effects? Or was it something else that was chiefly amiss?

If this boat had been intended for use as a runabout

to be operated at planing speeds in a relatively light condition of loading, its after bottom would definitely have been designed without rocker. Instead, it would have run back dead straight from the midsection to the transom. But the boat was planned as a working skiff for clamming, to be used in shallow water around the clam flats while digging was in progress, where it would frequently ground out and have to be dragged about. Also it would be rowed part of the time in water too shallow for running the motor. For rowing and dragging about on the flats, a rockered bottom is advantageous. And when the skiff is on its way in from the flats, heavily loaded with clams, enough weight can be distributed forward to keep the bow down and the stern from settling unduly. If the stern does settle slightly, this is all to the good, for then the boat will run drier and pound less when heading into a chop.

Rainey's intentions for the boat were quite different. It is clear he wanted a smooth-running runabout that would plane and show a fair turn of speed with his 25 h.p. outboard. Quite correctly he sensed it would help to get the weight out of the stern and move it forward in the boat, and late that fall, following his September launching, he had begun to install a center console and steering controls. At the same time he was considering ways to modify the after bottom with such devices as trim tabs, wedges (shingles), or extended planking.

There things stood over the winter. Then in April another letter arrived from Rainey, this one a much more reassuring report, the jist of which follows.

A few warm days in early March, and I turned the boat over, stripped the bottom, put on two coats of Chem-Tech L-26 and some hard bottom paint. Then I installed a center console and remote controls.... Wednesday's test run with all new rigging in place was a complete success. No sign of porpoising....Better visibility over the bow, a smoother ride in a chop, maybe best of all, my wife likes it better 'cause it drives more like a car. By the way the long bow and generous flare make for a very dry ride. She will run smoothly at full throttle.

No mention of trim tabs, wedges, or extended planking. No need to consider them anymore.

The first time around, Rainey ran out of lumber at the very end and left off the bottom rub stringers next to the chine. Might this omission have been "the key to the whole problem?" he queries. Definitely not for running performance, although the boat might have tracked better with the stringers in place.

What it all boils down to is weight distribution and trim. The weight of a large motor and the concentration of occupants in the stern of a lightly built 16-foot skiff are bound to make the stern settle, even a stern as wide as this one. A rockered bottom, especially in a boat as lightly built as this one, will add to this effect, but when there is only a small amount of rocker, as in this skiff, the prime cause has to be too much weight concentrated in the extreme stern. Unquestionably, the high-speed performance of this boat would be improved if the motor were mounted inboard in a well. This was not done, out of a desire to keep this ordinary working skiff simple and to not reduce its already restricted loading capacity.

As for porpoising, various factors are involved—not only trim and weight distribution but wave formation, running speed, and handling skill. Indeed, it is not uncommon for short, wide, lightly built outboard boats with heavy motors hanging over the stern, to start porpoising when driven at speed into certain wave formations. In fact, at least one of the most widely advertised and distributed small stock outboard runabouts of this kind has porpoised so severely as to flip over backward completely.

It hardly needs saying that the length of a boat has a lot to do with its performance. If this boat is not to be hauled about in a pickup truck—and there are no other restrictions on its length—I would recommend not only taking the rocker out of the after half of the bottom but also stretching the boat out to 18 feet, provided it is intended for recreation rather than use as a specialized work skiff. At 18 feet overall, and with a plywood bottom instead of cross planking, this skiff would be quite similar to the 19-foot Carolina dory skiff for which I made revised and expanded construction plans in 1979 for Texas Dory Boat Plans (P.O. Box 720, Galveston, Texas 77553). Some may recall the article in the September 1979 issue of the *National Fisherman* in which I described and commented on these revisions. These Carolina skiffs have since been built with gratifying success from the Arctic to the South Pacific, as well as here in the United States.

Although the Carolina skiff's motor is located in an inboard motor well, I do not recommend such a motor well for the clamming skiff lengthened to 18 feet. This is not because I do not think such an arrangement would give good results, but because it would require space and would add to the cost and difficulty of construction. I believe that if the motor is simply mounted over the stern, performance will be quite

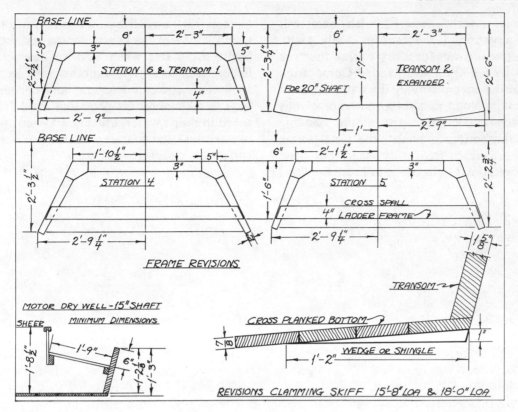

BASE LINE

STATION 6 & TRANSOM 1

FOR 20" SHAFT

TRANSOM 2
EXPANDED

BASE LINE

STATION 4

STATION 5

CROSS SPALL
4" LADDER FRAME

FRAME REVISIONS

MOTOR DRY WELL – 15" SHAFT
MINIMUM DIMENSIONS

SHEER

TRANSOM 2

CROSS PLANKED BOTTOM

WEDGE OR SHINGLE

REVISIONS CLAMMING SKIFF 15'-8" LOA & 18'-0" LOA

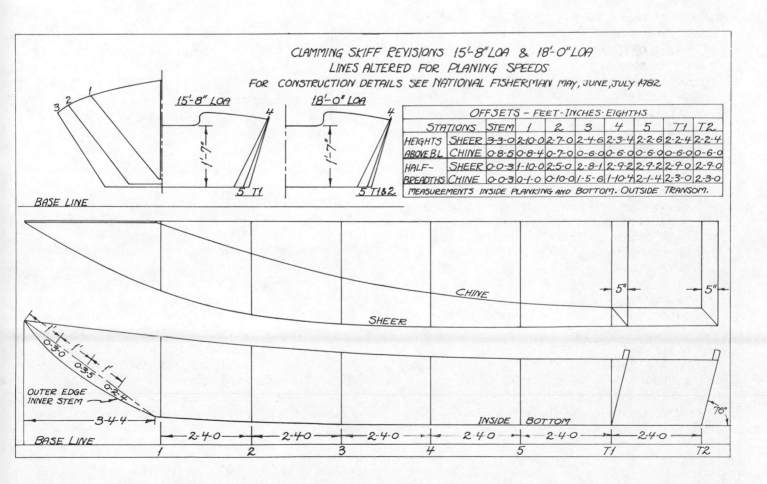

CLAMMING SKIFF REVISIONS 15'-8" LOA & 18'-0" LOA
LINES ALTERED FOR PLANING SPEEDS
FOR CONSTRUCTION DETAILS SEE NATIONAL FISHERMAN MAY, JUNE, JULY 1982

15'-8" LOA   18'-0" LOA

BASE LINE

OFFSETS – FEET·INCHES·EIGHTHS								
STATIONS	STEM	1	2	3	4	5	T1	T2
HEIGHTS ABOVE BL	SHEER	3-3-0	2-10-0	2-7-0	2-4-6	2-3-4	2-2-6	2-2-4	2-2-4
	CHINE	0-8-5	0-8-4	0-7-0	0-6-0	0-6-0	0-6-0	0-6-0	0-6-0
HALF-BREADTHS	SHEER	0-0-3	1-10-0	2-5-0	2-8-1	2-9-2	2-9-2	2-9-0	2-9-0
	CHINE	0-0-3	0-1-0	0-10-0	1-5-6	1-10-4	2-1-4	2-3-0	2-3-0
MEASUREMENTS INSIDE PLANKING AND BOTTOM. OUTSIDE TRANSOM.								

CHINE

SHEER

OUTER EDGE
INNER STEM

INSIDE   BOTTOM

BASE LINE

1   2   3   4   5   T1   T2

adequate. A motor with a long (20-inch) shaft will require hardly any cutout in the transom. A motor with a 15-inch shaft would call for a dry well of the type recommended by the Outboard Marine Corporation and detailed in the accompanying diagram.

The long, raking stem and sharp entrance of this skiff does much to eliminate one of the standing objections to flat-bottomed boats—the teeth-jarring pounding that occurs so frequently when they head into a hard chop. I don't believe the full benefit of this feature will be realized in a length of only 16 feet, which is one of the reasons I suggest increasing the length to 18 feet when work requirements or other imperatives do not dictate otherwise. Because of the 18-footer's increased length, and because it would have to take more of a pounding when driven at high speed in rough water, I would add narrow side decks (waterways) and coamings in order to strengthen and stiffen the topsides.

14

16-FOOT SWAMPSCOTT DORY

Every now and again I am contacted by prospective dory builders wishing to alter in some way the dimensions of the boat they are considering. Would it be possible to lengthen, shorten, widen, deepen, or otherwise change it without spoiling it? Generally the answer is yes, provided the change is not extreme and does not violate the basics of dory design. Dory design is more versatile, adaptable, and forgiving than most other small craft types.

Sometimes such a change turns out to be a distinct improvement, at least for the use for which the particular dory is built. That has been my aim in designing this modification of a proven rowing and sailing Swampscott dory. By moderately increasing the beam, the bottom width, and the size of the transom, I have significantly increased initial stability and stiffness, improved the dory's ability to stand up under sail, and added to its load carrying capacity.

This has been accomplished without detracting significantly from the craft's ability as a rowboat. In addition, there are alterations to the interior layout and the location of the centerboard that should improve performance and add to convenience.

The dory detailed here is descended from a typical Swampscott fisherman's 17-footer that I redesigned in 1974 for construction at the Mystic Seaport Museum. In late 1974 I reworked that design somewhat, shortening it to 16 feet, and I published plans and building instructions for the revision in a *National Fisherman* article and later in *Building Classic Small Craft, Volume I*. Both of these earlier designs have produced superior dories, including a fine 16-footer built by Dave Foster at The Apprenticeshop in Maine and the Mystic Seaport 17-footer that was rowed around Long Island by Dick Kohn, the Staten Island sailmaker, and two friends. On that trip, which took

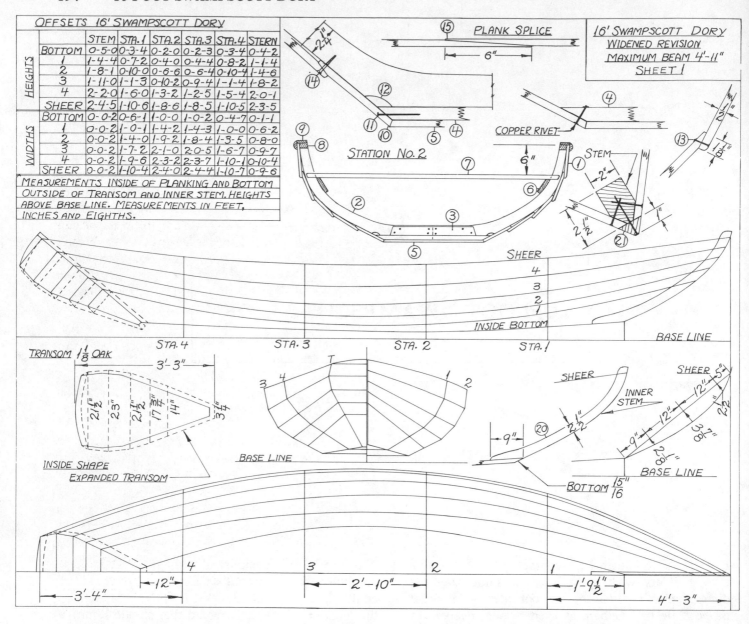

OFFSETS 16' SWAMPSCOTT DORY

		STEM	STA.1	STA.2	STA.3	STA.4	STERN
HEIGHTS	BOTTOM	0-5-0	0-3-4	0-2-0	0-2-3	0-3-4	0-4-2
	1	1-4-4	0-7-2	0-4-0	0-4-4	0-8-2	1-1-4
	2	1-8-1	0-10-0	0-6-6	0-6-4	0-10-4	1-4-6
	3	1-11-0	1-1-3	0-10-2	0-9-4	1-1-4	1-8-2
	4	2-2-0	1-6-0	1-3-2	1-2-5	1-5-4	2-0-1
	SHEER	2-4-5	1-10-6	1-8-6	1-8-5	1-10-5	2-3-5
WIDTHS	BOTTOM	0-0-2	0-6-1	1-0-0	1-0-2	0-4-7	0-1-1
	1	0-0-2	1-0-1	1-4-2	1-4-3	1-0-0	0-6-2
	2	0-0-2	1-4-0	1-9-2	1-8-4	1-3-5	0-8-0
	3	0-0-2	1-7-2	2-1-0	2-0-5	1-6-7	0-9-7
	4	0-0-2	1-9-6	2-3-2	2-3-7	1-10-1	0-10-4
	SHEER	0-0-2	1-10-4	2-4-0	2-4-4	1-10-7	0-9-6

MEASUREMENTS INSIDE OF PLANKING AND BOTTOM
OUTSIDE OF TRANSOM AND INNER STEM. HEIGHTS
ABOVE BASE LINE. MEASUREMENTS IN FEET,
INCHES AND EIGHTHS.

16' SWAMPSCOTT DORY
WIDENED REVISION
MAXIMUM BEAM 4'-11"
SHEET 1

most of a week, the dory demonstrated its excellent seakeeping qualities by handling late-season winds and rough seas with no particular trouble.

Dories have long been recognized as fine seaboats, but their low initial stability and active response to wave action is apt to be disconcerting to the sailor unaccustomed to dories. Their quickness to heel under press of sail can be alarming. What we have here is a somewhat stiffer, steadier boat than the general run of dories, yet one that retains all the advantages of dory construction. I believe these revisions will produce a boat more comfortable and less demanding when sailing, yet one that will still move easily and handle well under oars.

The true Swampscott dory, of which this boat is a good example, is essentially a round-bottomed boat, yet it has enough flat in its bottom to sit upright on the beach when it grounds out. For a boat that is to be beached frequently this is an especially desirable feature, particularly since it permits a double bottom, the outer layer of which is easily renewed when it wears thin from dragging over rocks.

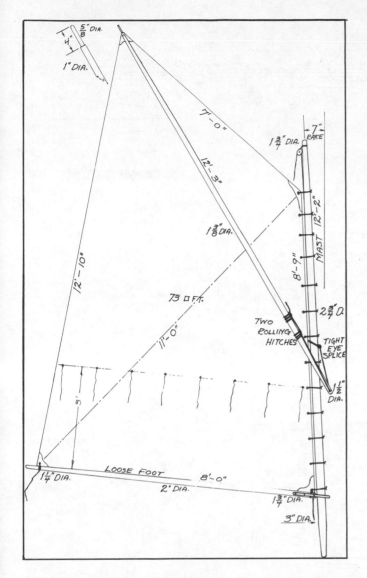

easily take six men or an equivalent load without undue reduction of freeboard. And because of its ample beam and depth, this boat will do well under sail.

In adapting this boat for sail the interior arrangements have been somewhat altered. The seat riser has been raised 1 inch, leaving 6 inches between the thwarts and the top of the railcap. One inch may seem a trivial amount, but it adds needed width to the centerboard without detracting from the rowing qualities of the boat. It is still a comfortable boat to row. In addition, the height of the centerboard trunk has been decreased slightly, bringing the top of its cap in line with the surface of the thwarts. With the sail furled and the mast down and stowed out of the way in the boat, a single oarsman can row from any one of the three thwarts without interference; when two oarsmen are present, they occupy the forward and after thwarts.

The sailing balance of a small boat is affected by so many variables that it is difficult, and often impossible, to predict just how the boat will behave in the water. It is to be expected that adjustments will have to be made after launching and the first trial runs.

Charles G. Davis, who knew a great deal about small craft both as a designer and a sailor, believed that all too many small-sailboat designs locate the centerboard too far forward. As it happens, this is especially true for some of the sailing dories, which in consequence have wicked weather helms.

Loading also has a lot to do with the sailing balance. Shifting weight forward or aft in a small boat can make all the difference under certain conditions, as is demonstrated by the behavior of the St. Lawrence River skiffs, which are sailed without rudders. One steers simply by moving back and forth in the boat to alter the trim.

In laying out the rig for this dory several features have been incorporated that will allow adjustments to be made in the sailing balance. For one thing, the centerboard has been made rather longer and larger than is usual for a boat of this size, and it is located well aft. By dropping it to different depths, or by raising it in the same manner, it will be possible to shift the boat's center of lateral resistance back and forth to some extent. To facilitate this, the board has a lead insert to give it positive drop. The board can be raised by means of a rope pendant that belays to a cleat bolted on the side of the centerboard trunk.

The indicated sail area is a moderate one, and

These Swampscott boats are the aristocrats of the dory clan, and are not to be confused with their clumsier, more crudely built cousins, the heavy, slab-sided working dories of the Grand Banks fishermen. True, in some features of their construction Swampscott and Grand Banks dories are similar, but in performance there is a vast difference. Swampscott dories row and handle much more easily. Whether they are faster under oars remains open to argument, but certainly they are every bit as good seaboats. Their principal superiority over the Banks model for recreational use lies in their greater ease of handling. In normal conditions a youngster could manage the boat under consideration easily, but he definitely could not handle a Banks dory of the same size.

Yet this is by no means a small boat. With an inside depth amidships of 19 inches to the top of the railcap and a maximum beam of 59 inches, this boat could

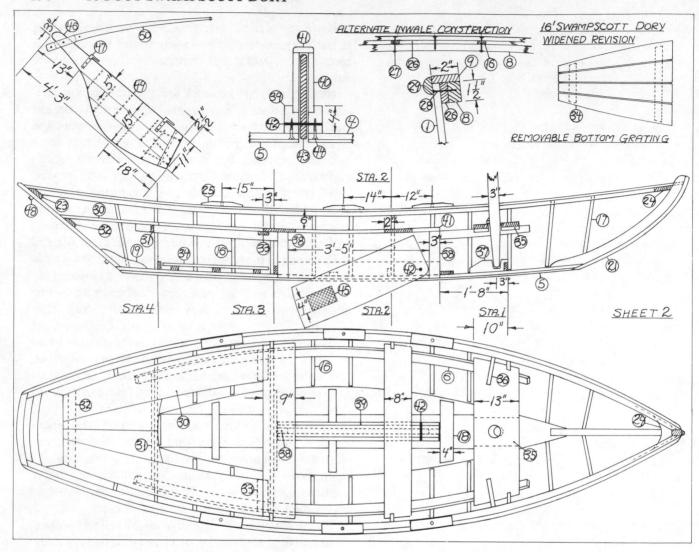

ALTERNATE INWALE CONSTRUCTION

16' SWAMPSCOTT DORY
WIDENED REVISION

REMOVABLE BOTTOM GRATING

SHEET 2

provision has been made for reefing down in heavy weather. Since there are no shrouds or stays, the entire rig is easily and quickly lifted out of the step for stowing in the boat. The spars are short enough to stow at one side, out of the way of the oarsman.

If desired, one might have one or more replacement rigs, smaller or larger or both, for different weather. This was a common practice early in this century at Marblehead, Beverly, and other towns on Boston's North Shore. Some dory fishermen there had as many as three separate rigs—a large sail for summer racing, a medium working rig for the summer, and a small sail for winter fishing.

Construction essentials are shown in the accompanying drawings. Needless to say, these should have close and careful study. Parts have been keyed for

ready reference to the listed supplementary information that follows. Those familiar with dory construction should find it plain sailing. The inexperienced, however, would do well to consult *The Dory Book*, in which I give a thorough and detailed explanation of all aspects of dory construction.

Most Swampscott dories of this size, and some even larger—including the 17-footer built at Mystic Seaport—are intended to be planked with four strakes to a side. This requires wide boards, especially those for the garboards, where widths of 16 inches and more will be needed. Boards of such width are rarely found today, and when they are, they are priced out of reach.

Mainly because of this, I have increased the number of strakes on this boat to five, which narrows the individual strakes considerably. As a result, one-piece garboards for this boat can be got out of 12-inch boards, and if the garboards are glue-spliced amidships, 9-inch boards will suffice. If need be, all the strakes may be spliced, provided the scarfs are well staggered.

Actually, this has advantages, for it avoids the cross grain in strakes that are curved to any extent. Splicing curved strakes in this way to avoid the weakness of cross grain was standard practice in the construction of Adirondack guideboats, which required the ultimate in strength together with lightness.

In the northeastern United States, northern white pine is the standard material for the bottoms and sides of dories. Knots, if they are sound and not too large, are quite acceptable. In fact, a plentiful distribution of sound knots in the ⅞-to-1-inch-thick pine bottom is desirable; such a bottom is stronger and wears better thereby. Even some small, loose knots are not to be ruled out, for they can be bored out and plugged. "Spike" knots, which extend across the width of a strake, are not acceptable, but in the strakes, too, a moderate distribution of round knots, provided they're not too large and are well scattered, is quite all right.

This means that relatively inexpensive lumber may be used—even number 2 common pine in some cases—if the boards are carefully picked over and cut so that the worst defects are avoided. Here is where glue splicing and the judicious arrangement of scarfs can work wonders. Splices should be kept at the ends of the boat, except for the garboards, and out of the midsection as much as possible.

To a great extent the strength of this hull will depend on its clinker construction; good lap fastenings are of particular importance. Copper rivets should be used. In any case, old-type chisel-point galvanized dory nails are no longer available. I strongly recommend the heavier English dished roves. The dished roves have greater holding power and grip the wood with greater compressive force when the rivet is made up, and are in every way far superior to ordinary flat roves or burrs.

First choice for the stem, sided 2 inches and molded 2½ inches, is dry white oak. Red oak is almost as good. If a plank can be found with a run of grain that favors the curve of the stem, so much the better. If not, straight grain will do, but the stem should be laid out so that the cross grain is equally distributed and does not come all in one end.

If oak is not to be had, any lasting hardwood can be substituted, preferably one with a grain that favors the stem curve. Locust, although heavy, would be excellent, and should it be used, the stem could be molded slightly smaller—say 2¼-inch instead of 2½-inch. Apple would also be fine. In fact, there is nothing better for dory frames than sound apple limbs of the right bend or curvature.

In case suitable hardwood is not available, good-quality Douglas fir or even longleaf hard pine may be substituted. When these softer woods are used, it would be wise to increase the molded dimension somewhat in order to compensate, say to 2¾ or even 3 inches. The extra weight would be negligible. Also, if softer wood is used for the stem, the fastenings through the hood ends of the planking should be larger.

Another possibility is a stem glued up with epoxy adhesive. This can be made of smaller pieces fitted together if a single large plank of sufficient size cannot be found.

There are a number of ways of doing this. One is to use several thin strips bent to shape on a curved form and clamped until the glue sets. Another is to build up the stem in layers. Short pieces can be used, distributed so that the grain in each is reinforced by the grain in those next to it.

I have shown the hood ends of the plank fastened into the stem with 2-inch galvanized boat nails; 1½-inch or 1¾-inch number 12 screws could just as well be used.

The transom can be Douglas fir or hard pine as well as oak. If oak is used, it could be planed to 1⅛ inches thick to save weight. Red oak would be better than white, which is heavier and more apt to pull out of shape in wide widths.

The boat should be planked bottom up. A setup is made for this purpose over a strongback—a wide 2-inch plank (1½-inch net thickness) secured on edge at working height, its upper edge cut to the curve of the inner bottom and notched to receive the frames and bottom cleats. The ends of the strongback are likewise cut to receive the stern knee and the bottom end of the stem.

Thus the strongback supports the preliminary assembly of bottom frames (which serve as molds), stem, and stern transom during the planking operation. After planking is completed, the planked-up shell is lifted off the strongback and turned right side up, and the laps are riveted in one operation. Of course, all the nails were previously in place, having been driven as the planks went on. The planks must be carefully fitted and properly beveled when building in this fashion.

The boat could be built right side up and the laps riveted plank by plank, but it would then be much harder to bevel the bottom correctly to receive the garboards and to fit the changing lap bevels. The planking operation is far easier and surer when done bottom up over a strongback.

Plank splices could be fitted and glued on the boat as the planking operation proceeds, but I don't recommend this. It will be far better and easier to lay out the splices and glue them ahead of time. They can then be planed smooth and the full-length plank spiled and laid out in one operation. There is much less chance of error this way.

In making the bottom and frame assembly, prior to securing it in position on the strongback, the bottom is laid out first. It is cut to shape and cleated together. Its edges may be beveled to receive the garboard planks, but anyone building a dory for the first time probably should leave this beveling operation until the completed frame and bottom assembly is secured bottom up on the strongback. When the bottom has been cut out and cleated, the stem, the frames, and the stern transom and knee, which have been made up separately, are put in position on the bottom and fastened. All of these members will have to be beveled.

Bevels can be taken ahead of setup from the full-size laydown of the lines, which, according to good boatbuilding practice, should be made and faired before any woodwork is started. Again, however, beginners who may not trust completely the bevels they take from their laydown are advised not to cut the bevels all the way in to the bevel lines until the boat has been set up and the bevels are checked with a batten. Wood is easily taken off when necessary, but it is difficult to pad out bevels that were cut too deep. Besides, in almost all cases it will be necessary to fair the bottom and frame assembly more or less extensively after it is set up and before planking starts.

1. *Planking:* Northern white pine, ½ inch thick. For a boat intended for very hard use, a plank thickness of $\frac{9}{16}$ inch is recommended. The weight of the boat would not be greatly increased thereby. The sheer plank had best be $\frac{9}{16}$ inch in any case. It has considerable curve and might need to be spliced from three pieces.

Where suitable sawn lumber is difficult to obtain, the boat can be planked with strakes of $\frac{3}{8}$-inch marine plywood. Strakes can be spliced from pieces cut from ordinary 4-by-8 and 4-by-10 panels, but even when plywood is used it would be desirable to make the sheer strake from sawn lumber $\frac{9}{16}$ inch thick. Increasing numbers of boats are now being planked in this way from marine plywood with satisfactory results. The use of plywood for planking is more fully treated in Chapter 1 and elsewhere in this book.

Three views of a 17-foot dory, forerunner of the design in this chapter, built at Mystic Seaport in 1974. **Opposite Page:** *Under construction, with stem, inner bottom, transom, and one frame clamped in place on a strongback.* **Left:** *The finished boat.* **Below:** *Under sail on the Mystic River. (Kenneth E. Mahler photos, Mystic Seaport)*

2. *Frames:* Oak, sided ⅞ inch, molded 2 to 3 inches wide, approximately 2¼ inches through the knuckles, tapering to 1½ inches at the top. While oak is first choice, substitutes such as Douglas fir can be used with a proportional increase in dimensions to give equivalent strength. As is shown here, the two sides of the sawn frames are joined and reinforced across the bottom by a strip or cleat set on edge of the same material as the side frames and 2¼ inches wide. If possible, sawn frames should be cut from lumber with grown crooks, to avoid cross grain.

There are a number of ways of making dory frames. They can be made in three sections that are cut out of ordinary oak boards and spliced where bottom and sides come together with galvanized-iron gusset plates located on either side and through-riveted. Instead of iron gusset plates, longer plywood gussets on either side of the frame, glued and screwed or riveted, are acceptable. It is even possible to laminate continuous one-piece frames from thin strips glued on a form. Detailed directions for framing dories can be found in *The Dory Book.*

3. *Frame bottom cleat:* Oak, ⅞ inch by 2¼ inches, set on edge.

4. *Bottom:* Pine, ¹⁵⁄₁₆ inch thick. To be not less than ⅞ inch or more than 1 inch. Three boards wide and solidly cleated together. Seams to be caulked with cotton and well payed with red lead primer.

5. *Outer, sacrificial bottom:* Pine, spruce, oak, elm, or other, put on with screws to be easily removable and replaced when thin from beach wear.

6. *Seat riser:* ⅝-inch pine, 3½ inches wide at the center and tapering to 2½ inches at the ends. Put on with 1½-inch number 12 wood screws.

7. *Thwarts:* Pine or spruce, ⅞ inch thick, three in number. Notched around frames and screwed to riser with number 12 screws. Center and after thwarts also fastened to the centerboard trunk, which they brace.

8. *Inwale:* Oak, ⅞ inch thick by 1½ inches wide, tapering to 1 inch at the bow and to 1¼ inches at the stern. Two different arrangements for installing it are shown. In one, the inwale is laid flat on top of the frame heads, which are cut so that the upper surface of the inwale comes flush with the top edge of the sheer plank, to which it is fastened. In the alternate construction the inwale is bent in on edge and riveted through the timberheads and sheer plank. Between the timberheads are filler pieces of ½-inch pine, glued in and nailed. The timberheads of the sawn frames are notched to receive the inwale, leaving ½ inch of wood against the sheer plank to line with the timberheads of

The 17-foot Swampscott dory built at Mystic Seaport in 1974 is shown here at the completion of a rowing voyage around Long Island in October 1980. This journey of 200 to 300 miles was accomplished by three men; when underway, one rowed, one steered from the stern sheets, and the man amidships bailed or slept. The boat proved seaworthy on this ambitious voyage. (Connie Marshall photo, Staten Island Advance)

the steam-bent timbers. Through rivets are also put in here. Finally, this construction is covered and made watertight by the railcap of oak, ½ inch thick, well bedded and pulled down with 1-inch number 10 wood screws.

Of the two methods, the first is more traditional but the second is undoubtedly stronger.

9. *Cap:* Oak, ½ inch thick. Two inches wide to cover inwale and top edge of sheer plank. Sawn to shape, not bent. Extends from stem to transom. Put on in several shorter lengths, butted, well bedded, and fastened with number 10 wood screws.

10. Note that the bottom edge of the garboard is not beveled off in line with the bottom, but is left square or approximately square to provide a fit for the false bottom.

11. At the ends of the boat where the bottom bevel is not suited to riveting, the lower edge of the garboard plank is fastened to the bottom with 10-penny nails, spaced 2½ to 3 inches apart. Nails can be galvanized-iron common nails, bronze-wire, or annular.

12. *Limber to drain bottom of boat:* When metal gussets are used to join frame futtocks, the joint in the frame is here.

13. The planking laps between the frames are fastened with copper rivets spaced 2½ to 3 inches.

14. The laps are fastened into the sawn frames with 1¾-inch number 10 bronze wood screws.

This 17-footer is one of a number of dories built by amateurs from the author's 1974 design. Weston Keyes built her to be rowed from three positions or to be rigged with a leg-o'-mutton sail. "It was a good boat for me to start out on," he reported.

A 16-footer constructed from the plans presented in Building Classic Small Craft, Volume I. *Jack MacKay of Sacramento, California, built her in his garage over a seven-month period. She was his first attempt at building a boat from scratch. (Leilani Hu photo,* The Sacramento Bee)

15. Plank splices are made 12 times the thickness of the plank—½-inch-thick plank, 6-inch splice. Scarfs are not planed to a sharp or feather edge, but are left ¹⁄₁₆ inch thick on the ends. The splice clamps better this way, and the extra ¹⁄₁₆ inch is planed off after the glue has thoroughly set. Scarfs are planed fair and true with a sharp block plane or smoother. Either epoxy or resorcinol glue can be used, but epoxy is best by far. Pressure is applied with a piece of oak on either side of the splice, held by four C-clamps. Wax the oak pressure blocks to prevent sticking.

16. *Intermediate bent timbers:* White oak, 1 inch wide by ½ inch thick. Two equally spaced between each pair of sawn frames. Steam-bent into place and fastened through the laps with copper rivets.

17. *Cant frames:* Same as *16*, but bent in on a cant better to fit the narrowing curvature of the sides at the ends of the boat.

18. *Three bottom cleats:* Oak, ⅞ inch thick. Laid flat against the bottom. Equally spaced between the sawn frames and solidly fastened through the bottom from the outside. Width of forward cleat increased from 2¼ inches to 4 inches for extra bracing forward of the centerboard trunk. Center cleat cut in way of the centerboard trunk but recessed halfway into the bed logs on either side, and fastened to them.

19. *Transom knee:* Oak, sided 2 inches. Overall length 16 inches.

20. *Inner stem:* Oak, sided 2 inches and molded 2½ inches.

21. *Outer stem piece:* Oak, 1 inch by 2 inches wide. Steam-bent to fit over plank ends and nailed in place. Trimmed to fair flush with the hood ends of the planking.

22. *Transom:* Oak, 1⅛ inches thick. Maximum width inside face, 23 inches. Made up from three full-length boards drifted together with ⁵⁄₁₆- or ⅜-inch galvanized drift rod. Cleated inside (see *23* and *32).*

23. *Transom cleat:* Oak, ¾ inch thick, molded 4½ inches and curved to conform to the curve of the upper end of the transom. Fastened with number 12 or 14 wood screws. The after ends of the railcaps *(9)* land on it and fasten to it.

24. *Breasthook:* Oak, 1 inch thick. Width of 3 inches to the after face of the stem. Railcaps extend over it on each side and fasten to it. Number 10 wood screws.

25. *Oarlock pads:* Oak, 1 inch thick and 12 inches long. Fastened through railcap with number 10 wood screws.

26. *Filler pieces:* Pine, ½ inch thick. They fill in the space back of the inwale and between the timberheads when the inwale is bent in on edge.

27. *Rivets:* 2½-inch 8-penny copper wire nails through sheer plank, timberheads, and inwale, headed over roves.

28. *Nails:* 1½-inch or 1¾-inch galvanized common or ring nails through sheer plank, filler pieces, and into inwale.

29. *Sheer guard trim:* 1¼-inch half oval of oak, tapered to 1 inch at the ends of the boat. Put on with 1¼-inch number 10 wood screws.

30. *Stern sheets and side benches:* Pine, ⅞ inch thick. Same material as the thwarts. Side benches 10 inches wide at the widest part. Extend as far forward as the after thwart at station 3.

31. *Cleat:* Pine or oak, ⅞ inch thick. Set on edge to support the forward end of the stern sheets. Similar to a deck beam. Ends cut for a tight fit between the seat risers just aft of the frame at station 4.

32. *Cleat:* Oak, ⅞ inch thick and 4 inches wide. Fastened flat to the inside of the transom to support and fasten the after ends of the stern sheets and side benches. Nail and glue.

33. *Cleats:* Oak, ⅞ inch thick, 3 inches wide. They support the forward ends of the side benches where these join the after thwart. Fasten with number 12 screws and glue.

34. *Bottom gratings:* Pine strips ⅝ inch wide cleated together to make removable gratings to cover the bottom.

35. *Mast partner:* Oak, ⅞ inch thick and 8 inches wide. Grain runs fore and aft. Well fastened through the thwart with number 12 wood screws and glue.

36. *Knees:* Oak, hackmatack, or other suitable wood, preferably grown crooks, to brace the thwart at the mast location. Fasten through the side of the boat with number 12 wood screws. Riveted through the inwale and thwart.

37. *Mast step:* Oak, 4 inches wide and 3 inches thick. Fitted against the bottom cleat of the frame at station 1. Well fastened through the bottom from the outside.

38. *Head ledges or end posts, centerboard trunk:* Oak, 1¼ inches thick and 3 inches wide. The lower ends mortise through the bottom to allow caulking but are covered by the outer false bottom. The bed logs are

fastened through the end posts with ¼-inch bolts from side to side. The sides of the centerboard trunk are riveted through the end posts. Glue will help to ensure a tight job.

39. *Bed logs, centerboard trunk:* Pine, 2 inches thick and 4 inches wide. Logs are rabbeted to take the sides of the trunk and scribed to fit the curve of the bottom. They are set in glue and pulled tight with 3-inch number 16 screws spaced about 6 inches apart.

40. *Sides, centerboard trunk:* Pine, ¾ inch thick. Glued to the rabbeted bed logs; copper riveted through the end posts of the trunk.

41. *Cap, centerboard trunk:* Pine, same thickness as the thwarts. Screwed down tightly.

42. *Centerboard pin:* Bronze rod, ½ inch diameter. Tight drive fit through the bed logs.

43. *Centerboard:* Oak, ⅞ inch thick and approxi-mately 40 inches long and 12 inches wide. Two boards fastened together with ⁵⁄₁₆-inch galvanized drift rod. Weighted with lead insert.

44. Number 16 wood screws, 3 inches long.

45. *Lead insert in centerboard:* 4 by 8 inches, set flush with the sides of the board and weighing approximately 10 pounds.

46. *Rudder:* Oak, ⅞ inch thick, tapered thinner toward the after edge. Made up as diagramed from several pieces and pinned together with ⁵⁄₁₆-inch galvanized drifts as shown. Fitted for easy removal when the boat is rowed.

47. *Pintle.*

48. *Gudgeon.*

49. *Drifts:* ⁵⁄₁₆-inch galvanized rod.

50. *Tiller:* Ash or oak slotted to fit over the rudder head and pinned to hinge up and down.

· 15 ·

MOWER DORY

Blueprints for this 18-foot Swampscott sailing dory came to me in a roundabout way. Although I was familiar with Mower dories, I did not know that plans for this one existed, until the prints turned up in 1978 in a letter from Maurice M. Wiley of Newport Beach, California. Wiley wrote:

> I purchased these plans from Mr. Mower many years ago (at least 40 or more) when I was searching for bank dory plans. At that time no one I contacted could give me any information as to where such plans might be available, if at all. I found out, not at all.
>
> Mr. Mower told me that he had the lines for a Swampscott sailing dory, and that he was sure I could finish the hull for oars, and that it would handle well. I never did anything with the plans after I received them but laid them aside and forgot about them. The other day I came across these plans and thought they would be better off in your hands than anywhere else. I hope

they will be of interest to you, if not, the waste-basket!

As I hastened to inform Mr. Wiley, not only was this dory of great interest to me, but I expected that it would prove interesting to amateur builders, a number of whom would probably construct it. This dory will sail well and will be nice to look at. As *Yachting* magazine said in its tribute to Charles D. Mower in its February 1942 issue, "Mr. Mower in his long career designed many famous boats and it was always said of his designs that he never turned out a bad boat or one that was not pleasing to the eye."

This dory is not too large and not too small. With a length overall of 18 feet and a maximum beam of 5 feet, it is large enough to sail well and be safe, yet not too large for one man to handle, or to transport over the road on a trailer.

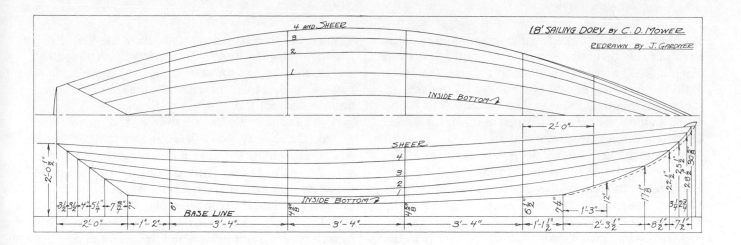

18' SAILING DORY BY C.D. MOWER
REDRAWN BY J. GARDNER

OFFSETS C.D. MOWER 18' SAILING DORY							
STATIONS	TRAN	4	3	2	1	A	STEM
HEIGHTS							
BOTTOM	0-7-0	0-6-0	0-4-3	0-4-5	0-6-4	—	—
1	1-0-5	0-9-5	0-6-7	0-7-1	0-10-6	1-2-2	1-5-1
2	1-4-3	1-0-3	0-9-3	0-9-5	1-2-0	1-5-7	1-10-4
3	1-7-2	1-3-4	1-1-0	1-1-4	1-5-4	1-9-0	2-1-4
4	1-10-0	1-7-0	1-5-6	1-7-0	1-10-0	2-0-2	2-4-4
SHEER	2-0-4	1-10-5	1-10-0	1-11-1	2-1-4	2-3-4	2-6-5
HALF-BREADTHS							
BOTTOM	0-0-0	0-2-0	0-6-0	0-6-4	0-2-4	—	—
1	0-4-0	0-9-2	1-1-6	1-2-0	0-10-0	1-4-6	0-0-1
2	0-6-5	1-2-7	1-8-7	1-9-0	1-3-4	0-9-1	0-0-1
3	0-8-6	1-6-3	2-1-4	2-1-5	1-7-1	0-11-6	0-0-1
4	0-10-4	1-9-4	2-5-0	2-5-0	1-9-2	1-1-1	0-0-1
SHEER	0-9-3	1-9-4	2-5-0	2-5-0	1-9-2	1-1-5	0-0-1

HEIGHTS ABOVE BASE LINE. MEASUREMENTS TO INSIDE BOTTOM & PLANKING, TO OUTSIDE TRANSOM & FORWARD EDGE OF INNER OR TRUE STEM. MEASUREMENTS IN FEET, INCHES & EIGHTHS.

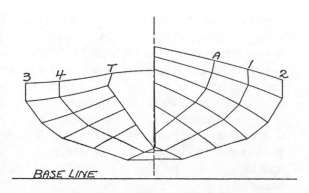

BASE LINE

"Few naval architects who devoted their talents to yacht designing were better known during the past three decades, or will be more missed, than Charles D. Mower," declared *Yachting* in summing up Mower's career following his death in January 1942. From his New York City design office, established at the end of World War I, came such yachts as *Junius,* S. Morgan's Class M *Windward,* the *Ardelle* and the *Ardette* of the R class, and a number of successful 6-meter and Q class boats. Another of his larger vessels was the cruising schooner *Windjammer,* and still another was the centerboard schooner *Shellback,* for Commodore Crabbe of the Cruising Club of America.

Mower was a member of the Cruising Club of America, the Manhasset Bay Yacht Club, and the New York Yacht Club, for which, as official measurer in 1903 and 1904, he measured *Shamrock III* and *Reliance* for the America's Cup races in 1903. At that time he was design editor for *The Rudder,* then the leading yachting publication. Before he left *The Rudder* in 1910 to join Thomas Bowes in Philadelphia and form the design firm of Bowes and Mower, he designed a boat for the editor, Thomas Fleming Day. This was *Sea Bird,* the 25-foot yawl in which Day made his famous crossing to Europe in 1911.

To list all the boats and yachts, both large and small, designed by Mower, many whose names are now inscribed in American yachting annals, would far exceed the limits of this chapter. Yet despite all the celebrated yachts that came from his board, there can be no doubt that the Swampscott dory stood very high in Mower's esteem and affections.

Mower was born in Lynn, Massachusetts, and grew up on the beaches of Lynn and nearby Swampscott. If he did not learn to sail in a dory, it is clear that he knew the boats of the Swampscott fishermen, and he must have sailed in them as a boy, like all of his friends and neighbors. The centerboard sloop *Vitesse,* which he built as a teenager in his backyard, proved so successful that the following year, at the age of 20, he found employment as a draftsman in the design office of Arthur Binney, Boston naval architect.

In 1898 he left Binney to go to work for B. B. Crowninshield, one of the most eminent and successful naval architects of the period. That same year Mower designed a 21-foot racing dory for the Swampscott Club. This boat came to be known as the X-dory, a winner from the start and rivaled only by the Beachcomber dories of Marblehead and the Alphas of Salem, nearly identical craft from William Chamberlain's Orne Street shop in Marblehead. Scores of X-dories were built and sailed, and they continued to sail and to win races well beyond the 1940s.

Around 1900 the Swampscott sailing dories were about the hottest thing in small racing craft afloat. From Swampscott dory shops, of which the Elbridge Gerry Emmons dory factory was the largest, sailing dories were distributed throughout the Northeast, as far north as the Adirondacks and as far west as the Great Lakes. For the next two decades the Swampscott dory was easily the most popular small-craft type in the Northeast.

As far as we know, the X-dory was Mower's first commissioned design, and its outstanding success speaks well for the ability of the 23-year-old naval architect.

In 1899 Mower went to New York to become design editor for *The Rudder* magazine, which, under the distinguished direction of Thomas Fleming Day, had grown from a slim sheet that in 1890 was devoted to sailing canoes and printed at Watertown, New York, at the eastern end of Lake Ontario, to this country's most influential yachting and boating publication with editorial offices in New York City.

In 1895 the talented Charles G. Davis, *The Rudder*'s first design editor, had initiated a new feature that caught on immediately and added immensely to the magazine's popularity—fully detailed how-to-build designs for small craft of a size and kind that suited the desires and abilities of amateurs and backyard builders of the time. There followed designs for flatties, catboats, dories, and other craft by Edson B. Schock, Fred W. Goeller, and, when he replaced Davis as design editor, Mower himself.

One of Mower's boats is *Bonito,* the construction of

which is fully explained in his article in the May 1904 *Rudder,* "How to Build a Power Dory." At this time the gasoline engine for marine use was quite new. A powerboat like this, therefore, was a very advanced design—indeed, a daring innovation.

If you examine *Bonito*'s hull lines and then turn to those of the X-dory, you will see at once that both have what is essentially the same hull, except that *Bonito* is scaled down to 18 feet. This, of course, is the length of the dory under consideration here, whose basic hull is remarkably similar to the other two. Furthermore, the same similarity exends to another Mower boat, his Massachusetts racing dory, an advanced sailing dory the rig and construction of which he worked out in great detail.

In fact, it appears that Mower had one basic dory hull that he considered the ultimate Swampscott dory hull. In adapting it to a number of varying requirements he made some minor and superficial changes, but always without altering the fundamental characteristics of his original 1898 design for the Swampscott Club. The success of the X-dory was so outstanding that there was little incentive to attempt to improve on it, and good reason not to risk spoiling it, even to a minor extent.

Before making this 18-foot Mower sailing dory available to readers of the *National Fisherman* in January and February 1979, I consulted with Mower's son, Charles P. Mower, who graciously stated that he would be happy to have any of his father's designs published for unlimited use by anyone interested.

Maurice Wiley's blueprints, however, were not suitable for direct reproduction. It was necessary to redraw them before they could be printed. In doing so I adhered closely to Mower's dimensions but changed his layout and presentation somewhat in order to adapt the plans to the printed page and make them easier for the novice to follow.

I have made a few very slight changes in the widths and angles of the planks in order to make the planking operation somewhat easier, but none that could affect the performance of the boat in the slightest or change its appearance enough to be noticeable. This is what would have been done by most professional builders anyway. Such adjustment during the planking operation was always the builder's prerogative, and the architect expected him to make such minor adjustments in the widths and run of the strakes as the actual planking required.

Also, I have drawn in a line for the top of the

garboard, which Mower did not show because there is no knuckle in the deadrise where the garboard and the plank above it come together. The location of this plank line was one of the things left to the builder to vary slightly as he saw fit to suit the widths of the planking stock at hand. I thought it best to lay out an acceptable plank line here for the benefit of the inexperienced builder.

For those not used to working with the standard offset table, I have dimensioned the four principal frames that serve as molds and remain in the boat as a permanent part of the hull structure. Mower did the same in his blueprint. It will not be necessary to lay this boat down full size in order to build it, although the inexperienced builder might want to make a full-size laydown to be on the safe side, and could undoubtedly learn from it.

This 18-foot sailing dory is partly decked with narrow waterways along the sides and a low coaming. Having a maximum beam of 5 feet, it is 8 to 10 inches wider than the average fisherman's working dory of 18 feet LOA. This increased width greatly increases initial stability and the ability to carry a press of sail. Its side decking and coaming allow the boat to heel steeply in a puff of wind and still not take water over the side.

With foam flotation (not available when the boat was designed) placed under the forward and after decks and out of sight under the waterways along the sides, this dory can be made unsinkable, and would float right side up and only partly submerged when full of water. Hence, she would be a safe boat for children and an ideal boat for youngsters to learn to sail in.

Although this boat has essentially a round hull as far as its performance in the water goes, its dory shape can be planked much more easily than a round hull. For that reason it is better suited to amateur construction.

In supplying construction details for this dory, I followed the old prints closely. Mower included but one sectional view, and only a few basic dimensions. Apparently he expected that prospective builders would be familiar with standard dory construction, which hardly needed to be explained and dimensioned in comprehensive detail 60 years ago, about the time this dory seems to have been designed.

For the modern builder inexperienced in dory construction and considering building a dory for the first time, I recommend in particular my *Dory Book* (Camden, Maine: International Marine, 1978) and

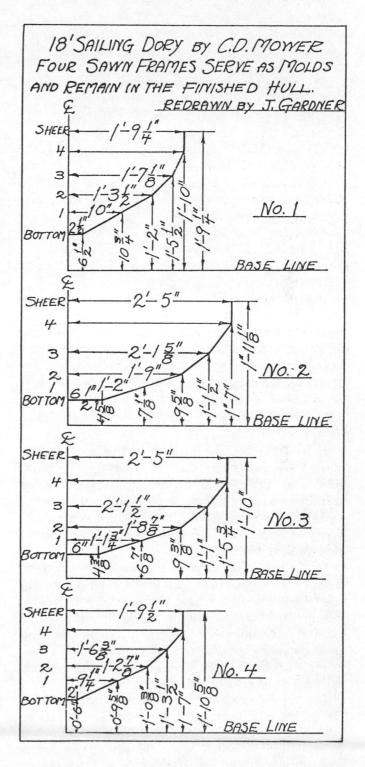

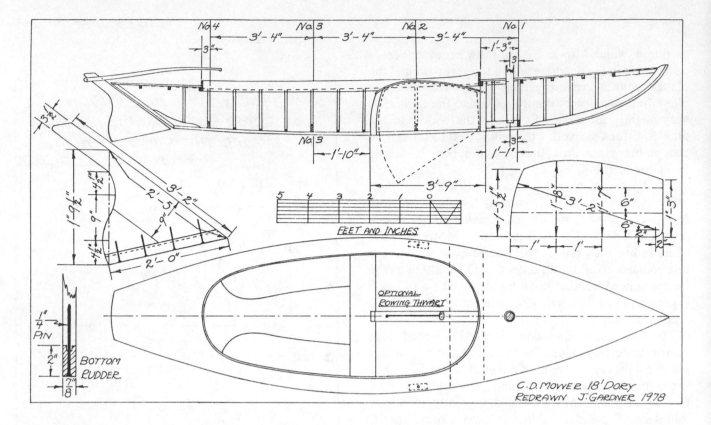

C.D. MOWER 18' DORY
REDRAWN J. GARDNER 1978

how-to-build dory articles by Schock and Mower, reprinted from early issues of *The Rudder* by Texas Dory Boat Plans, P.O. Box 720, Galveston, Texas 77553.

From these sources the prospective dory builder should be able to obtain answers to any questions that may arise. *The Dory Book,* a compilation of articles on dories and dory building published over the years in *National Fisherman,* was intended as a convenient, comprehensive, and authoritative source of information on dory building.

My principal departure from the original Mower blueprints has been to suggest the addition of a rowing thwart and the other minor changes that will make it possible to row this boat. If a boat is intended for general recreational use, and particularly if it is to be used by youngsters, there should certainly be provision for rowing it when the wind fails or becomes too strong, or on other occasions.

I have located the rowing position as far forward of amidships as the decking permits, to make it as easy as possible to keep the boat from blowing off when heading into the wind. When the rowing position is located too far aft, it is difficult and sometimes impossible to keep the boat on course when rowing into a head wind.

In order to locate the rowing thwart at a workable height, it was necessary to lower the forward end of the centerboard case. This in turn required alteration in the shape of the centerboard, but without any effective change in the area or location of its wetted surface. The shape resulting from lowering the forward end of the centerboard case may not be as aesthetically pleasing as what was drawn by Mower, but it is simpler and easier to build. If, however, one is not concerned about rowing and wishes a boat solely for sailing, it can be built as originally drawn.

As I mentioned, there is ample room out of sight under the decking along the sides and at the ends for the installation of foam flotation. The foam should be distributed so that the boat will float partly submerged, level, and on its waterlines, should it ever fill with water. Since the boat is built of wood and lacks outside ballast, it would undoubtedly float without foam flotation. But it would be better to have the foam, and the boat would float much higher with it. If the boat is to be used as a general-purpose family boat, and especially if it is to be used by children, I cannot recommend too strongly the addition of foam flotation attached inconspicuously to the underside of the decking.

The rig shown by Mower is the classic dory sailing rig, consisting of triangular leg-o'-mutton main with high-angled boom, and a small, loose-footed jib. The

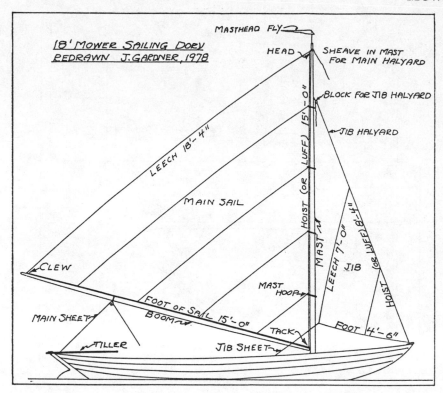

sail area is moderate, the mast unstayed. Such a rig is simplicity itself.

To lift up the boom and secure it and the bunched sail to the mast with a few turns of the main sheet, to unsnap the jib, and to lift the light mast out of its bury is but the work of an instant, and the whole thing stows easily in the cockpit. With the foot of the rig pushed up under the foredeck and the head tailing out over the cockpit's after coaming, the boat is ready to row with oars that are stowed conveniently under the foredeck.

Some may want more sail area, some less, depending on how the boat is to be used and who is going to use it. Many years ago in Marblehead some dory fishermen had as many as three rigs of different sizes, each with its own mast with sail and boom permanently attached to it: a small rig for winter sailing, a medium rig for summer fishing, and an oversize rig for racing.

No doubt there are others who will consider experimenting with other rigs. A sliding gunter mast might be more convenient to stow in the cockpit. Some might want to try a more modern high-aspect rig with fixed stays. There are many possibilities. Because of this dory's extra beam and its side decks and coaming,

it can safely handle more sail than narrower dories of the same length that are entirely open.

The construction views have been keyed wherever it seemed that detailed information would be required or helpful. The explanations and comments for the numbered references follow in order.

1. *Bottom:* The wood is pine. Mower indicated a thickness of 1 inch, which was slightly heavier than the ⅞ inch generally used. But the extra thickness is all to the good in providing ample wood for fastening the lower edge of the garboard, and it is insurance against leaks. Although the bottom is exceptionally narrow for a dory—only about 13 inches at the widest point— single boards of this width are not always to be had. When two boards must be used, they may be glued together. The location of the glue joint should be planned so that it is supported on the inside by bottom cleats and the bottoms of the sawn frames. White pine is the best bottom material. Acceptable substitutes are old-growth, rift-sawn Douglas fir, Port Orford cedar, southern longleaf pine, and Honduras mahogany, but not Philippine mahogany.

2. *Sawn frames:* Four sets of these serve as building molds and remain in the boat as principal

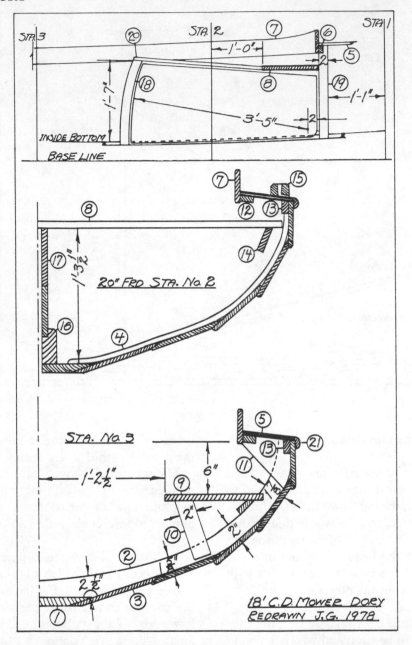

18' C.D. MOWER DORY
REDRAWN J.G. 1978

reinforcing members. Seasoned oak planed 13⁄16 inch to 7⁄8 inch thick is the standard material. Ideally, such frames are cut to shape from flitch-sawn ("live-edge") boards, the builder taking advantage of any curvatures to avoid cross grain, which is weak. When frames cannot be got out full length with a good run of grain, it will be necessary to splice them from shorter pieces. This is what is generally required. The splices are glued and reinforced with overlapping pieces set in glue and fastened with nails or screws.

3. *Planking:* As shown, this dory has five planks on a side, the customary number for Swampscott dories like this one. However, instead of two planks to fill up the space between the bottom and the first knuckle, as shown, three narrower planks could just as well be used. More work is required to fit and fasten three planks, but there is little choice if wide boards cannot be found.

These early dories were planked with northern white pine. At that time wide pine boards were plentiful and cheap. Cedar was rarely used because it was more expensive, and because cedar boards wide enough for dory garboards and broads were usually not to be had. As a replacement for pine or cedar I do not hesitate to recommend ⅜-inch marine plywood. Standard 4-foot-by-8-foot panels can be used if the strakes are glue-spliced. With careful planning, the plank sections can be laid out on these panels and cut with very little waste.

Plywood for clinker planking has a number of advantages. On the whole, it is more widely and more readily available than good-quality pine or cedar planking lumber. It will not split through a row of lap fastenings, which occurs too frequently in aging boats planked with sawn boards of natural lumber. Plywood planking does not develop splits or "rents," as often happens with sawn lumber, especially in the wide ends of dory garboards. When boats are clinker-planked with plywood the laps can be glued, since the strakes do not move with changes in width from swelling and shrinking. In all cases the raw edges of plywood planking must be sealed. This is probably best accomplished with liberal applications of a thin, penetrating epoxy resin.

It would also be possible to plank up to the first frame knuckles with a single width of plywood instead of two or three strakes of sawn lumber. Actually, this would be the easier, quicker way, since it would eliminate considerable fitting, beveling, and riveting. The plywood would be lighter than the sawn lumber and just as strong, if not stronger. Directions for splicing wide, full-length plywood planks from standard 8- and 10-foot panels are given in Chapter 13.

4. *Bent timbers:* Mower called for bent timbers or frames 1 inch wide by ½ inch thick put in on the flat and spaced between the sawn frames 10 inches apart. White oak is the standard bending stock for this, but in places where good oak bending stock is not to be had, a substitute must be found. Laminated timbers glued up from strips of spruce or fir ⅛ inch to 3/16 inch thick are one possibility. They can be glued at least double width on a form of the right shape, and if they are made somewhat thicker than the required ½ inch, there will be wood enough for them to be cut to shape or "joggled" for a snug fit against the inside surface of the laps. This may require additional labor and careful workmanship, but it makes for an extra strong job.

5. *Decking:* ⅜-inch marine plywood. For an extra light deck ¼-inch plywood could be used, but in that case deck beams should be spaced more closely together.

6. *Deck beams:* Laminated deck beams glued to shape from spruce strips will be light but amply stiff and strong. Because of the slight curvature, strips ¼ inch or even 5/16 inch thick can be used.

7. *Coaming:* Standard material for this would be steam-bent oak about ½ inch thick. When suitable bending oak is not available, glued laminations may be substituted. The coaming is not put in in one continuous length, but is made up of four segments spliced together. Gluing it up in segments like this makes lamination a relatively easy process.

8. *Rowing thwart:* A pine or spruce board ⅞ inch thick and a foot wide. In case a board this wide cannot be found, two narrower widths can be glued together.

9. *Side benches:* Same material as the rowing thwart, although fir, Port Orford cedar, or mahogany might also be used.

10. *Post:* A strip of oak, pine, or mahogany with the lower end cut so as to shoulder on the sawn frame and lie flush against one side of the frame for most of its width. Should be glued to the frame at station 3 as well as screwed or nailed to it. The other end of the post should be fastened to the underside of the bench.

11. *Side-deck gussets:* These are made of plywood ⅜ inch or ½ inch thick and are glued and screwed or nailed to the upper ends of the sawn frames.

12. *Side-deck reinforcements:* These strips, 1½ inches by ¾ inch, are glued and screwed or nailed to the underside of the side decks to provide landing and fastening for the coaming.

13. *Sheer clamps:* These strips, 1½ inches by ¾ inch, must be glued and screwed or nailed to the top of the inside of the sheer plank. They take the deck fastenings and ensure a solid union of deck and topsides.

14. *Rowing-thwart risers:* These short risers, 3 inches by ¾ inch, span sawn frames 1 and 2 to provide support for the ends of the rowing thwart.

15. *Rowlock pads:* Oak or mahogany, 1½ inches high, 2 inches wide, and 10 inches long, positioned so the center of the oarlock socket is 12 inches aft of the after edge of the rowing thwart. The hole for the socket is limbered so that it drains outboard.

16. *Bed logs, centerboard case:* These should be pine, 1¾ inches thick and 4 inches high. They can be bolted through the bottom with 5/16-inch carriage bolts

or drawn tight with 4-inch number 16 or number 18 wood screws. Bed logs should be cut to fit the curve of the bottom perfectly. The joint with the bottom should either be glued or bedded with some nonhardening bedding compound.

17. *Sides, centerboard case:* ¾-inch pine, fir, Port Orford cedar, etc.

18. *After headledge:* Preferably oak, 1¼ inches by 2 inches, sawn to curve as shown.

19. *Forward headledge:* Oak, 1¼ inches by 2 inches. Extends above the centerboard trunk to meet the underside of the deck. The upper end is notched to receive the afterdeck beam, which lets into it flush on the after side. This is a neat arrangement that supports the deck and braces the centerboard case. Both headledges extend through the bottom to cut off flush with the outside at either end of the centerboard slot. In this way they can be caulked from the outside.

20. *Cap, centerboard case:* ⅝-inch pine, fir, or mahogany.

21. *Half-oval trim:* 1⅛-inch oak or mahogany tapered slightly at the ends for appearance.

Fastenings: Lap fastenings are number 11 gauge copper nails riveted over burrs or roves. The garboard is fastened to the bottom with copper rivets in the midships section and with 2½-inch annular nails (ring nails) at the ends. For detailed information on fastenings for this boat, see construction drawings for various dories in *The Dory Book.*

Glue: Glue joints greatly increase the strength of the hull structure.

· 16 ·

BOATBUILDERS' PLANES

The amateur aspiring to the art of wooden boat-building had best familiarize himself with boatbuilders' wooden planes, both as to their use and their construction. For if he would build craft worthy of the old-time craftsmen, he will require a number of specialized boatbuilders' planes that are not now, and never have been, available ready-made at the hardware store. More than that, he will find few directions for making them in boatbuilding manuals, nor are there many old-time boatbuilders still hanging on who can show him how.

Since Dr. Henry C. Mercer's pioneer work *Ancient Carpenters' Tools* first appeared serially in the late 1920s in the bulletin of The Society for the Preservation of New England Antiquities, a flourishing literature devoted to old tools has sprung up. A substantial part deals with planes, but there is little on the subject of the specialized planes used in boatbuilding and shipbuilding, and how they were made.

I believe that the first published information on boatbuilding planes was an article I wrote for the December 1952 issue of the *Maine Coast Fisherman.* Then in the *National Fisherman,* in November and December 1971 and in January 1972, I published three articles on boatbuilding planes and how to make them. Combined, revised, and extended, these articles appear here. Although they were written over 10 years ago, and despite the fact that the literature on 19th-century woodworking hand tools has proliferated since then, little or nothing has been done to rescue boatbuilders' planes from their undeserved neglect. There is just one exception, a notable one—the section on the making of boatbuilders' wooden smoothing planes in Kenneth D. Roberts's *Wooden Planes in 19th Century America, Volume II,* pages 22–28. Yet the growing revival of traditional wooden boatbuilding has brought an increased need for these old-time planes, and more and more builders have become interested in making the specialized planes they cannot buy. The directions that follow outline the essentials and provide enough information to enable the aspiring planemaker to proceed on his own.

But before setting out to produce the planes he requires, the builder of wooden boats can well afford to give some attention to the historical background of boatbuilders' planes. It is a fascinating story, and he will find himself in the company of craftsmen with whom he can identify. Planemaking by boatbuilders in bygone days was a craft within a craft. In some respects it was more than a craft, coming close to being an art and a means of creative expression.

Henry Hall, in his 10th census entitled "Report on the Ship-Building Industry of the United States," gives the average number of hands employed in the shipbuilding industry during the census year 1880 as 21,345. Not all would have used planes, it is true, but since it was not unusual for a boatbuilder to have 15 or 20 planes in his kit, while sparmakers and outboard joiners sometimes had 40 or more, it seems reasonable to assume that considerably more than 100,000 boatbuilders' and shipwrights' wooden planes were in active use that year.

During the 18th century, more than a million planes must have been made, used, and worn out. All but a few have disappeared, and even how they were made—or that they were ever used—is now largely forgotten.

In his chapter on small craft in *The Common Sense of Yacht Design,* L. Francis Herreshoff extols the old-time builder of wooden boats. The boatbuilder, he writes, is very much of an artist whose work is of a much higher order than that of the cabinetmaker, requiring an elaborate kit of tools, often numbering more than 100 items, some quite expensive, and others peculiar to his trade, most of which he had to make himself.

This last, of course, refers particularly to his specialized boatbuilders' planes. According to Herreshoff, the boatbuilder excelled over all others as a maker of wooden planes, often supplying the ship carpenter as well as himself, and sometimes the cabinetmaker. This is borne out by my own experience and observation and what I have learned from older tradesmen.

Many instances come to mind. Cap'n Perry, employed for the average working lifetime at the Lawley yard in Neponset as an outboard joiner, was still planing boats at the age of 80 in the Sims Brothers yard in Dorchester in the late 1940s. Sims was then building double-planked yachts of African mahogany and cedar for Sparkman and Stephens, Nielsen, and others.

Starting with the adze and finishing off with scraper and sandpaper, Perry did most of the work with planes, of which he kept a trunkful at hand to select from as needed. The result was as smooth as the proverbial bottle. It is impossible to achieve equivalent results with power sanders. The yachts that are finished with power tools today would never have been accepted when yachts were smoothed by planing.

Like most of the old-time outboard joiners, Cap'n Perry made his own planes. The most he ever made in one winter, he told me, was 40, some of which he kept for himself and some of which he sold. I used to watch him planing the difficult African mahogany, marveling at the way the shavings came away tissue-thin, leaving the surface smooth without ever once catching or tearing the difficult cross grain of the mahogany.

He was secretive about his trade, like most of the old boatbuilders. For a long time he would not tell me how he did it, but finally he relented. He honed the cap on the oilstone until it was sharp and fitted the surface of the plane iron perfectly. Then he turned down the edge with a burnisher as if it were a scraper. He then fastened the cap to the iron with its burnished edge set very close to the sharpened edge of the iron, within ⅟₃₂ inch or thereabouts. A plane set in this manner is harder to push, but it will smooth the most difficult and treacherous cross-grain wood without catching, digging in, or tearing.

Another planemaker I have known was Charles W. Lawton, whose reputation as a boatbuilder still lingers in Marblehead. He worked until the age of 90 at the Graves yard on Beacon Street, building the finest varnished-cedar yacht tenders.

There was always a plane of some sort under construction at the back of his workbench, which he could turn to whenever he had a free moment. In this way, he kept up a more or less steady production of planes, providing relaxation as well as a minor source of pin money. I still have a couple of his planes—one a small spar plane with a quick radius, about right for boathook handles.

Planemakers who were gone before my time in Marblehead, but whose planes were prized by boatbuilders who had them, were Ed Howes of Essex and Jim O'Neil, the outboard joiner.

There was a mystique connected with planemaking

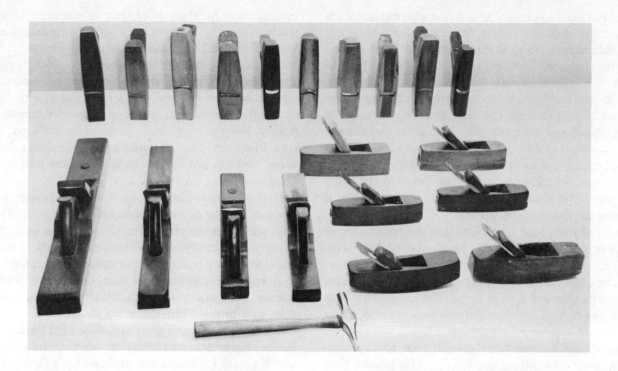

Two views of an assortment of boatbuilding planes made by the author. In the background are smoothers (flat sole), spar planes (concave sole), backing-out planes (convex sole), and a chamfer plane (third from right). In the left foreground are a wide Brazilian rosewood jointer, a normal-width jointer, an ironwood jackplane, and a lignum vitae jackplane. To the right of these (back to front and left to right) are a live-oak smoother, York pattern, angle of iron 60 degrees; a flat rosewood rocker; an ironwood rocker; a beech backing-out plane; a small ironwood rocker with sole curved both ways; and a large rocker. In the near foreground is a plane hammer for adjusting the set of the iron (or removing it from the stock) by starting, or loosening, the chip. (Mystic Seaport photos)

that is not easy to convey to anyone who did not work at the trade in days gone by. Wooden planes were not only valued for their utility, but were cherished as well for other reasons, some of which might be termed aesthetic or sentimental. Various kinds of fine and hard-to-get hardwoods were sought after as plane material. For example, the old Devereux Mansion in Marblehead was once enclosed by a great fence made of an extremely hard, dense, heavy tropical hardwood of a purplish red cast, which polished as smooth as marble and was known locally as "ironwood." This fence has long since been torn down, but pieces of it still live on in heirloom planes.

Junks of this fence that came into the possession of the true planemaker might be cherished for years under his bench or in some other safe, private place, until the time came for cutting it up into plane blocks. When this moment finally came, the prized balk was studied as carefully before the saw was put into it as if it had been a piece of gemstone.

Sometimes considerable stealth, not to say conniving, went into getting desired wood for planes. One of the shop floors at the Boston Naval Shipyard was originally laid with live-oak planks—the same material used to plank *Old Ironsides*.

Live oak (*Quercus virginiana*) has a dense, interlocked grain, is much heavier than other oaks, is highly resistant to checking and splitting, wears extremely well, takes a high polish, and is altogether ideal for making wooden planes. In times past, I have been told, when the planemaking urge reached a certain pitch at the shipyard, a suitable plank of live oak in the shop floor would be chosen. Then a substitute plank of ordinary timber, as nearly like the original in appearance as possible, would be carefully prepared. The switch was usually made late at night, and in the absence of foremen, snappers, and other supervisory personnel.

Junked-up blocks of the oak would then be parceled out to the conspirators, who would eventually transform it into planes. Thus planemaking at times was also a diversion, a means of relieving the tedium of the job and of outwitting the boss. Coups of this nature were always a favorite topic of conversation over the open dinner buckets, and no doubt were improved upon in the telling and retelling.

One such story, which I have heard more than once, took place on a large, expensive yacht under construction at the old Lawley yard in Neponset. A crew of joiners had come aboard to finish and fit out the interior. As the story goes, one of the crew took up quarters in the forepeak, where he improvised a workbench and proceeded to make planes for all hands. Signals were devised to give him ample warning when the yard foreman or the owner came aboard. He turned out the planes for weeks, and was never detected. Of course the crew enjoyed every minute of it hugely. Neither morale nor production suffered, I am sure. Planes made on the boss's time acquired a double value, and I'm not so sure he didn't know all the time what was going on.

If this seems like a long and roundabout introduction, it is because planemaking is something to be approached in the proper frame of mind in order to be savored and enjoyed. The true craftsman of former days, whether a boatbuilder or not, prized his tools and took enjoyment in them. In time, they came to be old friends, tried and trusted, familiar yet respected. But also, they brought him recurring pleasure just to touch and to look at, as well as to use. When Ed Perkins, the Essex ship joiner, was long past working, he would go into his shop for hours just to sit with his familiar and cherished objects around him. The modern tender of machines—who has neither tools of his own nor any need for them in his job—has been dispossessed of vastly more than he has any inkling of.

So we come to planes themselves: their shapes, sizes, and dimensions; the various woods from which their stocks are made; the tools used in their construction; the manner of laying out, shaping, and finishing; the procurement of suitable plane irons; their fitting, sharpening, and adjustment; and finally their use. There is more to making planes than some might think.

In general, boatbuilders' planes are slighter and better balanced than ordinary wooden bench planes. The reason, I surmise, is that the former are frequently used on the sides of vessels, overhead, or in other positions where ordinary planes would be clumsy and awkward. For the same reason, apparently, boatbuilders' jackplanes and jointers are razeed—that is, cut down aft of the bed to lighten them up and to bring the user's hand closer to the work for better balance.

The standard maximum width of irons for the boatbuilder's smoother is 1¾ inches, although many are narrower than this and some are only 1¼ inches wide. Jackplanes are also not infrequently made with 1¾-inch irons, but almost never with irons wider than 2 inches. As a general rule, boatbuilders' planes are from ¼ inch to ¾ inch narrower than the ordinary

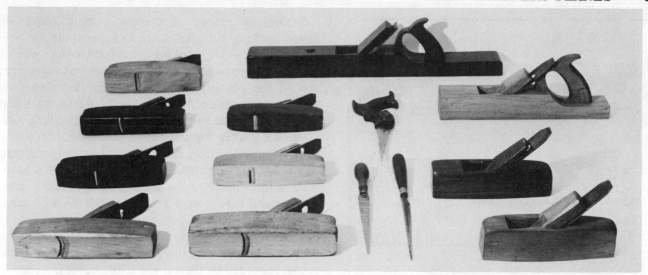

A few of the author's planes, with stocks made of woods such as ebony, live oak, lignum vitae, osage orange, beech, and ironwood. A rosewood jointer is in the background, and two spar planes are in the foreground. Also shown are a float and a stiff, pointed saw, specialized planemakers' tools. (Mary Anne Stets photo, Mystic Seaport)

beech bench planes that were formerly factory-made and sold to house carpenters and cabinetmakers.

Boatbuilders' long planes divide roughly into two groups according to their length—jacks and jointers. I cannot recall having heard a boatbuilder use any terms other than these in referring to his long planes. Jacks run between 12 inches and 16 inches, with irons almost never wider than 2 inches. Jointers are rarely over 2 feet in length, with more irons 2⅛ inches wide than 2½ inches. The standardized sizes adopted for commercially made planes—jacks, trying planes, fore planes, and jointers—do not obtain among boatbuilders.

The planes we are considering here are those found in the northeastern United States and the Canadian Maritime Provinces. There are in this area fairly uniform norms or patterns for planes, apparently handed down within the trade for several generations at least. Just how far back these go, or how they developed, is very difficult to determine, for there is virtually no written record. It is extremely difficult to date boatbuilders' tools found in this area earlier than the first part of the 19th century.

Boatbuilders' shorter planes are by far the most numerous. In one sense these are all smoothers, although perhaps that term should be reserved only for

The author getting out a plank with a wooden jackplane. (Mary Anne Stets photo, Mystic Seaport)

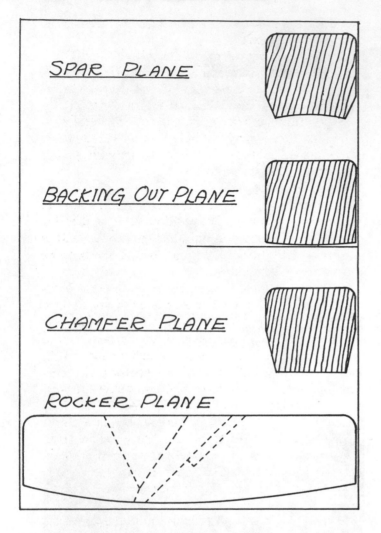

SPAR PLANE

BACKING OUT PLANE

CHAMFER PLANE

ROCKER PLANE

Cross sections of three types of boatbuilders' planes, with a side view of the rocker plane.

Smoothing planes of convex bottom curvature called backing-out planes are indispensable for hollowing the inside of planking to conform to the round of the ribs. Three or four, all of relatively flat curvature, are all the planker requires, but similar planes of greater round are occasionally useful in boat work and are usually found in the first-class boatbuilder's kit.

Rocker planes for smoothing the inside curves of deck beams, covering boards, taffrails, railcaps, and other sweeps are useful and necessary to have. Boatbuilders much prefer their wooden rocker planes to the metal variety now available with the adjustable sole of flexible steel.

A variation of the wooden rocker plane, with its bottom also curved athwartships like a backing-out plane, is needed by the outboard joiner, for instance in smoothing around the tuck of a vessel where hollow planking curves run both ways. In fact, the outboard joiner at one time or another will need almost every shape and size of plane there is, including even an occasional spar plane.

It should not be hard to see how the old-time boatbuilder came to make his own planes. He made them to fit the job, and to fit himself as well. He required such a variety that he could not afford to buy them ready-made. Considering the wages he got, purchasing the irons alone often meant a sacrifice. For wood, he could often find around the wharves and waterfront pieces of tropical hardwoods brought back from faraway places.

In a pinch, beech and even rock maple would do, but far better to have lignum vitae, rosewood, cocobolo, live oak, "ironwood," Turkish boxwood, ebony, black mesquite, horseflesh, or some other hard, exotic species.

The maker of planes—who will want them to work well, last at least during his lifetime, give him pleasure, and do him honor as a craftsman—will take great pains, if necessary, to secure suitable wood for the stocks. The ideal wood for boatbuilders' plane stocks is hard, heavy, close-grained, and not susceptible to checking, shrinkage, or warping. In addition, a pleasing grain pattern and a rich color are usually looked for. Obviously, only fully seasoned lumber is to be considered. However, nothing is to prevent the collection of blocks of green or wet plane wood, whenever available, to be put aside until they are thoroughly seasoned and dry. The boatbuilder who makes his own planes will generally have a number of such blocks or pieces stashed away under his bench, or

planes with flat soles. In addition, there are planes with hollow or concave soles of various radii, commonly called spar planes; planes with convex or rounded soles, plankers' "backing-out" types being the most common; planes with their soles curved fore and aft, called rockers or rocker planes; chamfer planes, which are able to do most of the work of a rabbet plane; and others. The length of such planes averages about 8 inches, and is rarely less than 7 inches or more than 9 inches. Spar planes tend to be the longest.

Nothing can quite equal a sharp spar plane of the right curvature for bringing a newly made spar to its final uniform finish. The old sparmaker had them by the trunkful, of all degrees of curvature from sprit-size up, accumulated during a working lifetime.

overhead on the rafters of his shop, or in some other secure place where they may lie for years, drying and seasoning until he gets around to using them.

Of course wood of the right sort is not to be found at the local lumberyard, and the few concerns that make a specialty of stocking tropical hardwoods for cabinet-makers may have trouble supplying it in the thicknesses required. Most plane blocks must be 2 inches thick or more.

Each species has its strong points, as well as its less desirable characteristics. Of the several species previously mentioned, I believe that live oak is the best. It is heavy, hard, and tough. It wears well, and when thoroughly seasoned it does not check, shrink, or warp. Not as hard as some of the more brittle woods, it has an interesting grain and, with age and use, acquires a marble smoothness and a rich golden-brown color. Rosewood—of which there are two somewhat different kinds, Brazilian and East Indian—is perhaps more handsome. Both kinds are excellent. They work well and wear well, but are not as tough as live oak. Cocobolo is somewhat similar to rosewood but harder.

Boxwood, when large enough blocks can be found, cannot be excelled for smoothness, but it is extremely brittle, and sooner or later it is apt to split out where the sides are cut thin for the slots that take the iron and the chip. Besides, when chiseling it, one requires goggles to keep flying chips out of the eyes. This is likewise the case with lignum vitae, which is nearly as hard and brittle as English boxwood. If it is not dried out thoroughly, lignum vitae is apt to check badly, and will shrink, twist, and warp. Some very fine planes have been made of lignum vitae, and, for want of adequate seasoning, some poor ones also.

Applewood that is the seasoned heartwood of large trees makes beautiful planes of a rich, reddish-brown color and a satiny texture. It chisels easily and wears quite well, but is only of medium weight, about the same as beech.

Beech, although not as heavy as live oak or lignum vitae, was adopted as the standard wood for commercially made planes. It wears well and becomes very smooth, cuts easily with sharp chisels, resists checking, and holds its shape well after seasoning. Formerly, beech lumber was plentiful in straight-grained, knot-free planks of any desired thickness, and was not expensive. Consequently beech was an ideal wood for the 19th-century plane factories. Good beech, if any can still be found, is not to be scorned as a utility material, but it is not quite in a class with the heavier tropical hardwoods.

Rock maple (not soft maple) can also be used. I have seen planes made of rock maple that worked very well, but like beech, it is not one of the heavier woods. Besides, it is not at all distinctive in appearance.

Well-seasoned cherry is not to be overlooked. About the same weight as beech and maple, it resists checking and holds its shape well. In addition, it has a pleasing reddish brown color.

Greenheart is a very heavy, hard wood, used for sheathing vessels against Arctic ice, which attests to its wearing qualities. In addition, it is a pleasing greenish golden-brown. But it has the serious fault of checking easily and badly, and so it is hardly to be recommended for planes.

Undoubtedly there are many more tropical hardwoods besides these that would make fine planes. One of the joys of planemaking is the search for materials.

Cherry, as well as applewood, is excellent for the totes of jackplanes and jointers, which require a firm, close-grained wood that resists splitting in short sections. Apple, it will be recalled, was long accepted as the standard wood for the handles of the best handsaws, which are quite similar to plane totes. Beech once furnished totes exclusively for commercially made planes, as it did for the stocks. Perhaps best of all would be rosewood, from which the wooden furnishings of the best iron planes were formerly made.

Shaping a plane stock, mortising it, and fitting the iron is not as difficult as it might appear to someone who has never done it—provided one goes about it systematically and has the right tools for the job. But before outlining the procedure, it will simplify the explanation to name the parts of the plane that we shall be considering.

Tote signifies handle. There are two kinds, open and closed. Only the latter is used on boatbuilders' planes. The *stock* is the body of the plane, exclusive of the tote and the chip. The bottom is the *sole*. The aperture in the sole through which the cutting edge of the iron protrudes and through which the shavings enter is the *mouth*. The shavings pass upward through the *throat* or the *escapement*. On either side of this opening through the stock are the *cheeks*. The incline on which the plane iron is seated is the *bed*; in iron planes it is called the *frog*. The angle of incline of the bed is the *pitch*. The after end of the stock is the *britch*. A *striker, button,* or *start,* as it is variously called, sometimes of

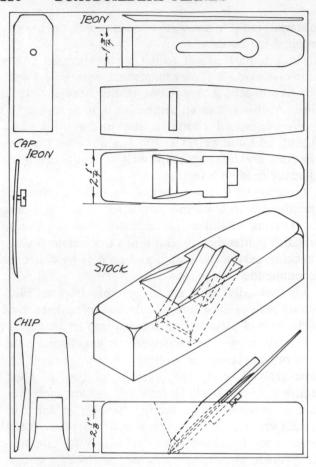

IRON

CAP IRON

STOCK

CHIP

A standard boatbuilder's plane, showing positions of the
iron, the cap iron, and the chip in the stock.

end-grain hardwood and sometimes of metal, is often
inserted in the britch end of smoothers and on top of
the forward end of jacks and jointers to take the impact
of the plane hammer when loosening the chip to adjust
the iron.

The iron is held firmly in position in the working
plane by the *chip*, which is little more than a thin
wedge the center of which has been cut away
somewhat to facilitate the egress of shavings from the
throat, leaving two narrow strips called *prongs* on
either side of the chip at its lower end. These prongs fit
into the shallow *slots* in the cheeks and wedge against
the forward sides of the slots, which are called the
shoulders or *abutments*. At the top, the slots are let in
to a depth of ¼ inch or slightly more, tapering to
nothing at the bottom (just above the mouth) to give as
much room as possible for the shavings to clear. As
planes are used, the prongs tend in time to reach too
deep, and their ends have to be trimmed to prevent
shavings from catching on them. They must not project
beyond the slots into the mouth of the plane. In making
the chip, the prongs should spread slightly wider than
the side-to-side distance between the inside of the
slots. This ensures a tight fit and prevents shavings
from wedging behind the points of the prongs.

Diagrammatic view of a boatbuilder's long plane.

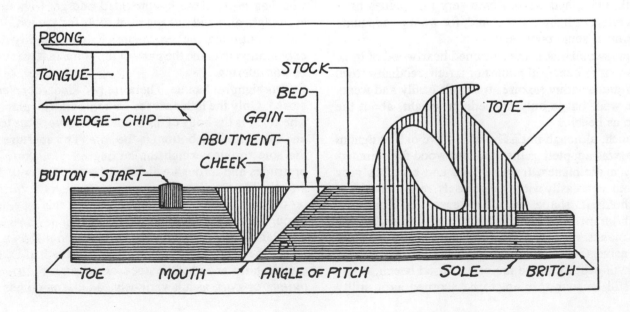

PRONG

TONGUE

WEDGE — CHIP

BUTTON — START

TOE   MOUTH   ANGLE OF PITCH

STOCK

BED

GAIN

ABUTMENT

CHEEK

TOTE

SOLE   BRITCH

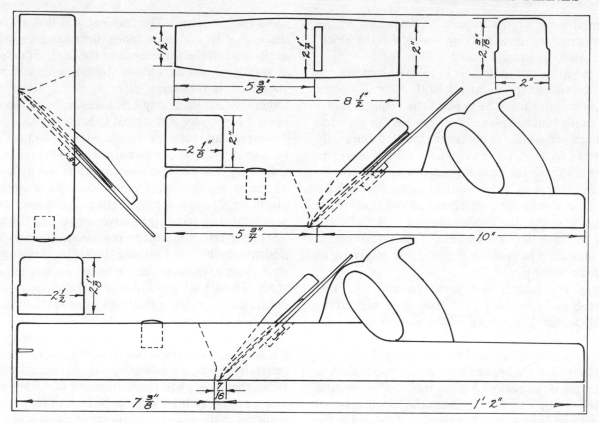

Plans for a smoother (top left), a jackplane (top right), and a jointer. Jackplanes and jointers are usually cut down aft of the throat to lighten them and to bring the user's hand closer to the work for better balance.

The wedge angle of the chip is critical, for if it is too great, the chip will not hold, popping up at the least jar or bump. But if the chip is made too flat, it will grip too tightly and will not loosen readily to permit adjustment of the iron. Ten degrees, plus or minus a degree, is about right for the angle of slope. To ensure getting this right is one reason for making a careful layout of the interior on the outside of the block, as will be described.

Undoubtedly there is more than one good method for making a wooden plane. The one we shall consider I have used successfully many times. I should not want to claim, however, that it cannot be improved, or that it should not be modified to suit different conditions or individual requirements.

First of all, and regardless of the kind of plane, the block is squared up to the desired size. It is necessary that its opposite surfaces be true and parallel to each other. After that, the ends are squared and cut to

length. But other than this, the stock is not given its final shape until it has been mortised for the iron, and the iron and the chip have been fitted in place.

After the block has been squared, the position of the iron is located and marked on one side. Ordinarily, the iron is set at an angle, or pitch, of 45 degrees. This differs, however, for some specialized planes, such as the York pattern, used for planing cross-grained hardwoods, which has a pitch of 60 degrees. The line marking the seat of the iron against the bed is next squared across the sole, and also across the top. Then a line indicating the position of the iron is marked on the second side to correspond with the first.

Next the iron, in most cases composed of blade and cap, is laid along the seat line already marked on the side of the block, and the outline of the iron is carefully traced. Then the width and taper of the chip are laid out and the position of the shoulder or abutment marked, with care taken to make the wedge angle of the chip approximately 10 degrees. The layout of the interior is now outlined fully on the side of the block, and the mortising can proceed.

The mouth is cut in first. It is located by squaring across the sole from the layout on the side. To begin with, the mouth should be kept a little smaller than it will be in the finished plane. It is very easy to get it too large if this precaution is not taken. Later, it can easily be enlarged to the desired width with a fine wood rasp. However, should the mouth inadvertently be cut too large, this mistake can be rectified either by setting a graving piece into the sole ahead of the iron, or by padding the seat of the iron on the bed with a piece of leather to bring the iron forward. This last device is sometimes used to cushion the iron and to give it an even, firm bearing.

Cutting the mouth first serves much the same function as does the "stop-cut" in wood carving. If the internal mortising is carried all the way through from the top, there is a danger of splitting pieces out of the sole when the chisel breaks through the bottom. This is particularly likely to happen with brittle woods such as lignum vitae or boxwood. Furthermore, if the mortise is carried all the way through from the top, it may not come out precisely where it is supposed to, and in the course of attempts to rectify this, the mouth is apt to become too large.

The safest and really the easiest way to start is by chiseling into the sole about ½ inch deep, or whatever shows on the diagram of the interior previously laid out on the side of the block. Just as the fore-and-aft width of the cut across the sole is kept small (and enlarged later, if necessary), so the width of the cut across the sole is kept narrow enough at first to come inside the cheeks, if it were carried through to the top of the block.

After the mouth has been cut through the sole to the required depth, and while the block is still in the vise bottom up, a series of holes, as close together as possible, are drilled through the mouth out through the top of the block. The drill is kept far enough away from the outside to allow for the thickness of the cheeks. This operation is done most accurately with a drill press.

As soon as these holes are drilled, the block is turned over and cutting proceeds from the top. The row of holes also serves as a stop-cut, and with a stiff, narrow, sharp-pointed saw, it is easy to connect them and to make a continuous cut across the inside of the block to work against from both ends. Several sharp

chisels are required. The smallest is ¼ inch wide, and the widest is 1 inch or more, depending on what is available and the preference of the user. For working in very hard woods, chisels should be ground with a shortened bevel—that is, at a rather steep angle. Otherwise the edge may break under the blows of the mallet, especially if the steel is extra hard.

Several fine-cut patternmakers' rasps and riffles are desirable, with one or two narrow enough to fit into the side slots. If one of these narrow rasps has safe edges, all the better. One who intends to make a number of planes might consider converting an ordinary narrow rasp for this by grinding its edges smooth on the wheel. There are also specialized planemakers' tools called *floats,* which are finishing tools for leveling and smoothing hard-to-get-at places in the interior of the stock. These have rows of large parallel teeth running across one side. Some floats are quite narrow, no more than $3/16$ inch. Others are pointed at the end and widen toward the handle to resemble a triangular flat file. Floats are not manufactured for sale; they are generally made by planemakers for their own use. Often they are made from worn-out files annealed to saw hardness so that they can be filed to shape and the teeth cut in them with a three-cornered saw file. With such specialized tools it is much easier to clean out and to smooth the side slots in the cheeks for the chip and iron.

As already mentioned, a special saw with a stiff, narrow, pointed blade is well worth going to some trouble to obtain, even if one is obliged to make over a saw for this purpose. Such a saw can be seen in the photograph of tools required for planemaking. This one was adapted from a worn-out compass saw. Its blade is a narrow triangle, about 1 inch wide at the base where the blade joins the handle, and about 6 inches long, running to a sharp point at the end. It is filed crosscut with 10 teeth to the inch.

The blade was thick to start with, and before the teeth were cut it was filed to a tapering section from back to front, leaving the back edge quite thin and the front or cutting edge its original thickness. Thus, the teeth need no set, and the saw runs true, cuts smoothly, and does not bind. With its narrow, stiff blade and sharp point, it can be started in a space no wider than a single drill hole, and it is the perfect tool for making shoulder cuts in the cheeks when it comes to fitting the chip and the iron. Without such a tool, shoulder cuts can be troublesome.

After the side slots are cut and the iron is seated, a

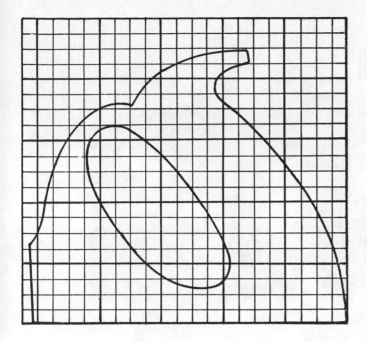

A pattern for a comfortable tote, or handle, of a jackplane or jointer. Cherry and applewood are fine materials for totes, which require firm, close-grained, split-resistant wood.

thin strip of pine is fitted in the tapered space between the iron and the shoulder to provide a template for making the chip, and also for checking to see if both side slots are the same size and slope. If they are not, one or the other must be trimmed to match. When the chip has been carefully fitted with the iron in place, and the throat has been smoothed and brought as near as possible at this stage to its final form, the outside of the plane is shaped and finished.

The sides of most boatbuilders' smoothers are cut on a convex curve so that the stock is narrow at the britch, somewhat wider at the fore end, and widest abreast of the mouth. It will be seen that this curved shape resembles a coffin, from whence comes the name *coffin plane* sometimes applied to them. This shape is traditional for boatbuilders' smoothers. The origin was clearly functional, for planes so shaped fit the hands better than if they were left straight-sided, and are easier to grasp and to push on the sides of a vessel, overhead, or in the other numerous awkward positions that occur in building wooden vessels. One exception, however, is that spar planes are sometimes left straight-sided.

Boatbuilding planes naturally vary in their shape, quality, size, and weight with the individual makers, yet for the most part they conform with remarkable fidelity to traditional patterns. As mentioned, the boatbuilders' long planes, the jacks and the jointers, are uniformly narrower and lower than the factory-made beech planes once supplied to house carpenters and cabinetmakers. But what particularly distinguished these long planes was their cut-down britch. This style of plane is often called a *razee,* the term formerly applied to ships whose upper deck was cut away.

Here again, the reason for shaping a plane in this way is functional. By lowering the tote, the force applied in pushing the plane is brought down more directly behind the iron, where it is most effective, improving both the balance and the efficiency of the tool. The tote can be shaped to fit the hand of the owner. Those formerly supplied on factory-made wooden planes are apt to be small and tend to cramp the user's hand. Not only is comfort affected, but also the control of the tool.

Not all planes are fitted with strikers or starts, but these are worth putting in. Smoothers that lack them are frequently disfigured and even split by continual pounding from the plane hammer in adjusting the iron. A small end-grain cylinder ¾ inch in diameter and about 1 inch long—of very hard wood inserted in a hole bored in the britch end of a smoother, with its end rounded over and protruding a little—makes a very good striking button. In a long plane, the striker is inserted in the top of the stock, near the forward end. Sometimes a metal pin is used, and occasionally a bronze carriage bolt, with the head serving as the striking button.

The blade of a wooden plane is properly called an *iron,* a name that has come down from antiquity. It is made principally of iron, except for the portion that does the actual cutting, which is a thin facing of the finest tempered steel welded on the inside at the lower end.

This type of iron, developed in Sheffield and standardized at the beginning of the 19th century, or perhaps even earlier, is not to be confused with the thinner, all-steel blade of the modern cast-iron bench plane. Such thin, lightweight blades are not well suited for wooden planes, being more apt than the heavier irons to jump and chatter when one is planing cross-grained wood.

The big problem facing the planemaker today is the scarcity of irons. These are no longer manufactured in this country, and old inventories on hardware shelves have long since been sold out.

Smoothers in various stages of construction, and the tools that made them. Left to right in the background are a block for a smoother with the mouth cut in; a block with completed mortise for chip and iron; a block shaped on the outside; a smoother cut away to show the interior; and a finished lignum vitae smoother. In the foreground are a wood carver's mallet; chisels; wood rasps and a riffle; the planemaker's special pointed saw; a Stanley block plane; a combination square; an Arkansas oilstone; and a back saw. In the near foreground are a plane hammer and a pattern-maker's vise. (Russell A. Fowler photo, Mystic Seaport)

Until a few years ago, a limited number of old-type irons by Marples and other Sheffield makers were obtainable from England, but that source has been exhausted. A few superior irons are still being imported from West Germany, notably Ulmia irons, and some apparently from Finland, but it is only a matter of time before these sources also dry up. At one time superior Swedish irons could be had—Shark Brand irons by Erik Anton Berg of Eskilstuna—but I have been informed that production has been discontinued.

There is another source of plane irons: secondhand ones, from old wooden planes, which are still to be found in considerable numbers. Only a few years ago such old planes, scorned and discarded by modern mechanics, were readily and cheaply available. The hockshops and secondhand stores were full of them, and many more found their way to the dump as attics and cellars were emptied and cleaned. More recently the antique industry has begun to take cognizance of the growing interest in old carpenters' tools, and the price of planes has gone up and will continue to rise.

Nevertheless, it is still possible to pick up an occasional bargain in secondhand plane irons. But don't delay, for these old irons are fast becoming

Planemakers' tools. In the foreground, left to right, are floats, rasps, chisels, a selection of double irons, and a plane hammer. Included in the background are the planemaker's saw (shown cutting an abutment) and two totes, one partly made and one finished. (Mary Anne Stets photo, Mystic Seaport)

collectors' items. Regretfully, what I am now writing can only hasten the inevitable.

In some cases the entire secondhand plane can be converted to boatbuilding use, even if it was not a boatbuilder's plane originally. A few simple changes or repairs to the stock may be all that is required, as I shall explain. But more frequently it is only the iron that is of interest.

Occasionally the stock will be so beat up and dilapidated as to appear next to worthless, yet it will contain a good iron. It does not matter if the iron is rusted, provided the steel facing is not pitted so deeply that the pits cannot be ground out without removing too much of the steel. Since the steel facing is generally about 1/16 inch thick, rust pits rarely go deep enough to spoil the iron. Unless all rust pitting is removed and the surface of the steel polished bright, however, it will be impossible to give the iron a perfect cutting edge.

Sufficient length of steel should remain on the iron to allow for enough grinding and sharpening to make it worthwhile to put the iron in a new stock. A new iron has about 2 inches of tempered steel, but even an inch of steel, provided care is taken to grind sparingly, will

last a long time in planes with special shapes that are used only occasionally.

Indeed, a mere half-inch of good steel is not to be scorned, for with careful grinding for occasional use it can be made to last for years. Should the steel be gone completely, the cap is worth having to match with irons missing their caps. Cap irons are also in short supply.

In reconditioning an iron that has rusted, there are a number of precautions to be observed. During grinding, the surface of the steel must be kept absolutely flat, and there should be no digging into it anywhere or lowering of the edges. The steel should not be heated to the point of drawing the temper. Grinding wheels coarse enough to leave deep scratches should be avoided. Such scratches are difficult to remove in the final polishing, which should result in a mirrorlike surface.

As previously mentioned, the width of iron most common in boatbuilders' planes is 1¾ inches for smoothers and jackplanes. Even in large jointers, an iron width of over 2 inches is rare. At the other extreme, a narrow smoother with an iron only 1¼ inches wide is one of the most useful tools a boatbuilder can have. I have one of this size in which I have worn out three irons during some 20 years of more or less continual use.

Wooden planes formerly used by house carpenters, joiners, and cabinetmakers were generally wider than boatbuilders' planes, and in adapting irons taken from them it is necessary to cut them down in width. If it is only a matter of $1/16$ inch or thereabouts that has to be removed, grinding on a coarse power wheel is the answer. But a sharp hacksaw is recommended for cutting down oversize irons from either side of which as much as $3/16$ inch or more must be taken.

Most of the iron—that is, what is actually iron—is soft enough to be sawn through readily. But the saw will not touch the tempered steel, which begins at about the base of the slot.

One way of handling this is to score the steel partly through on a thin, high-speed cutting wheel, and to complete the break by snapping off the nearly glass-hard steel in a machinist's vise. Care must be taken to score the steel deeply before clamping the iron, at the break line, between the jaws of the vise. Good contact the full length of the steel is essential. Otherwise there is a chance the break might not follow the scoring but instead run off into the center of the blade and spoil the iron. If this procedure is followed, including sawing through the soft iron backing of the steel behind where it is scored, a quick rap with a heavy hammer will snap the steel cleanly and instantly as if it were a piece of glass.

In grinding and polishing the steel facing of the iron after it has been cut down to the desired width, one must be careful not to overheat the steel to the point of drawing the temper. A buffing wheel is useful for bringing the steel facing to a bright polish. Afterward, the polished surface of the steel should be oiled to prevent further rusting, a critical precaution because in most cases the steel is not thick enough to stand grinding and polishing twice.

In sharpening the iron, the bevel of grind will be about 22 degrees, although for different work and different woods sometimes slightly more bevel, and sometimes slightly less, will be preferred. Unless the cap iron fits tightly against the face of the cutting iron it will be useless—and sometimes worse than useless, for shavings are sure to wedge themselves under a loose cap and become jammed there.

In his *British Plane Makers From 1700*, W.L. Goodman provides a check list of 48 British plane-iron makers, all but three of which were located in Sheffield. Many of these concerns exported plane irons to the United States; irons with various Sheffield marks are widely distributed in this country and constitute a considerable fraction of the secondhand irons. Sheffield names most commonly seen are William Ash, William Butcher, James Cam, Greaves, Graves, Hernshaw, Ibbottson, Moulson Brothers, William Marples, Newbould, Sorby, and Ward. Other Sheffield marks occasionally turn up. All such irons are of superior quality, as is any iron marked Sheffield and warranted cast steel. With enough steel left to justify putting it into a plane, such an iron should be considered a lucky find.

Irons by Moulson Brothers were highly esteemed by American boatbuilders and shipwrights, and must have been imported in quantity, considering the numbers to be seen in planes still in use. William Marples's irons were also popular and among the last to be sold commercially.

I have never seen a Sheffield iron that was not stamped *cast steel*. The unexcelled quality of Sheffield edge tools derived from the superior crucible cast steel produced by a process developed at Sheffield in the 1740s by Benjamin Huntsman for clock springs.

By the second quarter of the 19th century the forging of edge tools in this country was fast emerging from the local blacksmith shop to be carried on in mechanized factories. Tool manufacturing concerns founded by D.R. Barton at Rochester, New York, in 1832 and by L. and I.J. White at Buffalo in 1837 both produced superior plane irons faced with steel—although, for whatever reasons, they did not warrant their irons cast steel as most other plane-iron makers did.

White's irons were extra heavy, and in my judgment they were equal to any plane irons ever made anywhere. Buck Brothers, Sheffield edge-tool makers who removed to Millbury, Massachusetts, produced until about 40 or 50 years ago superior plane irons in great quantity, unquestionably a greater quantity than any other American concern. Their mark, a buck's antlered head, is still widely known and respected. One of the brothers, Charles Buck, left the original firm after a time, producing equally good irons under his own name.

On page 44 of his *Wooden Planes in 19th Century America*, Kenneth Roberts lists 32 concerns that formerly manufactured plane irons for wooden planes in this country. In addition to irons by Barton, White, and Buck, I can vouch from personal experience for

American irons marked Auburn Tool Company, Baldwin Tool Company, Chapin, Chapin-Stephens, Dwights French Company, Globe Manufacturing Company, Humphreysville Manufacturing Company, Ohio Tool Company, Providence Tool Company, Sargent and Company, and James Swan.

The would-be planemaker in search of irons will do well to familiarize himself with the lists by Goodman and by Roberts. Don't ask for these irons at the store. Chances are they wouldn't even know what you were talking about. Still, such irons in mint condition do turn up every once in a while in old tool chests, attics, dusty lofts, and cellars. Used irons with enough steel remaining to warrant consideration, while far from plentiful, can still be found. The places to look are flea markets, yard sales, tool auctions, and antique shops. Frequently, good irons can be salvaged from broken or wornout planes too far gone to be worth repairing. On the other hand, it is often possible to put worn or damaged plane stocks back in usable condition with only simple or minor repairs. Splits and checks are easily mended with epoxy adhesive. It is possible to renew the sole of a badly worn plane by gluing a new lift on the bottom. Sometimes a jack or a jointer is much improved by replacing the old loosened tote with a new one of improved design. Old beech planes are greatly improved in appearance by applying tung oil, Danish oil, or similar sealers or wood conditioners after they have been cleaned thoroughly.

Carpenters' or cabinetmakers' smoothers are readily converted to excellent backing-out planes for the use of the planker, merely by rounding the sole slightly from side to side and grinding the iron to match. In most cases a convex round of barely $\frac{1}{16}$ inch for a stock width of 2¼ to 2½ inches is quite adequate. More than this will be too much for most planking operations. A convex round of ⅛ inch in 2½ inches of stock width is certainly the maximum for a backing-out plane, but even though one with as much curvature as this will rarely be used, the boatbuilder will do well to have one in his kit.

A simple but effective method for converting an ordinary flat smoothing plane to a backing-out plane is as follows. One side of a piece of soft-pine board about a foot long and 6 or 8 inches wide is hollowed out to the shallow curvature desired for the bottom of the plane. This can be done in various ways, one of which is to use a flat gouge followed by a slightly curved block and coarse sandpaper.

Next a sheet of coarse emery cloth is placed over the hollowed-out surface and secured along the edges of the board with tacks. This is now ready for trueing up the bottom of the converted plane after it has been planed freehand as nearly as possible to the desired curvature with a sharp plane set fine and a curved template of thin wood. Vigorously scrubbing the converted stock back and forth over the emery cloth will make its curved bottom perfectly smooth and true. The iron is now inserted in the plane and allowed to protrude slightly through the mouth to show how much should be ground off to produce the required curvature. This can first be done close enough by eye, after which the iron is reinserted in the stock, allowed to protrude through the mouth ever so slightly, and scrubbed back and forth over the emery cloth. This will shape the iron to the precise curvature required. It is now removed, carefully ground sharp, and honed to a keen edge on the oilstone. The cap iron must be slightly reshaped to fit the curve of the blade and made to fit absolutely tightly against the surface of the steel. This may involve some slight hammering, filing, and a final trueing on the flat surface of a coarse stone.

For most work, rockers should not have too much longitudinal curvature either. Among the rockers in my own kit, the one that has seen the most use has only a scant ¼ inch of longitudinal curve in a sole length of 8 inches. My most extreme rocker, and one I rarely use, has 1 inch of curve in a length of 8 inches. Most of the concave curves that call for smoothing in boatbuilding are long, relatively flat sweeps—the underside of deck beams, the inside of waterways or covering boards, and the like.

Spar planes require some explanation. The spar plane, so called, is a finishing plane used to give the final smoothing after the spar has been sized and shaped and brought to a nearly perfect round by the successive use of a variety of other tools, including ordinary jointers, jackplanes, and smoothing planes. Thus, a great deal of planing gets done on a spar before the spar plane is applied. Before abrasives came into use, spars received their final finish from planing rather than sanding.

Best results are obtained from a spar plane whose curvature fits the round of the spar as closely as possible. Thus, the professional sparmaker had a chest, or maybe two chests, full of planes of different curvatures.

The method of making a plane to fit a spar of given diameter is first to lay out the spar's largest circumference with dividers on a piece of thin board in order

Planing a small mast with a spar plane. (Mary Anne Stets photo, Mystic Seaport)

to make two templates of its curvature—one concave, the other convex. Thin pine does nicely for this. Using the concave template, a block of pine or other soft wood wide enough to clamp in the vise with 4 or 5 inches protruding, and about as thick as the plane, is rounded to fit. When this is smooth and the template fits, a sheet of rough emery cloth, grit side out, is stretched over the rounded surface and tacked on the sides. The tacks must be far enough down the sides to be out of the way.

The convex template is needed when the sole of the spar plane is hollowed. This is usually started with gouges and often continued using a plane with a rounded sole when one of suitable curvature is available. Such a plane is not essential, however, and patient gouge work is all that is needed before the hollowed sole is ready for final trueing on the emery cloth. From here the procedure is the same as previously described for finishing the backing-out plane. One item not previously mentioned: Before the sole of the spar plane is hollowed, the mouth should be cut in, because it would be more difficult to cut it later.

The mouth is slightly curved to match the circumference of the spar for which the plane is made.

An alternate way to make a plane for a small-diameter spar, such as a small sprit, is to turn on the lathe a short section of cylinder of the same diameter. One end of this cylinder is cut off square, and this squared end is applied against the sole of the plane to mark the curvature of the mouth. The other end of the cylinder is cut at an angle of 45 degrees, the same angle or pitch at which the iron is set in the plane. The end so cut provides an elliptical template for grinding the iron, the curve of the cutting edge of an iron set at 45 degrees being elliptical rather than circular.

Traditionally, boatbuilders' planes were mortised and shaped from solid blocks. Now that we have reliable glues, some find it easier to make planes from two lengthwise halves that are glued together after the internal cutting and shaping has been done, so to speak, from the outside. An old worn-out plane too far gone to recondition, such as one of those frequently found at flea markets, can be split lengthwise with the saw to obtain a pattern to go by. In choosing wood for this type of construction, it should be remembered that some of the heavier tropical hardwoods, such as lignum vitae and cocobolo, do not glue well.

From the standpoint of utility alone, these glued-up planes work quite adequately, yet for many who take pride in having fine tools, they lack something aesthetically.

Instead of wedge-shaped slots in the cheeks, some European planes have a different arrangement for holding the chip. A section of metal rod (about ¼ inch in diameter) extends across the throat from side to side with its ends embedded in the cheeks. Between the cheeks is a strip of metal, flat on one side, curved on the other, and about 1 inch wide, through which the rod passes. This turns freely on the rod, adjusting its flat surface to the angle of the chip wedged against it. A variation of this arrangement is to have a thinner strip of flat metal brazed or silver-soldered to a section of rod, the rod turning freely in the holes in the cheeks, which carry it. This arrangement is well adapted to miniature modelmakers' planes with single-bladed irons.

Both variations of this alternate method of wedging the chip hold the iron securely while allowing it to be adjusted easily. In addition, the planes clear their shavings easily and seldom clog up. Furthermore, by inserting backing strips of various thicknesses between the bed and the iron, one can move the iron forward to narrow the mouth when fine work or cross-grained wood makes this desirable. This cannot be done, of course, when the chip wedges in side slots cut in the cheeks.

The novice planemaker tends to make the mouth of his plane too wide. In extreme cases, it is advisable to correct this fault by setting a graving piece in the sole at the forward side of the mouth to narrow it. In restoring old planes worn from long use, a graving piece is frequently let into the sole in this manner to bring the mouth back to its original width.

Some of the simpler molding planes useful at times in boat work are rounds and hollows, beading planes, narrow rabbet planes, and a few others, but boatbuilders rarely went to the trouble of making molding planes of their own. The standard shapes were too easily obtained ready-made.

A plane included in the outboard joiner's kit is the chamfer plane. This is little more than an ordinary flat smoother, but one whose sides are cut away from the bottom in a long, easy chamfer that barely exposes the corners of the iron. With a chamfer plane it is possible to plane up to protruding parts, such as moldings or trim, much as with a rabbet plane. For fine planing on the outside of the hull, a sharp chamfer plane works better than a rabbet plane, in part because of its wood sole and in part because of its double iron that can be set for a fine, smooth cut.

Occasionally the professional boatbuilder has need for a plane with a lot of round in its sole. One use for such a plane, similar to what house carpenters call a gutter plane, is for smoothing the semicircular hollow in split shaft logs for large power launches. There is nothing special about making such a plane, except that reworking the cap iron for a tight fit against the cutting iron can be fussy and exacting.

This is not all there is to boatbuilding planes and planemaking by any means, but it is enough for a start. From here, the capable mechanic will be able to strike out on his own.

BIBLIOGRAPHY

Chapter 1. Herreshoff Rowboat and Modified McInnis Bateau

Durant, Kenneth and Helen. *The Adirondack Guide-Boat*. Camden, Maine: International Marine Publishing Co., 1980.

Gardner, John. *Building Classic Small Craft, Volume 1*. Camden, Maine: International Marine Publishing Co., 1977.

Herreshoff, L. Francis. *The Common Sense of Yacht Design*. 1946. (Reprint: Jamaica, New York: Caravan-Maritime Books, 1974.)

Chapter 2. Pilot Gig

Hornsby, Thomas. "The Last Voyage of the *Thomas W. Lawson*." Nautical Research Journal, April 1955.

Larn, Richard. *Cornish Shipwrecks, Volume 3*. New York: Taplinger Publishing Co., 1971.

March, Edgar J. *Inshore Craft of Britain in the Days of Sail and Oar, Volume 2*. Camden, Maine: International Marine Publishing Co., 1970.

Chapter 3. Merrymeeting Bay Duckboat

Chapelle, Howard I. *American Small Sailing Craft*. New York: W.W. Norton, 1951.

Gardner, John. *Building Classic Small Craft, Volume 1*. Camden, Maine: International Marine Publishing Co., 1977.

Kunhardt, C.P. *Small Yachts*. New York: Forest and Stream Publishing Co., 1885.

Stephens, W.P. *Canoe and Boat Building, a Complete Manual for Amateurs*. New York: Forest and Stream Publishing Co., 1884. (4th edition, 1889, revised and extended, with 50 folding plates instead of original 30. Several subsequent editions.)

Chapter 5. Two 8-Foot Prams

Gardner, John. *Building Classic Small Craft, Volume 1*. Camden, Maine: International Marine Publishing Co., 1977.

Herreshoff, L. Francis. *Sensible Cruising Designs*. Camden, Maine: International Marine Publishing Co., 1973.

Chapter 6. Four Canoes

The American Canoe Association. "Sailing Canoes, a Brief History." June 1, 1935.

Crowley, William. *Rushton's Rowboats and Canoes: The 1903 Catalog in Perspective*. Camden, Maine: International Marine Publishing Co., 1983.

Kemp, Dixon. *A Manual of Yacht and Boat Sailing*. Fifth Edition. London: Horace Cox, 1886.

Manley, Atwood. *J. Henry Rushton and His Times in American Canoeing*. Syracuse, New York: Syracuse University Press, 1968.

Roberts, Kenneth G., and Philip Shackleton. *The Canoe: A History of the Craft from Panama to the Arctic*. Camden, Maine: International Marine Publishing Co., 1983.

Stephens, W.P. *Canoe and Boat Building, a Complete Manual for Amateurs*. Fourth Edition. New York: Forest and Stream Publishing Co., 1889.

Chapter 9. Sea Bright Skiff

Guthorn, Peter J. *The Sea Bright Skiff and Other Jersey Shore Boats*. New Brunswick, New Jersey: Rutgers University Press, 1971.

Chapter 10. Boston Fishing Power Dories

German, Andrew W. *Down on T Wharf*. Mystic, Connecticut: Mystic Seaport Museum, 1982.

Chapter 12. Two Garveys

Chapelle, Howard I. "Some American Fishing Launches." IN: *Fishing Boats of the World, Volume 1*. The Proceedings of the First FAO International Fishing Boat Congress, 1953. Ed. Jan-Olof Traung. Surrey, England: Fishing News (Books) Ltd., 1955.

Chapter 13. Clamming Skiff

Gardner, John. *The Dory Book*. Camden, Maine: International Marine Publishing Co., 1978.

Chapters 14 and 15. 16-Foot Swampscott Dory and Mower Dory

Gardner, John. *The Dory Book*. Camden, Maine: International Marine Publishing Co., 1978.
Mower, Charles. "How to Build a Power Dory." The Rudder, May 1904.
Schock, Edson B. "How to Build an Auxiliary Cruising Dory, *Fish Hook*." The Rudder, June 1904.

Chapter 16. Boatbuilders' Planes

Herreshoff, L. Francis. *The Common Sense of Yacht Design*. 1946. (Reprint: Jamaica, New York: Caravan-Maritime Books, 1974.
Mercer, Henry C. *"Ancient Carpenters' Tools."* Fourth Edition. Doylstown, Pennsylvania: The Bucks County Historical Society, 1968.
Roberts, Kenneth D. *Wooden Planes in 19th Century America*. Fitzwilliam, New Hampshire: Ken Roberts Publishing Co., 1975.
Roberts, Kenneth D. *Wooden Planes in 19th Century America, Volume II*. Fitzwilliam, New Hampshire: Ken Roberts Publishing Co., 1983.

· INDEX ·